The Golden Peninsula

CULTURE AND ADAPTATION IN MAINLAND SOUTHEAST ASIA

CHARLES F. KEYES

UNDER THE EDITORSHIP OF JOHN MIDDLETON

THE GOLDEN PENINSULA

CULTURE AND ADAPTATION IN MAINLAND SOUTHEAST ASIA

CHARLES F. KEYES
Department of Anthropology
University of Washington, Seattle

Macmillan Publishing Co., Inc.
New York

Collier Macmillan Publishers
London

Macmillan Publishing Co., Inc.
866 Third Avenue, New York, New York 10022

Collier Macmillan Canada, Ltd.

Library of Congress Cataloging in Publication Data

Keyes, Charles F
   The golden peninsula.

   Bibliography: p.
   Includes index.
   1. Ethnology—Asia, Southeastern.
2. Asia, Southeastern—Social life and customs.
3. Hinayana Buddhism—History. I. Title.
GN635.A75K48   1977   301.29'59   76-15175
ISBN 0-02-364430-3

Printing: 1 2 3 4 5 6 7 8   Year: 7 8 9 0 1 2 3

TO NICHOLAS AND JONATHAN, FOR WHOM MAINLAND SOUTHEAST ASIA HAS PROVIDED PART OF THEIR CULTURAL HERITAGE.

PREFACE

In this book I have attempted to provide a general survey for those who wish to gain some understanding of the ways in which cultural traditions in mainland Southeast Asia have emerged from and have guided the experiences of peoples as they have adapted themselves to a variety of circumstances in the history of the region. I have sought to interpret the cultural traditions of the region as they are expressed in the everyday lives of people residing in specific places. These particular places include upland communities, lowland peasant villages, and cities located in what today are the countries of Burma, Thailand, Laos, Cambodia, and Vietnam. The cultural traditions I have considered are of several different types, including highly localized primitive and tribal traditions, historic Theravada Buddhist and Sino-Vietnamese traditions, and such new traditions as Karen nationalism, Buddhist socialism, and Vietnamese communism. My purpose has been not only to show how local manifestations of these types of cultural traditions provide meaningful patterns whereby people in mainland Southeast Asia adapt to specific contexts but also to show how cultural traditions in the region have been transformed and, in some cases, supplanted by other traditions in the wake of radical changes in people's experiences. Thus, I have attempted in this study to trace such major cultural changes as those that have occurred as a consequence of the processes of Indianization (including the spread of Theravada Buddhism as a popular religion), Sinification, and Western colonialization.

I have purposely excluded consideration of Malay culture from this work for two reasons. First, I have followed many of my colleagues in Southeast Asian studies in recognizing that from a cultural perspective Malay culture is better considered with reference to the cultures of the Southeast Asian archipelago than with reference to the cultures of the mainland. More importantly, if Malay culture were to be interpreted in the same manner as I have interpreted Theravada Buddhist and Vietnamese cultures, it would have been necessary to discuss in some detail the spread of Islam to Southeast Asia and the development of Islam as a popular religion in the region. To have undertaken such a discussion would have added greatly to the length of this book and would also have necessitated a much longer delay in seeing it to press.

I have drawn my material primarily from the results of recent research by historians, orientalists, anthropologists, and other social scientists. Rather than list my sources in a bibliography at the end, I have keyed them in footnotes to discussions of various issues in the text. By this method, I hope to have identified some of the lacunae in the scholarship on mainland Southeast Asian society and culture as well as to have provided a more useful guide to the literature. I have provided an author index which will also facilitate any search for sources.

In the subject index I have given glosses for some of the more important Southeast Asian terms used in this work. The subject index also includes many of the technical terms, mainly anthropological in origin, which I have employed in the book.

My interpretations have been formed, in part, by my own experiences during the five and a half years I spent in mainland Southeast Asia. I am deeply grateful to villagers in the community in northeastern Thailand where I lived, to monks with whom I worked in Mae Sariang and Chiang Mai in northern Thailand, and to my former colleagues in the Faculty of the Social Sciences at Chiang Mai University for their guidance in my efforts to understand the cultural life of the region.

I have also benefited by discussion with many colleagues and I should like to express my particular debt of gratitude to A. Thomas Kirsch and T. G. McGee. Moreover, the book has been much improved by the editorial help Jane Keyes has given so generously. Finally, I should like to thank Kenneth Scott, Senior Editor of the College and Professional Division of Macmillan, for his patience during the long genesis of this book.

Seattle, Washington   CHARLES F. KEYES

CONTENTS

Ecological adaptation and economic organization
Local communities and the political organization of rural life
Religion, social structure, and rural life

MAPS AND PHOTOGRAPHS

MAPS

PHOTOGRAPHS

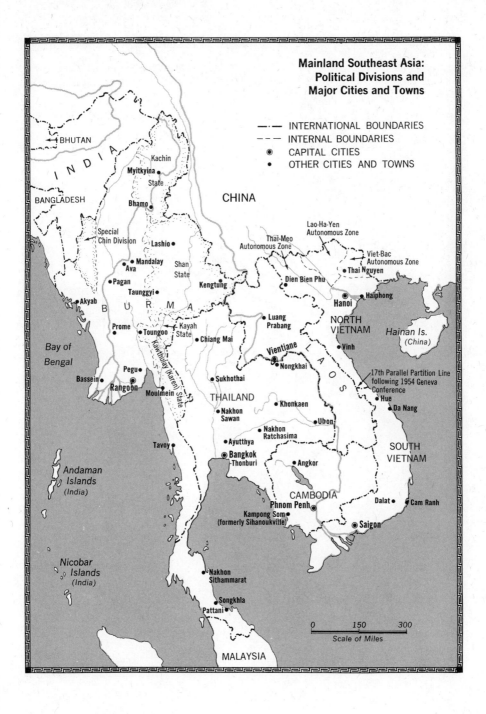

**Mainland Southeast Asia:
Political Divisions and
Major Cities and Towns**

—·— INTERNATIONAL BOUNDARIES
——— INTERNAL BOUNDARIES
◉ CAPITAL CITIES
• OTHER CITIES AND TOWNS

BHUTAN

INDIA

Kachin

Myitkyina •
State

BANGLADESH

Bhamo •

CHINA

Special
Chin Division   Lashio •

Lao-Ha-Yen
Autonomous Zone

Thai-Meo
Autonomous Zone

• Mandalay   Shan
Ava   State

Viet-Bac
Autonomous Zone

• Thai Nguyen

• Pagan

Taunggyi •

Kengtung •

Dien Bien Phu •

• Akyab

B U R M A

Haiphong •

Hanoi ◉

Prome •
• Toungoo

• Kayah
State

• Chiang Mai

Luang •
Prabang

NORTH
VIETNAM

Hainan Is.
(China)

Bay of
Bengal

Vientiane ◉
• Nongkhai

L   A   O   S

• Vinh

17th Parallel Partition Line
following 1954 Geneva
Conference

Pegu •

Bassein •

• Sukhothai

THAILAND

Rangoon ◉
Moulmein •

Kawthulay (Karen) State

• Khonkaen

• Nakhon
Sawan

• Hue

▲ Da Nang

• Nakhon
Ratchasima

• Ubon

SOUTH
VIETNAM

Tavoy •

Andaman
Islands
(India)

• Ayutthya

◉ Bangkok
Thonburi

• Angkor

CAMBODIA

Dalat •   • Cam Ranh

Phnom Penh ◉

Kampong Som •
(formerly Sihanoukville)

◉ Saigon

Nicobar
Islands
(India)

• Nakhon
Sithammarat

• Songkhla

Pattani •

0   150   300

Scale of Miles

MALAYSIA

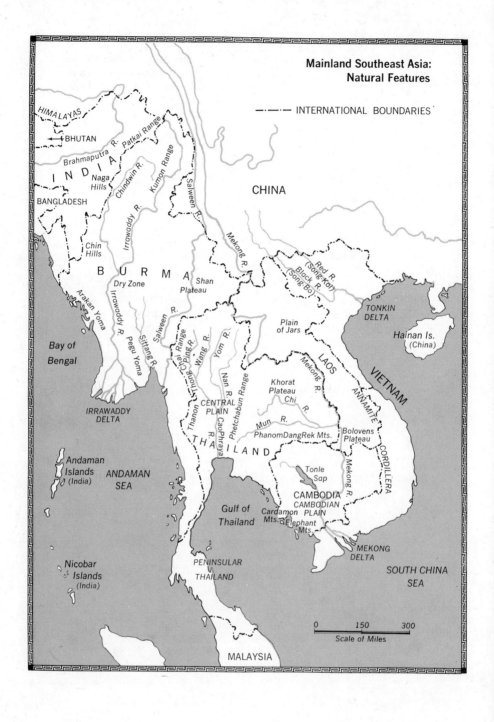

**Mainland Southeast Asia:
Natural Features**

— · — · — INTERNATIONAL BOUNDARIES

HIMALAYAS

←BHUTAN

Brahmaputra R.

Patkai Range

Naga
Hills

I N D I A

BANGLADESH

Chindwin R.

Kumon Range

Salween R.

CHINA

Chin
Hills

Irrawaddy R.

B U R M A

Dry Zone

Shan
Plateau

Mekong R.

Red R.
(Song Koi)

Black R.
(Song Bo)

TONKIN
DELTA

Arakan Yoma

Irrawaddy R.

Salween R.

Pegu Yoma

Sittang R.

Thanon Thong Chai Range

Ping R.

Wang R.

Yom R.

Nan R.

Salween R.

Plain
of Jars

Hainan Is.
(China)

Bay of
Bengal

CENTRAL
PLAIN

Chao Phraya

Phetchabun Range

Khorat
Plateau

Chi R.

Mekong R.

LAOS

VIETNAM

ANNAMITE

IRRAWADDY
DELTA

T H A I L A N D

Mun R.

PhanomDangRek Mts.

Bolovens
Plateau

CORDILLERA

Andaman
Islands
(India)

ANDAMAN
SEA

Tonle
Sap

Mekong R.

Gulf of
Thailand

CAMBODIA

CAMBODIAN
PLAIN

Cardamon
Mts.

Elephant
Mts.

MEKONG
DELTA

Nicobar
Islands
(India)

PENINSULAR
THAILAND

SOUTH CHINA
SEA

0   150   300
Scale of Miles

MALAYSIA

INTRODUCTION: THE STUDY OF SOCIOCULTURAL DIVERSITY IN MAINLAND SOUTH-EAST ASIA

... Indochina, in the sense of the Indochinese Peninsula (the " India beyond the Ganges " of the ancient world) ... [is] a " crossroads " where the most diverse racial groups came into contact with each other and mixed with each other, and where since ancient times the two main civilizations of Asia have confronted each other. In Indochina these civilizations were trans- formed, in varying degrees, through contact with the indigenous societies, and the civilizations resulting from this contact reacted upon each other and were subsequently enriched or changed by later influences from abroad, such as Buddhism from Ceylon, and European civilization.

George Coedès, *The Making of South East Asia*[1]

In this book, we will be concerned with the sociocultural systems found in that part of the world bordered by India and Bangladesh on the west and northwest, by China to the north, and by peninsular and insular Southeast Asia (Malaysia, Indonesia, and the Philippines) to the south and southeast. This part of the world has been called by various names throughout history. For the reasons cited by Coedès, Indochina might seem to be the most appropriate name; however, as the French preempted this name for the colonial domain they contructed out of territories that are today in Laos, Cambodia, and Vietnam, it would be misleading to use this term. In ancient times, the region was known as the " golden country " (the Indian *Suvannaphumi*), the " golden peninsula " (Thai *laem thong*), or the " golden chersonese." Although the mineral gold is not an important commodity in the region, the term " golden " country or peninsula is still evocative for the student of culture. Here in the lands that today include the modern nations of Burma, Thailand, Laos, Cambodia, and Vietnam can be found cultures whose value have only begun to be appreciated.

Indigenous Models of Sociocultural Diversity

The sociocultural diversity of mainland Southeast Asia is obvious to the people of the region as well as to outsiders. Southeast Asians have developed a number of indigenous models in their attempts to make sense of this diversity. Most of these models are known to us not from theoretical treatises, but from

1

myth, legend, and traditional histories. There is a common theme in many of these myths, positing as they do a symbiotic relationship between two types of people, the one living in the lowlands, following a literate tradition, and being organized into some form of state, and the other living in the uplands, following an oral tradition, and lacking state structures. I shall explore this theme more fully when I discuss the traditional form of relationship between tribal and civilized peoples.

A more comprehensive model is evident in some of the indigenous chronicles that combine myth, legend, and history. Consider, for example, the Jinakālamalī, a sixteenth-century chronicle composed in Pali by a Buddhist monk living in Chiang Mai, then a court center of a minor kingdom located in northern Thailand.[2] In this work the author was concerned, as is typical in many traditional chronicles of Southeast Asia, with tracing the origins of the religion practiced by his compatriots and, more specifically, with establishing the line of legitimacy for his own Buddhist sect. The first chapters of the Jinakālamalī are what might be described as a cosmogonic myth, a myth that defines the significant parameters of the world as it is lived in. In this case, the myth is expressed in the form of a life of the Buddha, or, rather, the lives of previous Buddhas including that of Gottama Buddha, the Buddha known to history. The next chapters trace the history (including legendary history) of Buddhism as it developed in India, spread to Ceylon, and then to the Mons of lower Burma. The author also dwells at some length on the history of the kingdom of Haripunjaya, an early kingdom in northern Thailand, which preceded the establishment of the Tai states of which Chiang Mai was one. Next he links the spread of Buddhism with the history of northern Thailand as found during the period since the thirteenth century when Chiang Mai supplanted Haripunjaya.

The author of the Jinakālamalī makes two basic distinctions that constitute, in our terms, a classification of sociocultural types. On the one hand, he distinguishes between those who have become Buddhists and those who have not, the latter being the aboriginals of the various countries he mentions. Thus, there is a fundamental distinction between the " civilized " and the " uncivilized." In addition, he also recognizes differences among the civilized themselves based on the polity to which they belong.

These basic categories of classification between the pagan aboriginals and civilized peoples and between different polities in which civilized people live define the dominant model used by the peoples of Southeast Asia in dealing with sociocultural diversity. It should be added that this model was rarely, if ever, a " conscious " one; that is, it was never explicitly stated or reflected upon.[3]

Southeast Asian Ethnography During the Colonial Period

The first significant attempts by Westerners to make sense of the sociocultural diversity found in mainland Southeast Asia were made by scholars who were usually also colonial officials or missionaries. Among the most outstanding examples of early western enthnological surveys, or works that attempted to classify peoples according to their sociocultural characteristics, were the

Gazeteer of Upper Burma and the Shan States written primarily by Sir James George Scott,[4] and the compendium of observations, local chronicles, and folklore of the peoples of present-day Laos and north and northeast Thailand collected under the supervision of Auguste Pavie[5] and published under the title, *Mission Pavie*. Scott and Pavie epitomized the colonial builder *cum* scholar *cum* adventurer in British Burma and French Indochina, respectively. Both Scott and Pavie attempted to make sense out of the sociocultural complexity and heterogeneity that exists in the mountainous areas of northern mainland Southeast Asia. Their motivations, however, were far from simply scholarly. Scott, in particular, felt the need to identify distinctive ethnolinguistic differences that would be useful to officials charged with administering the region. Both Scott and Pavie were interested in identifying the cultures that were the " same," in order to justify their inclusion within the British or French domains. Although these works had an " applied " orientation, their scholarly quality cannot be denied. The *Gazeteer* helped to standardize many of the ethnolinguistic categories still used today, and the *Mission Pavie* represented one of the first efforts to compare different versions of chronicles and folklore in the reconstruction of the history of the region.

Throughout the colonial period and up to World War II, there was a steady accumulation of first-hand reports, or ethnographic accounts as they are called by anthropologists, of the customs and ways of life of various peoples living in different parts of Southeast Asia. A very few of these ethnographic accounts were produced by academic anthropologists, a larger number were produced by officials or missionaries with anthropological training, and the majority were written by untrained people who felt impelled to record something of what they had seen during their intensive contact with certain peoples of the region. Such ethnographic accounts were produced not only by Westerners, but also by a small number of Western-trained Southeast Asians. Probably the most well-developed indigenous development of ethnographic reporting occurred in Thailand, where the central Thai government faced administrative problems in outlying areas comparable to those of the colonial governments in Burma and Indochina.

Cultural Diffusion

Prior to World War II, the ethnographic literature compiled on Southeast Asian cultures and societies was, for the most part, rarely taken into account by anthropologists concerned with theoretical issues. By the same token, anthropological theory was only rarely used by those who wished to make sense of sociocultural patterns found in mainland Southeast Asia. One major exception contradicts this generalization, however. The anthropological theory known as *diffusionism* was developed in a significant sense with reference to ethnographic data from Southeast Asia.

Father Wilhelm Schmidt, a founder of the Vienna school of anthropology and a leading figure in the development of diffusionist theory, was one of the first anthropologists to undertake research on Southeast Asia.[6] He was followed by other members of the Vienna school who also carried out research in the area. One of Schmidt's students, Robert Heine-Geldern, was the first anthropologist to attempt a general systematic ordering of Southeast Asian ethnography within a broader framework informed by anthropological theory.[7] Heine-Geldern's influence still remains strong, especially in Europe, among both anthropologists and historians interested in Southeast Asia.

Diffusionist theory postulates that certain " bundles " or " complexes " of cultural traits " adhere." Where these complexes are found in different cultures, such must be taken as evidence of historic contacts between these cultures or of diffusion of the complex of these cultures from a common source. Different complexes are associated with different waves of influence or migrations, which are postulated to have occurred at different periods of time in Southeast Asian history. For example, the " megalithic complex," which has perhaps received the greatest attention by diffusionists working with Southeast Asian materials,[8] is believed to have diffused in prehistoric times from Central Asia and ultimately from Europe. The elements of the complex, including ancestor worship, buffalo sacrifice, head-hunting rituals, graveposts (characteristically, but not invariably, made of stone and thus the megaliths diagnostic of the complex), and elements of decoration are claimed to " abound and can even still be studied as integral parts of living cultures " in Southeast Asia today.[9]

Diffusionary theory has often been carried to extremes as can be seen, for example, in the arguments of some diffusionist-influenced Southeast Asian historians who see Southeast Asian civilization as merely transplanted Indian or Chinese cultures. Cultural traits, in such a view, are significant only if they can be shown to link one society with another. Such extreme positions have led many critics of diffusionist theory, including most British and American anthropologists, to dismiss it as having no merit whatsoever. To do so would lead one to overlook the very considerable contribution certain diffusionists, particularly Heine-Geldern, have made. Heine Geldern's work presents considerable evidence to support the thesis that cultural forms cannot be understood *only* in terms of the context in which they are found. This argument is strengthened by the recognition that those cultural forms which can be treated independently of local context are related to each other in some coherent " complex."

Social Structure and Adaptation

Such a view of culture is directly refuted by E. R. Leach, whose *Political Systems of Highland Burma*, first published in 1954,[10] has had a greater theoretical influence on anthropological studies of Southeast Asia than perhaps any other single work. Leach views the cultural symbols structured as myth and ritual as a language for the expression of social relations. Leach asserts that " ritual . . . serves to express the individual's status as a social person in the structural system in which he finds himself for the time being."[11]

Given this position, Leach looks for the basis of social action elsewhere than in the culture. In his study of the Kachins of the Kachin Hills in Northern

Burma, Leach sees Kachin social structure as a function of the adaptation made by Kachins to the environment in which they live. Although Leach recognizes the importance of the ecological adaptation the Kachins have made, he sees the environment to which the Kachins are adapted as including more than the natural characteristics of the Kachin Hills. In addition, he also recognizes sociodemographic factors as relevant; in this case, adaptation is manifested in a system of exchange of wives among descent groups. Leach further argues that the environment in which the Kachins live must be understood to include other peoples, specifically other Kachins and lowland-living Shans. The adaptation to this part of the environment, Leach sees, as structured politically. It was Leach's argument that there could be a common social structure for peoples who were members of two different societies, in this case the Kachin and the Shan, that has come to be recognized as a major contribution to anthropological theory.

Since Leach, most studies concerned with the adaptation of societies in Southeast Asia have given much greater stress than did Leach to ecological adaptation. This focus has followed the theoretical developments in anthropology that have made " cultural ecology " a major research strategy. Cultural ecology does not view environment and culture as separate systems that influence each other but as components of a single system, the ecosystem.[12] Cultural ecologists, following Julian Steward,[13] recognize that there are cultural similarities between different societies that have resulted from similar strategies of ecological adaptation in similar environments. It follows, then, that a typology of sociocultural systems can be constructed according to a type of ecosystem or *ecotype.* Such was done, for example, in Wallace's recent book on the peoples of island Southeast Asia.[14] Burling's ethnological survey of mainland Southeast Asia is also organized primarily around the contrast between two different ecotypes.[15]

As we have already observed, Leach recognized the importance of the Kachin adaptation to sociodemographic conditions as well as to the conditions of the natural world in which they lived. Most anthropological theory prior to World War II had stressed " descent " as the basis whereby various peoples adapted to these conditions. That is, societies were seen by anthropologists as divided into descent groups whose functions provided the society with a continuity through time and whose structured relationships also provided a basis for social solidarity. In Southeast Asia this theory was apparently confounded by the fact that many societies were not organized according to principles of unilineal (matrilineal or patrilineal) descent. Southeast Asia is not, of course, the only area of the world in which one finds such " nonunilineal " kinship systems. However, some of the studies made of groups in Southeast Asia— mainly groups from island rather than mainland Southeast Asia—did provide the context in which some of the theoretical issues raised by nonunilineal systems were discussed. Moreover, one of the most influential theoretical papers on the question, George Peter Murdock's " Cognatic Forms of Social Organization," was written primarily with reference to ethnographic data from

Southeast Asia.[16] Murdock's argument, like that of others who also attempted to make sense of nonunilineal kinship systems, stressed that factors other than descent must be taken into account in understanding the role of kinship in society. These other factors include rules of post-marital residence and rules regulating marriage.

Marriage rules are brought to stage front in the theory developed by Lévi-Strauss, which he presented to the world in a book, *Les structures élémentaires de la parenté*, first published in 1949.[17] In this work Lévi-Strauss draws heavily on the ethnographic literature of Asia, including that on many groups of mainland Southeast Asia. Lévi-Strauss makes a convincing case for seeing marriage systems as social structures functioning to promote social order in the face of the entropic pressures of nature, that is, to ensure the persistence of at least certain types of societies. Such a function obtains whatever the cultural idiom in which such a marriage system might be expressed.

Lévi-Strauss' ideas have been championed by Rodney Needham who has made his own case primarily in reference to ethnographic data from Southeast Asia.[18] Unlike Lévi-Strauss, Needham is concerned with a particular type of society, one in which an ideology of alliance, as encoded in the myths and rituals of the society, functions to promote social solidarity. Lévi-Strauss' interest is much more comprehensive. As Leach has observed, Lévi-Strauss' "ultimate concern is to establish facts which are true about 'the human mind' rather than about the organization of any particular society or class of societies."[19] Although I would agree with Needham that Lévi-Strauss' theory does offer insights into a type of society in Southeast Asia, it does so, apparently, in spite of the ultimate purpose for which he constructed his theory.[20] Needham also, in my opinion, gives undue stress to the ideology of alliance as against other structural bases for society.

Lehman has pointed out that the Southeast Asian societies discussed by Needham that appear to be structured primarily with reference to an ideology of alliance are " closed " societies involving " a small, remnant people living in alien territory, with perhaps a reduced population and range of lineages."[21] Most Southeast Asian societies wherein an ideology of alliance is found do not follow this pattern. Rather, they are " open " societies whose structures reflect long-standing relations with neighboring societies. This recognition that social structure may reflect the adaptation of one society to another—an idea first proposed by Leach—has proved to be an extremely powerful idea not only for the study of Southeast Asia but for the study of societies in general. With this perspective, societies can no longer be thought of as being comprised of peoples who share a common culture and speak a common language. Although there has been dissent from this view, other studies from Southeast Asia, including those of other than tribal societies, have provided additional support for Leach's position.[22]

While Leach, and other anthropolgists, have argued that competition for power provided the basis for structural differences in certain mainland Southeast Asian tribal societies in which there was considerable interaction between tribal peoples and those of neighboring civilizations, political economist J. S. Furnivall[23] put forward a rather similar argument regarding the social systems of entire societies under colonial rule. Furnivall constructed the model of the " plural society " to explain the relations between groups of differing cultural backgrounds, which compete for control over access to the same resources. Furnivall's ideas, which have been influential in the social sciences generally, were forged by his experience as a colonial official in Burma. In his studies of the political economy of British Burma, Furnivall took into account the ethnic differences not only between Burmans and tribal minorities, but also between all Burmese (be they Burman or tribal peoples) and those living in Burma who were not of Burmese origin, namely the immigrant Indians who came to Burma in great numbers during the colonial period, the Chinese, and the Europeans. Such a perspective obviously has implications (as we shall see) for the study of other large immigrant populations—especially the Chinese—found in other countries of Southeast Asia.

Most who have considered the structure of ethnic relations a function of the political economy have also argued that the cultural differences among ethnic groups are meaningful only insofar as they are used as a type of language in which to express such structural differences. We are brought back, thus, to the Leach argument that would see culture as providing codes whereby the structure of social action can be expressed. I accept that the structure of social action is, following Leach and others, a function of ecological adaptation, sociodemographic adaptation, and political economic adaptation, but I also argue that culture itself provides a basis for the structure of social action. However, before I can pursue my argument, we first need to look at another theoretical orientation that has been influential in the study of Southeast Asia but has developed tangentially to the orientations discussed thus far.

Culture and Personality

During World War II, Ruth Benedict, then one of the best-known anthropologists in the United States, prepared a study, based on written sources, of Thai culture and behavior.[24] Benedict's study was the first, to my knowledge, to attempt to explain social behavior in mainland Southeast Asia with reference to psychological factors.[25] Since World War II a number of other studies have adopted this orientation,[26] the most important by far being Spiro's recent studies of Burmese religion.[27]

In *Burmese Supernaturalism*, Spiro set forward the following position as the basis for explaining similarities found among different sociocultural systems:

It is my personal assumption ... that the regularity which underlies the manifest (cross-cultural) diversity in cultural *forms* rests on a common psychobiological " human nature," and that within any cultural domain (and frequently across domains) the *wide* range of diverse forms constitutes a set of structural variations for the satisfaction of a *narrow* range of common psychobiological needs.[28]

In *Buddhism and Society*, he pursues the same position and argues that Burmese Buddhism, despite the content that is often ascribed to it on the basis of studies on written sources, reveals " most of the defining characteristics of religion in general."[29] For Spiro, cultural symbols that comprise a religion provide a mode of expression for " a restricted set of needs, fantasies, wishes, conflicts, aspirations, and so on which are deeply rooted in a universal human nature."[30]

Spiro is very convincing in his argument that the behavior of any people must be studied with reference to the adaptation that humans make to their " psychobiological ' human nature '." However, to consider only this " human nature " in an effort to understand sociocultural systems is as reductionist as it would be to consider only what is true about the " human mind " as advocated by Lévi-Strauss. As we have already seen, it is equally important to take into account ecological adaptation, sociodemographic adaptation, and political economic adaptation.

Although we have a broadened view of the nature of human adaptation, we are still left, in the works of Spiro, Leach, and the other postwar anthropologists we have considered, with a view of culture as functioning only to provide expression for the various forms of adaptation. This position is clearly contrary to the view of the diffusionists who accorded culture an autonomous power to orient people in their social action. But it is not necessary to become a diffusionist to adopt such a position. A number of other traditions of anthropological scholarship in Southeast Asia also espouse a similar position.

Culture and Adaptation

Such an espousal is particularly marked among French anthropologists and cultural historians who have carried out research in Southeast Asia. Perhaps, because Oriental studies—Sinology and Indology—first dominated the efforts of the French to understand Southeast Asian societies and cultures, the emphasis on culture was established and later perpetuated in anthropology. Whatever the reason may be, the commanding figures in the French anthropological tradition who have studied Southeast Asia have been men who have pursued studies of specific Southeast Asian cultures in immense detail. One could not find better examples of what Clifford Geertz has termed " thick description "[31] than in the works of Paul Mus, Charles Archaimbault, Eveline Porée-Maspéro, or Georges Condominas.[32] Mus' *Sociologie d'un Guerre* provides an excellent example of this *genre* of French anthropological studies not only because Mus bridged the orientalist and anthropological worlds but also because this particular study addressed itself to the problem of elucidating the culture not of a stable society but of one in revolution, the Vietnamese revolution. Mus demonstrates, quite convincingly, that the success that the Communist Viet Minh had in persuading the Vietnamese (and particularly the north Vietnamese) peasantry to support them was not merely because the peasantry found the conditions of life under French colonialism unbearable.

After all, other anticolonial movements competed with the Viet Minh for the support of the peasantry. Rather, Mus argues, it was because the Viet Minh were able to make their message meaningful in cultural terms the peasants understood.[33] Confronted with studies such as those of Mus and other French anthropologists, it is difficult indeed to question that culturally derived meanings do not orient people toward social action.

It is my position that the sociocultural diversity of mainland Southeast Asia can best be understood if it is recognized that culture is both an expression of the adaptation by humans to the conditions of their existence and also a set of conditions to which humans must adapt. To make this position clear, I need at this point to be precise as to what I mean by culture.[34] *Culture*, as I understand it, is a system of meaning. Such meaning is expressed in forms that are directly observable and also invested with a content that must be elicited.

Cultural forms include all types of expressive actions (such as speech, gestures, play, ritual, and music), art, written documents, architecture, as well as more mundane implements of daily life, tools, dress, and so on. In short, cultural forms are as observable as are aspects of the landscape, as the number of people living in a settlement, or as the rice placed in a granary. They are certainly more easily observable than the psychological needs that motivate people to action. Cultural forms in and of themselves have only a limited utility for the student; one must also know what content these forms carry for the people for whom they are meaningful. Cultural content can be gleaned by eliciting exegeses from informants, by noting the contexts in which the forms appear, and by comparing forms with unknown meanings with similar forms with known meanings.[35]

The content of cultural forms derives in part from the experiences that humans undergo in relating to the conditions of their existence, for example, from such experiences as having been weaned at the age of two, raising a crop, arranging a marriage, paying taxes, coping with grief, and so on. Yet at the same time these conditions themselves are perceived, in part, in terms of meanings derived from the historical tradition in which a person has been raised. People acquire meanings with which they can invest their experiences as a consequence of socialization, repetitive exposure to the same cultural expressions, didactic teaching, and personal study. In addition, meaning may also be arrived at by the process of rational thought. However derived, cultural meanings serve to provide both a basis for understanding experience and a source of values that orient people in determining courses of action.

In the following pages I will attempt to use this view of the dialectical relationship between culture and experience to provide an interpretation of the types of sociocultural systems found in mainland Southeast Asia and an analysis of the processes of change these systems have undergone and are still undergoing. My approach leads me to focus on culture, both as adaptive strategies employed by people living in particular conditions and as systems of meaning to which humans must also adapt.

NOTES

Introduction

1. George Coedès, *The Making of South East Asia* (tr. by H. M. Wright; Berkeley and Los Angeles: University of California Press, 1966), pp. v–vi.

2. Ratanapañña, Thera, *Jinakălamălipakarnam: The Sheaf of Garlands of the Epochs of the Conqueror* (tr. by N. A. Jayawickrama; London: Luzac for the Pali Text Society, 1968).

3. For further discussion of indigenous models employed for classifying varieties of sociocultural systems see the following: F. K. Lehman, " Ethnic Categories in Burma and the Theory of Social Systems," in *Southeast Asian Tribes, Minorities and Nations*, ed. by Peter Kunstadter (Princeton: Princeton University Press, 1967), pp. 93–124; Michael Moerman, " Ethnic Identification in a Complex Society: Who Are the Lue? " *American Anthropologist*, LXVII (1965), pp. 1215–30; Ch. Archaimbault, " L'histoire de Campăsăk," *Journal Asiatique*, CCXLIX (1961), pp. 519–95 and Archaimbault, *Structures Réligeuses Lao* (Vientiane: Editions Vithagna, 1973); Donald K. Swearer, " Myth, Legend and History in the Northern Thai Chronicles," *J. Siam Society*, LXII (1974), pp. 67–88; and Charles F. Keyes, " The Karens in Thai History and the History of Karens in Thailand," in *Ethnic Adaptation and Identity: The Karens on the Thai Frontier with Burma*, ed. by Charles F. Keyes, forthcoming.

4. J. G. Scott and J. P. Hardiman, *Gazeteer of Upper Burma and the Shan States*, Part I, 2 vols; Part II, 3 vols. (Rangoon: Supt. Govt. Printing and Stationery, 1900–1901).

5. A. Pavie, *et al.*, *Mission Pavie (Études Diverses)*, 3 vols. (Paris: Leroux, 1898, 1898, 1904); *Mission Pavie (Géographie et Voyages)*, 7 vols. (Paris: Leroux, 1900–1919); and *Mission Pavie (Atlas)* (Paris: A. Challumel, 1903).

6. Schmidt was interested in the question of the diffusion of culture from India to Southeast Asia, a question that led to linguistic research whereby he discovered a link between the speakers of Austroasiatic languages in Southeast Asia and the speakers of Munda languages in India. See W. Schmidt, " Die Mon-Khmer Volker," *Archiv fur Anthropologie*, XXXIII (1906); translated as " Les peuples Mon-Khmer," in *Bulletin de L'Ecole Française d'Extrême-Orient*, XL (1940), pp. 239–313.

7. Robert Heine-Geldern, " Sudoestasien," in *Illustrierte Volkerkunde*, ed. by G. Buschan (Stuttgart, 1923), vol. 2, pp. 689–968.

8. See the survey of the literature on the " megalithic complex " given in *Elements of the Megalithic Complex in Southeast Asia: An Annotated Bibliography*, by H. H. Loofs (Canberra: Australian National University, Centre of Oriental Studies, Oriental Monographs Series, No. 3, 1967).

9. Loofs, *op. cit.*, p. v. The list of elements of the complex is also taken from Loofs (p. vi). Also compare Robert Heine-Geldern, " Some Tribal Art Styles in Southeast Asia," in *The Many Faces of Primitive Art*, ed. by D. Fraser (Englewood Cliffs, N. J.: Prentice-Hall, 1966), pp. 165–214. In this article, Heine-Geldern argues again that the " megalithic complex " has a European origin.

10. E. R. Leach, *Political Systems of Highland Burma* (Cambridge: Harvard University Press, 1954); reprinted with a new introductory note by the author (Boston: Beacon Press, 1965).

11. *Op cit.*, pp. 10–11.

12. See Clifford Geertz, *Agricultural Involution* (Berkeley and Los Angeles: University of California Press, 1963).

13. Julian Steward, *The Theory of Culture Change* (Urbana: University of Illinois Press, 1955).

14. Ben J. Wallace, *Village Life in Insular Southeast Asia* (Boston: Little, Brown, 1971).

15. Robbins Burling, *Hill Farms and Padi Fields* (Englewood Cliffs, N. J.: Prentice-Hall, 1965).

16. George Peter Murdock, " Cognatic Forms of Social Organization " in *Social Structure in Southeast Asia*, ed. by George Peter Murdock (Chicago: Quadrangle Books, Wenner Gren Foundation for Anthropological Research, Publications in Anthropology, No. 29, 1960), pp. 1–14. The other articles in the volume concern peoples living in Vietnam, the Philippines, Borneo, Java, Ceylon, Formosa, and South China.

17. Claude Lévi-Strauss, *Les structures élementaires de la parenté* (Paris: Press Universitaires de France, 1949). The second, revised edition of this work has been translated into English by James Harle Bell, John Richard von Sturmer, and Rodney Needham, edited by Rodney Needham, and published in English as *The Elementary Structures of Kinship* (Boston: Beacon Press, 1969).

18. Needham's arguments have been developed in numerous articles, a few based on his own researches in Indonesia, but most being reanalyses of older ethnographic writings, in introductions to the writings of various Dutch anthropologists whose works he has translated, and in a treatise written in defense of Lévi-Strauss. See, especially, Rodney Needham, " A Structural Analysis of Purum Society," *American Anthropologist*, LX (1958), pp. 75–101 and *Structure and Sentiment* (Chicago: Chicago University Press, 1962). See also Frank B. Livingstone, " A Further Analysis of Purum Social Structure," *American Anthropologist*, LXI (1959), pp. 1084–87 and Needham's reply, " Structure and Change in Assymetric Alliance: Comments on Livingstone's Further Analysis of Purum Society," *American Anthropologist*, LXII (1960), pp. 499–503.

19. E. R. Leach, *Claude Lévi-Strauss* (New York: Viking Press, 1970), p. 2.

20. Lévi-Strauss takes Needham to task for misinterpreting his theory in the introduction to the English version of *Elementary Structures* . . . (*op. cit.*, p. xxxi). This he does to the consternation of Needham who had organized the translation project.

21. F. K. Lehman, *The Structure of Chin Society* (Urbana: University of Illinois Press, 1963), p. 99.

22. The argument has been pursued in an exchange between Raoul Naroll, who disputed Leach's position on theoretical grounds, and Michael Moerman who supports it on the basis of his researches in a Tai-Lue community in northern Thailand. See Raoul Naroll, " On Ethnic Unit Classification," *Current Anthropology*, V, 4 (1964), pp. 283–91, 306–12; Naroll, " Who the Lue Are," in *Essays on the*

Problem of the Tribe, ed. by June Helm (Seattle: University of Washington Press, Proceedings of the 1967 Annual Spring Meeting of the American Ethnological Society, 1968), pp. 72–79; Michael Moerman, " Ethnic Identification in a Complex Civilization: Who are the Lue?" *American Anthropologist*, LXVII (1965), pp. 1215–30; Moerman, " Being Lue: Uses and Abuses of Ethnic Identification," in *Essays on the Problem of the Tribe*, ed. by June Helm, *op. cit.*, pp. 153–69.

23. J. S. Furnivall, *Netherlands India: A Study in Plural Economy* (Cambridge: Cambridge University Press, 1939); Furnivall, *Colonial Policy and Practice* (Cambridge; Cambridge University Press, 1948; reprinted New York: New York University Press, 1956).

24. Ruth Benedict, *Thai Culture and Behavior: An Unpublished War Time Study Dated September, 1943* (Ithaca, N. Y.: Cornell University Southeast Asia Program, Data Paper No. 4, 1952).

25. It is worth noting that some of the pioneering studies in psychological anthropology were carried out in island Southeast Asia. See, for example. Gregory Bateson and Margaret Mead, *Balinese Character* (New York: New York Academy of Sciences, 1942) and Cora DuBois, *The People of Alor* (Cambridge: Harvard University Press, 1944).

26. See, for example, Herbert P. Phillips, *Thai Peasant Personality* (Berkeley and Los Angeles: University of California Press, 1965) and Lucian Pye, *Politics, Personality, and Nation Building: Burma's Search for Identity* (New Haven: Yale University Press, 1962).

27. Melford E. Spiro, *Burmese Supernaturalism* (Englewood Cliffs, N. J.: Prentice-Hall, 1967) and *Buddhism and Society: A Great Tradition and Its Burmese Vicissitudes* (New York: Harper and Row, 1970).

28. Spiro, *Burmese Supernaturalism*, p. 6; emphasis in original.

29. Spiro, *Buddhism and Society*, p. 14.

30. *Loc. cit.*

31. Clifford Geertz, " Thick Description: Toward an Interpretative Theory of Culture," in *The Interpretation of Cultures* (New York: Basic Books, 1973).

32. See, for example, Paul Mus, *Viet-Nam: Sociologie d'un Guerre* (Paris: Editions du Seuil, 1952); Charles Archaimbault, *Structures Réligieuses Lao* (*op. cit.*); Eveline Porée-Maspero, *Etude sur les rites agraires des cambodgiens* (3 vols, Paris: Mouton, 1962, 1964, 1969). Georges Condominas, *Nous avons mangé la forêt* (Paris: Mercure de France, 1957) and *L'exotique est quotidien* (Paris: Librairie Plon, 1965).

33. Mus, *op cit.*, pp. 248–67. See also The *Vietnamese and Their Revolution* by John T. McAlister, Jr., and Paul Mus (New York: Harper and Row, 1970). This book includes a partial translation of *Sociologie d'une Guerre*.

34. The approach to the study of culture taken here has been formulated, in part, with reference to the interpretative sociology of Max Weber and to the more recent ideas of Clifford Geertz who has adapted the Weberian tradition for anthropological uses.

35. For a more extended discussion of the methodology for eliciting cultural meanings, see Victor Turner, *The Forest of Symbols* (Ithaca, N. Y.: Cornell University Press, 1967).

CHAPTER 1
PRIMITIVE AND TRIBAL WORLDS
AND THEIR TRANSFORMATIONS

PRIMITIVE AND TRIBAL CULTURES IN SOUTHEAST ASIAN PREHISTORY AND HISTORY

Throughout the uplands of mainland Southeast Asia, from the rugged mountains of northern Burma to the highlands of southern Vietnam, live peoples whose ways of life are more primitive than those of their neighbors in the valleys, plateaus, and plains of the region. The ways of life of these peoples represent an adaptation to conditions in areas peripheral to the major civilizations of mainland Southeast Asia. This was not always the case; in prehistoric times primitive and tribal peoples dominated the region.

Early Humans in Mainland Southeast Asia

Southeast Asian prehistory has recently become an extremely exciting field. In the past few years discoveries, primarily in northeastern Thailand, have led to radical reassessments about the beginnings of agriculture, especially rice cultivation, the dating of pottery traditions, the origin of bronze manufacture, and the development of town life in mainland Southeast Asia. Although these reassessments have not yet been fully completed, it has become clear that the long-standing view of Southeast Asian cultures as little more than receptacles for influences emanating from India and China can no longer be sustained. The cultural traditions of Southeast Asia, however much they may have taken over cultural elements from their more powerful neighbors to the north and west, have always shown what certain Southeast Asian historians have referred to as " local genius."

The peoples who have settled in mainland Southeast Asia over the centuries have adapted themselves to the particular geographical features of the region. Most of the area is characterized by high temperatures and monsoonal rainfall, but both rainfall and temperature have significant local variations owing to differences in wind patterns and relief. The dominant feature of the physical relief of the region is the alternation between what the geographer Fisher terms ridge and furrow.[1] The ridges of the Indo-Malayan ranges, as the mountain

13

ranges of the region are collectively called, are extensions of the Himalayas, which, having previously swept from west to east, take a sharp turn to the south in upper Burma. The mountains of mainland Southeast Asia, although rugged, do not reach great heights except in the far north of Burma, where some peaks rise to about 19,000 feet. The other ranges, from the Chin Hills and Shan-Tenasserim range in Burma to the Annamite Cordillera of Indochina, are considerably lower.

The furrows that lie between the hills and mountains are dominated by watercourses, the more important ones serving as channels for the great rivers of the region: the Irrawaddy-Chindwin and Salween of Burma, the Cao Phraya in Thailand, the Song-koi or Red River of northern Vietnam, and the Mekong, which runs through Laos, forms much of the border between Laos and Thailand, continues on through Cambodia, and then passes through the Mekong Delta in southern Vietnam to empty finally in the South China Sea. With the exception of the Cao Phraya, all these rivers have their sources in the Himalayas. Almost all rivers in the area, including all the great rivers except the Song-koi, flow in a more or less north to south direction. The Song-koi, as well as some other smaller rivers in Vietnam, such as the Pearl, whose mouth is near Hué, flows from west to east.

From prehistoric times to the present, the population has moved from the northern part of the region and from what is today southern China southward into mainland Southeast Asia. Some peoples, as for example the Meo and Yao tribal peoples, who are the most recent migrants from southern China into the region, have followed along the ridges, moving from one hilltop to the next. Larger scale migrations, such as that by the Tai-speaking people, who began filtering into mainland Southeast Asia from southern China sometime before the 10th century A.D., followed along the river courses. Yet another pattern of migration can be seen in the Vietnamese, whose " push to the south " from the Tonkin Delta from about A.D. 1000 on took place along the coastal lowlands of the South China Sea. The mountains have made transverse movement across the region difficult and have tended to separate peoples who have followed separate paths of cultural and social development. Moreover, the peoples who have inhabited the uplands have also generally been culturally and socially different from their neighbors who have settled in the lowlands.

The earliest human occupation of Southeast Asia appears to date from the latter part of the Lower Pleistocene or, more likely, from the Middle Pleistocene period. These early human groups were Pithecanthropoid, and their stone implements " were fashioned primarily in the chopper-chopping-tool tradition —consisting of crudely flaked unifacial and bifacial implements on pebbles with big secondarily retouched flaking surfaces."[2] During the Upper Pleistocene period, the Pithecanthropoids were succeeded by *homo sapiens*. At what point and where racial differences between Mongoloids and Australoids (also called Oceanic Negroids, that is, ancestors of such peoples as the Semang, the Andaman Islanders, and the Australian aboriginals) first appeared is still unclear, but by the end of the Pleistocene period it would seem that two races had emerged and were living together on the continent of Asia. The Australoids occupied primarily the area that today forms Southeast Asia, while the Mongoloids lived to the north in what is now China.

The Paleolithic tool industry associated with chopper-chopping-tools continued through the Upper Pleistocene period, gradually evolving into a complex referred to as the Hoabinhian industry. At Hoa Binh, in northern Vietnam, and at sites throughout Southeast Asia, similar assemblages of tools, shells, and fish bones have been found. From them we can deduce that the peoples associated with these sites lived by hunting small game, gathering molluscs, and, at the later stages of their development, trapping fish.

The question of when cultures associated with agriculture first appeared in Southeast Asia has become a subject of considerable debate. Until quite recently, the prevailing view among students of Southeast Asian prehistory was that the complex of traits which included the domestication of plants, the domestication of animals, and the manufacture of pottery originated in China and gradually filtered down into Southeast Asia. Meantime the emergence of agriculture in Southeast Asia was generally considered to have begun no earlier than about 1500 B.C., or considerably later than the time at which cultures based on agriculture are known to have first arisen in China.

These views have been seriously challenged by recent archaeological findings in Southeast Asia and, in particular, by findings from sites in Thailand. Following the work of Solheim and his associates[3] who carried out these studies in Thailand, we can propose the following tentative reconstruction of the prehistory of mainland Southeast Asia. It would seem that sometime around 10,000 B.C. a shift in the type of subsistence patterns practiced by certain of the peoples of mainland Southeast Asia occurred. Although hunting and gathering remained an important means of obtaining food, certain plants were domesticated; with their domestication, slash-and-burn horticulture was developed as a planting system. Among the more important plants to have been domesticated at this time were certain tubers, especially taro, and other plants such as gourds, cucumbers, beans, peas, and black pepper. In certain of what Solheim has termed " late Hoabinhian " sites, evidence of bark cloth, cord, and cord-marked pottery appears in association with domesticated plants. The horticulturalists of the late Hoabinhian period appear to have adapted themselves to the lower flanks of the hills and to areas along the sea coasts.

During the ensuing millennia, certain animals such as the pig and fowl were domesticated, as were a number of new plants. The most important of the latter was rice. It now seems clear that rice was first domesticated in Southeast Asia, and that this most important element in the Asian diet was diffused from Southeast Asia to neighboring areas in China and India. During the Neolithic period, however, millet, rather than rice, formed the staple crop of most of the peoples of Southeast Asia.[4] Not until the development of wet-rice cultivation in Southeast Asia, a practice that came into being rather late in the area, did rice come to hold its currently preeminent place in the diet of Southeast Asians.

Around 4000 to 3500 B.C. changes began to take place in the pottery styles of the area. In northeastern Thailand, where these changes have been best documented, incised pottery appeared and was succeeded by a red-on-tan painted pottery now referred to as Ban Chiang ware. Studies of the designs and sequence of changes in style found in Ban Chiang pottery are still in their infancy, but once completed, they should provide a revealing source of information on the cultural life of prehistoric humans in mainland Southeast Asia.

Around 3000–2500 B.C., we find the beginnings of bronze metal working in Southeast Asia. It had long been thought that bronze working was not an indigenous Southeast Asian craft, but that it had been introduced from China during the first millenium B.C. Bronze was also thought to be associated with the beginnings of town-based civilizations in Southeast Asia. Findings from northeast Thailand, together with related findings from Cambodia and South Vietnam, have now established, however, that bronze working began in Southeast Asia before it began in China or India, and that it was carried out at the village level rather than by people living in town-based societies.

The so-called " bronze age " of Southeast Asia now turns out to have been a somewhat specialized, localized, and late development in Southeast Asian prehistory. Although the great bronze drums that are one of the hallmarks of this period have been found as far afield as the hinterlands of Sulawesi in Indonesia, they were apparently manufactured in only a small area of North Vietnam around Dong-Son, from where they were traded to the more outlying parts of the region.[5]

At some point during the late Hoabinhian period, the dominant racial type in mainland Southeast Asia shifted from Australoid to Mongoloid. The story of this change has yet to be unfolded fully, but it seems clear that throughout this period there was a movement of peoples from the Asian mainland to the islands. As the Mongoloids came in contact with the Australoids, they either interbred with or displaced them. Remnants of the Australoid peoples continued to exist in a few pockets in the regions, but they remained only as isolated interbred groups.

Linguistic Groupings and Culture History in Mainland Southeast Asia

A number of works on Southeast Asian history still put forward the theory that the Australoid peoples were displaced first by a " proto-Malay " people who spoke Austronesian (or Malayo-Polynesian) languages, and that these people were then in turn displaced throughout mainland Southeast Asia, save in the Malay peninsula and parts of South Vietnam and Cambodia, by peoples speaking Austroasiatic (or Mon-Khmer) languages.[6] Robert Heine-Geldern, the first scholar to attempt a synthesis of Southeast Asian prehistory, was responsible for this theory.[7] Heine-Geldern equated the quadrangular axes found in the region with Austronesian-speaking peoples, whereas he believed shouldered axes to be the product of Austroasiatic-speaking peoples. Such a thesis is, however, fraught with many dangers. As von Heekeren so correctly observes: " It seems to me . . . rather speculative to identify culture waves or migrations with the spread of a language."[8]

The acceptance of Heine-Geldern's thesis, or of any subsequent theses that attach ethnolinguistic labels to prehistoric cultures must rest on the type of evidence that linguists can provide. In theory it would seem that historical linguistics could furnish us with significant insights in this field. The establishment of genetic connections between languages provides a picture of the spread of members of a language family. Linguistic reconstructions provide historical clues about when and where languages diverged. So far, however, work on Southeast languages has either been inconclusive or even contradictory in regard to theories about prehistoric origins and distributions of ethnolinguistic groupings in Southeast Asia.

One of the first linguistic theories about Southeast Asian ethnic group relationships and origins was predicated on the discovery of apparent genetic relationships between Austroasiatic languages in Southeast Asia and Munda languages in South India.[9] On the basis of this evidence a number of scholars have proposed that " there was a community of culture between pre-Aryan India on the one hand and Farther India on the other."[10] Although this theory has never been totally refuted on linguistic grounds, archaeological evidence suggests that during Neolithic times, Southeast Asian connections were with China rather than with India.

In recent years, linguistic evidence has also been adduced to support a theory concerning the origin of the Austronesian-speaking peoples that is very different indeed from the one long held by prehistorians. Dyen, working with a sample of 245 Austronesian languages,[11] indicated that the greatest diversity of Austronesian languages within a single region was to be found in Melanesia. Following a hypothesis advanced by such linguists as Sapir and Greenberg that " the homeland of the ancestral speakers of any group of related languages is likely to have been located in or near the region exhibiting the greatest genetic diversity,"[12] Dyen and his advocate, Murdock, proposed that the original home of the Austronesian peoples was in Melanesia. Murdock then went on to suggest that the dispersal of Austronesian peoples took place well before Neolithic agriculture had appeared in Melanesia.[13] This alternative theory has been challenged by a number of archaeologists and even by another specialist in Oceanic linguistics.[14] Even if we assume that Dyen's classifications are correct,[15] other cases exist to contradict the fundamental hypothesis. For example, the greatest diversity of Sinitic languages is to be found in Southeastern China—a region that few Sinologists would propose as the homeland of Chinese languages.[16]

Questions of Austronesian and Austroasiatic origins and migrations remain unresolved. As with other theories about the relationships between Vietnamese and Tai, Vietnamese and Austroasiatic, Tai and Chinese, Tai and Austronesian, and so on, the solid linguistic data necessary to substantiate such theories have not yet been fully collected or analyzed.[17] At this stage, the question of ethnolinguistic identity of prehistoric cultures must be left open. With the protohistoric period in Southeast Asia, for which we have contemporary evidence from Chinese sources, we are, however, on firmer ground.

Wet Rice and the Emergence of Civilization

The earliest evidence available to us concerning the emergence of wet-rice agriculture in mainland Southeast Asia comes not from archaeological findings, but from Chinese written records. From these records we know that irrigated rice culture existed in southern China and the Tonkin delta from at least the middle of the first millenium before Christ onward.[18] It may well be that wet-rice cultivation developed earlier than this in other parts of mainland Southeast Asia, and that the practice arose independently of outside influences emanating from China. However, the archaeological evidence to support this supposition has yet to be reported.[19]

It would seem that during the early stages of development after the introduction of wet-rice cultivation in Southeast Asia, societies in the interior of the peninsula were village based. Chang has suggested that for this early type of society based on irrigated rice the term " stratified village-farmers " might be coined—*stratified*, to stress the internal differentiation in status between villagers, and *village-farmers*, to underline their autonomy.[20] The southern Chinese " kingdom " of Tien provides a case in point. In Tien,

> Settlements do not seem to cluster in groups in which each of them served a specialized set of functions. Single settlements seem to be the basic unit of economy, politics, and religion: internally the settlement's populace was apparently stratified, and there was a highly privileged aristocracy at the top. Externally, however, such single settlements do not appear to form a coherent and stable superstructure, and the alliance among them, if any, must have been based on military conquest and only to a lesser extent on trade.[21]

This characterization has been echoed by Bayard in his summary of his findings regarding neolithic sites in northeastern Thailand:

> In summary, the picture that emerges at present for Non Nok Tha in particular and perhaps for most of Central and Northeastern Thailand as a whole is, in my view, one of semi-isolated but vaguely related cultures with an apparently low level of political organization but possessing a hitherto unsuspected sophistication of technology [i.e., bronze-casting].[22]

From about the middle of the first millenium B.C. onward, major changes began to take place in Southeast Asia. With the expansion of Han Chinese control over the borderlands of southern China and Tonkin, small town societies based on the Chinese model began to arise in the area. Meanwhile in the interior of Southeast Asia, even in areas relatively distant from China and possible Chinese influences, an independent development toward town life appears to have occurred.[23] At the same time entrepôts established to facilitate the growing trade between India and China were being set up along the coasts of the Malay peninsula and what is today South Vietnam. These entrepôts became centers for the spread of Indian civilization in Southeast Asia.[24]

As these early civilizations began to develop in the first centuries of the Christian era, the primitive and tribal peoples began to lose their dominant position in Southeast Asia. The new civilizations centered around the major river valleys and the Great Lake of Cambodia. Only in hilly areas ill suited to wet-rice cultivation were primitive and tribal cultures perpetuated.

At the dawn of civilization in mainland Southeast Asia, or around the early centuries of the Christian era, the differences between primitive and tribal peoples, on the one hand, and civilized peoples, on the other, were probably not very great. The Chams, for example, who founded the kingdom of Champa in what is now South Vietnam, were probably not greatly different from the Rhadé and other Austronesian tribal peoples in the vicinity. So, too, the Yueh, the ancestors of the Vietnamese, were probably little different from the Mu'ong, or the Mons from the Lawa, and so on. However, as the civilizations evolved, and perhaps even more importantly as the ethnic composition of the area was altered by migrations, the relationships between the lowland and the hill peoples of Southeast Asia began to undergo changes.

Structure of the Traditional Relationship between Hill and Lowland Peoples

Despite a growing distinction between the hill and lowland peoples, sharp boundaries did not develop between the two. Rather, throughout most of Southeast Asia, hill peoples were incorporated into social systems dominated by the lowland peoples. They remained " the holders of the wild," " the people of the upland fields " who rendered periodic obeisance to the lowland rulers in return for recognition of their status as the first inhabitants of these lands. These relationships found symbolic expression in rituals involving both lowland and upland peoples. One of the most famous of such symbolic acts was the triennial exchange of gifts between representatives of the Khmer ruler and the *sadets*, or Lords of Fire and Lords of Water, of the Jarai tribe. This exchange took place from about A.D. 1600 until A.D. 1860, when King Norodom of Cambodia brought the practice to an end. The basis for the relationship was a myth that told of a sacred sword, originally belonging to a Cham ruler. The *sadets* had obtained possession of the sword itself, whereas the Khmers held only the scabbard. This unequal division was reflected in the gifts subsequently exchanged between the two parties. The Khmer would send a convoy of bull elephants and richly decorated palanquins along with buffaloes, clothes, musical instruments, dishes, mattresses and cushions, salt, iron, lead, silk, needles, and other gifts. In return the Jarai sent the King of Cambodia a little ivory, rhinoceros horn, and some beeswax. The fact that the two *sadets* were hereditary sorcerers whose power was probably recognized by the Khmer as well as by the Jarai may also be relevant to understanding the disparity in the gifts exchanged.[25]

Another example, from Luang Prabang, Laos, has continued until the present day. In Luang Prabang, ceremonies are held twice yearly, " which act out a historico-mythical scenario, permit us to witness the genesis of the world by the dancing ancestors, the organizing of a territory seized from the aborigines, and the installation of the ruling line."[26] At these ceremonies, the aborigines, who are Austroasiatic-speaking hill peoples, make an offering to the ruler of gourds, called " fruits of strength, fruits of longevity " that emphasizes that " the aborigines were in fact the support of the prosperity of the kingdom and the longevity of the monarch."[27] The very fact that the aborigines are involved in a royal Lao ritual signifies Lao recognition of the tribal people as the first to tap the fertility of the lands of the realm. However, having so recognized them, the Lao insist on their present political primacy through a ritual wherein the hill people are chased back to their villages. This ritual is enacted when the monarch is installed in a new palace.

> [T]he aborigines . . . had to shoot arrows against its facade to drive out evil. The king then rubbed a small ball of rice over his body, and turning towards the aborigines, called out, " May the aborigines living in the mountains perish before I do! " In chorus, the aborigines shouted, " Yes! " The king then threw the ball in their direction and the aborigines fled in fright back to their village, which, however, they could only enter after having been purified. If one of them were touched by the royal ball he would die, they said, within the year.[28]

In addition to the symbolic relationship that traditionally existed between many, if not most, of the hill and lowland peoples of Southeast Asia, were more tangible relationships. The hill people provided the lowlanders with forest products such as lac, beeswax, wild animal hides, tusks and horns (used in medicines), herbs, and exotic flowers. From the lowlands, the hill peoples obtained metal (which they did not manufacture themselves), salt, and such heirloom or ritual items as trade pottery and bronze drums. The hill peoples were also viewed by the lowlands peoples as potential laborers, to be acquired not through the corvée system used among the lowland peoples themselves, but through slave raids. The practice of slave raiding tended to pit one tribe against the other, by encouraging individual groups of hill peoples to procure slaves from other groups and sell them to lowlanders.

In short, the emergence of lowland civilizations led to the emergence of new relationships between the hill and lowland peoples of Southeast Asia. The relationship between tribal and lowland peoples was not everywhere as highly structured as in the Lao case described above. In some of the more remote hill areas, life went on in hill villages without much reference to events in the lowlands. In at least one instance, in what is today South Vietnam, a conscious attempt was made to minimize contacts between lowlanders and hill people. After the Vietnamese moved south into territory previously dominated by the Chams and the Khmers, a military organization along the frontier between the lowlands and uplands was established by the mandarins. This effectively reduced the relations between hill and lowland peoples to the payment of tribute and a restricted amount of trade.[29]

Even where population movements such as the Vietnamese move to the south from the fifteenth century on disturbed the traditional symbiotic relationship between lowland and hill peoples, the structure almost invariably remained. Only with the establishment of European rule over parts of Southeast Asia did the structure itself come under serious challenge.

Tribal Peoples During the Colonial Period

Colonial interest in Southeast Asia initially focused on the lowland state societies. Neither the British in Burma nor the French in Indochina made a concerted effort to bring the tribal peoples of their territories under colonial rule until very late in the nineteenth century. In Burma, the tribal areas of northern Burma were the last to be pacified. Even after peace was imposed in 1890, it remained a very uneasy one. In the highlands of central Indochina, resistance against the French was kept up by the montagnards until well into the twentieth century. Indeed, in parts of the Pays Montagnards du Sud, as the French referred to this area, resistance to French rule persisted throughout the colonial period. In the upland regions of Tonkin and northern Laos, the French only succeeded in establishing a few posts from which they could "show the flag."

Despite the difficulties the British and French underwent in establishing political control over the hill peoples of their colonies, colonial rule radically affected the lives of many of them. Of particular significance was the exposure of a significant number of hill peoples to the teachings of Christian missionaries. Christian missionaries established themselves in both Burma and Indochina prior to the beginnings of colonial rule, and indeed, their existence in Indochina provided at least one aspect of the rationale for the French conquest of the area. Although missionaries in Burma, most of whom were Protestant, had little success in converting the lowland peoples of that country, from around the third decade of the nineteenth century onward they started to achieve notable success among the hill peoples. The conversion of large numbers of Karens, sometimes whole villages at a time, by members of the American Baptist Mission, is one of the most dramatic stories of missionary activity in Asia in the nineteenth century. In Indochina, Catholic missionaries worked among both Vietnamese and highland peoples, making steady progress among both until by the end of the nineteenth century both the lowlands and the hill areas contained significant Christian communities. In the highlands, Catholic communities were everywhere conspicuous by their prosperity.

In addition to advancing religious teachings, missionaries also introduced schools and health centers into the upland areas of Burma and Indochina. Those who patronized these institutions were by no means exclusively Christian. Later in the colonial period, the colonial governments of both Indochina and Burma increased the educational and medical opportunities available to the highland peoples. Although the number of hill people attending mission or government schools was never very great at any one time, there was a steady output of graduates whose literacy and knowledge of the larger society marked them as totally different from any tribal people in the past. The improved medical care provided the tribal peoples also appears to have contributed to a growth in population in the hills—a growth that was to create strains on resources in many upland areas of mainland Southeast Asia.

In Burma, the British attempted, insofar as was possible, to administer the hill peoples separately from the lowland peoples. They allowed the Shan chiefs to continue to govern their states, although they had to accept a representative of the British government who was to keep check on their administrative practices. British administration was also indirect in the hill areas inhabited by the Chins, Kachins, and other tribal peoples. A number of the Karens lived intermingled with the Burmans, but during the colonial period the British also recognized the independence of three small Karenni states to the south of the Shan states. In central Indochina, the French created the Pays Montagnards du Sud as a " crown domain." This had the effect of separating it from the other administrative entities of Indochina. In northern Indochina, the French administered the highland areas through existing Tai chiefs rather than by creating a political structure common to both the lowland and upland peoples of the area. In Laos, the indigenous political system, which involved a symbiotic relation between lowland Lao and upland peoples, was left intact. In Cambodia, the hill peoples of the northeastern area tended to be treated by the French as belonging to the Pays Montagnards du Sud. In sum, colonial rule did nothing to further the integration of the hill people into national politics. Meanwhile, the emergence of an educated tribal elite, produced through the mission and government schools, tended to exacerbate the now institutionalized separation between the lowland and upland peoples of Southeast Asia.

Another, and perhaps the most significant, change that occurred in the highland areas during the colonial period was economic in character. The highlands of both Burma and Indochina were seen as sources of important economic resources that could profitably be exploited. The highlands of Burma were viewed as sources of teak; those of northern Tonkin as sources of coal. The highland areas also came to be viewed by a number of enterprising Europeans as areas well suited for the introduction of new cash crops. In the 1920s French, and some Vietnamese, entrepreneurs began to open rubber plantations on the highland plateaus of what is now South Vietnam on, for the most part, land previously used by montagnard peoples as fields for upland crops. The establishment of plantations brought Vietnamese laborers into the highlands and provided cash employment for a number of montagnards as well. In the highland areas of the Shan States in Burma, tea plantations were established. These had effects on the resident upland peoples similar to those of the rubber plantations in the highlands of South Vietnam. An exceptional cash crop that was raised in the highlands of Southeast Asia toward the end of the colonial period, and one that remains extremely important today, was opium. Although the opium trade was very important in French Indochina and to a lesser extent in Thailand and British Burma, throughout the colonial period, opium was raised in only relatively small quantities in Southeast Asia prior to World War II. The war made it difficult to import opium into Southeast Asia from traditional sources of supply. Faced with this situation, French officials in Indochina began to encourage the upland Meo of Laos and Tonkin to expand opium production.[30] Meanwhile considerable quantities of opium raised by upland tribal groups in South China also found their way into Southeast Asian markets.

All tribal peoples in British Burma and French Indochina were by no means touched equally by the introduction of cash crops and the exploitation of hill resources that began during the colonial period. However, few tribal areas remained where cash was not used more than it had been in precolonial times.

Some of the transformations wrought in tribal society in British Burma and French Indochina produced echoes in Thailand. There was, for example, no place made for a symbiotic relationship between upland and lowland peoples such as had existed in premodern Siam in the new political order created by King Chulalongkorn and his advisors at the end of the nineteenth century. In fact, no formal administrative policies toward the tribal peoples of Thailand were adopted by the Thai government until after World War II. Thus, for about half a century, the tribal peoples were left in a state of political limbo. This state of affairs permitted the migration of tribal people into Thailand from neighboring countries, where population pressures were beginning to be felt. Most important among the new migrants were the Meo and Yao who brought opium production with them to their new homes in Thailand. Some of the tribal people of Thailand also became involved in the teak trade. In contrast with the peoples of both Burma and Indochina, however, few tribal peoples in Thailand received any education, and no tribal leaders emerged as spokesmen for the hill peoples of the country until well after World War II.

Tribal Peoples in Modern Mainland Southeast Asia

The tribal peoples of Southeast Asia found themselves caught up in the nationalist struggles that swept the region after World War II. In Burma they were confronted with the prospect of being ruled by Burmans rather than by the British—a prospect that a number of the tribal peoples did not relish. The largest of Burma's tribal minority groups, the Karen, rose in rebellion almost immediately after Burma gained her independence in 1948. Although the Karen rebellion was unsuccessful, it has still not been fully put down. Moreover, tribal dissent had continued to ferment throughout Burma, encouraged by all manner of outsiders, including Communists of at least two stripes, missionaries, opium middlemen, the CIA from time to time, and others. Today Burma has more " ethnic rebellions " per square mile than almost any other place in the world. The basic concern motivating tribal minorities in Burma to rebel is a fear that the Burmans will insist on implementing a policy of total assimilation in a heavy-handed way.

In what was formerly French Indochina, the tribal peoples have also been caught up in wars. In northern Vietnam the tribal Tai, Tho, and other groups were divided in their support for the French and the Viet Minh during the long French-Indochinese war. However, the final battle of that war, Dien Bien Phu, was fought in the heart of the hill country, and the success of the Viet Minh, who could not have triumphed without the support of some of the tribal people, left a strong impression on the minds of tribal groups throughout the whole of what had formerly been Indochina.

Following the establishment of an independent Democratic Republic of

Vietnam (DRV) an autonomous zone for the tribal peoples of northern Vietnam was established. Tribal rather than Vietnamese cadres were appointed to work in the tribal villages, and a variety of public institutions such as schools and health centers were founded in the tribal areas, staffed, insofar as was possible, by tribal peoples. Members of the traditional ruling elite of the tribal areas— the families of Tai chiefs—were, however, deprived of their positions, partially because these created political obstacles for the new government of the DRV, and partially because this elite had largely supported the French during the French-Indochinese war.

Whereas the DRV accorded its tribal minorities some semblance of autonomy, the Republic of Vietnam, after 1954, appeared intent on pushing a Vietnamization program in the highlands. This program involved the resettlement of Vietnamese in the region and the assimilation of the montagnards into Vietnamese culture. Given this policy and the long history of resistance to outside political pressure that has characterized the highlands, it is not surprising that a major uprising should have occurred in the region in 1958. Subsequently the South Vietnamese government backed away somewhat from its Vietnamization program, created a Ministry of Montagnard Affairs, and attempted, in consultation with tribal leaders, to promote a number of welfare and development programs for the benefit of the montagnard people. Most of these efforts were greatly frustrated by the war, the central highlands being an area of intense fighting.

The 1958 uprising in the highlands of South Vietnam brought to the fore, for the first time, a number of leaders who claimed to speak for tribal coalitions in the highlands. These leaders, and their coalitions, have become an important element in the recent political scene in South Vietnam. In 1964, a number of these leaders joined together to form the United Front for the Protection of Oppressed Races (FULRO), an organization sponsored by Prince Sihanouk, then the head of the state of Cambodia. FULRO originally represented a neutral force between the South Vietnamese government and the National Liberation Front (NLF), although it later became allied with the NLF and the Khmer Rouge.

The highlands continued to be the scene of fighting. Thousands of tribal people were killed or died as a consequence of illness, starvation, and other causes consequent upon the war. Still more were uprooted and resettled, often in areas where it is impossible for them to earn a living. Some land previously cultivated by tribal peoples was also denuded by defoliation, making it unsuitable for cultivation even now that the fighting has ended.

The situation of the tribal people of northern Cambodia and Laos appears to be much the same as that of the montagnards of the southern Vietnamese highlands. The lives of these people were equally disrupted by the war since their communities lay on the supply routes between North Vietnam and Laos, Cambodia, and South Vietnam. The Meo of northern Laos were swept up into the war in a number of different ways. One concerns Meo production of opium, since this long served as a source of cash for both the Pathet Lao and the Royal

Lao armies during the Lao conflict. In addition, Meo were recruited as soldier, into the armies of both sides. Finally, their homelands were the scenes of many battles, and were also often subjected to bombing. Given that opium production is now being strongly discouraged by the authorities of the new Lao governments it does not seem likely that even peace can bring renewed prosperity to the Meo of Laos. The position of the Meo, as well as that of other tribal people—not a few of whom live in refugee camps around Vientaine, on the Plain of Jars or across the border in Thailand—poses some very difficult questions for those concerned with the reconstruction of Laos.

The tribal people of Thailand have not escaped the turmoil of the period since World War II. Since Thailand first assumed its role as the leading anti-Communist and pro-American state in Southeast Asia (a role it was not to alter until 1973), successive Thai governments pushed a policy of assimilation of tribal minorities into the kingdom of Thailand. Only through assimilation, it was felt, could the loyalty of the people who lived along Thailand's strategic borders be ensured. Concomitantly with this policy, Thai governments took a strong stand against the use of forest lands for swidden cultivation. Further, the Thai government became increasingly concerned over tribal aliens migrating

Sgaw Karens, a mainland Southeast Asian tribal people, at the edge of an upland village in northern Thailand. [C. F. Keyes photograph]

into Thailand from neighboring countries. At the same time the Thai government promoted programs designed to improve the welfare and ensure the development of the tribal people. Although not all these policies were pressed with equal vigor or consistency throughout the upland areas, the general impact was such as to ensure that life in the hills will never be the same as it was before World War II.

Few studies of tribal society in Southeast Asia have attempted to present the life of a particular tribal group without demonstrating the ways in which that group has adapted to neighboring lowland peoples. Nonetheless, there is a significant difference between such studies since some stress the relationship as it existed before the colonial period and have presented the tribal society as it appeared in traditional times, whereas others have stressed the ways in which the relationship has been, and still is being, transformed by various forces first unleashed during the colonial period. In the discussion of specific cases, I shall attempt to portray both types of relationship.

TYPES OF PRIMITIVE AND TRIBAL SYSTEMS IN MAINLAND SOUTHEAST ASIA

Modes of Production

The primitive and tribal cultures found in Southeast Asia, both today and in the past, serve and have served as modes of adaptation for peoples living on the margins and in the interstices of the major civilizations of the region and having patterned relationships with representatives of these civilizations. Although most of the primitive and tribal peoples of the region are found in its highland areas, not all of them are. Of particular fascination are the so-called " sea nomads," groups of people—most of whom appear to speak Austronesian languages—who are found along the coasts from Tenasserim in lower Burma down through southern Thailand and Malaysia, and as far east as the Philippines. These sea nomads fish for their livelihood and trade the products of the sea with sedentary agricultural peoples living near the coasts.[31]

Other than these sea nomads, only very small numbers of primitive and tribal people in mainland Southeast Asia live primarily by hunting and gathering. The only groups known to do so are the Mrabri and/or Yumbri of northern Thailand, groups that are often known by the Thai sobriquet, *Phi tong luang*, " the spirits of the yellow leaves," and the Negrito Semang who live in Southern Thailand and northern Malaya.[32] We shall discuss the Semang in some detail below.

By far the majority of the primitive and tribal peoples of mainland Southeast Asia employ " swidden " or " slash and burn " agriculture. Although the basic features of swidden agriculture, including the preparation of fields through the cutting and burning of foliage, the cultivation of fields for only several years in succession at most, and allowing fields to lie fallow for a number of years before cultivating them again, are common to all the Southeast Asian systems, major differences exist between these systems. For example, rice is by no means the only or even the major crop raised by all the swiddening peoples in Southeast Asia. The Meo and Yao often grow no rice at all and raise maize and opium-producing poppies as their major crops. The Chin, as we shall see, often raise millet and beans to the exclusion of rice. Even when rice is the major crop, it is normally interplanted with other crops, such as gourds, which provide dietary supplements for their cultivators. Swidden cultivators also differ in the type of tools they use, in the ways in which they fire their fields, in the number of successive years a field is planted, in the number of years the field is allowed to fallow, and in other such particulars.[33]

Some tribal people, such as the Black Tai of northwestern Tonkin, have long been wet-rice agriculturists. In recent years they have been followed by other groups, as a number of tribal people have increasingly abandoned swidden cultivation and adopted wet-rice cultivation. In some hill areas, this change to wet-rice cultivation has been accompanied by the construction of elaborate terracing systems, although none in mainland Southeast Asia can rival those found in Java or in northern Luzon in the Philippines.

A small number of tribal people has long engaged in specialized occupations. This was particularly characteristic of communities located near a resource in demand in the lowlands, or those located at a strategic location on a trade route. The Lawa village of Baw Luang, located to the west of Chiang Mai in northern Thailand, enjoys both advantages. The village is near a vein of iron, which can be mined with very primitive implements. Furthermore, it lies along the main route from Chiang Mai to Moulmein in Burma, on the one hand, and that leading toward Red Karen country on the other. Very few communities such as Baw Luang existed traditionally in the tribal areas, however. Within the past century, the tribal peoples have increasingly come to specialize in occupations that fill a market need. Among the more striking examples are certain Karen, Khamu, Lamet, and a few others, tribal groups that have come to assume important roles in the teak trade. These tribal peoples raise, train, and manipulate the elephants without which teak could not be extracted from the forests. Other tribespeople have taken on wage-labor jobs on tea and rubber plantations or in the new mines that have opened up in tribal territory. Although such employment still accounts for only a very small percentage of the tribal labor force, it is continuing to increase.

Sociopolitical Characteristics

Although all primitive and tribal societies in Southeast Asia have had economic and other links with the lowland civilizations of the region, very few of the tribal peoples have succeeded in establishing political units that extend beyond more than a small number of communities. Most tribal societies are segmentary societies, that is, they are divided into a number of descent groups—most patrilineal, but some matrilineal—integrated at the local level through the exchange of wives and goods. In *Political Systems of Highland Burma*—perhaps the most well known of all studies of tribal peoples in Southeast Asia—E. R.

Leach has argued that the Kachin, with whom he worked, and other tribal peoples in Southeast Asia pass through a cycle of structural change, moving from a " democratic " segmentary system toward an " autocratic " system, modeled on the structure of lowland societies. However, such autocratic systems, wherein one lineage obtains a monopoly on wealth and potency, are, he argues, inherently unstable. When they merge, they normally survive only a short time before collapsing, sometimes as a consequence of rebellion, and reverting to the previous democratic structure.[34]

Although Leach's argument has been the subject of considerable debate, there is no question that contrasting " autocratic " and " democratic " structures can be recognized among many tribal peoples from northern Burma to southern Vietnam. Many, perhaps even most, of the tribal systems of Southeast Asia as they existed in the recent past can be understood with reference to the model proposed by Leach and elaborated in the work of C. Lévi-Strauss[35] and R. Needham,[36] among others. However, some tribal systems did achieve permanent autocratic structures. A number of such tribal " chiefdomships " existed until quite recently in the South China borderlands of mainland Southeast Asia and included such groups as the Lolo, Minchia, and Nakhi. In Southeast Asia proper, perhaps the best examples of chiefdoms could be found in northwestern Tonkin and northeastern Laos among Tai-speaking peoples.

The peoples of this region include the Black Tai, the White Tai, the Red Tai, the Phu Tai, the Neua, and so on, with the Black Tai being numerically dominant. The distinctions among these groups, based primarily on differences of dress and dialect, are apparently not very significant. The more important distinctions in this region are sociopolitical in character. The area was divided into divisions known as *muang* and ruled over by a chief (*cao*) who was a member of a chiefly lineage. This chief held superior title to all the irrigated land in his domain and had the power to redistribute land according to need. The cultivators each paid a tax to the lord for their right to use the land they cultivated.[37]

Religious Characteristics

The Tai chiefdomships differ from the feudal-like principalities of the Lao and the Shan primarily in regard to religion. The Tai chiefdomships derived their legitimacy from a cult of a spirit of the domain, whereas the legitimacy of Shan and Lao lords was grounded in Buddhism. Although some tribal peoples have converted to Buddhism—for example, the Pa-O or Taungthu, a Karen-speaking people of the southern Shan States—until quite recently most tribal people in Southeast Asia adhered to religious systems that were not versions of or affiliated with any of the major world religions. During the colonial period, and indeed from somewhat before that time, Christian missionaries enjoyed a certain amount of success in their work among tribal peoples. Today, a significant percentage of tribal people in every country in Southeast Asia are Christian: some Protestant and others Catholic. As Christians, tribal people continue to remain distinct from the lowland peoples who in the main adhere to either Buddhism, one of the traditional or new religions of Vietnam, or Islam.

As part of their effort to convert the tribal peoples to Christianity, the missionaries sought to render the scriptures into the languages of the tribal peoples. Prior to the arrival of the missionaries, literacy was extremely rare among any of the tribal peoples, although what one might call " craft literacy " existed among the Tai and certain other tribal peoples. The Yao (Iu Mien, Man), for example, had their own ritual specialists who learned to read and write an archaic form of Chinese so that they could communicate with spirits, which " have difficulty understanding other languages."[38] Since World War II, all the governments of Southeast Asia have introduced programs for promoting literacy among the tribal peoples who live within their territories. With the exception of the Democratic Republic of Vietnam, which has modeled its program on that of the Peoples Republic of China, such literacy programs have been carried out in the national languages of the countries concerned, that is, in Burmese, Thai, Lao, or Khmer, rather than in tribal languages. These programs have, thus, perpetuated the pattern that tribal traditions are not literate traditions.

Linguistic Characteristics

Tribal languages are not limited to any one language family, as can be seen by referring to Appendix A. However, certain patterns of language distribution are of some relevance in understanding the nature of primitive and tribal societies in Southeast Asia. Hill peoples speaking Austroasiatic languages are found scattered throughout the region, from Assam in northwestern India to the uplands of Malaya and the highlands and lowlands of South Vietnam and Cambodia. Austroasiatic languages spoken by hill peoples differ almost from village to village, thus giving rise to the extremely large number of ethnolinguistic groups identified as existing among the Austroasiatic-speaking peoples of the area.[39] Austronesian-speaking tribal peoples are restricted to a much smaller area, being found only in the highlands of South Vietnam and Cambodia and in the Malay Peninsula. Tai-speaking tribal peoples are similarly restricted, being found primarily in northern Laos and northwestern Vietnam, as well as in neighboring parts in South China. Although Tai-speaking tribal peoples are thus found only in a fairly small area, it should be noted that when Tai-speaking lowlanders are added to the picture, the Tai speakers are found to be as widely distributed geographically as Austroasiatic speakers. Tibeto-Burman speaking tribal peoples are confined mainly to northern Burma and neighboring areas of northwestern India and Bangladesh and China. Some Tibeto-Burman-speaking tribal peoples have settled relatively recently in northern Thailand and in Laos. Miao-Yao speakers, who are distantly related to Tibeto-Burman speakers in the larger Sino-Tibetan language family, are found in northern Thailand, Laos, and northern Vietnam, with by far the largest percentage of them existing in South China. Although many scholars believe that Karen languages are also related to Sino-Tibetan, the status of these languages remains uncertain. Karennic languages are spoken by peoples who live mainly in eastern Burma, but who are also found in hill tracts across the border in western Thailand. The most restricted of all tribal languages found in mainland Southeast Asia is that spoken by the Muong whose language belongs to the Viet-Muong family. The Muong are found almost exclusively in an area bordering the Tonkin delta in northern Vietnam.

Researches on Primitive and Tribal Peoples

Although there are few truly primitive peoples left today in mainland Southeast Asia, tribal peoples continue to live in all the countries in the region. As can be seen from the statistics presented in Appendix B, the percentage of tribal peoples in the total populations of mainland Southeast Asian countries ranges from as little as less than 1 per cent in Cambodia to as much as 15–17 per cent in Burma.

Studies of primitive and tribal peoples prior to World War II were carried out primarily by nationals of the countries that held power over the respective countries of Southeast Asia: the British in Burma, the French in Indochina, and the Thai in Thailand (although there were very few in this last group). There were a few exceptions, such as the studies of the Karen made by Americans affiliated with the American Baptist Mission or the studies made by such Austrian ethonologists as Paul Schebesta and Hugo and Emily Bernatzik. It is probable that during World War II the Japanese recorded observations and experiences regarding the tribal peoples; however, such records are not generally available.

Since World War II, research on the hill peoples of Southeast Asia has been limited by the unsettled conditions that have prevailed in many parts of the region. Very few studies of Burmese tribal peoples have been made since World War II by native or foreign scholars, and those that were made were carried out almost exclusively before 1962 when General Ne Win and the Army seized power. A few studies in North Vietnam have been made since 1954 by Vietnamese and Russian ethnologists, although these are not widely known. Research on South Vietnamese and Lao tribal peoples has continued in the postwar period, but on a small scale. Such research has been undertaken mainly by a few French and American scholars, a few American missionaries, and some American " advisors." Cambodia's tribal peoples, who are concentrated in the war-ravaged northeastern sector of the country, have been inaccessible to researchers. In the postwar period Thailand has been the only country in which it has been possible to undertake research untrammeled by major political restrictions and without fear of impending disturbances.

Given the greater opportunities for research that have existed in Thailand in the postwar period, the tribal peoples of that country have come to be rather better known than those of neighboring countries even though the tribal population in Thailand does not comprise as high a percentage of the total population of that country as does the tribal populations of any of Thailand's neighbors save Cambodia. Research among tribal peoples in Thailand has been carried out primarily by Americans, a function of the fact that America has played a major role in Thailand's political and economic development during the period from World War II to the early 1970s. However, Americans have not been the only people working among tribal peoples in Thailand; researchers have come from Australia, Great Britain, France, Austria, Germany, Scandanavia, Japan, New Zealand, as well as from Thailand itself.

In the following pages, I shall draw on some of the research undertaken among tribal peoples in both the pre-World War II and post-World War II periods. I have chosen to examine the life of three groups, the Semang, the Chin, and the Karens, in some detail. The Semang hold a particular fascination for

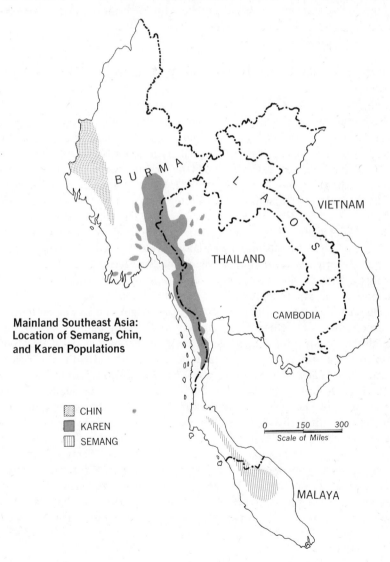

**Mainland Southeast Asia:
Location of Semang, Chin,
and Karen Populations**

CHIN
KAREN
SEMANG

anthropologists partially because their physical characteristics, which are usually subsumed under the quasi-racial term *Negrito*, suggest that they have remained genetically distinct from their neighbors since prehistoric times. They are also of particular interest because they are one of the last remaining groups in mainland Southeast Asia that support themselves primarily through hunting and gathering. I shall then turn to the Chins, whose culture includes the traits of cross-cousin marriage, oscillation between autocratic and democratic systems, and feasts of merit that have been the foci of considerable attention by anthropologists. Lastly, I shall discuss the Karens, who hold particular interest because they are the most numerous tribal people in mainland Southeast Asia and because they have been the tribal people who have most nearly succeeded in establishing themselves as a separate nation.

THE SEMANG OF THE MALAY PENINSULA

The Semang and Their Context

Nomadic bands of hunters and gatherers have almost disappeared from Southeast Asia. On the mainland, the only remaining groups appear to be the elusive Mrabri or Yumbri, the *phi tọng luang* or " spirits of the yellow leaves," who live in the forests of northern Thailand and the Semang, a Negrito people living in southern Thailand and northern Malaya. The Semang are often grouped together, because of their physical characteristics, with the Andaman Islanders and the Aeta of the Philippines. Although it is true that the Negritos are a remnant, biologically speaking, of a premongoloid population that once existed in the region,[40] it does not follow, as many have suggested, that Negrito culture preserves the original character of paleolithic Southeast Asia. Semang culture can only be understood as a form of adaptation to the particular environment of the area of the Malay Peninsula in which the Semang live.

The term *Semang* appears to be of Malay origin and has come to be used by anthropologists to refer to the Negritos who live by hunting and gathering, although the term is not so restricted by the Malay. The Semang themselves call themselves by a variety of names, depending on the band with which they are affiliated. The Thai sometimes call them *khon pa*, " forest people," a term that finds a parallel in the *orang bukit* or *orang liar*, used sometimes by the Malay. More commonly, the Thai call the Semang *ngọ' pa*, " wild rambutan," owing to the putative similarity that the Thai claim to see between the frizzy-headed Semang and the prickly rambutan. This term, as well as the term " forest people," carries a derogatory flavor, implying that the Semang are savages, little better than wild animals. Yet the appelations of " forest " or " wild " people do convey some truth, for the Semang inhabit the dense rain forests of the upland areas of northern Malaya and southern Thailand. The true habitat of the nomadic Semang lies in the interior, where the jungle has never been cut for the creation of cultivated plots.

Semang hunters with blowguns.
[Photo from Paul Schebesta, *Among the Forest Dwarfs of Malaya*, tr. by Arthur Chambers (New York: Oxford University Press, 1974).]

Over the centuries there appears to have occurred a steady assimilation of the Semang into the societies of the neighboring peoples. Father Schebesta, one of the main ethnographers of the Semang, tells us that " I saw many Malays whose Negrito origin was written on their faces, and on enquiry I have found that their mothers were Semang."[41] He reports that he also met settled swiddening peoples who were also obviously Semang in origin. This continuous assimilation has probably kept the population of the nomadic Semang low for centuries. In the late 1960s the total population of Semang in both Malaya and Thailand was somewhere between 1,000 and 3,000 people.[42]

That the Semang have had long relationships with neighboring peoples is evidenced in the fact that the language they speak is related to the Senoi languages despite the fact that speakers of Senoi languages are mainly Mongoloid rather than Negrito in physical type. Semang-Senoi languages are recognized by linguists as being Austroasiatic, although there has been considerable borrowing of Austronesian vocabulary since the neighboring Jakun and Malay peoples speak Austronesian languages. Other indications that the Semang have adapted themselves to an environment in which other more civilized peoples are also present can be found in the metal tools and other goods that the Semang have obtained through trade, since they do not manufacture such goods themselves. With the arrival of the British colonialists, Western technology also left its mark on Semang culture. Semang relations with peoples of other cultures are graphically represented in a cave painting recently made by the Semang and photographed in the 1930s. The painting depicted not only Semang hunters, but also rice cultivators (Senoi?), Malay-style houses on piles, figures with guns, bicycles (or motobikes), and automobiles.[43]

The Semang also have a place in the cultures of neighboring peoples. For the most part, this place is a negative one, the Semang being viewed as brutish, filthy savages. This image was clearly evident in the Semang displays I viewed at New Year's fairs in Bangkok in 1964 and again in Chiang Mai, northern Thailand in 1973. On both occasions, a small group of Semang were kept in cage-like structures in one of the booths at the fair. For a price, fairgoers could see the Semang perform such feats as using a blow gun on balloons. On the other hand, the Semang have also been portrayed as the Thai equivalent of the " noble savage " by no less a playwright than King Chulalongkorn (1868–1910). On a trip to the south, a young Semang boy had been presented to the King. The king took the boy back with him to Bangkok and had him made a page. The king took the opportunity to interview the boy about his home and about the traditions of his people. From his notes, King Chulalongkorn wrote the play *ngǫ' pa*, which is still popular, having in recent years been turned into a musical and made into a movie.

Despite the fact that Semang culture has been strongly buffeted by influences from neighboring peoples, it still retains a definitely primitive cast. In the following portrait, I have drawn mainly on the works of Igor Evans and Father Paul Schebesta, the two foremost authorities on the Semang, who carried out their research in the 1920s and 1930s.[44] In addition, some more recent information has been gleaned from the work of Charles Brandt, who carried out some research on Semang living in Thailand in the 1960s.[45]

Semang Economy and Society

The Semang gain their livelihood primarily through gathering wild fruits and vegetables and secondarily through hunting and fishing. The mainstay of their diet would appear to consist of wild roots and tubers, which the Semang women dig up in the forest. Some of the tubers are poisonous in their raw state and must be prepared in a special way in order to make them edible. For example,

> The *tulegn* tuber (*hubi kapor*) is poisonous. To make it edible [the Semang]
> burn the leaves of the *gobin* tree and mix the ashes with the *tulegn*, which is
> first pounded to a pulp. This dish is edible and tastes like paste.[46]

To this dish of *tulegn* paste may be added some roasted fish or birds caught by Semang men on their fishing or hunting expeditions.

Unlike the lowland peoples of Malaysia and Thailand, the Semang do not fish in a systematic way, although this may be as much a function of the relative paucity of fish in upland streams as it is the methods that the Semang employ.

Semang men use a variety of equipment to fish and hunt with, including nets, harpoons, and bows and arrows, although the last are used only rarely, but their most distinctive weapon is the blowgun. The darts used with the blowguns are tipped with a poison obtained from the *ipoh* tree. This poison is strong enough to kill not only birds but small animals such as monkeys, rats, and squirrels, although it is not effective against larger animals such as deer, wild pigs, or wild buffaloes. To capture these latter animals, the Semang employ spears and bows and arrows, although reportedly such large-scale hunting is very rare among them.

Schebesta, who carried out his research among the Semang in the 1920s, found that " Many Semang groups have begun the laying out of small plantations, which, however, are far from adequate to support the people permanently."[47] These plantations are privately owned by individual Semang families[48] and are planted primarily with *ipoh* trees, from which the Semang obtain poison for their blowgun darts, and also with *durian* trees whose fruit is greatly prized not only by the Semang but by most peoples in Southeast Asia.

The Semang include rice among their food whenever they can obtain it. However, as they do not themselves cultivate rice, they can only acquire it through trade with neighboring peoples such as the Senoi and Malays who do raise it. In addition, the Semang also seek tobacco, metal, and cloth from their neighbors. For these goods, the Semang trade forest products such as rattan, sticklac, resins, and medicinal herbs, together with goods that they make themselves, such as blowguns, although it is reported that in recent years the Semang no longer make their own blowguns, but buy them from the Senoi.[49]

The Semang live in small bands of between 10 and 55 people. Each band is divided into residential kin groups, that is to say groups of kinsmen who share a common hearth. These groups number from 3 to 17 per band and each builds its own temporary lean-to at encampments. These bands have been grouped together on linguistic grounds into seven subdivisions, one of which is found in Thailand, and six in Malaya. These linguistic groupings have often been misleadingly referred to as " tribes," although they have no sociopolitical significance.

One becomes a member of a band either by being born into it or by marrying into it. Although Schebesta suggests that band exogamy is preferred and usual,[50] Evans seems to suggest that band endogamy is more usual, for he says that " a bachelor who can find no girl in his camp whom he is entitled to marry, goes to other camps in search of a bride."[51]

Both Evans and Schebesta indicate that marriage between first, and in some bands, second, cousins is prohibited. Brandt, on the other hand, quotes one informant, interviewed in southern Thailand, as asserting " that incestuous relations between brother and sister were permitted."[52] This assertion must certainly be suspect, if, for no other reason than the informant was only one of three remaining members of a band, the other two being his wife and child. When exogamous marriages are contracted, there appears to be some pressure on the young man who initiates marriage proceedings to find a bride in a band in which marriage connections already exist. This seems to suggest the existence of an embryonic marriage exchange system, but there is certainly nothing prescriptive about Semang marriage patterns. The significant rule is a prescription against incestuous marriages, not a prescriptive rule determining whom one should marry.

Marriage is extremely important for the Semang as their economy is based on a strong division of labor by sex. Women provide the staple food for their families through the collecting of wild plants such as tubers, roots, leaves, and wild fruits. Men provide supplementary foodstuffs from their hunting and fishing, although Schebesta notes that the Semang men are not avid hunters or fishermen. In gathering wild plants, the women may use a digging stick. Men use blow guns, bows and arrows, spears, nets, lines and hooks, and so on for hunting and fishing. Many of the implements used by the men are obtained from the neighbors of the Semang. Some Semang also own their own gardens, where they raise mainly fruit trees as an additional food source. Food collected on any one day is never preserved or even allowed to go to waste. If one family has a surplus, it shares it with other families in the band.[53]

Given the importance of the sexual division of labor, few adult Semang remain unmarried for very long. If a spouse dies, the survivor quickly takes another. Divorce is not uncommon and is invariably followed by (if not preceded by) another marriage. As this last statement indicates, polygamy, and apparently even polyandry, does occur, although the normal union is monogamous.

Although postmarital residence may temporarily be in the wife's band, final residence is with the husband's band. Consequently, the band takes on the character of a group of agnatically related kinsmen. Membership in a band determines access to most productive resources, since a band tends to operate within a particular territory. However, some resources, notably certain trees (e.g., *ipoh* and *durian*), are held as private property. Rights to these resources are inherited patrilineally in some groups, bilaterally in others.

Semang Religion and Changes in the Semang World

The leadership of a band is determined by age as well as sex, the oldest male being the leader. In addition to social differentiation on the basis of age and sex, there is one specialized role among the Semang—that of the " shaman," called *hala* by Schebesta and *halak* by Evans. According to Evans, a man becomes a *hala* because of a dream or because he gains access to a sacred quartz stone. Schebesta, on the other hand, claims that the role of *hala* is inherited, passing " from father to the eldest, or youngest son."[54] However he gains his role, the *hala* possesses his special power because he is, or becomes during the time he performs his role, equated with the *chenoi*, ubiquitous spirits, because he is the son of Karei, the supreme god, because he alone among men can speak to Karei, and because he possesses the *chebuch* stone that makes such communication possible. The *hala* is consulted for curing and on occasions of crisis. There are two types of *hala*, a " greater " and a " lesser," the latter knowing

" the diseases of his patients, but not the remedies," whereas the former, " knows both the disease and its appropriate remedy."[55]

As already noted, the *hala* is equated with the *chenoi*, the largest class of spirits. The *chenoi* are present in flowers; thus, people decorate themselves with garlands. The *chenoi* are also present in other animals, in mountains, in rivers, in birds, and in fetuses. The *chenoi*, as a category of Semang thought, thus, permit the equation of the realm of humans (specifically *hala* and fetuses) with the realm of nature. Such an equation of nature and humans is also present in the belief that the Semang were once buffaloes just as the Malays were once pigs; thus, the food taboos on buffalo meat and on pork which the two peoples observe. The *hala* also becomes, on occasion, *bidog*, " Old Man," who is in turn an incarnation of a particular avatar of *chenoi*, that of tiger. In turn, *hala*, on death, may become such *chenoi*-tigers.

The *chenoi* are not the only beings in the Semang pantheon. Two other beings are of particular importance: Karei and Ta Pedn, variously described as Father and Son and as brothers. Karei is the embodiment of all human misfortunes, which he imposes for their transgressions. The Semang explain such deaths as those caused by lightning and by wild tigers with reference to Karei. In addition, diseases are to be explained as the result of having committed *lawaid karei*, sins against Karei, such sins including mocking of animals that have been captured and are being kept or killing of certain types of insects and birds. If one has committed such sins, one must sacrifice one's own blood, drawing blood and presenting it to Karei as expiation of guilt. This blood sacrifice, according to Schebesta, is the only ritual performed by the Semang, although one would also have to count as ritual behavior the acts performed by the *hala*.

Although Karei oversees the actions of humans, Ta Pedn created the world, and its elements, in which the Semang live. According to some Semang, there are also other gods, all relatives of these two high gods, but they appear to play relatively unimportant roles in the lives of the Semang.

The Semang believe that their spirits hover around their camps after death and can kill their kinsmen if they are not properly dispatched to the land of the dead. Feasts are held on several occasions after a death to ensure the departure of the spirits of the dead. In the afterworld, life is an inversion of ordinary life; " the dead eat only the shadows of things; while they sleep in the daytime, they wander at night in search of food."[56]

Although a belief in an afterlife appears to implicate a belief in absolute change, of historic time, in Semang culture, this is misleading. The afterworld is not a heaven to be attained, but merely the abode of the dead, a world inverted. The Semang world view presupposes, in fact, no actual change from times past; no postulated change in times to come. Rather, there is a stable relationship between humans and nature, mediated by a supernatural world.

Although the culture of the Semang orients them toward a world that always was and evermore shall be so, the actual lives of the Semang, both in the past and at present, have been ones in which many major changes have occurred. As already noted, the Semang have been assimilated into the cultures of their neighbors for centuries. This assimilation presupposes the movement of the Semang from their environments to the environments of others. During the colonial period, the terrain occupied by the Semang became of great interest to others for it was recognized to contain timber and minerals that could be profitably exploited. Semang were recruited as foresters in some of the enterprises begun during the colonial period. After World War II, Malaya was torn asunder by what the British euphemistically termed the " Emergency," what was in fact a civil war between Communist-led Chinese and the British and Malays. As the government succeeded in denying the lowland villages and towns to the rebels, the rebels, in turn, sought the sanctuary of the jungles— areas that had previously been inhabited almost solely by the Semang. In order to keep track of the Semang, the government resettled many of them, thereby either stimulating more rapid acculturation, or undermining the traditional character of Semang culture, or, in some cases, both.[57] Some Malayan Semang appear also to have migrated north into Thailand during the Emergency.[58] The future—a future that the bands of Semang who continue to roam the jungles of northern Malaya and southern Thailand may not even recognize as existing— does not augur well for the perpetuation of Semang culture.

THE CHIN OF NORTHERN BURMA

Models of Tribal Social Structure and the Chin

Chin-speaking people have attracted the attention of anthropologists not only because they form one of the largest tribal populations in Burma—indeed, in the whole of Southeast Asia—but also because they follow certain cultural patterns that can be explained only by raising certain fundamental questions about human society in general. The Chin are adapted to a rugged terrain where their form of swidden or slash-and-burn cultivation permits the production of only very small surpluses. In some areas of the Chin Hills, these surpluses have been monopolized by " aristocratic " lineages through the manipulation of marriage alliances. These aristocratic lineages have used their capital both to acquire prestige goods from lowland Burman civilization and to give great " feasts of merit " whereby they acquire enhanced status in this world and assurance of a good place in the Chin afterworld. Such " autocratic " systems with their class-like divisions have never encompassed the whole of the Chin population. Many Chin communities, while also forming marriage alliances, engaging in trade with the lowlands, and holding " feasts of merit," have not developed the class-like divisions of their " autocratic " cousins. Moreover, those " autocratic " systems that did develop never, except when they were " frozen " by the British during the colonial period, turned into stable and lasting chiefdomships.

The Chin are by no means the only tribal society in the region to be characterized by the above-mentioned patterns. Other societies in northern

Burma, in neighboring Assam in India, in the Chittagong hills in Bangladesh, and, apparently, in other hill regions of Southeast Asia including those of the highlands of Vietnam, also show this contrast between democratic and unstable autocratic systems. Anthropologists, in trying to describe and interpret these societies, have attempted first to elucidate the structures whereby these societies are organized, then to ask why some members of these societies seek monopolies of the small surpluses produced by the society in question, and finally to unravel the question of why the evolution of these societies toward an autocratic structure is usually aborted. The most elaborate answers to these questions are those offered by Claude Lévi-Strauss in his monumental *Elementary Systems of Kinship*, a work that draws extensively on the ethnographic literature on tribal Southeast Asia.[59]

Lévi-Strauss has argued that the fundamental driving force among humans is the need to create a social order in contrast to the entropic tendencies of nature. The most primitive form of social structure is that which recognizes an artificial division of society into two groups or two moieties. These moieties are then integrated through an incest taboo against sexual relations among members of the same moiety and through a rule prescribing the exchange of wives between moieties. In this system of prescriptive exchange of " sisters " between moieties, a system that Lévi-Strauss calls " restricted exchange," one group, moiety A, is wife giver to the other group, moiety B, and vice versa. Societies with " restricted exchange " are structually very limited and examples of such societies are rare.

More common—particularly in Asia, according to Lévi-Strauss—are societies structured according to " generalized exchange." Such exchange is created by the institution of " matrilateral cross-cousin marriage " (in contrast to the " sister exchange " in restricted exchange systems). It must be pointed out quickly that although the rule underlying matrilateral cross-cousin marriage is that a man should marry his mother's brother's daughter, actual marriages under this rule are not so restricted. Rather, a man is expected to marry a woman who belongs to a class for which the kin term meaning " mother's brother's daughter " is appropriate (often a very large class of cousins) and, in some cases, merely to a kin group to which a man's mother's brother belongs. In societies—such as the Chin and other tribal societies in mainland Southeast Asia—that have such a marriage rule, the kin groups of the society are integrated through a " circular connubium," that is, kin groups take wives from one group and give wives to another group, and so on, until all groups within a society could be arranged in a circle vis-à-vis other groups that are either wife takers or wife givers.

Such integration is threatened, however, if the relationships between wife givers and wife takers become associated with differences in status such that, for example, a man marries a woman of a higher status, while women in his kin group are married to men of lower status. When such status differences associated with wife takers and wife givers occur, the connubium is broken since at one end are groups with a surplus of women while at the other end are groups that can find no wives for their men. Lévi-Strauss thus argues that systems of " generalized exchange " contain within their structures the seeds of their own destruction. For this reason one finds among the Chin, as with other similar societies, an oscillation between autocratic and democratic types, since when systems of " generalized exchange " approach the point of absolute status differentiation between wife givers and wife takers, a point that would be impossible to maintain, they undergo " regression " back to a simpler form.

At this point, it is important to note that Lévi-Strauss does not argue that all marriages actually contracted within a society be between matrilateral cross-cousins for the society to be organized according to a principle of generalized exchange. Rather, what is important is that the society has an ideology that prescribes such exchange and this ideology makes all marriages, including " wrong " marriages, meaningful.

E. R. Leach, in his study of the Kachins, another tribal people in northern Burma, recognized the importance of cross-cousin marriage as a structuring principle in tribal society and took into account the argument that Lévi-Strauss had made about the inherent instability of systems of generalized exchange.[60] However, Leach also argued that understanding the marriage system of such societies was not sufficient to answer all the important questions about the nature of these societies. In addition, it is necessary to take into account that the Kachin, and similar tribal societies, are adapted to an environment in which the influences of neighboring lowland civilization are as relevant as are the topography and the climate. Kachin social structure cannot be fully under-stood, in other words, unless it is seen as part of a larger social system in the Kachin hills, which includes both Kachins and Tai-speaking Shans. Leach concludes

> A part of my objective in writing this book has been to demonstrate that in contexts such as we find in North Burma the ordinary ethnographic conven-tions as to what constitutes *a* culture or *a* tribe are hopelessly inappro-priate.[61]

In his study of Chin society, Lehman has reiterated this same argument:

> The structure and organization of the society and culture of the hill Chin . . . reflect their adaptation to an environment in which the neighboring civiliza-tions are as important as their own physical habitat. Chin society and culture, therefore, must be understood in terms of a dual adaptation: first, an adap-tation to local resources by means of a particular technology, and second a response to Burman civilization.[62]

Lehman goes on to propose that societies such as the Chin and the Kachin be recognized, by virtue of their adaptation to lowland civilizations, as a particular type of society, that which he calls " subnuclear society." Subnuclear society " is distinct both from peasant society and from purely tribal society."[63]

Leach argues that the differentiation of status between kin groups in Kachin society was not simply a function of an emergent status differentiation between wife-giving and wife-taking groups. Rather, this status differentiation, as well as the drive toward monopolization of surpluses within the Kachin economy, was a function of Kachin efforts to emulate the Shan model of a feudal-like polity. Moreover, Leach sees this emulation as being grounded in a desire for power: " a conscious or unconscious wish to gain power is a very general motive in human affairs."[64]

Lehman agrees with Leach that the tendency among hill societies to evolve into autocratic systems is a function of the adaptation of such societies to neighboring lowland civilizations. He does not agree with Leach, however, in seeing what the hill peoples borrow from the lowland civilizations as being a conception of power. Rather, what really attracted the Chin, at least, " was the sheer quantity of cultural possession, material and nonmaterial (e.g., named social roles) " possessed by the lowland civilization.[65] The drive toward autocratic structures, according to Lehman, was grounded in the desire, acted on by some Chin, to gain control of unusual wealth[66] rather than to gain power.

Kirsch has offered yet another interpretation of the culture of such Southeast Asian tribal societies as found among the Chin, Kachin, and others. For him, " religion is the repository of cultural values and conceptions which provide the cognitive and affective framework within which social action takes place."[67] He goes on to argue that

> [M]y assumption about the motivational basis of the dynamism found in these upland Southeast Asian societies . . . is that the individuals within these groups are seeking for " ritual efficiency," " potency," " enhanced ritual status," or some religiously defined goal, not seeking simply to possess "political power."[68]

Kirsch recognizes, with Lehman, the importance of acquiring wealth in tribal society, but he sees the wealth that accrues as significant only insofar as it is transformed into " enhanced ritual status, increased control of ritual rights, and an increment of imputed " innate virtue."[69] For this reason the " feasts of merit " are central to tribal culture. All social action, including marriage alliances, striving for greater control of wealth and power by autocratic lineages, and obtaining prestige goods through trade is informed by the desire of some tribal peoples to hold increasingly more elaborate " feasts of merit." Moreover, the acts leading up to the " feasts of merit " are themselves charged with religious significance, each signifying control of humans over their environment. The " feasts of merit " accomplish even more, improving an individual's status not only in this world but in the afterworld as well.

Kirsch does not offer a cultural determinist argument; rather, he recognizes that the actions that follow on the religious conceptions held by tribal people are adaptive for these people in the environment in which they live:

> Given the uncertainties with respect to rainfall and land fertility, adequate agricultural production could potentially become problematical. In particular, the motivation to maximize production cannot be left to chance . . . Every unit of production . . . must be *highly* motivated to produce.[70]

Kirsch's view is that there is a cybernetic relationship between the culture of a people and the mode of adaptation the people have made to their environment. The culture develops as one solution to the problems confronting a people in adapting to their environment, but, once developed, this culture itself conditions the mode of adaptation:

> The upland peoples of Southeast Asia have adapted themselves to a narrow niche which is defined by their own cultural conceptions and resources as a total world.[71]

Kirsch's cybernetic model succeeds, I believe, in making possible a better interpretation of tribal societies such as the Chin than was heretofore possible with the models offered by Lévi-Strauss, Leach, and Lehman. However, I believe Kirsch errs in downgrading the importance of the influences of neighboring civilizations on tribal societies.[72] It is very important, as Leach and Lehman have both argued, to recognize lowland cultures as being part of the environment to which tribal societies are adapted.

The Chin and Their Context

With these various arguments in mind, let us now consider some facts about Chin society. Chins, who speak languages belonging to the Tibeto-Burman language family, are found in Burma, within the Chin Special Division, which lies along the northwestern border of Burma with India and Bangladesh. In addition, Chins are also found in both hill and lowland areas peripheral to the Chin Special Division and in those areas of India and Bangladesh that border on Burma. It is very difficult to obtain exact figures on the population of Chin speaking peoples, because almost no census was undertaken in Burma between 1931 and 1974 and the 1974 census figures are still unavailable. According to the 1931 census, there were 344,000 Chins in Burma, about half of whom lived in the Chin Special Division. Given an estimate (conservative) of 2 per cent natural increase per year there would be on the order of 800,000 Chin-speaking peoples in Burma in 1975. Approximately $1\frac{1}{2}$ times as many Chin-speaking people live in India and Bangladesh as live in Burma. Thus, the total number of Chin-speaking people would be on the order of 2 million in 1975.

The history of when Chins first settled in the area they now occupy is not known, but it is known that Chins lived here before the Burmans settled the plains to the east and south. Thus, for perhaps as much as a thousand years prior to the British annexation of upper Burma in the 1880s, Chins lived in proximity to Burman civilization. In this period, Chin society developed as an adaptation to Burman civilization. With the arrival of the British, Chin society was fixed according to some mistaken ideas of the British about the nature of that society as well as according to their own ideas about local administration. Since the independence of Burma in 1949, the Chins have been attempting to work out new modes of adaptation to a transformed Burma.

The area in which most Chin live is among the most rugged in all of Southeast Asia. Stevenson says of the Falam subdivision in the northern Chin Hills that " the most noticeable characteristic of the country . . . is its steepness. Deep valleys rise to the very tops of ridges and leave but little level land even for the building of villages."[73] In the southern Chin Hills one finds Mount Victoria, at 10,018 feet the highest peak in the division. Given the altitudes reached in the Chin Hills, much of the area is considerably cooler than the plains below.

The climate in the Chin Hills changes seasonally, temperatures ranging from freezing at night in the cold season, which runs from mid-November to mid-February, to an occasional high of 90°F in the hot dry season, which runs from late February through April. May brings the rainy season, which lasts into early November. During this period the hills are cool and wet. The rainfall, which varies markedly from locality to locality owing to the changes forced by the mountainous terrain, determines, in part, the crops that the Chin raise.

Chin Mode of Production and Economy

Most Chin are swidden agriculturalists, although some Chin living on the periphery of the Chin Hills are wet-rice cultivators and a number of hill-dwelling Chin have recently taken to cultivating wet rice in terraced fields. Among the southern Chin, the staple is rice, and few other crops are grown with it. Among the northern Chin, rice is rarely grown, and the main staples are millet and maize supplemented by beans. Millet or maize are planted in the same fields as beans, but the latter are harvested later than the former. In addition, the northern Chin also plant taro and, in recent years, potatoes, which are eaten when the stores of staple grains are exhausted. In a small area in the northern Chin Hills, commercial production of oranges and tea was begun during the colonial period.

As swidden cultivators, the Chin plant fields with crops for one or more years and then allow the fields to remain fallow for a number of years. Among the southern Chin, where the staple is rice, fields are planted for only one year and are then allowed to lay fallow for about twelve years. Among the northern Chin, most fields are planted for a number of years in succession (sometimes as many as nine), a practice that requires a fallow period of " up to forty years to regenerate satisfactorily, though such fields are usually recut much sooner because they are urgently needed and there is no other choice."[74] The Northern Chin also cultivate some fields for only one or two years, then allow them to lay fallow for seven to nine years.

The Chin also engage in animal husbandry, raising pigs, chickens, goats, dogs, and mithan, the latter being a bovine especially associated with hill-dwelling peoples in India, Bangladesh, and Burma. All the animals the Chin raise are used for food, not as work animals, although meat is usually consumed only on sacrificial occasions.

In addition to agriculture and animal husbandry, the Chins also obtain foodstuffs by hunting, fishing, and collecting wild produce that can be found in the surrounding forests and nearby streams and rivers. Hunting is particularly important to the Chin, figuring predominantly in their religious life.

Some Chin have specialized in the production of pottery, in smithing, in the manufacture of jewelry, in the making of mats, and so on. Only in rare instances is such production undertaken by individuals who are full-time specialists.

The Chin economy could not be sustained without the import of certain items that are not produced locally. Among such imported items are salt and metal used for forging the implements the Chin use. Equally important are goods that enhance the owner's prestige rather than enable him or her to use them for utilitarian purposes. Among such imported prestige goods are metals made into jewelry, brass and bronze vessels and gongs, glazed pottery, and silk for embroidered blankets.[75] Although historically some of the goods obtained outside the Chin Hills were gained through raids, most such goods were brought in through trade. With the advent of British rule, trade became the only means whereby such goods could be obtained. For these imported goods the Chin trade such local products as maize husks, beeswax, stick lac, and other forest products. Beginning in the colonial period, some Chins also acquired cash by working on government projects or serving in the armed forces. This cash was also used to purchase trade goods rather than to buy locally produced goods.

Wealth among the Chin is calculated in terms of grain (including grain that has been transformed into beer), mithan, and prestige goods. Even among the so-called democratic Chin, some differences of wealth existed. Among the autocratic Chin, surplus wealth was monopolized by a few lineages. A significant accumulation of wealth could not be built up, however, if it rested on the resources of only a single village.

> Great differences of wealth between powerful families and others can . . . only arise where the political conditions provide for their accumulation and perpetuation. Such wealth cannot be accumulated locally in such a poor country as the Chin Hills, unless there is a well-organized system for the circulation of wealth over large regions.[76]

In other words, accumulation of wealth and acquisition of power are two sides of the same coin for the Chin.

Chin Society

Both the accumulation of wealth and the acquisition of power begin at the village level. Here we find a community, ranging in size " from a small group of about ten houses to a powerful collection of over 300."[77] Access to the productive resources of a community and to the wealth generated through local production is a function of three different principles: descent, marriage alliance, and village headmanship.

Every Chin is a member of a patrilineal descent group. A village is made up mainly of members of one or more lineage segments, which consist of agnatically related men and their wives. Some property and some rights to resources are passed through lineage lines, with the eldest son inheriting in some areas, the youngest in others, and both the eldest and youngest in others. Even in democratic villages, not all lineage segments are equal. In these villages, the rank of the lineage is a function of status, which varies according to the wealth possessed by members of the lineage. In autocratic communities, rank is a function of class, " a hereditary, fixed attribute of certain descent groups."[78]

Whatever the basis of rank, those that are higher can demand a larger bride price for its women than can those of lower rank. Since men are supposed to marry up, the kin group of the wife giver normally has greater rank than the kin group of the wife receiver. Through the marriage transaction, the wife-giving group also increases its wealth vis-à-vis the wife-receiving group. Although some Chin groups have a rule that prescribes marriage between matrilateral cross-cousins, the important rule, according to Lehman, is not this prescription, but a negative prescription " which state[s] that once a marriage has been made, a reverse marriage may not be made without legal penalty; any marriage establishes a categorical alliance."[79] It is desirable to establish marriage alliances with as many groups as possible " as a means of expanding or strengthening a relatively complex network of political relations."[80]

The really significant power in Chin society was wielded by the village headman. His power was that of the " entrepreneur " who was expected to " ' manage ' the group resources to the mutual advantage of all."[81] In autocratic villages, the headman had absolute right, at least in theory, " of division and disposal, sequestration and redistribution of land within their village boundaries."[82] Headmen in autocratic villages had the right to have a house built free by villagers, the right to receive flesh dues from animals killed in hunt or animals sacrificed, rights to a portion of the natural resources (beeswax, salt, and so on) obtained from his domain, rights to free labor on his fields by members of the villages, and rights to dues, paid in beer, from every cultivator on the occasion of the opening of new fields.

In democratic villages, all the responsibilities for managing the land and the rights to various dues and labor from the village members were, again in theory, shared by the headman with a village council.[83] The real difference, according to Lehman, between autocratic and democratic village politics was whether the role of headman was hereditary or achieved in recognition of acquisition of wealth. To use Stevenson's terms, the difference was whether or not " entrepreneurship " was a function of office, as in the autocratic villages, or a prerequisite to office, as in the democratic villages.

The fact that headmen, in autocratic villages, or headmen plus councils, in democratic villages, had the power to reallocate the lands used by villagers provided a basis for acquisition of access rights to productive resources other than through descent or marriage alliance. This fact underlies a pattern that Stevenson notes was very marked, at least in the Falam subdivision—namely, the pattern whereby individuals would leave their home village and resettle in a new village. When an individual found himself at odds, for whatever reason, with the powers that be in his home village, he could move to another village where he was assured that the headman of his adopted village would arrange to have a house built for him and to provide him with land for cultivation. Often, the village in which a migrant settled was one in which both the customs and language differed from those of his home village. In the Falam subdivision, Stevenson reports:

> Almost all villages have a sprinkling of " foreigners," and in some cases one finds as many as five different tribes represented in a village of less than 30 houses. [84]

The choice of which village a migrant would settle in was usually made because the migrant had determined that the headman of his adopted village was likely to be more " entrepreneurial " than the headman of the village the migrant had left.

Entrepreneurial skills also provided the basis for claims to power exercised by the " chiefs " found in some parts of Chin society. Such chiefs were headmen of their own villages and, in addition, held the power, because of the strategic location of their villages, to " manage " trade within Chin society or between the Chins and lowland Burma. Historically, some chiefs also held their position because of their ability to " manage " the warfare forever being waged between rival villages and the forays the Chins carried out in the lowlands. When the British arrived, they froze the system and recognized these traditional " chiefs " (some of whom had only the most tenuous claims to chieftainship) as the heads of districts created for the administration of the Chin Special Division.

Whether entrepreneurship was an inherited quality or an acquired characteristic, it had to be validated through the giving of increasingly more elaborate " feasts of merit." Before we can consider these " feasts of merit," we first need to understand certain fundamental ideas of Chin religion.

Chin Religion

Lehman has argued that Chin religious thought was characterized by a basic duality between *khua*, " settled area . . . [that which] is inhabited, what has feeling, ' soul ' . . . that in which life is felt to exist . . . culture," and *ram*, " countryside . . . abode of unnamed spirits and the abode of the spirits which control the wild game . . . forest." [85] Following Kirsch, we can see Chin religious action as being granted to the transformation of potency or fertility, from *ram*, where it is dangerous, to *khua*, where it can be employed to humanity's beneficial uses. This transformation is effected in the essential religious act of the Chin, that of sacrifice. For some purposes almost any animal raised by the Chin is suitable for sacrifice; however, for really important occasions, only the pig and especially the mithan are appropriate.

Religious acts of sacrifice are undertaken either because of the threat to order posed by some actual experience—for example, illness, the potentiality or reality of crop failure, the killing of a wild animal, the killing of a human enemy, " unnatural " death, and so on—or in order to ensure the prosperity and material well being of the local Chin community. For illnesses, it is quite common for the afflicted person or his kinsmen to consult a " shaman "—who is always a woman—that is, a person who as the medium through whom the offending spirit can reveal itself or through whom the source of witchcraft can be identified. The " shaman " also determines, for these purposes, the appropriate sacrifice. For agricultural rites, which are held at a village shrine, a ritual specialist—sometimes called a priest—is called on to officiate at the sacrifices.

Rites held after the killing of a wild animal fall into a special category. On the one hand, the killing of a wild animal is an invasion of *ram*; on the other hand, it is a demonstration of the skill of particular men in converting that which is *ram* into something useful (i.e., food) for men who are *khua*. After the killing of animals, the hunters will sponsor feasts of celebration, the size of which depends on the significance of the animal killed. Feasts of celebration are obviously closely related to feasts of merit, and for some Chin feasts of merit cannot be held until one has previously sponsored an appropriate feast of celebration.

The purpose of the feast of merit is to create " potency," which will benefit all those who are participants in the feast. As Stevenson says, it is only through such feasts that the Chin feel that they can control the spirit world, which, in turn, controls material prosperity.[86] Those who create " potency " in the feasts of merit are neither shamans nor priests; they are one and the same as the " entrepreneurs " of wealth and power in Chin society. The essence of the feasts is the sacrifice of one or more animals (pigs and/or mithans) and the serving of large amounts of food to a quantity of guests. The number of guests invited, the amount of food served, and the number of days over which the feasts is held depend on the previous feasts a man has held and the amount of his wealth that can be used for these Asian potlatches.

> In a *bawi* [" lord "] Feast of Merit, which takes several days to perform, many people from one's own village and guests invited from other villages are fed and entertained with dancing and drink. One's achievement of status is proved by one's ability to entertain all these people on a grand scale. One attempts to put on as much show as possible and, in particular, to sacrifice as many mithans as possible. There is also a special ritual meal given to selected guests ... The performer forces excessive amounts of food and brandy ... upon these guests, and they are forced by attendants armed with sticks to consume it all.[87]

Although the sacrifices performed at a feast of merit are dedicated to a variety of spirits, the major religious significance of the feast is that it ensures that the performer will hold a rank in *mithi khua*, " the village of the dead," after his death commensurate with the rank he now holds in the society of the living by virtue of having held the feast. The ritual statement being communicated here is that the establishment of order, as against the chaos of *ram*, is ensured even against the fact of death. Chin are not, in fact, overly concerned about the afterworld; there is no heaven to which they aspire. Rather, they are concerned that death does not destroy the " potency " created through an arduous life of " entrepreneurship," " One overpowering concern of all Chin men and even women," Lehman informs us, " is that they should not be forgotten after they have died."[88] The feasts establish an unbreakable link be-

Sacrifice of a mithan at a Chin feast of merit. [Photo from F. K. Lehman, *The Structure of Chin Society* (Urbana: University of Illinois Press, Illinois Studies in Anthropology, No. 3, 1963), with permission from F. K. Lehman.]

tween the living and dead, a link that is given ultimate manifestation in the memorials erected for a man at his death. These memorials traditionally consisted of posts on which were carved a symbolic recapitulation of the man's significant deeds during life. Today, with some Chins having gained literacy through the teaching of missionaries, stone slabs, not unlike Western gravestones, are engraved with a written history containing the same facts—namely, the animals he killed, the ranks he achieved, the wealth expended at feasts of merit, and the like. Such memorials are also found among tribal peoples in neighboring areas of mainland Southeast Asia and in certain parts of island Southeast Asia as well. On the basis of the distribution of these memorials to the dead, Heine-Geldern posited the existence of a " megalithic " tradition, which had, in the distant past, " spread over most of Southeast Asia, continental as well as insular."[89] Rather than seeing these memorials as being evidence of the existence, prehistorically, of a megalithic tradition that was diffused throughout Southeast Asia, I would see them, as I would see the totem poles of the Northwest Coast of America, as a cultural manifestation of a fundamental mode of human thought, namely one that would deny to death its final victory.

Sociocultural Change among the Chin

Lehman, who was able to study Chin culture in the late 1950s, found it little different from what it had been when it was previously studied during the period of colonial rule. However, there is some evidence that the Chins are developing new modes of adaption in order to adjust to life in a postcolonial Burma, and such developments cannot but be reflected in Chin culture.

During the colonial period, missionaries—mainly from the American Baptist Mission—undertook to bring Christianity to the Chins. Few Chins were actually converted, but the missionaries left their mark on Chin society. Chin spoken languages were reduced to a written language, thus creating a Chin literate tradition. Mission schools not only exposed some Chins to this tradition but also stimulated a desire on the part of certain high-ranking Chins to acquire an education for use as an important tool in their entrepreneurial activities. Education has not been the only development to serve this function. Experience in the police and army and service in public work projects outside the Chin domains also opened new horizons for a small number of Chins.

As already noted, the British tended to give greater recognition to traditional Chin chiefs than Chin culture would itself have allowed. These chiefs were not slow to use the colonial administrative system to their advantage in advancing their own interests. Since Burma achieved independence, the power and authority of these chiefs has been seriously undermined by the Rangoon government. When Ne Win assumed office in 1962, the Burmese government set itself the task of integrating all local administration into a national system, a task that thereby also entailed eliminating all privileges previously accorded to local chiefs. The direct threat posed by the Burmese government to the political system of the Chin hills is a major factor, if not the major factor, underlying the emergence of a Chin independence movement.

This movement has its roots in the colonial period in more ways than one. By no means did all Chins accept the exceptional powers accorded to their chiefs by the British. Large number of Chins used ideas introduced by missionaries to form a religious movement, the Pau Chin Hau, which rejected the ideas that tended to legitimate the autocratic structures.[90] In short, the present-day political upheavals in the Chin Hills must be seen in terms of both a traditional conflict between democratic and autocratic structures within Chin society and a more recent conflict between Chins and Burmans over the political future of the Chins. This latter conflict was carried to a much greater intensity among the Karens, the tribal people to whom we now turn.

THE KARENS OF BURMA AND THAILAND

Expansion of Karens in Burma and Thailand

Karen-speaking people are the largest " tribal " minority in both Burma and Thailand, numbering three million or more in the former, although in Thailand they probably do not number more than 200,000. Prior to about the middle of the eighteenth century, Karen-speaking peoples were confined mainly to hill areas in what is today eastern Burma. Here they practiced swidden cultivation and had developed a system of relations with neighboring civilizations. Like the Chins, the Karen also appear to have lived traditionally in societies that consisted mainly of democratically structured villages, but which on occasion were organized into unstable autocratic chiefdoms:

> [T]he unit of political and social life among the Karen is the village. In consequence, the village chief is the highest civil authority in his little community. In the early days a chief of strong personality . . . would extend his control over several villages and perhaps weld them into a kind of state; but, unless [his] son and heir possessed an equally dominating nature, the fabric would fall apart as soon as the controlling hand was removed. The organization of the village was patriarchal, but the government was really democratic.[92]

Since at least the middle of the eighteenth century, large numbers of Karens have moved out of their original hill habitats and have settled in the lowlands of Burma. Some also moved eastward into what is today Thailand, where they settled in both the uplands and the lowlands.

The movement of the Karen into the lowlands of Burma and into Thailand was associated with political changes in Karen society as well. Whereas Karens had previously lived in areas that were relatively inaccessible from the centers of political power in Burma and Thailand, now many Karens lived in lowland areas that could be reached with relative ease. Moreover, as both Burma and Thailand developed new roads, railroads, and air systems in recent years, even those Karens living in areas that had previously been remote came to have regular contact with governmental agencies. Although British rule provided something of a buffer between the Karens and Burmans, it failed to give the Karens lasting political equality of status with the Burmans. And although some Karens undeniably benefited from commercial rice production and involvement in the teak trade, it did not bring them equality of economic status with either the Burmans or the Thai. In short, the experience of the past two hundred years has created among many Karens in both Burma and Thailand a sense of being " an oppressed peasantry which through acculturation may gradually become assimilated into the lower ranks of the dominant population."[93]

This status has not been accepted passively by the Karen. During the same two centuries, the Karen have made many attempts to set up autonomous Karen political entities. Most of these attempts have failed, in part because of the same type of contradictions within Karen society that prevented the creation of lasting autocratic systems among a number of other tribal peoples in Southeast Asia. Some Karens did, however, succeed in transcending these contradictions in the nineteenth century. The Red Karen or Kayah, who live in an area bordering on the southern Shan States of Burma, northern Thailand, and hill tracts occupied by other Karens, succeeded in establishing three chiefdomships that survived from the early nineteenth century until the end of British rule over Burma. Moreover, these chiefdomships were deemed sufficiently important at the founding of an independent Burma for the area in which they are located to be recognized as a separate state, that of Kantharawadi.[94] Some other Karens, who had settled in Thailand, also developed higher levels of political organization, and established semifeudal systems under the Siamese monarch. Three small " domains " (*mụang*) that had Karens as their lords existed in western Thailand from about the middle of the nineteenth century until well into the twentieth century. These " domains " were abolished, however, in the wake of political reforms instituted by King Chulalongkorn and implemented both before and after his death in 1910.[95]

Even though only the Karen who lived in the Kayah area or in western Thailand succeeded in transcending the structural barriers inherent in traditional Karen culture, which tended to prevent the establishment of lasting supralocal political entities, the push to overcome these barriers existed among many Karen. Although this push was encouraged somewhat by the British, both the governments of independent Burma and Thailand have strongly resisted it. This has led the Karen to suffer from a sense of oppression at the hands of their neighbors.

The demographic, political, and economic changes that Karen society has undergone since the middle of the eighteenth century have also been accompanied by intense religious agitation. Much of this has been in the form of massive conversions of Karens to Christianity, a missionary success story for which no equivalent exists elsewhere in Southeast Asia unless it be among the Vietnamese. Many Karens who have not embraced Christianity have nonetheless abandoned their traditional religion. Some have become Buddhists, taking on forms of Buddhism practiced by their neighbors. Others have joined certain of the many indigenous sects that have sprung up among the Karen. Many of these sects have been millenarian in character, that is to say they have looked to the imminent establishment of some type of heaven on earth. Stern has argued that the religious agitation that has characterized Karen society over the past two centuries can be explained in terms of the experiences of the Karens relative to their more powerful neighbors:

> [B]oth the envy toward the superior civilizations of their neighbors . . . and the bitterness of their lot when those neighbors became oppressors combined to drive them to seek redress in religion.[96]

Stern also sees the new religious ideas of the Karen, including those associated with Karen millenarian movements, as having been borrowed either from their Buddhist neighbors or from Christian missionaries.[97] Although not denying in any way the importance of the experiences of the Karens with their neighbors or the cultural influences of these neighbors and missionaries on Karen religious life, I would also argue that to understand Karen religious change and the political aspirations associated with this change, we must also look to traditional Karen culture.

Traditional Karen Religion

In Karen mythology can be found a conception of Karen culture that is contrasted with nature, on the one hand, and the cultures of civilized peoples, on the other. In a cosmogonic myth found in one form or another among all Karens, the story is told of Y'wa, the divine power who creates nature, including the first man and woman. This ancestral couple live among wild trees that bear seven types of fruits, six of which they are permitted to eat by Y'wa, but the seventh of which is forbidden to them. One day a large serpent persuades them to eat of the seventh fruit, after which the couple becomes subject to the processes of suffering, aging, and death. The serpent, which is but one manifestation of the basically feminine divinity, Mü kaw li, then teaches the couple the elements of their culture, including the technology of rice production, the names of the various spirits who inhabit the world in which they live, the identity of the ancestral spirit, *bgha*, the rites of propitiation for the various spirits that cause illnesses, the methods for securing the life principle (*k'la*) that must not wander from the body lest illness also ensue, and so on.

In a related myth, Y'wa is said to have given books to his various children, sometimes said to number seven, who are the ancestors of the major ethnic groups in the world known to the Karen. This gift of a book was, of course, the gift of literacy. The Karen, however, are negligent with the book given to them and it is eaten by animals or, in some versions, consumed in the fires built by the Karen in the course of tilling their fields. Y'wa offers the Karen the consolation that at some future date, " foreign brothers " will bring the gift of literacy—in the form of a golden book—back to them.

These two myths greatly impressed the American Baptist missionaries who began work among the Karens in the early part of the nineteenth century. The first story so paralleled the Biblical story of the Garden of Eden, including the fact that the name Y'wa was very similar to the Hebrew Yaweh, that the missionaries concluded that the Karens must be the descendants of one of the ten lost tribes of Israel. Moreover, they quickly presented themselves as the foreign brothers bringing the Karens the golden book. The fact that missionaries were the first to record these myths has led to their interpretations coloring the understanding of them ever since. Contrary to such interpretations, Y'wa cannot in fact be seen (at least prior to Christian missionization) as a high god that approximates the Biblical conception of God. For the Karen, Y'wa represents a natural state, including the distinctions between men, some of whom are literate and others of whom, like the Karens, are not. Mü kaw li (whom the Christians came to identify as Satan) represents the cultural state wherein the life of the Karen is meaningful.

The cosmogonic deities, Y'wa and Mü kaw li, are but one type of supernatural power recognized by the Karen. In addition are the rather large number of animistic divinities, that is, minor gods and spirits, that belong to the Karen pantheon. Of these animistic beings, the most important are the " Lord of Land and Water," that is, a territorial god, and the ancestral spirit, called *bgha*. In addition, the Karen also conceive of human beings, certain animals and plants (especially rice), and even certain inanimate objects as possessing a " life force," known as *k'la*. Finally, Karens further conceive of humans, animals, and plants, and some inanimate objects as partaking in unequal ways of an impersonal power known as *pgho*.[98]

The Lord of Land and Water provides the supernatural protection necessary for the well being of the people living in a village. Sacrificial rites are held at least once a year to propitiate this spirit, such rites being led by a man who is both headman of the village and village ritual specialist. As each locale is associated with such a divinity, it is difficult for this belief to be used by village headmen as a claim to supralocal authority. On the contrary, if a village is not prosperous, this can be interpreted as being a consequence of the headman's inability to please the local spirit. In such cases, some of the people living in a village might secede and migrate to other villages or establish a new village of their own.

Perhaps the most important supernatural power for traditional Karens is the *bgha*, the ancestral spirit. The *bgha* does not appear to be the spirit of any particular ancestor:

> The family " Bghas " are said to be eternal. As new unions take place and households are set up generation by generation, each family finds itself provided with a " Bgha " of its own. But what the relation of the new crop of " Bghas " is to that of the preceding generation, no one is able to explain.[99]

Although some concern is focused on the *bgha* associated with particular households, the more important *bgha* is that worshipped by a group of kinsmen living in different households and often in different villages. This group of kinsmen are related matrilineally. For Pwo Karen in one area in northern Thailand, the size of the membership of the matrilineal ancestor cult range from 6 to 55.[100] The *bgha* must be propitiated lest it consume the " vital substance " (*k'la*) of family members, thus causing them to fall ill and perhaps even die. At least once a year, all the members of the matrilineal cult group must collect for a sacrificial feast for their collective *bgha*. The officiant at this feast is the eldest woman of the senior line. Every member of the group must attend; if he or she does not, the *bgha* will be offended and one or more members of the group will fall ill. Conversely, no person—including all in-laws—who is not matrilineally related to the officiant can attend, lest the *bgha* be offended for another reason. Iijima has seen in this ritual propitiation of the *bgha* the essence of traditional Karen identity.[101] It is certainly true that Karen could sustain a refusal to participate in the rituals of the matrilineal cult group only by recognizing some power superior to that of the *bgha*. And such power must belong to supernatural beings of forces that the Karen have come to know only through contact with other traditions, reinterpretation of other elements in their own tradition, or both.

Most of the spirits of the Karen pantheon, other than the two already discussed, have much more particular functions. There is, for example, the Karen version of the Rice Goddess, the god of the rainbow, and deities of the trees, water, rivers, and so on. Although these spirits are important for such Karen concerns as health, production, natural disasters, hunting, and so on, none of them have ever been associated with more than a local cult.

The next important religious concept of the Karen is that of the *k'la* or life principle. The *k'la* can become detached from the bodies of humans (or animals) that they vitiate. Such commonly occurs during sleep, or when one shifts his place of residence, changes status, as at marriage, or comes into contact with the *k'la* of a dead person. Thus, one must on these occasions have one's *k'la* securely fastened to one's body. This " securing of the k'la " is often done by ordinary people themselves, but sometimes by specialists who have acquired through learning or contact with other sources of power the ability to call and fasten *k'la* belonging to others.

In traditional Karen culture, the power that could be called on by some humans, such as the specialists mentioned above, and not by others was *pgho*. The possession of *pgho* was not limited to humans; objects, which thus became fetishes, could also partake of *pgho*. However, *pgho* was most significant when it was a quality of a human. The man who was endowed with *pgho* was believed to have established a personal communication with supernatural beings, particularly with those divine wellsprings of Karen life, Y'wa and Mü Kaw Li.[102] Such men of *pgho* included the " prophets " (*wi*), " medicine teachers " (*k' thi thra*), and " witches," who because they used their power for evil purposes were known as " false prophets " (*wi a' bla*). Some men of *pgho* were villagers who had immersed themselves deeply in traditional Karen lore. Others, and apparently more powerful ones, were village outcasts who had been forced to make their lives in the jungle. Such outcasts included orphans and men who had broken some major sexual taboo. In rare cases men of *pgho* were village headmen.

Religious Change Among the Karens

Although most men of *pgho* contented themselves with acting in terms of Karen culture, some linked themselves to the culture of neighboring Buddhist civilizations and, after the entrance of the missionaries, some linked themselves to Christianity. Both links had their sanction within Karen culture. As we saw above, mythology provided the Karen with a rationale for seeing those of a literate civilization as superior.

The literate civilizations with whom Karen had the most intensive contact were those of the Buddhist Burmans, Mons, Shans, and Thai. It is hardly surprising, then, that Karen who possessed *pgho* should sometimes be thought of as men who possessed " merit " in the Buddhist sense of the term.[103] This equation was all the more apparent in the event that a Karen entered the monkhood of one of the Buddhist orders. There is a long tradition of Pwo Karen joining the Mon monkhood in lower Burma and of Taungthu Karen joining the Shan monkhood in the southern Shan States. The Karen affiliated with the temples in which such monks live must be seen as having been integrated, albeit often imperfectly, into either Mon or Shan civilization. Other Karen men of *pgho* have also been seen as men of " merit," but have not expressed their power through the role of the Buddhist monk. Rather, they have become focal figures in syncretic religious movements, which often look to the establishment of a new order on earth, one in which the Karen themselves will be powerful. Most such new orders are but millenial dreams; however, for the Kayah such a dream was realized. In the early nineteenth century the Kayah were able to establish three small chiefdomships modeled on Shan principalities. The rulers of these chiefdomships combined the role of political leader with that of *phre phrow*, the Kayah equivalent of the man of *pgho*. These chiefs succeeded in combining traditional Karen concepts of supernatural power with Buddhist cosmocratic conceptions borrowed from the Shan.[104]

With the arrival of the missionaries and the beginning of their intensive work among the Karen, which started shortly after the British annexed lower Burma in 1826, the Karen were presented with another literate religious tradition to emulate. Under Christian influence, some men of *pgho* saw themselves as the prophets of Y'wa who were to tell Karens the news of the arrival of the " foreign brothers " bringing the " golden book." Thus, some traditional Karen prophets paved the way for the introduction of Christianity. The missionaries, for their part, responded by drawing wherever possible on Karen ideas in making the Christian message meaningful. They were influenced in this by the strong

Sgaw Karens taking part in a ritual dedication of a Buddhist shrine in a Karen village in northern Thailand. [C. F. Keyes photograph]

parallels they professed to see between traditional Karen religion and Old Testament Christianity. The combination of the receptivity of Karens to religious ideas that would permit them to transcend their localities and to confront the oppressive tendencies of their neighbors, the adaptation by the missionaries of the Christian message to Karen culture, and the mediation of men of *pgho* are the major factors explaining why by 1919 some 335,000 Karens, that is about 17 per cent of all Karens in Burma, had become Christian.[105]

Christian influences did not result only in conversion to Christianity. Some Karen men of *pgho* who had been exposed to Christian ideas, often in mission schools, also became leaders of syncretic cults involving Christian and Karen and sometimes Buddhist elements. These cults do not appear to have been as successful as the cults drawing only on Buddhist and Karen traditions. The reason for this may be that the syncretic cults that draw on Christianity had little to offer Karens that Christianity did not.[106]

Karen Nationalism

The activities of the Christian missionaries among the Karen must be recognized as perhaps the most important factor in the development of a Karen national movement, a movement that has attracted many non-Christian Karens. The missionaries promoted the development of a school system for the Karen. At these schools, the Karen were taught some subjects in the Karen language by way of a Burman script adapted to Karen by missionaries. They were also taught Burmese and English and were given education in skills that could not be properly used at the village level. The missionaries initiated the development of a Karen literate tradition, beginning with the translation of the Bible into Karen but also including, from a very early time, publication of Karen folklore supportive of Christian ideas. The construction of printing presses to serve both religious and educational needs also stimulated the emergence of a Karen press and a tradition of secular literature. The Karen Christian churches (which are mainly Baptist) have provided a network of connections and an organization that is more than local. Missionaries have also attracted support for the Karen from non-Karen circles in Burma, India, England, and the United States.

During the period of British rule, the Karen were accorded distinctive recognition, a function, as J. S. Furnivall has observed, of the unity wrought by Christian missionization. The Karen, he said, were

> [F]ormerly a wild jungle folk oppressed by the Burmese, large numbers had accepted Christianity, with a rise in status and prosperity that attached them to the British.[107]

As Britain accorded Burma some semblance of self-government in the years just prior to World War II, so too did it accord special recognition to the Karen, who along with such other minorities as the Chinese, Indians, Eurasians, and Europeans were given special representation in the Burmese Legislative Assembly.

World War II was a shattering experience for the Karen in Burma. They suddenly found that their former patrons, the missionaries and the British, had gone from the scene and that the Burmans, under the tutelage of the Japanese, held political ascendancy. During the War numerous incidents occurred in which there was conflict between the Burmans and the Karen. These were but preludes to the more violent conflict to come. Following World War II, the British were forced rather quickly to realize that they would have to grant Burma independence within a very short period of time. Karen leaders then began to make representations, both to the British and to the nationalist leadership, for some sort of guarantees for a distinctive Karen political identity. Although Karen leaders had good personal relations with Bogyoke Aung San, the architect of Burmese independence, they were not able to gain any promises of substance on the issue. A Commission of Inquiry set up to report on the question of the type of administration to be established in areas populated mainly by non-Burmans provided no clear guidance about the action to be taken regarding the Karen.

Shortly before the British relinquished suzerainty over Burma, assassins broke in on a meeting of Bogyoke Aung San and his advisers. Those killed included Aung San and Mahn Ba Khaing, one of the Karen leaders. Although some of the more moderate Karen leaders attempted to maintain a dialogue with the Burmese government led by U Nu, that is, with the first independent government of Burma, many Karen leaders despaired of working out any satisfactory status for the Karen within the framework of the Union of Burma. Although U Nu adopted a conciliatory position toward the aspirations of the Karen, the die was cast. In the latter part of 1948, just a few months after Burma became independent, the Karen went into rebellion. By early 1949, the Karen rebels held Moulmein and were threatening Rangoon, the Burmese capital, itself. However, the attack failed, and the Karen rebellion began to subside, a function as much of conflict within the rebel movement as it was of the military superiority of the Burmese government. Although most of the Karen eventually made their peace with the Burmese government, albeit without gaining any lasting guarantees for their distinctive status, some Karens remain in rebellion to this day. An area of Burma in what is now the Karen state (Kawthulay State) that borders on Thailand is still mainly in rebel hands.

Place of the Karens in Contemporary Burma and Thailand

Since General Ne Win took power in 1962, the Burmese government has embarked on a program of centralization. The designation of Karen State, like that of the Shan State and others, is mainly an empty form. Under Ne Win's administration, education and military activities are all geared to produce the integration, if not the assimilation, of the ethnic minorities into a society dominated by Burmans.

In Thailand, some Karens continued to be accorded a distinctive political identity even into the 1920s. In 1924, one district head in western Thailand was still a Pwo Karen. However, this man was but a relic of the old order being eliminated in the wake of reforms instituted by King Chulalongkorn at the end of the nineteenth century. These reforms had as their intent the centralization of administration and the elimination of local bases of power. They were associated with policies that sought to play down the cultural and ethnic differences within the country. By 1932, when Thailand changed from an absolute to a constitutional monarchy, Karens had totally disappeared as a distinctive element in the Thai polity. They were not to reemerge until the 1950s, when their location along the Burmese border, and particularly their proximity to the area in Burma in which the Karen rebels were most firmly entrenched, led Thai officials to take note of them again. However, the new government policies that directly affected the Karen were not constructed for the Karen alone. Rather the Karen were lumped together with others in a general category of " hill people " (*chao khao*). Thai policies toward the " hill people " have sought to eliminate swidden cultivation as being detrimental to programs of forest conservation, to educate them in the Thai system, and to convert them to Thai Buddhism. In short, the Thai policies have—at least until the early 1970s—sought to deny to the Karen a distinctive identity within the Thai state.

Karens continue to attempt to alter their status as a submerged minority in both Burma and Thailand. Some Karens remain active participants in the politico-military movements that seek to create an independent Kawthulay, and probably many more in both Burma and Thailand are sympathetic to this rebellion. Other Karens, however, have sought a solution to their difficulties through religion. In northern Thailand, where I was in 1972–1974, at least four different Karen religious movements were active. One was centered on a charismatic northern Thai Buddhist monk, a second on a defrocked northern Thai monk, and third on a Karen orphan who was believed to possess miraculous powers derived both from Karen supernatural sources and from his Buddhist " merit " acquired when he was a novice in a Thai temple. The fourth drew on a source of power that could be learned from Burmese and/or Shan texts and involved a ritual break with the ancestral spirit, the *bgha*. Moreover, the Telakhon sect that Stern[108] had observed in the mid-1960s in Kancanaburi province in central Thailand was reported to be very active still in the early 1970s.

The variety of religious forms adopted by Karens in both Thailand and Burma reflects a continuing crisis in Karen society. This crisis, which has its equivalent in many parts of the world, derives from the desire of the Karen to be distinctive, a desire that is contradicted by their experience as a submerged minority.

NOTES

Chapter 1

1. Charles A. Fisher, *South-East Asia* (London: Methuen, 1964).

2. K. C. Chang, " Major Problems in the Culture History of Southeast Asia, *Bull. Inst. Ethnology, Acad. Sinica*, XIII (1962), pp. 2–3.

3. See, especially, the following: Wilhelm G. Solheim II, " Reworking Southeast Asian Prehistory," *Paideuma*, XV (1969), pp. 125–39; Solheim, " Early Bronze in Northeastern Thailand," *Current Anthropology*, IX (1968), pp. 59–62; D. T. Bayard, *Non Nok Tha: The 1968 Excavation* (Otago, N.Z., University of Otago, Studies in Prehistoric Anthropology, Vol. 4, n.d. [1971]); C. Gorman, "Hoabinhian: A Pebble Tool Complex with Early Plant Association in Southeast Asia," *Science*, CLXIII (1969), pp. 671–73; Karl Hutterer, and others, " An Evolutionary Approach to the Southeast Asian Cultural Sequence," *Current Anthropology*, XVII (1976), pp. 243–62.

4. See Chang, *op. cit.*, p. 12.

5. See Richard Pearson, " Dong-So'n and Its Origins," *Bull. Inst. Ethnology, Acad. Sinica*, XIII (1962), p. 44.

6. See, for example, G. Coedès, *The Making of South East Asia* (Berkeley and Los Angeles: University of California Press, 1966), pp. 22 *et seq.*

7. Robert Heine-Geldern, " Urheimat and Früheste Wanderungen der Austronesier," *Anthropos*, XXVII (1932), pp. 543–619.

8. H. R. van Heekeren, *The Stone Age of Indonesia* (The Hague: Nijhoff, 1957), p. 131.

9. See Father Wilhelm Schmidt, " Les peuples Mon-Khmer, trait d'union entre les peuples de l'Asie centrale et de l'Austronesie," *Bull. de l'Ecole Française d'Extrême-Orient*, VIII (1907), pp. 213–63. Also see Heinz-Jürgen Pinnow, " The Position of the Munda Languages within the Austroasiatic Language Family," in *Linguistic Comparison in South East Asia and the Pacific*, by Eugenie Henderson, *et al.* (London: School of Oriental and African Studies, University of London, 1963), pp. 140–53.

10. G. Coedès, *The Indianized States of Southeast Asia* (Honolulu: East-West Center Press, 1968), p. 8.

11. I. Dyen, " The Lexicostatistical Classification of the Malayapolynesian Languages," *Language*, XXXVIII (1962), pp. 38–46 and *The Lexicostatistical Classification of Austronesian Languages* (New Haven, 1963).

12. G. P. Murdock, " Genetic Classification of the Austronesian Languages," *Ethnology*, III (1964), p. 122.

13. Murdock, *op. cit.*, p. 124; *cf.* Dyen, *op. cit.*, 1962, p. 86.

14. " Movement of the Malayo-Polynesians, 1500 B.C. to A.D. 500," *Current Anthropology* V (1964), pp. 359–406.

15. G. W. Grace has questioned the Dyen/Murdock hypothesis on the basis of his own linguistic reconstruction of Austronesian languages. See " Movement of the Malayo-Polynesians . . .," *loc. cit.*

16. I am indebted to Professor F. W. Mote for bringing this example to my attention.

17. Paul Benedict has argued that Tai (or Daic) languages are genetically related to Indonesian (i.e., Austronesian) languages. See Benedict, " Thai, Kadai, and Indonesian: A New Alignment in Southeastern Asia," *American Anthropologist*, XLIV (1942), pp. 576–601 and Benedict, *Austro-Thai: Language and Culture with a Glossary of Roots* (New Haven: HRAF Press, 1974). Although Benedict's thesis has been accepted by some cultural historians, it has not been generally

accepted by linguists. Nor has an older theory that Tai languages belong to the Sino-Tibetan language family (see Kurt Wulff, *Chinesisch und Tai: Sprachvergleichende Untersuchungen* [København: Levin, Mungsgaard, Ejnar Munksgaard, 1934]) been accepted, although there is evidence to suggest that there may have been ancient contacts between Tai and Sinitic languages (see G. B. Downer, " Chinese, Thai, and Miao-Yao," in Henderson, *et al., op. cit.*, pp. 133–39). The thesis that Viet-Muong languages (including Vietnamese) belong to the Austroasiatic language family, a thesis first advanced by Schmidt in 1906, has received wider support (see Pinnow, *op. cit.* for relevant sources); however, there is also an alternative thesis that would relate Viet-Muong and Tai languages (see, for example, P. J. Honey and E. H. S. Simmonds, " Thai and Vietnamese: Some Elements of Nominal Structure Compared," in Eugenie Henderson, *et al., op. cit.*, pp. 71–78). It should be noted here that the term " Tai " is used to refer to any group speaking a Tai (or Daic) language wherever the group is found while the term " Thai " refers to citizens of the nation-state of Thailand.

18. On the Tonkin area see P. Wheatley, " Discursive Scholia on Recent Papers on Agricultural Terracing and on Related Matters Pertaining to Northern Indochina and Neighbouring Areas," *Pacific Viewpoint*, VI (1965), pp. 123–44.

19. Chang (*op. cit.*, p. 15), however, believes that wet-rice cultivation was not an indigenous development in Southeast Asia, but was the result of influence from China.

20. *Ibid.*, p. 19.

21. *Ibid.*, pp. 18–19.

22. Bayard, *op. cit.*, p. 40.

23. See Benett Bromson, " Excavations at Chansen, Thailand: An Interim Report," *Asian Perspectives*, XIV (1973); Thiva Supajanya and Srisakra Vallibhotama, " The Need for an Inventory of Ancient Sites for Anthropological Research in Northeastern Thailand," *Tonan Ajia Kenkyu* (Southeast Asian Studies), X (1972), pp. 284–97; C. F. Keyes, " A Note on the Ancient Towns and Cities of Northeastern Thailand: *Tonan Ajia Kenkyu*, XI (1974), pp. 497–506.

24. See Paul Wheatley, *The Golden Khersonese* (Kuala Lumpur: University of Malaya Press, 1961), and Wheatley, *Impressions of the Malaya Peninsula in Ancient Times* (Singapore: Eastern Universities Press, 1964).

25. See Bernard Bourotte, " Essai d'histoire des populations montagnards du Sud-Indochinois jusqu'à 1945," *Bull. de Société des Etudes Indochinoises*, XXX (1955), pp. 1–133 (English translation by U.S. Department of State, Division of Language Services [Washington, D.C.: Agency for International Development, n.d.]). References from English translation: on the Jarai/Khmer relationship see pp. 23, 33–34.

26. Charles Archaimbault, " Religious Structures in Laos," *J. Siam Society*, LII (1964), p. 59.

27. *Ibid.*, p. 65.

28. *Ibid.*, pp. 65–66.

29. Bourotte, *op. cit.*, p. 39.

30. Alfred W. McCoy, *The Politics of Heroin in Southeast Asia.* (New York: Harper and Row, 1972), pp. 77ff.

31. See David E. Sopher, *The Sea Nomads: A Study Based on the Literature of the Maritime Boat People of Southeast Asia* (Singapore: Memoirs of the National Museum, No. 5, 1965).

32. On the Mrabri/Yumbri see Hugo and Emmy Bernatzik, *The Spirits of the Yellow Leaves* (London: Robert Hale, 1958), Kraisri Nimmanhaeminda and Julian Hartland-Swann, " Expedition to the ' Khon Pa ' (or Phi Tong Luang?)," *J. Siam Society*, L, 2 (1962), pp. 165–86, and the special issue of the *Journal of the Siam Society*, LI, 2 (1963), entitled " The Mrabri: Studies in the Field."

33. For a discussion of types of swiddening systems found in Southeast Asia see J. E. Spencer, *Shifting Cultivation in Southeastern Asia* (Berkeley and Los Angeles: University of California Press, University of California Publications in Geography, Vol. 19, 1966).

34. E. R. Leach, *Political Systems of Highland Burma* (Cambridge: Harvard University Press, 1954).

35. C. Lévi-Strauss, *Elementary Structures of Kinship* (2nd. rev. ed. tr. by James Harle Bell, John Richard von Sturmer, and Rodney Needham, ed. by Rodney Needham, Boston: Beacon Press, 1969).

36. R. Needham has published a large corpus of studies of tribal systems in the Assamese/No. Burma area by reanalyzing the data first collected by field researchers. His argument, as well as references to most of this work, can be found in *Structure and Sentiment* (Chicago: Univ. of Chicago Press, 1962).

37. For a summary statement regarding the Tai based on the reports of a number of observers, see Karl Izikowitz, " Notes about the Tai," *Bull. of the Museum of Far Eastern Antiquities*, XXXIV (1962), pp. 73–91.

38. Peter Kandre, " Autonomy and Integration of Social Systems: The Iu Mien (' Yao ' or ' Man ') Mountain Population and Their Neighbors," in *Southeast Asian Tribes, Minorities, and Nations*, ed. by Peter Kunstadter (Princeton; Princeton University Press, 1967), vol. 2, p. 599.

39. See Frank M. LeBar, Gerald C. Hickey, John K. Musgrave, *Ethnic Groups of Mainland Southeast Asia* (New Haven, Conn.: Human Relatiosn Area Files Press, 1964).

40. Cf. Carleton S. Coon, *The Living Races of Man* (New York: Knopf, 1965), p. 179. Coon classifies the Negritos together with the Australian Aboriginals and the " Papuans " of New Guinea as members of an " Australoid subspecies." Brandt disputes this and follows the more traditional classification in seeing the Negritos as pygomoid Oceanic Negroids—see John H. Brandt, " The Southeast Asian Negrito," *J. Siam Society*, LII (1965), p. 27.

41. Paul Schebesta, *Among the Forest Dwarfs of Malaya* (tr. by Arthur Chambers, London: Hutchinson, 1927), p. 41.

42. LeBar, Hickey, and Musgrave (*op. cit.*, p. 182) state that: " The Malayan Department of Aborigines now places the number of Semang in Malaya unofficially at between 2,000 and 3,000." Kunstadter (*op. cit.*, p. 316) gives 841 as the number of Semang appearing in the Census of the Federation of Malaya in 1957. J. H. Brandt in his article, " The Negrito of Peninsular Thailand," *J. Siam Society*, XLIX (1961), p. 133, places the number of Semang in Thailand at 300.

43. Ivor Evans, *Negritos of Malaya* (Cambridge: Cambridge University Press, 1937), pictures following pp. 170 and 174.

44. Evans, *op. cit.*; Schebesta, *op. cit.*

45. Brandt, " The Southeast Asian Negrito," *op. cit.* and Brandt, " The Negrito of Peninsular Thailand," *op. cit.*

46. Schebesta, *op. cit.*, p. 116.

47. *Ibid.*, p. 378.

48. On hunting and on plantations among the Semang, see *ibid.*, pp. 77–83.

49. P. D. R. Williams-Hunt, *An Introduction to the Malayan Aborigines* (Kuala Lumpur: The Government Printer, 1952), p. 58.

50. *Ibid.*, pp. 98, 114.

51. Evans, *op. cit.*, p. 251.

52. Brandt, " The Southeast Asian Negrito," *op. cit.*, p. 39.

53. Schebesta, *op. cit.*, p. 84.

54. *Ibid.*, p. 233.

55. *Ibid.*, p. 228.

56. *Ibid.*, p. 236.

57. See G. C. Madoc, "Jungle Fort" in *Straits Times Annual for 1961* (Singapore: Straits Times Press, 1959), pp. 70–73; T. Stacey, *The Hostile Sun* (London: Duckworth, 1953); T. Westwood, *The Face of the Beloved* (London: G. Allen, 1962); and Williams-Hunt, *op. cit.*

58. Brandt, " The Southeast Asian Negrito," *op. cit.*, p. 35.

59. Claude Lévi-Strauss, *op. cit.*

60. E. R. Leach, *Political Systems of Highland Burma*, 2nd ed. (Boston: Beacon Press, 1964; copyright 1954), p. 9.

61. *Ibid.*, p. 281.

62. F. K. Lehman, *The Structure of Chin Society* (Urbana: University of Illinois Press, 1963), p. 1.

63. *Ibid.*, p. 2.

64. Leach, *op. cit.*, p. 10.

65. Lehman, *op. cit.*, p. 30.

66. *Ibid.*, p. 103.

67. A. Thomas Kirsch, *Feasting and Oscillation* (Ithaca, N.Y.: Cornell University, Southeast Asia Program, Data Paper No. 92, 1973), p. 3.

68. Kirsch, *Loc. cit.*

69. *Ibid.*, p. 8.

70. *Ibid.*, p. 9.

71. *Ibid.*, p. 6.

72. *Ibid.*, p. 31.

73. H. N. C. Stevenson, *The Economics of the Central Chin Tribes* (Bombay: The Times of India Press, 1943), p. 29.

74. Lehman, *op. cit.*, p. 56.

75. *Ibid.*, p. 166.

76. Lehman, *op. cit.*, p. 146.
77. Stevenson, *op. cit.*, p. 22.
78. Lehman, *op. cit.*, p. 140.
79. *Ibid.*, p. 96.
80. *Ibid.*, p. 100.
81. Stevenson, *op. cit.*, p. 8; compare Lehman, *op. cit.*, p. 170.
82. Stevenson, *op. cit.*, p. 82.
83. *Ibid.*, p. 90.
84. *Ibid.*, p. 15.
85. Lehman, *op. cit.*, pp. 172–73.
86. Stevenson, *op. cit.*, p. 156.
87. Lehman, *op. cit.*, pp. 178–79.
88. *Ibid.*, p. 188.
89. Robert Heine-Geldern, " Some Tribal Art Styles of Southeast Asia; An Experiment in Art History," in *The Many Faces of Primitive Art* ed. by D. Fraser (Englewood Cliffs, N. J.: Prentice-Hall, 1966), p. 167.
90. See Kirsch, *op. cit.*, p. 32, and Stevenson, *op. cit.*, pp. 161–63.
91. The main sources I have used for this portrait of the Karen include H. I. Marshall, *The Karen People of Burma* (Columbus: The Ohio State University Bulletin, vol. 26, no. 13, 1922); Theodore Stern, " *Ariya* and the Golden Book," *J. Asian Studies*, 27, 2 (1968), pp. 297–328; Peter Hinton, *The Pwo Karen of Northern Thailand: A Preliminary Report* (Chiang Mai, Thailand: Tribal Research Centre, 1969); F. K. Lehman, " Kayah Society as a Function of the Shan-Burman-Karen Context," in *Contemporary Change in Traditional Societies, Vol. II: Asian Rural Societies*, ed. by Julian H. Steward (Urbana: University of Illinois Press, 1967), pp. 1–104; and Charles F. Keyes, ed., *Ethnic Adaptation and Identity. The Karens on the Thai Frontier with Burma*, forthcoming.
92. Marshall, *op. cit.*, p. 143.
93. Stern, *op. cit.*, p. 298.
94. Lehman, *op. cit.*
95. Theodore Stern, " A People Between: the Pwo Karen of Western Thailand," and Charles F. Keyes, " The Karen in Thai History and the History of the Karen in Thailand," both in *Ethnic Adaptation and Identity: The Karens on the Thai Frontier with Burma*, forthcoming.
96. Stern, " *Ariya* and the Golden Book," *op. cit.*, p. 299.
97. *Ibid.*
98. The native terms here used are taken from Marshall (*op. cit.*) and are based upon a Skaw Karen dialect.
99. Marshall, *op. cit.*, p. 248.
100. Hinton, *op. cit.*, p. 14.
101. Shigeru Iijima, " Ethnic Identity and Sociocultural Change among Sgaw Karen in Northern Thailand," in *Ethnic Adaptation and Identity: The Karens on the Thai Frontier with Burma*, ed. by Charles F. Keyes, forthcoming.

102. See Marshall, *op. cit.*, pp. 268–9.

103. See Stern, " *Ariya* and the Golden Book," *op. cit.*, p. 303.

104. See Lehman, *op. cit.*, esp. p. 26 and pp. 38–40.

105. Marshall, *op. cit.*, pp. 300–301. Russell E. Brown in his book *Doing the Gospel in Southeast Asia* (Valley Forge, Pa.: Judson Press, 1968) gives the figure of 450,000 for all Christians in Burma. By far the majority of these would be Karens. Although we have only gross figures to work with, they do suggest that growth of the Christian community among the Karens occurred primarily in the period up to World War I and that since then the percentage of Christian Karens to all Karens in Burma has remained more or less constant.

106. See Stern, " *Ariya* and the Golden Book," *op. cit.*, and Marshall, *op. cit.*, pp. 264–65.

107. J. S. Furnivall, *Colonial Policy and Practice* (New York: New York University Press, 1956), p. 180.

108. Stern, " *Ariya* and the Golden Book," *op. cit.*

CHAPTER 2
DEVELOPMENT OF THERAVADA BUDDHIST CIVILIZATION IN MAINLAND SOUTHEAST ASIA

Tribal societies in mainland Southeast Asia, as we have seen, can be fully understood only by taking into account their relationships with neighboring civilizations. Two major types of civilizations have developed in mainland Southeast Asia, the Theravada Buddhist civilization of Burma, Thailand, Laos, and Cambodia and the Sinitic civilization of Vietnam. In this chapter, we will examine the development of Theravada Buddhist civilization in the region and in the next we will look at how this civilization has been adapted to rural life in Burma, Thailand, Laos, and Cambodia. In Chapter 4 we will turn to consider the Sinitic civilization of Vietnam.

THE CLASSIC INDIANIZED CIVILIZATIONS

Formation of Indianized Civilizations

The Theravada Buddhist civilizations of mainland Southeast Asia have their roots in what have been termed " Indianized " civilizations, that is, the civilizations that first began to emerge in mainland Southeast Asia in the early centuries of the Christian era. The formative period during which the classic Indianized civilizations of mainland Southeast Asia developed lasted from about the second century before the Christian era until about the ninth century A.D. During this period, a number of Southeast Asian societies, societies that were tribal in character, began to incorporate into their cultural traditions themes borrowed from India. From this synthesis of local and Indian cultures, a process historians have termed " Indianization,"[1] emerged the first significant civilizations of the region.

The process was spurred by the well-developed trading relationships between India and Southeast Asia that had existed since prehistoric times. This trade was part of a larger trade between India and China that passed through Southeast Asia. The trading system of which Southeast Asia was a part, and in which Southeast Asians actively participated,[2] made possible the introduction of Indian culture into the region.

Indian traders themselves were not, however, the transmitters of the Indian high tradition, for they were neither members of the Brahmanical caste nor members of the Buddhist monkhood. In other words, they were not in possession of the knowledge used by Southeast Asians in the development of their " Indianized " traditions. Neither were these traders, as was once thought, the forerunners of a large-scale Indian colonization of Southeast Asia. Although some Indians did settle in the entrepôts located along the coasts of Southeast Asia, there is no evidence of any significant immigration of Indians to the region. Nor were Indian traders an advance guard for Indian rulers who wished to extend their power into Southeast Asia. With only minor exceptions, Indian rulers took no interest in extending their domains across the Bay of Bengal. What the trade connections did do was make possible the transport of Brahman priests and scholars and Buddhist monks from India to Southeast Asia and, probably also, the transport of Southeast Asian " students " to India.

Those who initiated the process of Indianization were, most likely, the rulers of Southeast Asian societies. Through their contacts with bearers of Indian culture, some of these local chiefs must have come to perceive that Indian culture offered a new basis for their power. In other words, the earliest Indianization of Southeast Asia involved a welding together of indigenous and Indian conceptions of potency. This process is evident in the myth of the Naga princess, a myth related in a third century Chinese account and in a seventh century Cham inscription from what is today Vietnam. These sources tell of the founding of two early Indianized states, Funan and Champa, the former centered in what is now Cambodia and the latter in central Vietnam.[3] According to the myth, an Indian Brahman, by the name of Kaundinya, arrives in Southeast Asia. With him he carried a spear (or a bow and arrow) obtained from the " best of Brahmans." He throws the spear (or shoots an arrow) and it lands at the spot where the future capital of Funan or Champa will be constructed. He then marries a local princess, Soma (called Willow Leaf in the Chinese version), who is the daughter of the King of the Nagas, the giant serpents. Kaundinya and Soma then found the ruling line of Funan and Champa.

The myth of the Naga Princess can be interpreted at several different levels. At the deepest level, it expresses a dualism between nature, symbolized by the Naga king and his daughter, and culture, symbolized by the Brahman Kaundinya, which is mediated through their marriage. Both the Naga and the sword of the Brahman (or arrow) are symbols of male potency and fertility. However, the Naga symbol becomes transformed into feminine fertility by its expression in the form of Soma. The Brahman's spear also symbolizes the potency of an ideology, that of Brahamanism. The spear is used to locate a city, which, as we shall see, is oriented according to Brahmanical ideas. The marriage of Kaundinya and Soma also ensures the fertility and prosperity of the land that they and their line rule. A thirteenth century account by Chou Ta-kuan, a Chinese visitor to Angkor, recounts a popular story that the King of Angkor (the latter day successor to the King of Funan) must have intercourse each night with the Naga Princess who lived in a tower in the palace lest the kingdom suffer ill consequences. The same assurance of fertility is carried by a version of the myth, *Phra Daeng Nang Ai*, still told today in Northeastern Thailand in association with a fertility-producing ritual known as the " firerocket festival " (*bun bong fai*).[4] On an historical level, the myth tells of civilization being brought in the form of " Brahmanism " to a land that previously had followed localized cults involving the worship of a snake-god deity whose power was linked with that of the chieftain. This latter point is not conjecture, for a late fourth or early fifth century Cham inscription " contains an imprecatory formula ordering respect for the ' naga of the king '."[5]

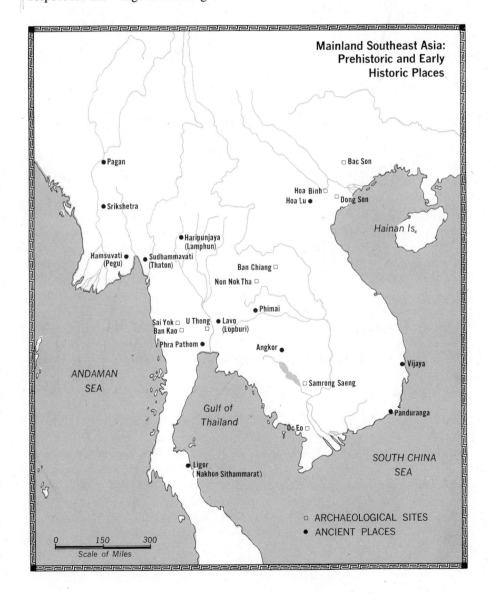

Mainland Southeast Asia:
Prehistoric and Early
Historic Places

□ ARCHAEOLOGICAL SITES
● ANCIENT PLACES

The myth also suggests why the peasantry of Southeast Asia came to accept a new form of kingship as a consequence of " Indianization." The king was viewed as a source of power that ensured the prosperity of the land, this power deriving from association with both locally recognized supernatural forces— e.g., the Naga King—and from new supernatural forces, those introduced by Brahmans. It is important to note that royal legitimacy, whether couched in pre-Indian or Indian terms, could not simply be asserted. It was also necessary that the King undertake acts that established that he indeed had such power. Such acts, as we shall see, were expressed in both politico-religious and politico-economic ways.

During the course of the period between about the second century before the beginning of the Christian era and the ninth century A.D. several rulers in Southeast Asia experimented with a variety of Indian motifs as the basis for their power. These motifs were as often Buddhist as they were Hindu. Yet, despite the wealth of Hindu and Buddhist iconography that dates from this period, the people of the region were neither Buddhists nor Hindus. Both Hindu and Buddhist motifs were used to clothe conceptions that were as much indigenous as they were transplantations of Indian culture. Insofar as there was any Hindu or Buddhist orthodoxy in Southeast Asia prior to about the thirteenth century, such was practiced only by a very small number of religious virtuosos living in centers supported by the ruling elites. For the rest of the populace, the new civilization was a " syncretic " tradition, comprising a blend of motifs drawn from Hinduism and/or Buddhism together with motifs drawn from indigenous Southeast Asian traditions. These syncretisms were not everywhere the same. Hindu themes came to dominate (although never to the point of exclusivity) in the traditions that developed among the Khmer and Chams living in the eastern part of the region, whereas Buddhist themes came to dominate among the Mons and Burmans living in the central and western parts of the region. Yet whether Hindu or Buddhist themes were dominant, the classic Indianized civilizations were structurally very similar. This point can be best discussed with reference to the two major classical civilizations that existed in the ninth to the thirteenth centuries, the Khmer empire of Angkor and the Burman empire of Pagan.

The Classic Indianized Civilizations of Angkor and Pagan

The civilization of Angkor, which flourished between the ninth and the fifteenth centuries A.D., centered on the basin of the Tonlé Sap, or Great Lake of Cambodia. This lake, which Coedès has called " that regulator of irrigation and inexhaustible fish pond "[6] made possible a concentration of population in the region rivaled throughout this period only by that found in the Red River valley and delta of northern Vietnam, and the Kyauksè region of upper Burma. The Tonlé Sap provided food, in the form of fish and aquatic products, and the water supply necessary to support a sizeable population: The population, in turn, made it possible for the rulers of Angkor to draw on a labor force large

Angkor. Faces of the Compassionate Bodhisattva on the Bayon, the architectural sacred center built by Jayavarman VII at the end of the twelfth century.
(*C. F. Keyes photograph*)

enough to enable them to build the great architectural monuments that still stand as the glory of Angkorean civilization.

Although the capital of Angkor was shifted from reign to reign for politico-religious reasons, which will be discussed shortly, the rulers of Angkor dwelt in the same general vicinity from the ninth to the fifteenth centuries, always remaining close enough to the Tonlé Sap to be able to draw on its fish, yet far enough away to avoid the devastations of annual floods.

The term *Angkor* comes from the Sanskrit word *nagara*, " a city." However, the Khmer capital was not a city in the modern sense; rather, it was the center for a cult, that of the *devarāja*, the divine king.

Angkorean kings claimed to be incarnations of Siva, or of Vishnu, or to be Bodhisattvas, future Buddhas. Whatever divine claim the ruler made, he attempted, if possible, to validate the claim through the construction of a pyramidical structure that housed the essence of his divine royalty. For most kings, this divine essence was believed to reside in a *linga*, a phallic representation of Siva, which was " ensconced in a pyramid in the exact center of the royal city which in turn was located in the center of the world."[7]

Despite the importance of the Siva cult, the great monuments of Angkor Wat and Angkor Thom, the latter with the Bayon at its center, were not Sivaite monuments. Angkor Wat, built by Suryavarman II (1113-1150) was " a sanctuary to Vishnu, but the Vishnu worshipped there is not the ancient god Vishnu, nor any of the forms of his traditional incarnations, but King Suryavarman II."[8] Angkor Thom, which is the city, and the Bayon, its central monument on which appears the famous four-faced image of the Boddhisattva Lokesvara, were built by Jayavarman VII (1181-c. 1218) who saw himself as a Buddha-to-be.

Whether housing a *lingam*, symbolizing the *devarāja*, depictions of the works of Vishnu, or an image of the Boddhisattva as *Buddharāja*, the monuments were of the same significance. They were architectural models of the cosmic order that served to harmonize the human world with cosmic reality:

> In order to achieve this harmony, men tried to build the kingdom, the capital, the palace, the temple, in the form of microcosms, which were the replicas of of the structure of the macrocosms.[9]

The conception of the cosmic order had been borrowed from India, although the idea of a sacred mountain at the center of the universe was probably also an indigenous Southeast Asian conception.

The immense monuments of Angkor required the labor of thousands of men. To give but one example, the temple of Ta Phrom, built during the reign of Jayavarman VII and dedicated to the female Boddhisattva, Prajnaparamita, the " Perfection of Wisdom," who was the divine counterpart of the queen mother, required the services of 79,365 people in 3,140 villages.[10] The major politicoeconomic concern of the rulers of Angkor, then, was the assurance of a sufficient labor force. This concern was most usually translated into action in the form of warfare to increase the population of the empire rather than to increase its territorial domains. The king who was a successful conqueror not only demonstrated that he was a true representative of the gods on earth but also gained sway over a large enough labor force to be able to translate his power into architectural symbolism of monumental proportions. The great monument builders of Angkor were also mighty conquerors. At its greatest extent, the Angkorean empire included all of present-day Cambodia, the Mekong delta region of southern Vietnam, what are today central and northeastern Thailand and southern Laos, and probably much of southern Thailand and central Laos as well.

The rulers of Pagan, like the rulers of Angkor, were also conquerors, and Pagan, also like Angkor, was built upon foundations laid by earlier Indianized states. Among these were the kingdoms established prior to the eighth century by the Tibero-Burman speaking Pyu in central and upper Burma and by the Mons in lower Burma. The kingdom of Pagan itself apparently began as a small kingdom or chiefdomship in the dry zone of upper Burma. Pagan appears a curious anomaly in that its capital, located in an unfertile area next to the

Irrawaddy river, was separated from the major area of peasant settlement near Kyauksè by about 80 miles:

> Compared to the fertile . . . areas, Kyauksè and Minbu, Pagan is almost a desert. . . . There is no rice-cultivation mentioned in Old Burmese around Pagan, on more than a quite modest scale.[11]

The choice of location for Pagan appears to have been partially a function of proximity to the Irrawaddy River, a main highway of traditional Burma, and partially a function of its proximity to Mount Popa, an ancient sacred place.

Pagan was founded in the middle of the ninth century, but it was not until the middle of the eleventh century that it gained more than local importance. According to legends told in the Burmese chronicles, the Pagan king, Anorahta (Aniruddha; Anuruddha), was converted to Theravada Buddhism by the Mon monk, Shin Arahan, shortly after Anorahta ascended to the throne in 1044. Anorahta was anxious to spread the new religion among his people and thus sent to Thaton, the Mon capital in southern Burma, for copies of the Buddha's scriptures. The Mon king, Manuha, declined to send the scriptures. Anorahta was angered at this refusal and led a large force in invasion of lower Burma, destroyed the capital of Thaton, and brought back to Pagan not only the scriptures, but Buddhist monks, and the Thaton royal family.[12] Although the invasion of lower Burma by Anorahta is attested to in inscriptions, Luce doubts that Anorahta introduced Theravada Buddhism into Pagan after the conquest,[13] Whatever the cultural influences actually introduced into Pagan following Anorahta's conquest, it is clear that until the late twelfth century at the earliest, the religion of Pagan was as syncretic as was the religion of Angkor. Moreover, Pagan, like Angkor, was a cult center at which Kings, their relatives, and some high religious leaders constructed large monuments, equivalent in their monumentality to those of Angkor.

Pagan art, architecture, and civilization probably reached its supreme development in the reign of Kyanzittha (1084–1113), although Pagan was to remain the dominant political power of upper Burma until the end of the thirteenth century. Kyanzittha was the builder of the two monuments, one a *cetiya* or reliquary and the other a " temple," which are to this day the most famous of approximately 1000 remains at Pagan: the Shwé Zigon *cetiya* and the temple of Ananda.

Legend has it that the Shwé Zigon, which is located near the present-day town of Nyaung-u, and about three miles from the main gate of Pagan city, was begun by Anorahta and only finished by Kyanzittha. Luce has pointed out, however, that the major inscription at the shrine erected by Kyanzittha makes no mention of Anorahta; thus, it seems likely that the Shwé Zigon was built solely by Kyanzittha himself. The Shwé Zigon was built on a site that was " auspicious," thus the name of the temple, which is derived from the Pali word meaning " victorious land " (*jayabhūmi*). The *cetiya* itself is believed to enshrine a number of actual relics of the Buddha: a collar bone, his frontlet bone,

Pagan. Ananda temple, built by Kyanzittha in the twelfth century. (*C. F. Keyes photograph*)

and a tooth, magically produced from the famous tooth relic of Ceylon. The Shwé Zigon is more than a Buddhist shrine, however. At the shrine are also found images of the " 32 Nats," the main spirits of the Burmese pantheon. Oral legend has it that Anorahta, when he began the building of this shrine, said " Men will not come for the sake of the new faith [Theravada Buddhism]. Let them come for their old gods and gradually they will be won over."[14] Whether this was ever said by Anorahta or Kyanzittha, who was probably the actual builder of the Shwé Zigon, it is clear that Kyanzittha used every possible religious motif as the basis of legitimizing his reign.

In various inscriptions left by Kyanzittha, we find a prophecy of the Buddha about the coming of Kyanzittha, a claim that he was an incarnation of Vishnu, a claim that he was a Boddhisattva and a Cakravartin, a universal emperor, and a claim that he was " the lord abounding in merit." In the rituals accompanying the dedication of his palace he also employed Mon spirit mediums and other practitioners of magical-animistic rituals. In short, he attempted, as Luce concludes, to make use of the widest syncretism possible in order " to lay a broad and strong foundation of a united Burma."[15]

Although Kyanzittha may have been willing to be accepted as divine regardless of the particular conceptions of divinity held by the peoples of Burma, he sought to realize his own apotheosis in a way similar to that of his contemporaries in Cambodia. We can, I believe, see the Ananda as a funerary temple for Kyanzittha. It represents a model of cosmic reality, a world wherein dwell those who have achieved enlightenment. Kyanzittha has spent his life as a Boddhisattva and on his death he achieves translation into the realm of the Buddhas.

During his lifetime, Kyanzittha was incessantly at war, attempting, as we have already noted, to bring the peoples of Burma under his power. Like the rulers of Angkor, warfare was necessary for mobilizing sufficient labor to construct the monuments at Pagan; successful wars also established the rule of Pagan's claims to divinely inspired power.

In sum, both Angkor and Pagan have similar civilizations. Both were informed by a conception of a supernatural order that was unchanging, absolute, and well defined. Although the characteristics of this order were somewhat different in Angkor and Pagan and also varied at different times in the history of each, the structure remained the same. The role of kings was to harmonize the human world with the cosmic order. This they did by constructing architectural models of the cosmos that were dramatic statements to all subjects about the power of the kings. Yet these statements could only be made if there were sufficient labor available to construct the monuments. To gain labor in underpopulated Southeast Asia, it was necessary to go to war. If the wars succeeded, they were self-fulfilling prophecies. If they failed, which they sometimes did, it was necessary for the king to mount a new and successful war within a short time or else he would be deposed, often violently. The deposed king was one who had failed to demonstrate that he could actually draw on the divine powers he claimed. The successful king ultimately demonstrated his divinity by creating a model of some heavenly realm, where after death he would dwell as Siva, as Vishnu, as a Buddha, or a Boddhisattva.

The world of social action and the world of religious belief were, then, related tautologically in the classical civilizations of Southeast Asia. As Geertz has said of the similar civilizations of Java prior to the coming of Islam, the power of such a tautology " lies in the fact that it pictures the ultimate structure of existence in such a way that the events of everyday life seem repeatedly to confirm it."[16] As we shall see in the next section, this circle was broken by the events of the thirteenth and fourteenth centuries. Although societies based on new cultural world views replaced the old classical Indianized civilizations, the ideas of these civilizations did not completely die with them.

For example, there remained in both Cambodia and Thailand the archaic conception of the world being centered on a point at which is concentrated the potency/fertility of the realm. The court centers of Ayutthaya, and later Bangkok and Phnom Penh, had their sacred mountains and their versions of a *linga*. In Bangkok, for example, the *san cao lak muang*, the " Shrine of the Pillar of the Lord of the Land," which is located near the Grand Palace, even today perpetuates, albeit in an altered form, the ideology of the *linga* cult.[17] In Burma there remained the idea, greatly elaborated on in Pagan times, that through the architectural representation of the cosmos one can attain salvation. Many Burmans, for example, still believe that if they are able to acquire sufficient wealth they should sponsor the construction of a reliquary, a *cetiya*, since this act ensures that they will attain Nirvana, the ultimate salvation of Buddhists.

In Northern Thailand, I have found beliefs that use Buddhist symbols to imply a fixed cosmic order rather than a world of constant change, which is a basic doctrine of Theravada Buddhism.[18] Although archaic ideas that were once dominant during the period of the classical Indianized civilizations have continued to hold some attraction for peoples of mainland Southeast Asia, they were, however, overshadowed by the Theravada Buddhist orthodoxy that became dominant after the thirteenth century.

THE TAI AND THE RESTRUCTURING OF SOUTHEAST ASIAN SOCIETIES

The Expansion of Tai-Speaking Peoples

According to Professor George Coedès, the thirteenth century was a watershed in the history of the Indianized states of Southeast Asia:

> One gets the impression that in the second half of the thirteenth century the kingdoms that had been Indianized since the first centuries of the Christian era no longer had the resilience to withstand a major shock, or even to survive a minor disturbance of the foundations upon which their civilizations rested. The shock administered by the Mongols was their undoing.[19]

In the latter part of the thirteenth century, the Mongols launched a number of attacks on parts of Southeast Asia. In 1283–1285, the Mongols staged a prolonged attack on the kingdom of Champa in what is today southern Vietnam. This attack proved ultimately unsuccessful for the Mongols, but it shook the foundations of Champa. In upper Burma, the Mongols were more successful. After a long period of conflict, they succeeded in capturing Pagan in 1287. However, although the Mongols administered a severe blow to a number of the Indianized states of Southeast Asia, they did not bring about a restructuring of the sociopolitical systems of the region. In that part of Southeast Asia, which was to become the Theravada Buddhist world, it was Tai-speaking peoples who were to effect this restructuring.

Tai-speaking people from southern China had probably been moving into mainland Southeast Asia for some centuries before the Mongol rise to power. This migration was not a sudden shift of population, but a slow and steady infiltration:

> Actually the Thai " invasion " was . . . a gradual infiltration along the rivers and streams that had undoubtedly been going on for a very long time, part of the general drift of population from the north to the south that characterizes the peopling of the Indochinese Peninsula.[20]

By the eleventh century, the Tai had established themselves on the peripheries of the Indianized states of Southeast Asia. These Tai were probably " barbarians," that is, they were neither " Indianized " nor " Sinified." The Tai introduced into the region a new type of social structure, which had similarities to that of the Mongols. The Tai were organized into territorial units, known as *mµang*, which were ruled by chiefly families. The sons of the chief of a strong and well-established *mµang*, with the exception of one son, usually the youngest, were expected to found their own mµang and were provided the necessary personnel for conquest or colonization as the case might require. By this method, the Tai brought under their control during the eleventh to fourteenth centuries large areas of Southeast Asia including areas previously settled by other ethnic groups.[21]

The expansion of the Tai brought them into increasing contact with the civilized peoples of Southeast Asia. As happened with the barbarians of Europe at an earlier time, the contact between the Tai barbarians and the civilized peoples of Southeast Asia resulted in the Tai achieving political dominance while also adopting much of the civilization they conquered. Although the Tai had founded some " beachhead " states in mainland Southeast Asia prior to the mid-thirteenth century, the ascendancy of the Tai was most dramatic in the period between the mid-thirteenth and the mid-fourteenth centuries. During this period, the Tai founded a number of new states in what are now Thailand, Burma, India, and Laos and also succeeded in becoming the rulers of a large part of Burma and in effecting the demise of the Khmer Empire. The first of these dramatic changes took place in what is today Thailand.

The Earliest Tai Civilizations

During the latter half of the thirteenth century, several Tai chiefs in northern Thailand succeeded in expanding their domains at the expense of the Mons who ruled the kingdom of Haripunjaya from what is today the town of Lamphun. At the very end of the thirteenth century, the Tai chief Mengrai captured Lamphun and brought the kingdom of Haripunjaya to an end. Mengrai founded a new kingdom with its capital at Chiang Mai, a kingdom that, although it was never the only Tai polity in northern Thailand, became and remained until the end of the nineteenth century the dominant political entity in the region.

The collapse of the Mon kingdom of Haripunjaya is to be interpreted less as a product of military defeat of one people, the Mon, by another, the Tai, than as the emergence of a new historical tradition known as the Yuan, which was the successor to both Mon (civilization) and Tai (barbarian) traditions. The chronicles of northern Thailand do not indicate that the Tai conquerors embarked on any genocidal campaign against the Mons. On the contrary, relations between the northern Tai principalities and the Mon states of Lower Burma remained close after the Tai conquest of northern Thailand, and Mon monks continued to play very important roles in the spread of Buddhism under the Tai rulers of Chiang Mai.[22] The Yuan cultural tradition, which was the successor to both Tai and Mon traditions in northern Thailand, came to be the dominant cultural tradition of northern Thailand, of what is today the state of Kengtung in Burma, of parts of Yunnan in southern China, and of parts of northern Laos.

Another Tai tradition, and one that was to become the wellspring of the contemporary national tradition of Thailand, was developed at Sukhothai in what is today north central Thailand. This area had been brought under Khmer control by the early part of the twelfth century at a time when the Khmer also annexed the Mon statelet Lavo whose capital is present-day Lopburi in the lower Cao Phraya valley of central Thailand. Tai colonists had settled in north central Thailand from perhaps as early as the eleventh century, and by the time the Khmer assumed control over the area they had become the dominant population in this area lying between the two Mon domains of Haripunjaya and Lavo. Although the Khmer exercised ultimate control over the Sukhothai region, they appear to have administered it indirectly through local Tai chiefs.[23]

Under the tutelage of the Khmers, the Tai of the Sukhothai area adopted many new cultural elements, one of the most important being the Khmer system of writing, which was modified by the famous King Ram Khamhaeng (ca. 1279–1299) for writing a Tai language. This writing system was to be adopted by Tai-speaking people who lived throughout central Thailand and is the ancestor of the present-day national writing system of Thailand. The Tai of Sukhothai also adopted Khmer models in devising their irrigation system and probably also borrowed some Khmer ideas of statecraft and some Brahmanistic beliefs.[24]

Although Khmer influences were important, the new Tai state of Sukhothai, which came into existence after a rebellion of Tai chiefs against Khmer suzerainty in the early part of the thirteenth century, was not structured in the mold of the classic Indianized state. Certain Tai patterns, including some that were related to the exercise of power, were retained. Moreover, the culture that eventually became dominant at Sukhothai was not the syncretism of Angkorean civilization but was founded in orthodox Theravada Buddhism. The kings of Sukhothai from the end of the thirteenth century through the middle of the fourteenth century supported the efforts of missionary monks, most of whom were of Mon origin, to establish orthodox Theravada Buddhism in the kingdom.[25] These same monks carried the message northward to the Yuan principalities. We will return to a consideration of the spread of orthodox Theravada Buddhism in the next section.

Although Sukhothai enjoyed a brief period of dominance over much of what is today central and southern Thailand, its power was challenged by yet another Tai state that emerged in lower central Thailand in the mid-fourteenth century. This area, which is the lower Cao Phraya valley, had long been the locus of a Mon civilization. Tai settlers who arrived in this region, from about the eleventh century or earlier, were incorporated into the Mon kingdom with a capital at Lavo. Between the eleventh and thirteenth centuries when Lavo was struggling to maintain its independence from Angkor, the Tai subjects of Lavo undoubtedly formed a component of the Lavo armies. These struggles may also have permitted the emergence of strong Tai leaders who ruled their own local domains, located in the western part of the region, without too much interferences from the Mon capital. Finally, in 1350, a Tai lord succeeded in becoming ruler of all the Mons and Tai in the lower Cao Phraya basin. Although the rulers of this new kingdom, called Ayutthaya after its capital, were Tai-speaking people, the kingdom itself was also unquestionably the successor to the Mon state of Lavo.[26]

In the following century, the two states of Ayutthaya and Sukhothai struggled for supremacy in the region that is today central Thailand. Ayutthaya ultimately triumphed and absorbed the kingdom of Sukhothai. It was in the area now dominated by Ayutthaya that the culture we know as Siamese developed.

Conflicts Between the Tai States and the Angkorean Empire

The Siamese culture that emerged in central Thailand resulted from the adaptation of barbarian immigrant people to a context long dominated by the Indianized Mon and Khmer. The Mon made this adaptation peacefully; indeed, after the fourteenth century, the Siamese and the Mon of central Thailand differed in little else than language. In the case of the Khmer, however, the rise of Ayutthaya initiated a period of conflict that was to result in the collapse of the Angkorean empire.

By the time the conflict with Ayutthaya began, the Angkorean empire was beset with internal contradictions that had begun to undermine the state. The demands levied by the Angkorean rulers on the populace to support the construction and maintenance of the enormous shrines dedicated to the cult of the God King had become excessive. As Coe has noted,

> A social order founded on the sanctions necessary to enforce tribute and corvée labor is extraordinarily brittle to social change, whether internal or external. [27]

At the end of the thirteenth century, a Chinese envoy to Angkor, Chou Ta-kuan, reported that Theravada Buddhism was dominant among the populace. [28] This observation suggests that the cult of the *deva rāja* was on the decline by this time. The attacks on Angkor by Ayutthaya in the fourteenth and fifteenth centuries proved in fact what had already been questioned in thought, namely that the rulers of Angkor could no longer draw on the potency of the cosmos.

In the fifteenth century, Angkor, the now no longer sacred capital, was abandoned. In the wake of Angkorean civilization came a new Khmer culture, one based on Therevada Buddhism. Historic Cambodian culture, that is, the culture of the Khmer from the mid-fifteenth to the mid-nineteenth centuries, showed strong similarities to historic Siamese culture. Whereas the Tai barbarians had borrowed from the Khmer in the process of becoming civilized, the post-Angkorean Khmer borrowed from the Siamese in their establishment of a postclassic cultural tradition.

Another Tai-speaking people, the ancestors of the present-day Lao, had also settled on the peripheries of the Khmer empire when the empire was still very much the dominant power of the region. From Lao legends we learn that the Tai of the middle Mekong were civilized through the borrowing of culture from the Khmer, although the culture they are said to have borrowed in the early fourteenth century was not that of classic Angkor but that of an Angkor in which Theravada Buddhism had become the dominant religion. [29]

Although the Lao may have been first civilized by the Khmer, they were also greatly influenced by their other Tai-speaking neighbors, the Yuan of northern Thailand and the Siamese of central Thailand. In other words, the culture of the Lao represents the adaptation of Tai to an environment in which Khmer, Yuan, and Siamese influences were important.

The Tai and the End of Pagan

Tai-speaking people also played a key role in the transition in Burma from the classic civilization of Pagan to the historic cultures of postclassic Burma. In the early fourteenth century, in the wake of the Mongol defeat of Pagan, Tai chiefs from small Tai principalities founded in what is now the Shan state of Burma succeeded in uniting much of Burma under their rule. The Tai rule of Burma, however, was not to be permanent. By the mid-fourteenth century a new Burman state, with its capital at Toungoo, had emerged. Meanwhile, the Mons in lower Burma had reasserted themselves and established another state. The collapse of Pagan, thus, was followed by the emergence of three rather than one historic cultures. In lower Burma, the tradition was that of the Mon. In Upper Burma, it was Burman. And in the Shan states, it was Shan, a new tradition born by Tai-speaking people who had adapted themselves to Burman civilization. Eventually the Mon tradition was to be almost absorbed, after a long period of violence, by the Burman.

The historic traditions that emerged from the thirteenth century on were, in part, the product of a period of great turbulence caused by the expansion of Tai-speaking peoples in the region. The new historic cultures of the Yuan, Siamese, Lao, Khmer, Burmans, Shans, and Mons were not, however, simply the products of political conflict between the Tai and the classic civilizations. The new historic traditions were also associated with a new ideology, one that not only legitimated new types of political systems, but had marked implications for all aspects of social life. This ideology was Theravada Buddhism. We must turn now to the story of the introduction and triumph of Theravada Buddhist orthodoxy in Southeast Asia.

THERAVADA BUDDHISM IN SOUTHEAST ASIA

Development of Theravada Buddhism

Buddhism has its origins in the teachings and the exemplary life of Siddhattha Gotama who was born in north India in 563 B.C. and who passed away 80 years later.[30] Early Buddhism was the religion of a small number of religious virtuosos, that is of monks (*bhikkhu*) and nuns (*bhikkhunī*) who attempted to practice as closely as possible the way taught by Gotama Buddha. These monks and nuns together made up the *Sangha* or Buddhist order.

Buddhism underwent a marked change in the third century B.C. when it received the royal patronage of the great Indian king Asoka (269–232 B.C.). Asoka is credited in legend with the sending of Buddhist missionaries to Southeast Asia and of sending his own son, Mahinda, who was a Buddhist monk, to establish Buddhism in Ceylon. This legend has a certain plausibility, but archaeological evidence does not attest to the presence of Buddhism in Southeast Asia before about the third century A.D. Although it may not be possible to trace the spread of Buddhism to Southeast Asia to the reign of Asoka, it is possible to trace to this king the encouragement of a distinctive tradition of lay, as distinct from clerical, Buddhism. These lay adherents of the Buddhist religion were, however, drawn almost exclusively from the elite. It was not until about the twelfth century A.D. that Buddhism was to become a truly popular religion.

Early Buddhism was divided into a number of different schools of thought, associated in some cases with different languages used for the communication of the tradition. The most well-known division of Buddhism, and one that persists to the present, is that between Mahayana Buddhism and Theravada Buddhism. Mahayana Buddhism, the Buddhism of the " Greater Vehicle," used a textual tradition written in Sanskrit, whereas Theravada, the " Way of the Elders," the Buddhism the Mahayanists call Hinayana, the " Lesser Vehicle," uses a textual tradition written in Pali. Mahayana and Theravada Buddhism are also associated with quite different interpretations of certain fundamental Buddhist doctrines. Mahayana Buddhism spread through northern India, to China, and thence to other parts of East Asia. It also spread to Vietnam, and we will consider Mahayana Buddhism again when we look at the Vietnamese tradition.

Although Theravada doctrines were probably transmitted orally in Pali from the time of Asoka, they were not written down until about the first century B.C. In the fifth century A.D., the Theravada Buddhist tradition was interpreted by the famous monk Buddhaghosa, and his interpretations have remained the orthodox interpretations for Theravada Buddhists to this day. It is perhaps worthy of note that a legend from lower Burma has it that Buddhaghosa was a native of that area; it is more likely, however, that he came from India.

Orthodox Theravada Buddhism, the Buddhism that used the Pali texts and followed the interpretations of Buddhaghosa, did not flourish in either Ceylon or Southeast Asia until many centuries after Buddhaghosa's death. Although Buddhism was an important element in the syncretic traditions of the classic civilizations in Southeast Asia, such Buddhism was most usually that of a school other than Theravadin. Moreover, it was often found as one among several Indianized traditions as can be clearly seen, for example, in the case of Angkor. Indeed, at times, Theravada Buddhism all but disappeared; however, a few centers in southern India, Ceylon, and lower Burma and perhaps central Thailand continued to preserve the tradition despite the vicissitudes to which it was subjected.

By the ninth century A.D., Buddhism of all schools was very much in retreat in its homeland India. From the ninth to eleventh centuries, Hindu Tamils waged continuous attacks against those kingdoms in southern India and Ceylon where Buddhism continued to exist. In southern India, Buddhism was finally extinguished; it was almost extinguished in Ceylon as well. Early in the eleventh century, the Singhalese had been forced by the Tamils to leave their old capitals of Anuradhapura and Polonaruva and to take refuge in the mountainous country of southern Ceylon. In the middle of the eleventh century, the Singhalese king Vijaya-Bahu I was able to rally a significant force and, in 1065, he succeeded in reconquering the country. He found that Buddhism had practically disappeared from the kingdom: monasteries had been destroyed and sacked, the order of nuns had completely disappeared, and there were not even sufficient monks left to perform a higher ordination (it takes a chapter of five monks to perform the ordination ceremony that initiates a new member into the monkhood). In order to reestablish the religion, he sent to Burma for some monks.

Spread of Theravada Buddhism to Southeast Asia

Burma at this time was dominated by King Anoratha (1044–1077), the founder of the great classical Burman kingdom of Pagan. As we have already seen, although legend has it that Anoratha had been converted to Theravada Buddhism by the Mon monk Shin Arahan, epigraphical and archaeological evidence prove that Anoratha was far more eclectic in his choice of religious sources for the construction of the ideology that was to be dominant at Pagan. Nevertheless, he was a patron of Buddhism and there were at least some well-established centers of Buddhism within his domains. From these centers, Anoratha was able to supply the necessary personnel to Vijaya-Bahu so that the Sangha could be reestablished in Ceylon.[31]

The monks (who were probably Mon) who went to Ceylon returned to Burma with copies of the Theravadin texts and commentaries preserved there. Moreover, they established a pattern of exchange of personnel and texts between Burma and Ceylon that was to prove critical in the history of Theravada Buddhism.

In the twelfth century, the great Singhalese king Parakkama-Bahu I undertook to reform the Buddhist Sanga. Before his accession to the throne, there were three different sects of Buddhism, each associated with a specific monastery as its center. One of these, the Abhayagiri, was associated with Mahayana Buddhism, a second, the Mahavihara, with Theravada Buddhism, and a third, the Jetavana, alternated between these two.[32] Parkkama-Bahu called a council to determine which of the three sects preserved and perpetuated the true doctrine. In 1165, the king himself decided in favor of the Theravada Buddhism of the Mahavihara sect, and he undertook to suppress the other two sects. From the time of King Parakkama-Bahu, Theravada Buddhism became the dominant religion of Ceylon.

Monks from Burma who traveled to Ceylon during the reign of King Parakkama-Bahu found Theravada Buddhism being promoted as the " true faith " with a militancy that had not heretofore been the case. The dynamism with which Theravada Buddhism had been infused deeply impressed some of these monks, and they returned to their homes to report about it. This message was carried, apparently, to other centers of Buddhism in Southeast Asia. In about 1180, a group of monks and novices traveled from Burma to Ceylon to study the Theravadin tradition as it was followed by the Mahavihara sect of Ceylon. Legend has it that this group of five monks, led by the Mon monk

Chapata, included a prince of Cambodia, another who had originally come from Conjeevaram in south India, and two from other parts of Southeast Asia. The members of this group were ordained in Ceylon and spent ten years there, thereby becoming elders who could perform ordinations. They returned to Burma in 1190 to establish the Singhalese form of Theravada Buddhism.[33] Whether this legend is in fact true, it is certain that by the beginning of the thirteenth century the Singhalese form of Theravada Buddhism had been established and was spreading in Southeast Asia.[34]

Although our information about Chapata and his associates is scanty, we can make certain conclusions about the religion they promoted on the basis of the few facts we have. First, they insisted that monks strictly adhere to the rules of the *Vinaya*, the scriptural regulations that define the roles of monks. Second, they strongly emphasized the line of pure succession as being that which was traced to those who had been ordained in Ceylon. For this reason this form of Buddhism is sometimes referred to as the Singhalese sect. Given that they had been trained in Ceylon at a time when there was strong political support for adherence to Theravada Buddhist orthodoxy, these monks can also be supposed to have insisted on that orthodoxy. They promoted this orthodoxy not only by oral teachings and sermons, but also through the composition of texts:

> Chapata . . . was the author of a series of works in Pali, notably the gram-matical treatise *Suttaniddesa* and the *Sankhpavaṇṇanā*, a commentary on the compendium of metaphysics named *Abhidhammathasangaha*.
> Another Mon monk of the same sect, Dhammavilasa . . . was the author of the first collection of laws composed in the Mon country, the *Dhammavilasa Dhammathat*, written in Pali. . . .[35]

Given that these monks were of diverse nationalities, we can see in them the expression of the idea of Buddhism being a universal religion, not one associated with a particular society. By extension it is likely that they did not see their religion as the religion of a single strata of society, but as a religion that drew its support from whomever took refuge in the Buddha, the doctrine, and the Sangha. Whether or not this last point was consciously promoted by the members of the Singhalese sect, it came to be practiced as those in this order sought recruits not only in the royal capitals but also in the villages.

One of the most intriguing facts about the monks associated with Chapata was that one was a prince of Cambodia, presumably, as Coedès has suggested, the son of the famous King of Angkor, Jayavaraman VII (1181–c. 1218).[36] Jayavarman VII, the builder of Angkor Thom, the Bayon, and other major monuments and the Angkorean king who extended his boundaries throughout much of present-day Thailand as well as Cambodia, had broken from the tradition of his predecessors in making the state religion the worship of the Buddharaja rather than the worship of the Sivaite Devaraja. Structurally, the Buddharaja cult differed little from the Devaraja cult. However, it was important for the subsequent history of Southeast Asia that Jayavaraman VII saw himself as a Buddhist. It was probably for this reason, as well as for political reasons, that he sent (or permitted) a son to Ceylon to enter the monkhood there.

The aggressiveness with which the monks associated with the Singhalese sect promoted their religion finds a later parallel in the actions of Christian missionaries. However, their success cannot be explained by the fact that these monks felt that they knew the truth and sought to communicate it to others. Rather their message succeeded because it provided a meaningful way of relating to the world for many who had previously been marginal to the classical civilizations or who had been seriously affected by the disruption of the classical civilizations in the thirteenth and fourteenth centuries. The first converts to Theravada Buddhism were Mons, living in what is today lower Burma, a people who had been relegated to a minority position within the Pagan empire. They were followed shortly thereafter by the Tai—the Yuan, the Siamese, the Lao, the Shan—who were newcomers in Southeast Asia. With the collapse of Pagan and Angkor, the Burmans and Khmer in turn accepted the new religion. By the early fifteenth century at the very latest, the vast majority of the people living in what is today Burma, Thailand, Cambodia, and Laos had become adherents of Theravada Buddhism.

It is important to stress that whereas Buddhism had been the religion of a small number of virtuosos and a small number of elite lay persons prior to the twelfth century, the Therevada Buddhism introduced by those who had been to Ceylon became a popular religion. Whereas prior to the thirteenth century Buddhism was practiced in only a few centers, mainly urban, after the thirteenth century it came to be practiced in thousands on thousands of villages. We need to consider now the essence and appeal of the doctrines of a religion that has so permeated the lives of the peoples living in much of mainland Southeast Asia from the thirteenth century to the present.

THERAVADA BUDDHISM AS A POPULAR RELIGION

Essence of Theravada Buddhist Doctrine

Religion provides its adherents with a perspective for interpreting reality and an orientation for engaging in meaningful social action. If a religion is " popular," the perspective and orientation it offers must allow for the fact that most of the existential concerns of the adherents are mundane. Buddhism, at least Buddhism as it has often been interpreted in Western literature, would appear to be a poor candidate for a " popular " religion, since it is portrayed as a religion in which worldly action of any type whatsoever is seen as a hindrance in the attainment of *Nirvāṇa*,[37] that is, of ultimate salvation.

Buddhism was founded by Siddhatha Gotama, a man born into the world a Prince, the heir to the throne of a small principality in northern India. Although his early life was full of portents of the life he would ultimately live, his childhood, youth, and early adulthood were spent surrounded by luxury. He married Princess Yasodhara who in proper time bore him a son, Rahula. But the life of a king, even a king who would be a universal monarch as was predicted at this birth, was not to be his. One night as his wife and child lay sleep,

The Buddha as represented in images from Chiang Mai, northern Thailand.
(*C. F. Keyes photograph*)

ing, he stole from their side and rode away from the palace on his favorite horse to a forest. There he discarded his royal garb, cut his hair, and assumed the life of a wandering ascetic, a seeker of truth.

After six years of rigorous asceticism, he determined that such was not the way to truth. One day he accepted a bowl of milk from a merchant's daughter, thus breaking his fast. At the same time he felt that he would that day achieve the supreme enlightenment of a Buddha. He withdrew to a grove of trees and there under a Bodhi tree he spent the night in deep meditation. During this night he came to understand the essential nature of the universe and by dawn he had become the Buddha. He spent four weeks in this grove under the Bodhi tree and then set forward to teach the " Way " to salvation as he had realized it. Those who heard the message and undertook to follow the " Way " became members of the " community," the *Sangha*.

The " Way " taught by the Buddha was developed in the numerous sermons he is said to have delivered during his life. The discourses of the Buddha, together with the sayings of some of his disciples, were collected a book called the *sutta-piṭaka*, " the basket of discourses." The *sutta-piṭaka*, together with the *vinaya-piṭaka*, " the basket of discipline," which contains the regulations for the lives of those who become members of the Sangha, and the *abhidhamma-piṭaka*, " the metaphysical basket," which contains elaborations on the Dharma or " doctrine," together constitute the *Tripiṭaka*, the " Three Baskets," the scriptures of Therevada Buddhists.

The teachings of the Buddha entail a radical devaluation of sentient existence. Such existence is suffering or sorrow (*dukkha*); one's experience in sentient existence is impermanent (*anicca*); even one's self (ego) is not permanent (*anatta*). What is absolute insofar as sentient existence is concerned is the Law of Karma, the Law of Action. Good actions have good consequences; they lead to a lessening of suffering. Bad actions have bad consequences; they lead to increased suffering. These consequences may follow on the act in a single lifetime or they may occur in successive lifetimes. Thus, there is a transmigration of Karma across the threshold of death and birth, although there is no rebirth of the self. So long as one is bound to the Law of Karma, there can be no absolute cessation of suffering, since even the good consequences of Karma are ultimately impermanent and when they end one must again experience suffering. As the Buddha expressed it in the " Noble Truth of Suffering ": " Birth is [suffering], age is [suffering], disease is [suffering], death is [suffering]; contact with the unpleasant is [suffering], separation from the pleasant is [suffering], every wish unfilled is [suffering]—in short all the five components of individuality [forms, sensation, perceptions, psychic dispositions, and consciousness] are [suffering] ".[38]

Salvation (*nirodha*), according to the Buddha is the transcendence of sentient existence and the Law of Karma, thus effecting a total cessation of suffering. The Way to Salvation begins with a recognition that attachment to sentient existence is caused by desire or craving (*taṇhā*). Salvation can be attained when passion has been completely extinguished, when craving has been

A Buddhist monk who has spent his life as a member of the Sangha in rural northeastern Thailand. (*C. F. Keyes photograph*)

completely stopped. To effect an end to desire, one should follow the " eightfold path," which has been divided by Therevada Buddhists into three types of action:

1. Wisdom (*paññā*).

2. Morality (*sīla*).

3. Mental Discipline (*samādhi*).

1. Right Understanding.
2. Right Thought.
3. Right Speech.
4. Right Action.
5. Right Livelihood.
6. Right Effort.
7. Right Mindfulness.
8. Right Concentration.

" Wisdom " both begins and ends the path. One must first have an understanding of the teachings of the Buddha before entering the Path. When one has truly followed it, one also gains wisdom. Morality consists of all those actions that produce good consequences and the avoidance of these actions that produce bad consequences. One must be a moral person before one can undertake mental discipline. Through mental discipline, one transverses the path of purity and, ultimately, one reaches absolute purity, which is Nirvana itself.

Most Western writers who have discussed Buddhism have given emphasis to the ultimate goal of Buddhism, that is, they have stressed the quest for Nirvana. " The Buddhist point of view," according to Edward Conze, one of the leading Western Buddhologists, " will appeal only to those who are completely disillusioned with the world as it is, and with themselves, who are extremely sensitive to pain, suffering, and any kind of turmoil, who have an extreme desire for happiness, and a considerable capacity for renunciation. ... The Buddhist seeks for a total happiness beyond this world."[39] If the true Buddhist is one who seeks to become an Arahat, the fully perfected monk who attains enlightenment, then quite obviously Buddhism could never be a popular religion. It would be a religion of only a small number of adepts. Ancient Buddhism may have been such a religion, but it underwent a transformation first in the third century B.C. when it was brought under the patronage of King Asoka who set an example for other ruling elites. Theravada Buddhism was further transformed in the fifth century A.D., through the theological interpretations of Buddhaghosa and several of his contemporaries. Finally, it went through yet another transformation in the twelfth to thirteenth centuries when it became a universal religion, a religion for peasant farmer as well as for monk and king.

Buddhist Belief and Everyday Life

On the basis of recent research, mainly by anthropologists, it is possible to describe the interpretations of Buddhist doctrine that have made it a popular religion. Although there are differences in the popular religion as found in Thailand, Laos, Cambodia, Burma, and Ceylon, as well as between the population in each country, there is an underlying and fundamental similarity in the religion as it is found in almost all cases.[40]

Aspirants to arahatship, to becoming fully perfected and enlightened beings, are extremely rare in all Theravada Buddhist societies and appear to have always been so. Indeed, it would be surprising to find more than a handful of such aspirants in any society. For almost all Theravada Buddhists, be they monks or laity, Nirvana is a very remote goal, a goal that can only be achieved after many, many existences. Such a view does not imply, as some observers would have it, that the quest for Nirvana has no significance in popular Buddhism. Buddhists do attempt to traverse the Path of Purity insofar as the conditions of their existence permit. That most find that they can travel only a little way along the Path reflects their realistic appraisal that they are still bound to sentient existence.

For all Theravada Buddhists, the reality of sentient existence is determined by the Law of Karma. For those who find it impossible to strive immediately for ultimate salvation, for the transcendence of sentient existence and the cessation of suffering, the belief in the Law of Karma provides an alternative religious goal, that of the reduction of suffering. Suffering can be reduced by positive or meritorious actions and the avoidance of negative or demeritorious actions. Acts of " merit making " are mainly ritually manifest and are basically similar in all Theravada Buddhist societies. Avoidance or demeritorious action finds ethical expression, which again is basically the same in all Theravada Buddhist societies.

The Law of Karma provides a cognitively satisfying way of relating to the world. Inequalities among people, whether manifest as differences in physical characteristics, differences in the propensity for illness, differences in wealth and power, differences in intelligence, differences in motivation, and so on, can all be explained as the consequence of previous Karma. The Law of Karma also provides a guide for action that will ensure the improvement in one's existential condition, although this improvement may not be effected until a future lifetime. Psychologically, the Law of Karma is less than satisfying. One cannot predict whether one will fall ill, whether one will experience a rise or fall in social status, whether one will suffer an accident that will result in permanent bodily damage, whether one will gain an end for which one strives. Moreover, although it may be comforting to know that in a future existence one's meritorious deeds will result in a reduction in suffering, it would be far preferable if that reduction in suffering could occur in the present lifetime.

Given that the Law of Karma is psychologically unsatisfying, people in all Theravada Buddhist societies have also held to other beliefs that are not Buddhist in origin. Thus, most peoples in Theravada Buddhist societies believe that spirits and ghosts can interfere with their lives, that the constellation of heavenly bodies at birth can effect their ability to act, that deities can cause improvements in fertility and potency. In all the Theravada Buddhist societies of Southeast Asia there is also a belief that one's life force must be securely attached to the body lest one be subject to illness, social failures, and even death. In addition to adherence to beliefs with non-Buddhist sources, Theravada Buddhists have also reinterpreted Buddhist symbols such that they have acquired other than orthodox Buddhist meanings. Thus, certain images of the Buddha are believed to be more than simply " reminders " of the Buddha; they are believed to have innate power that can be tapped for immediate ends by those who worship the images. Throughout Southeast Asia there are shrines believed to hold relics of the Buddha, these relics again believed to have innate power that can be drawn by those who worship them. Certain monks are also believed to have attained supernormal powers, which they can use for those who seek them out.

That people in Theravada Buddhist societies adhere to beliefs in spirits, in divinities, in astrology, in life essences, and in the magical power of Buddhist sacra has led some students of these societies to conclude that the people in these societies are not really Buddhists—or, at least not orthodox Buddhists. The argument runs that according to orthodox Theravada Buddhism, the only cause of suffering is Karma. Therefore, if one adheres to beliefs in other causes of suffering, the Buddhist belief system has been compromised, at the very least, and perhaps even negated.[41] Such a conclusion is, at best, misleading. It is more correct, as Tambiah has argued with regard to northeastern Thailand, to see beliefs in karmic causation and beliefs in magical animistic causation as operating " within a total field " of belief characterized by " complementary and hierarchical ordering " of all beliefs.[42]

Buddhist Cosmology

It is important to stress that the orthodox Buddhist theory of karmic causation is not a theory of absolute determinism of one's place along a continuum of suffering. As Gombrich has argued: " Determinism is heresy . . . *Karma* is a doctrine of free will."[43] If Karma were totally deterministic, it would be impossible to engage in actions that will alter one's future Karma. Such a conception of Karma, quite obviously, runs directly counter to Buddhist doctrine. Karma does not determine one's every change of fortune in life (and death). Rather, it determines one place along a moral continuum, each place being associated with a generalized lesser or greater degree of vulnerability to the forces (such as spirits, gods, actions of other humans and germs) that cause suffering and with a generalized lesser or greater degree of freedom of action whereby one can alter one's Karma. This moral continuum is expressed in terms meaningful to Southeast Asian Buddhists in the form of Buddhist cosmology. Although Buddhist cosmological ideas are contained within the Tipitaka, the scriptures themselves, they have been given various interpretations throughout the history of Theravada Buddhism. Perhaps the most systematized Buddhist cosmological treatise ever written was the *Trai phūmi gāthā*, known colloquially as the " Three Worlds (*trai phūmi*) of Lord Ruang," which was compiled in 1345 by a Thai prince, the future King Lithai of Sukhothai.[44] This work in its various versions was, and still is, widely known, even in the villages of Thailand, Cambodia, and Laos.

Buddhist cosmology has provided for most people in Theravada Buddhist societies the " total field " that can accommodate both karmic and other forms of causation. According to this cosmology, one's karmically determined state of existence is that of an animal, a spirit, a human, a god, or one of the other of the eleven states in the realm of sensation, of the sixteen states in the realm of form, or of the four states in the realm of the formless. The human state is not totally undifferentiated in karmic terms; one may be born a man or woman, rich or poor, prince or peasant, whole or deformed. One may also have, if one is born a male, sufficient Karma to enter and remain for life within the Sangha, or one may have only enough Karma to enter the Sangha temporarily; some men may not have sufficient Karma to take on the yellow robes for even a brief time. Depending on the karmically determined state into which one is born, one is subject to a particular set of influences or forces that have the power to inflict or ameliorate suffering. For example, most human beings are subject to the influences of spirits, although those who become monks are much less vulnerable than are those outside the Sangha. Gods, on the other hand, are invulnerable to the influences of spirits. The same interpretation holds for all other forms of proximate causation, including scientifically based forms of causation

Lay members of a Buddhist congregation at a Shan temple–monastery
in northern Thailand. (*C. F. Keyes photograph*)

—such as germs—which have been adopted by many in Theravada Buddhist
societies in recent times.

To say that Buddhist cosmology provides a total field that accommodates
beliefs in both karmic and other forms of causation is not to say that there is
no tension between these beliefs. Such a tension exists in all the traditions of
Theravada Buddhism, and it has probably existed since earliest Buddhism. This
tension does not compromise the orthodoxy of Theravada Buddhism unless
other forms of causation are made equal to karmic causation. There is a tendency in this direction in every Buddhist tradition. For example, in northern
Thailand, relics of the Buddha, images of the Buddha, texts from the Dharma,
acts of the Sangha, and acts of lay piety have been interpreted as implicating an
ultimate reality of sentient existence that is absolute and unchanging rather than
an ultimate reality that is, according to the Law of Karma, constantly in flux.[45]
Despite such tendencies, karmic theory has never been displaced in any Buddhist
society as the interpretation of ultimate reality of sentient existence. People in
northern Thailand have always been concerned with making merit and avoiding
demerit as well as orienting themselves to a fixed cosmos. Karmic theory may
coexist with such competing theories as that of cosmic permanence, but since
the thirteenth century at least it has never been replaced or subordinated to
such theories anywhere in Buddhist Southeast Asia.

Salvation in Theravada Buddhism

The Buddhist doctrine of ultimate salvation has, in contrast to the doctrine
of Karma, undergone radical reinterpretation among some Theravada Buddhists.
Although most Theravada Buddhists have viewed and still do view Nirvana as
a very distant goal, some have attempted to find shortcuts or ways to this goal
other than by the route taught by the Buddha himself. In Burma, for example,

there is a common belief that if one is able to sponsor the construction of a *cetiya*, a shrine for a relic, one will ensure that one will be reborn at the time of Sri Ariya Maitreya, the next Buddha (who, it is believed by many, will come 5,000 years after the death of Gotama Buddha). And, by being in the presence of this future Buddha, one will attain enlightenment. In Thailand, Laos, and Cambodia there is a similar belief, although the significant act is listening to the whole sermon that relates the story of the life of Prince Vessantara, who was the Buddha in his last incarnation before being born as Siddhatha Gottama. Again, this act ensures rebirth at the time of Ariya Maitreya. From time to time in Buddhist Southeast Asia, some people have found in a king, a monk, or some other individual one who appears to have the attributes of a Boddhisattva, a future Buddha. Such persons are believed to be so endowed with merit that they are able to share it with others. The effects of this merit ensures that all who share it will enjoy a marked reduction in suffering if not its cessation.[46]

Although ultimate salvation, Nirvana, has been sought by some Theravada Buddhists through unorthodox magical and messianic ways, and a few have sought Nirvana through the orthodox practice of meditation, most people in Theravada Buddhist societies have not and do not focus on the attainment of Nirvana as their religious goal. Rather, they have sought and still seek to attain a reduction in suffering, first in this life and next in a future existence, postponing the quest for total cessation of suffering to a remote future many lifetimes away. In historical terms, it is clear that in the process of becoming a popular or universal religion, Buddhism ceased to be a religion of radical salvation.

The primary message carried by the monk revolutionaries of the thirteenth and fourteenth centuries was not one whose main theme concerned the Path to ultimate salvation but one that stressed that beneath the impermanence of sentient existence was an underlying reality, that of the Law of Karma. Moreover, they also taught that through an understanding of Karma, of which actions bore evil fruit and which bore good, one could undertake action that would result in a surcease, albeit temporary, from suffering. The actions necessary to effect such an end were possible for everyone, be one peasant or prince, ethnically marginal or ethnically a part of the majority of the great states. In the turbulent times of the thirteenth and fourteenth centuries, this message must have found a highly receptive audience among the general populace of the Indianized states of Southeast Asia.

TRADITIONAL THERAVADA BUDDHIST SOCIETIES AND THE CHALLENGE OF COLONIALISM

Traditional Societies in Theravada Buddhist Southeast Asia

The period of the classic Indianized civilizations in Southeast Asia had been a period of centralized power, albeit power that was exercised more theatrically than actually. The period from the thirteenth to the nineteenth centuries, that is, the period between the demise of the classic civilizations and the impact of European colonialism, was one of fragmented power.[47]

The greatest fragmentation of power was among the Tai-speaking peoples. The Tai living in northern mainland Southeast Asia—that is, the Tai living in what are today the Shan states of Burma, southern Yunnan in China, northern and northeastern Thailand, and Laos—were organized politically into literally hundreds of small polities that were hierarchically arranged. A few of these, such as Hsenwi and Kengtung (Chiang Tung) in Burma, Kenghung (Chiang Hung) in Yunnan, Chiang Mai in northern Thailand, Luang Prebang, Vientiane, and Campasak in Laos, had rather greater influence than most of their neighbors and enjoyed some periods of independence. However, each was eventually absorbed as a vassal state by the more powerful Burmans and Siamese.

Of all the Tai polities, only Siam in what is today central Thailand developed a strong centralized state, and this development was a long time in the making. It was not really until the end of the eighteenth century—after the fall of the old Siamese capital of Ayutthaya and the founding of a new capital at Bangkok (following an interregnum when the capital was across the Cao Phraya River from Bangkok at Thonburi)—that Siam finally became a major power in Southeast Asia.

A powerful Burma was similarly a long time in the making. From the fourteenth to the mid-eighteenth centuries, Burma was in constant turmoil. There were wars between the Burmans and the Shans of the Shan States, between the Burmans and the Arakanese (a people closely related to the Burmans) living in what is today western Burma, and, most importantly, between the Burmans of upper Burma and the Mons and Burmans of lower Burma. In the 1750s, Burma was finally united under a new Burman dynasty, the Konbaung. The Konbaung kings built several capitals in the Burman heartland in upper Burma, the last capital being at Mandalay. The Konbaung court, located far inland, tended to be far more isolated from Europeans than was the case with the court at Bangkok, which was located near the coast. This isolation was one factor in shaping the relationship between Konbaung Burma and the British, which began with a war in 1824–1826 and ended with another war in 1885 during which the British destroyed the Burman monarchy. The promise shown by the early Konbaung kings was thus aborted by wars with the British.

During the period between the fourteenth and early nineteenth centuries, Cambodia was a residual state in Southeast Asia, a remnant of the once-great Khmer empire. From the fourteenth century on, Cambodia lost more and more of its territory to its neighbors. By the early part of the nineteenth century, Cambodia was under strong pressure from both the Vietnamese and the Siamese, and, if the French had not intervened, it is not unlikely that Cambodia would have ceased to exist altogether. Cambodia's political system in premodern times perpetuated some aspects of the classical system; of equal importance, if not greater, were those aspects that developed as an adaptation to the constant threat posed by Cambodia's neighbors. This dual legacy of a glorious past and of a constant threat posed by Thailand and Vietnam has continued to shape Cambodia's political actions to this day.

The overwhelming majority of villagers who lived in the traditional Buddhist states of Southeast Asia were producers of rice. Some specialized in other occupations, the most important being fishing, which was engaged in particularly by peoples living along the coasts of the Bay of Bengal, the Gulf of Siam, and the Tonlé Sap (the Great Lake of Cambodia). A few villagers also specialized in such craft production as pottery manufacture, lacquer-making, blacksmithing, bronze working, and silversmithing. Villagers produced first for their own needs, including the need to expend wealth in merit-making activities in order to ensure ultimate well-being. In addition, the peasants had to produce a surplus that was appropriated by local lords or agents of a king. Throughout the whole of Buddhist Southeast Asia, taxes were legitimated by the belief, acceded to by peasants as well as advanced by rulers, that the kings and/or lords held ultimate rights to the land on which the peasants lived and worked.

In addition to the payment of taxes, which were normally in kind, villagers had to provide their lords or the agents of their kings with labor service on a regular basis. For those who lived near the court centers, this labor service could be a heavy burden; for those living in more distant villages, it appears to have been irregularly demanded. Some men owed permanent service to others; these men were slaves. Some who became slaves had been freemen who had given up their freedom in order to pay off a debt. Other slaves had been captured in war or by raiding parties of tribal people who sold their captives to lowland peoples.

Warfare was nearly endemic in traditional Southeast Asia. Wars were fought far less often over territory than they were over people, as all the states in traditional Southeast Asia were underpopulated. After a war, the victors normally would force a part of the population of the vanquished state to uproot and resettle in areas already under the control of the victors. Other peoples moved of their own initiative when their lives were disrupted by war. Wars also unsettled villages and towns located far from the actual places of battle, as young men from all communities in a domain were mobilized to fight.

As the fact of endemic warfare demonstrates, traditional Theravada Buddhist societies in Southeast Asia were not tranquil worlds. Indeed, both socially and politically traditional Theravada Buddhist societies were in constant turmoil. Kings and lords often did not live out their natural span, but were forcibly deposed by sons or other claimants to their offices. Peasants were periodically mobilized for warfare, and the peasantry of defeated states were quite often moved from their home communities or chose to move and resettle elsewhere. Some tribal peoples living on the peripheries of the Theravada Buddhist states engaged in regular slave raiding and those who did not do so were not infrequently subjected to slave raids. Yet, for all this social and political flux, both peasant and ruler in traditional Theravada Buddhist society lived in meaningful worlds. Kings and lords held office because of their previous

The shrine of That Phanom in northeastern Thailand, a *cetiya* believed to contain a breastbone relic of the Buddha. (*C. F. Keyes photograph*)

A Burmese-style ordination hall in a northern Thai temple-monastery in Mae Sariang, northern Thailand. (*C. F. Keyes photograph*)

" merit "; they were deposed because their " merit " had been exhausted. Families, villages, feudalities, and states waxed and waned, because all social structures were subject to *anicca*, all were subject to impermanence. Rulers and peasants all also knew that underlying the turmoil of existence was a permanent moral order, that which was grounded in Karma.

The Buddhist religion thus flourished despite the constantly changing political scene. Almost the only enduring edifices constructed on the landscape of the traditional Theravada Buddhist societies were the *cetiya*, or reliquary shrines, and the various buildings of the temple monasteries (called *kyaung* in Burmese and *wat* in the various Tai languages and in Khmer). Most males spent at least a temporary period as a member of the Sangha and there was no dearth of men who chose to remain within the Sangha for life. In short, the world as lived in by people in the Theravada Buddhist societies of Southeast Asia was also the world as it was expressed in the teachings of their religion. For people in the Theravada Buddhist societies of Southeast Asia, the validity of traditional life came under sharp challenge after the British annexation of Arakan and Tenasserim following the first Anglo-Burmese war of 1824–1826.

European Colonial Expansion

There had been a European presence in Southeast Asia for over three centuries prior to this first Anglo-Burmese war. In 1511, a Portuguese force led by Alberquerque took Malacca on the Malay Peninsula, thereby establishing the first European outpost in the region. Throughout the next three centuries, various Europeans, some representing the great European trading firms, some serving as missionaries, and some being adventurers, involved themselves in various ways in Southeast Asia. Although this involvement led to the creation of several European entrepôts in the region, it did not initially lead to an attempt by Europeans to dominate the Southeast Asian societies. There was one aborted move in this direction in the late seventeenth century, when a group of men representing French interests attempted to gain preeminent political influence at the Siamese court of Ayutthaya. The Siamese reacted strongly to this effort, however, killing the main leader of the move and expelling the rest of those involved from the country. The next, and more successful, attempt by European powers to impose their will on Southeast Asian societies was made by the British.

British involvement in Southeast Asia represented, initially at least, an extension of their interests in India. The first footholds the British established in the region were on the island of Penang (1786) in what is now Malaysia, in Singapore (1819), and in Malacca (confirmed by the Anglo-Dutch treaty of 1824). These Straits Settlements, as they came to be known, were founded by the British primarily in order to protect their trading interests in the Bay of Bengal. British interests in this area as well as British concerns with border conflicts between Burma and British India culminated in the Anglo-Burmese wars.

The creation of British Burma was accomplished through three successive wars between the British and the Burmese, the first in 1824–1826, the second in 1852, and the last in 1885. In the first, the Burmese ceded Arakan and Tennaserim to the British and gave up claims to Manipur, which lies in what is today Assam in eastern India. In the second, the British took over the Irrawaddy delta and surrounding areas. And in the last war, the Burmese monarchy was overthrown and the whole of upper Burma was added to British Burma. It took a number of years more for the British to " pacify " the Shans and the tribal peoples living on the peripheries of Burma proper.

The extension of the British Empire into Southeast Asia became a major concern to those in France who were advocates of French expansion in Asia.[48] Goaded by these advocates, the French government found pretext in the purported persecution of French missionaries by the Vietnamese to undertake military operations in the late 1850s in what is today southern Vietnam. From these operations, the French succeeded in creating the colony of Cochin China. Almost simultaneously—in 1864–1867—France also succeeded in persuading King Norodom of Cambodia to make Cambodia a French protectorate. It is clear that King Norodom turned to the French in order to safeguard the integrity of his country against the very serious threats posed by Thailand and Vietnam. It was not until two decades later that the full implications of becoming a dependency of France was impressed upon the Khmer.

Laos was, in a very real sense, entirely a creation of the French. French interest in the middle Mekong area was stimulated in the first instance by the hope that Mekong would prove to be a passageway to China. After explorations of the Mekong proved this hope to be unrealistic, owing to the impassable rapids at a number of places along the Mekong, the French temporarily lost interest in the region. This interest was renewed, however, in the 1880s in the wake of French expansion into northern Vietnam and westward into territories formerly dependent on Vietnam. The French expansion into Laos was essentially the work of a single individual, Auguste Pavie. Pavie first undertook to win the support of the king of the small statelet of Luang Prabang, which was, at the time, a vassal of Siam. This done, he then persuaded the French to acquire all the territory west of the Annamite range and east of the Mekong. Most of this territory, which today constitutes middle and southern Laos, had been organized previously into small feudalities under the Siamese king. The Siamese were, quite naturally, reluctant to cede territory they had come to consider an integral part of their kingdom. However, in 1893, the French blockaded the Port of Bangkok with gunboats and forced Siam, through an ultimatum, to accede to their demands. By 1907, the Siamese had also been forced to cede the right-bank territories of Sayaboury in the north and Campasak in the south to the French. The French then welded together the old Kingdom of Luang Prabang (comprising the four present-day Lao provinces of Luang Prabang, Hua Phan or Sam Neua, Phong Saly, and Sayaboury), territories taken from the Lue (another Tai people) confederacy in South China, the small feudality of Chiang Khuang, which had formerly been under both the Siamese and Vietnamese, a number of Thai tribal chiefdomships, and the feudalities that had been under the Siamese into a single administrative unit called Laos.

Thailand, or Siam as it was then, was the only country in Southeast Asia that was not incorporated into one of the colonial empires. Nonetheless, Thailand was as radically affected by the influences of the colonial period as were its neighbors. Following a treaty between Great Britain and Siam negotiated by Sir John Bowring in 1855, Siam became exposed to new economic forces manipulated by Westerners. Moreover, by the end of the nineteenth century, Thailand had become, economically, a client state of Great Britain, a status it retained until World War II. Thailand's leaders also found it necessary to undertake radical, political, social, and cultural changes in order to maintain the independence of the kingdom. During the 1890s and early 1900s, King Chulalongkorn and his advisors instituted reforms, which could only be termed revolutionary.

Although the colonial period began for the Theravada Buddhist societies in the early part of the nineteenth century, it was not until about 1880 that colonial influence became most intense. This period of intensity lasted until World War II, when the Japanese shattered the myth of European dominance in the region. Although the colonial powers returned to Southeast Asia after the war, they resumed power only for a brief time. The Union of Burma gained its independence from Great Britain in 1948. France recognized the independence of Cambodia in 1946 and the independence of Laos in 1949, although true independence did not come until 1954 after the French defeat by the Viet Minh at Dien Bien Phu and the holding of the Geneva Conference.

THE IMPACT OF WESTERN COLONIALISM ON THE THERAVADA BUDDHIST SOCIETIES

Political Economy During the Colonial Period

During the colonial period the most conspicuous changes in the Theravada Buddhist societies of Southeast Asia were political in nature. In Burma, the British abolished the monarchy and established " direct " role over Burma proper. That is, the administration of this area of the country was centralized under a British Governor. Some of the tribal areas were also administered directly, although their administration was separated from that of Burma proper. In the Shan states and in Karenni, the British instituted " indirect " rule whereby the local lords were permitted considerable autonomy, although ultimate power lay with British officials.

The French administered both Cambodia and Laos in a manner rather similar to the " indirect " rule of the British in parts of Burma. Although the king of Cambodia and the ruler of the Lao principality of Luang Prabang had no real power, the territories of these two states were administered in the names of these monarchs. The local political structure with provincial governors in Cambodia and local lords throughout Laos was left intact by the French. Siam, of course, retained its independence, although Britain came to wield con-siderable influence in the Siamese court, particularly in economic matters. King Chulalongkorn of Siam himself instituted political changes that were almost as radical in some instances as those instituted by the British and French. At the end of the nineteenth and beginning of the twentieth centuries, the Siamese court successfully eliminated the autonomous power previously exercised by local lords in northern, northeastern, and southern Siam. Power was centralized in Bangkok and administered by officials appointed by the court.

The political changes effected during the colonial period were accom-panied by the introduction of new concepts of administration. In traditional Theravada Buddhist societies, officials carried out their duties in terms of their personal relationships with their subordinates and superordinates. The colonial powers introduced in their administration and their dominions the Western conception that bureaucrats should carry out their duties in terms of abstract principles. In Burma, it was not only the few Europeans at the upper echelons of the bureaucracy who were expected to follow the new principles, those Burmese and Indians recruited to serve in posts in Burma proper also were expected to be " modern " bureaucrats. The rationalization of the bureaucracy in Burma was studied by high Siamese officials who used the British-Burma model of administration for their own administrative retorms instituted at the end of the nineteenth and the beginning of the twentieth centuries. In Cambodia, in Laos, and in the areas of indirect control in Burma, however, a dichotomy developed between the European officials who were " modern " bureaucrats and the native officials who continued to follow traditional practices. Even in Burma proper and in Siam, a tension between the old and new principles was often manifest, even in the same individual. This tension has remained to the present day.[49]

The economic transformation of the Theravada Buddhist societies during the colonial period was perhaps even more radical than the politicoadmini-strative transformation. Although it is simplistic to see European colonialism as being primarily an extension of European capitalism, it remains true that a primary interest of the European powers in Southeast Asia, as in other parts of the colonialized world, was to effect economic development, which would produce profits for both government and business in the home countries. This became particularly true from about the mid-nineteenth century on.

The economic development promoted during the colonial period centered on the export of foodstuffs and natural produce from the areas under colonial domination or influence and on the import into these areas of manufactured goods from the home countries in Europe. Although a number of different commodities produced in the Theravada Buddhist societies were promoted for export—for example, teak from Burma and Thailand, rubber from Thailand and Cambodia, and tin from Thailand—rice was by far the most important. De-mand for rice on the world market had increased greatly in the 1860s, a func-tion in part of the cutting off of sources in the American south during the Civil War, of the opening of the Suez canal, and of population growth outstripping production in parts of the Dutch East Indies and British India. This demand remained high, albeit with some fluctuations, until the Great Depression of the 1930s. After World War II, the demand again grew and has continued, again with some fluctuations, until the present.

The response to the world demand for rice was met primarily through the commercialization of rice production in lower Burma and central Thailand. Both areas had been rather underpopulated in the precolonial period, but with the commercialization of rice production these areas grew rapidly in population. Villagers from other areas of the two countries left their homes and moved into lower Burma and central Thailand where they opened new lands and founded new villages. With commercialization came a radical transformation of the relationship between humans and land in these areas of Burma and Thailand. Land, labor, and capital came to be conceived of by the peasants themselves as commodities that could be transferred through impersonal market transactions rather than as extensions of kin groups that could be transferred only through inheritance. What Silverstein has said of Burma could also be applied to central Thailand, although to a lesser degree, " The conversion of Burma into a commercial granary and the world's largest rice exporter brought with it tenancy, money lending, and land alienation."[50]

While the peasants of lower Burma and central Thailand were being swept up into a market economy, most of the peasantry elsewhere in the Therevada Buddhist societies of Southeast Asia continued to follow traditional economic ways. This division between market-oriented peasants and traditional peasants was the source of some tension, a tension that remains to this day. We will examine this in more detail in the next chapter, and return to a general consideration of the economic transformations of Theravada Buddhist society in Chapter 5.

The economic transformations of the colonial period also brought other divisions to the Theravada Buddhist societies. In Burma, large numbers of Indians migrated into the country, often with the encouragement of the British, to take up commercial and proletarian occupations. Large numbers of Chinese migrated into Thailand, where they assumed many of the same roles played by the Indians in Burma. By the turn of the century, the Chinese had gained a near monopoly on rice milling and on the internal trade of Thailand as well as on other entrepreneurial activities. Chinese and Vietnamese migrated into Cambodia and Laos, although in relatively fewer numbers, where they also came to play the same roles as the Indians in Burma and the Chinese in Thailand. In all the countries of Theravada Buddhist Southeast Asia, Europeans dominated the firms involved in the export trade. They also dominated the highest administrative positions in Burma, Cambodia, and Laos. The colonial society in which different ethnic groups predominated in different sectors of the economy became what J. S. Furnivall called a " plural society."[51] This ethnic division of labor has remained a major problem in Theravada Buddhist societies to this day (see Chapter 5 for further discussion with reference to urban life).

The promotion of exports of foodstuffs and raw materials from colonial societies and the promotion of imports of manufactured goods into these societies necessitated some investment in the economic infrastructure of these societies. By far the greatest concentration of investment was in the major port city of the countries concerned. As a result of the economic opportunities created by the expansion of what became the " primate " city in the country, these cities grew far more rapidly in population than did the countries as a whole or other towns in these countries. During the colonial period Rangoon in Burma and Bangkok in Thailand became classic examples of the " primate city." Prior to the British annexation of upper Burma, Rangoon had been approximately equal in size to Mandalay, the old Burmese royal capital. By 1911 Rangoon was more than twice the size of Mandalay and it continued to grow, becoming four times larger than Mandalay in the 1950s. Bangkok had an even more dramatic growth vis-à-vis other cities in the country. It was already several times larger than the next largest city, Chiang Mai, before the end of the nineteenth century. By 1947 it was nearly 15 times larger and by 1960 it was 30 times larger.[52] Whereas the towns and cities of Burma and Siam had not been radically different in both size and quality of life from the peasant villages in traditional times, in the colonial period Rangoon and Bangkok became very different types of places with very different ways of life from those found in the countryside or in other towns. Although life in the cities will be examined in greater detail in Chapter 5, it is important here to point out the growing differences between village and city life that developed during the colonial period.

The investment in economic infrastructure was not limited to the primate cities, however. Both the British in Burma and the Siamese in their own country invested in the building of railways, in improving communications, in developing waterways for transportation and irrigation, and so on. These improvements were not carried out solely for economic reasons; they were also made to ease government communication and administration.

The economic development of Cambodia and Laos during the colonial period was far less dramatic than was the case in Burma and Thailand. As Smith has said of Cambodia: " France's primary interest in Cambodia was defensive . . .; only secondarily was it interested in the development of natural or human resources."[53] There was some development in Cambodia, however; rubber plantations were founded in eastern Cambodia, some commercialization of rice agriculture took place, and communication and transportation facilities —roads, railways, and shipping—were improved to a certain extent. Phnom Penh also developed some of the same characteristics of Rangoon and Bangkok as a colonial " primate " city, although these were not so accentuated as they were in the other cities.[54]

Laos was hardly developed at all. Although Laos was recognized by French officials and certain agents of French commercial interests to have natural wealth—lumber, minerals, water that could be harnessed for power, and so on

—no serious effort was ever made to exploit these resources. Only telegraph lines and roads necessary for administration were constructed during the colonial period. Vientiane remained a sleepy backwater town; it never developed into a major colonial city.

Although the political, bureaucratic, and economic changes wrought during the colonial period were far fewer in Laos and Cambodia than in Burma and Thailand, all the countries of Theravada Buddhist Southeast Asia were forced to make a break from their traditional systems. Such a break was not always accepted passively. The Burmese fought three wars against the British to protect their traditional society and resistance continued for at least five years after the British conquest of upper Burma. In 1930–1932 there was a major uprising in Burma, the Saya San rebellion, which represented a popular attempt to reinstitute the traditional Burman monarchical system.[55] Although Thailand did not lose its monarchy, the Yuan of northern Thailand, the Lao of northeastern Thailand, and the Malay of southern Thailand all lost their local political autonomy in the wake of the reforms instituted by King Chulalongkorn and his associates at the end of the nineteenth century. Again, there was resistance to this action on the part of the local populace. In 1900–1902 there were rebellions in Thailand in the north, the south, and the northeast. The latter was part of a wider uprising, which also involved people in French Laos. It is important to note in this regard that the French were in the process of implementing their rule in southern Laos just prior to the time this uprising occurred.[56] In Cambodia, the transition from an independent monarchy to a French protectorate was initially accomplished without much trauma. However, in the early 1880s the French began to take their role in Cambodia seriously and to interfere directly in administration in the provinces as well as in the capital. This action was met by resistance, perhaps even supported by the king himself, climaxing in a rebellion of Khmer provincial elite in 1884–1886.[57]

All the efforts to preserve the traditional system in the face of the socioeconomic and sociopolitical changes introduced during the colonial period ended in failure. These changes had brought to an end, once and for all, the traditional life of the peoples living in the Theravada Buddhist societies. These changes also came to pose for these peoples a severe crisis of meaning. That is, the cultural forms inherited from the traditional past no longer adequately served to inform and guide action in the world of experience transformed by the forces of the colonial period.

Although the various uprisings mentioned above represented efforts to assert the validity of the traditional culture despite the changes in experience, these assertions failed as the uprisings themselves failed. The Buddhist millennium looked to by adherents to such movements as the *phu mi bun* uprising in northeastern Thailand and southern Laos in 1900–1902 never came. Millennial ideas continue to attract some followers,[58] but they are peripheral to the political culture of Theravada Buddhist societies. The successful resolutions to the cultural crisis in Southeast Asia have taken other forms.

Change in Educational Systems

Cultural transformations during the colonial period in Theravada Buddhist societies were not consequences of socioeconomic and sociopolitical changes, but went hand-in-hand with such changes. The rationalization of the bureaucracy in both Burma and Thailand, for example, necessitated a radical restructuring of education, so that those who were recruited for the bureaucracy would be properly trained. In Burma, educational reform resulted in the creation of two very different types of educational systems. On the one hand, there was the educational system, made up of private and government schools and of missionary-run schools, whose curriculum was basically secular and Western and whose medium of instruction was partially if not completely English. On the other hand, there remained the monastery-based educational system whose curriculum was basically religious and traditional and whose medium of instruction was Burmese (or Shan in the case of the Shan states). The cultural orientations obtained by those who passed through these two systems were radically different. As a consequence, there emerged in British Burma an almost unbridgeable gulf between the culture of the elite and the culture of the rest of the population.[59]

Although the French created something similar to the " two cultures " of Burma through bifurcation of education, the effect was not nearly so great since very few in Laos or Cambodia were educated in the French system. At the end of the World War II in Laos " only 1 per cent of the population, estimated at just over 1.1 million persons, was receiving an elementary education (in Lao), while secondary education (in French) was being provided for only 200 students."[60] In Cambodia, the record for primary education was slightly better. In 1941, there were 192 primary schools in which instruction was given in French and 845 Buddhist temple schools in which " modernized " primary education was given in Khmer. However, beyond the primary level, education was comparable to Laos in that there was but one secondary school giving instruction in French to 537 students.[61]

Thailand presents rather a sharp contrast with Burma with regard to educational changes during the colonial period.[62] Both King Mongkut (1851–1868) and his son, King Chulalongkorn (1868–1910), recognized the importance of Western knowledge, particularly scientific knowledge, if Thailand were to rationalize its bureaucracy and to promote economic development. To some extent, both kings, as well as later governments, sponsored the acquisition of such knowledge by sending a few Thai on scholarships to study in Western countries. This small group of Western-educated Thai did develop cultural orientations that were markedly different from those of their fellow countrymen. However, this difference was diminished in importance by the necessity of Western-educated Thai to readapt themselves on returning home to a society whose political elite remained culturally Thai. In the 1890s, King Chulalongkorn and his counselors also developed a comprehensive reform of education, a reform that would bring the rudiments of modern education to the village level. Although this compulsory education plan was not fully implemented until the early 1930s and the division between traditional monastic-based education and this new secular education was also not fully effected until the 1930s, the educational reforms instituted under King Chulalongkorn did succeed in perpetuating an articulation between popular and elite education, which was not the case in Burma and in many other colonialized countries.

Cultural Crisis and the Buddhist Response in Burma

Secular education, whether restricted to an elite as in Burma, Cambodia, and (to a very small extent) Laos or carried down to the village level, albeit in a very attenuated form, as in Thailand tended to exacerbate the cultural crisis of the colonial period. The old truths provided by the religious traditions were brought into question not only because of changed socioeconomic and sociopolitical circumstance but also by the new truths offered by secular education. Another direct challenge to the old truths was offered by Christian missionaries. These missionaries actually found little success among the Buddhist peoples of Thailand, Laos, Burma, and Cambodia. Converts to either Catholicism or Protestantism in these countries were overwhelmingly drawn from minority groups, that is, from tribal peoples and the Chinese and Vietnamese imigrants. Although the Christian missionaries converted few who were Buddhists by birth, they contributed significantly to the rethinking of the cultural tradition undertaken by some of the elite in all the Theravada Buddhist societies.

Briefly, then, the cultural crisis in the Theravada Buddhist societies of Southeast Asia was born of the growing discrepancy between life as the changes of the colonial period led people to experience it and the world as tradition led people to conceive of it. For some, primarily the elite, this crisis was exacerbated by having been exposed to alternative cultural orientations, namely those derived from Western secular and, in some cases, Western religious sources. Given the different ways in which the cultural crisis was felt by people in the Theravada Buddhist societies, it follows that the ways of confronting the crisis were also different.

The Buddhist Sangha, both as an institution and as a collection of individuals concerned with the Buddhist tradition, has played an extremely important role in the confrontation with the cultural crisis of Theravada Buddhist societies. The institution of the Sangha in Burma was dealt a severe blow when the British captured Mandalay and brought the Burmese monarchy to an end. Not only was royal support for the Sangha terminated, but the British also greatly undermined the office of the Buddhist patriarch. Thus, the religion became disestablished and the Sangha lost its unifying focus. This, in turn, led to an exacerbation of the sectarianism in the Burmese Sangha, which had always existed. Although most monks continued to perform their roles as they had always done, some felt compelled to rethink Buddhism in light of the changed circumstances of colonial Burma. This rethinking of Buddhism in Burma took two radically different directions.

Most well known is the direction represented by those who became " political monks," that is, monks who actively involved themselves in the nationalist movement in Burma. These monks worked with a number of lay nationalist leaders who had found the Young Men's Buddhist Association (modeled on the YMCA) in 1906. The political monks also organized associations of their own, such as the General Council of Monkhood Associations, which was founded in 1922. The political monks found themselves working side by side with some secular nationalist leaders who had been strongly influenced by Marxist thought. From this interaction came an attempt on the part of some to create a Marxist Buddhism, that is, a Buddhism that stressed the importance of reducing suffering not only for the individual but for the whole society. Although the nationalist movement in the period prior to independence in 1948 accommodated those who adhered to secular Socialist and Communist ideologies and, in the case of minority peoples. to Christianity and Hinduism, Buddhist socialism was unquestionably one of the dominant ideological strains in Burmese nationalism. This ideology was promoted after independence by U Nu, the man who was the dominant political figure in Burma from 1948 to 1962. Indeed, it was partially U Nu's efforts to give primacy to Buddhism that led to his downfall in 1962, because a number of groups in Burmese society felt threatened by this action.

Another reinterpretation of Buddhism during the colonial period was undertaken by several monks who sought to return to the essence of the Buddhist tradition by stressing the importance of meditation. Of the monks who promoted an emphasis on meditation, the Leidi Sayadaw (1846–1924) and the Jetavan or Mingalun Sayadaw (1868–1955) were the dominant figures during the colonial period. The meditation tradition founded by such monks was not meant for monks alone, but for the laity as well. Through meditation one could transcend the tribulations of worldly existence and the person who had mastered meditation could engage in worldly activity without attachment to the results of that activity. The Burmese form of " popular " meditation has had a marked influence on Buddhist practice throughout the Theravada Buddhist world. Its appeal is greatest for members of the educated elite, that is, for those who most feel the contradictions between experience and traditional Buddhist meaning.[63]

Buddhist Reform in Thailand, Cambodia, and Laos

A rethinking of Buddhism also took place in Thailand during the colonial period, the results of which were to have an impact not only in Thailand but also in Cambodia and Laos. The Buddhist reformation in Thailand was predominantly the work of two men: Mongkut, the ruler of Siam from 1851–1868 but a member of the Sangha between 1824 and 1851, and his son Wachirayan who dominated the Thai Sangha from the early 1890s until 1921.

Owing to the caricature of Mongkut in the novel, play, and movie, *The King and I*, Mongkut is often viewed by Westerners as an Oriental despot, a buffoon, and an unbeknighted semibarbarian chief. Nothing could be further from the truth. In 1824, Mongkut was ordained a monk at a point in time when he, rather than his brother, might have been expected to inherit the throne from his father. During the reign of Rama III (1824–1851), Mongkut lived the life of a monk. As a monk, Mongkut undertook a rethinking of Siamese culture, a rethinking that was stimulated in part by his exposure to Western thought, introduced mainly by missionaries. Out of this rethinking came a religious reformation that bears some striking similarities to the Protestant Reformation of Europe. As Mongkut's son, Prince Damrong, later wrote, Mongkut undertook the reorientation of Siamese culture because he had become aware that Siam " had met the time [when] the situation in the East would be changed by the [Europeans] who came with increasing power." Of equal importance, he also felt that: " It was not enough to follow what had been done before, just for the sake of protecting custom."[64]

The instrument for Mongkut's religious reformation was a new Buddhist Order, the Thammayut. This order has its origins in a new tradition or ordination initiated by Mongkut in about 1833.[65] Although the distinctiveness of the Thammayut order was manifest in forms of practice, that is, in the ways in which certain aspects of the Discipline (*vinaya*) were followed by monks, the order had a function far more important than disciplinary reform. The Thammayut monks became a clerical vanguard of a movement promoting a new interpretation of Buddhism, one that sought to demythologize the religion.[66]

During Mongkut's reign as king (1851–1868), the Thammayut order spread beyond the confines of the two temple monasteries in which it had been located while Mongkut was still a monk. New Thammayut communities were founded not only in Siam, but also in Cambodia and Laos. In Cambodia, as in Thailand, the Thammayut order received royal patronage.

Neither Mongkut nor his son Chulalongkorn, who reigned from 1868 to 1910, allowed the Thammayut to develop into a separate sect. Through careful allocation of senior positions in the Sangha during the period from 1851 to 1910, the Thammayut was kept within the Thai Sangha, albeit it eventually did achieve separate administrative status within the Sangha. Instead of sectarian separation, the Thammayut Order attempted to provide the lead for a reform of the whole Sangha.

The leadership role in the Buddhist reformation in Thailand reached its apogee in the person of Prince Wachirayan, a son of King Mongkut and brother of King Chulalongkorn. Prince Wachirayan became a monk in 1879, at the age of 20, and by 1890 was clearly the leading monk in the country. In 1893, King Chulalongkorn made him head of the Thammayut Order and *de facto* Patriarch of the Sangha, although he did not formally assume this position until 1910 after the death of Chulalongkorn. Prince Wachirayan was Prince Patriarch from 1910 until his death in 1921.

Prince Wachirayan played the role in the transformation of Thai cultural life comparable to the role played by others of Mongkut's sons and Chulalongkorn's brothers in effecting the transformation of the sociopolitical system of Thailand. Prince Wachirayan wrote voluminously, and his writings can be considered a systematic theology of the demythologized Buddhism promoted by the

Thammayut Order. He was also responsible for drawing up the Sangha Law of 1902, which sought to effect the integration of the Sangha throughout the kingdom. Although the implementation of the Sangha Law of 1902 took many years, it was well under way by the time of Prince Wachirayan's death in 1921. The integration of the Sangha throughout Thailand necessitated the de-emphasis of the local and regional religious traditions and the acceptance by all monks of centralized authority, particularly in the important matter of ordination. As a consequence of these reforms, Thailand emerged from the period of colonial transformation with a strong and unified national Sangha. In contrast, the Burmese Sangha during the colonial period had become even more fragmented than it had been during the premodern period. Laos and Cambodia emulated the model of Thailand, although adapting it to a colonially dominated context.

The reform Buddhism promoted by the Thammayut Order in Thailand, Laos, and Cambodia has not been fully accepted by a large portion of the Sangha, especially those members of the Sangha who are still firmly rooted in village society. Moreover, although reform Buddhism, owing to its established character, has offered the most important resolution to the cultural crisis in Thailand, Laos, and Cambodia, it has not offered the only resolution, not even the only Buddhist resolution. As in Burma, there emerged in Thailand during the colonial period a few monks who gave particular stress to the importance of meditation. Although an emphasis on meditation appears to have an independent origin in Thailand, it has become linked with Burmese developments in recent years. In Thailand, as in Burma, there was also some effort to develop a socialistic Buddhism, an effort mainly promoted in Thailand by a lay political leader, Pridi Phanomyong. However, this effort was strongly resisted by most of the Thai elite and has never become a strongly viable ideological option in Thailand, at least not prior to 1973.

Non-Buddhist Solutions to the Cultural Crisis

Buddhism in any of its manifestations—traditional, millennarian, reform, meditational, or socialistic—has not offered the only cultural strategies whereby people in the Theravada Buddhist societies of Southeast Asia could confront the cultural crisis posed by the changes of the colonial period. Although Christianity has not proved to be a viable alternative ideology, Western secular ideologies—notably Socialism and Communism—have become so. When these ideologies were first introduced into Southeast Asia, they attracted only a very small number of the educated elite. Moreover, they existed as hot house plants with no real connection to the cultural traditions of the societies in question Through time, however, these ideologies have been reworked to make them more meaningful to Southeast Asians themselves. In the Theravada Buddhist societies, the first major success of Socialist/Communist ideology was in Burma. The adaptation of these ideologies to Burma was facilitated by the efforts made by Burmese nationalist leaders to effect a meaningful synthesis between Marxism and Buddhism. Some introduced Marxist ideas into Buddhist thought; others used traditional Buddhist meanings to give expression to Marxist ideas. Members of the Burmese nationalist movement (leaving aside for the moment the minority interests) eventually divided into those adhering to a Socialist Buddhism, to secular Socialism, and to Communism. (Communism came to be championed by two hostile parties.) None of these has succeeded fully in attracting a mass following, although Socialist Buddhism has been more successful than the others.

Both secular Socialism and secular Communism have had adherents in Thailand since at least the 1930s, but their importance has been almost insignificant compared with that of both traditional and reform Buddhism. Nonetheless, the persistence of a Communist-led insurrection, mainly in northeastern Thailand, and the minor successes of Socialist parties, again mainly in northeastern Thailand, prove that Communism and Socialism cannot be wholly dismissed as alien ideologies without resonance in Thai society.

Given the relatively minor disruption of life in Cambodia and Laos during the colonial period, neither country would seem likely to have been receptive to radical secular ideologies. However, an important aspect of colonial rule changed this situation. Cambodia and Laos were linked inextricably through colonial rule with Vietnam. In Vietnam (as we shall discuss in Chapter 4), the ideology that succeeded in becoming dominant was Communist. Proponents of Communist ideology, some indigenous Lao and Khmer and some Vietnamese living in Laos and Cambodia who were given the backing first of the Viet Minh and later of the government of the Democratic Republic of Vietnam, were able to exert an influence that they might otherwise not have been able to do.

The political, economic, social, and cultural transformations of Theravada Buddhist societies that were initiated during the colonial period have not yet been fully completed. In the final chapter we shall examine the ongoing processes of change that continue today in these societies, as well as in Vietnam, and that are particularly marked in the cities of the region. First, however, we shall look at rural life in mainland Southeast Asia, beginning with that found in Burma, Thailand, Laos, and Cambodia. In the villages of these countries, Theravada Buddhism, either in its traditional popular forms or in its more recent reformed guises, has continued to provide, at least until quite recently, the grounding for the world view that makes life in the rural areas meaningful.

NOTES

Chapter 2

1. The foremost authority on early Southeast Asian history, Professor George Coedès, first used the term *hindouisé* for those societies that borrowed elements from India. However, most authorities writing in English have preferred the term " Indianization " to avoid the misleading implication that only Hinduism was diffused from India to Southeast Asia. For a recent excellent study of " Indianization " and of the characteristics of " Indianized " civilization, see Paul Wheatley, " Satyānrta in Suvarṇadvīpa: From Reciprocity to Redistribution in Ancient Southeast Asia," in *Ancient Civilization and Trade*, ed. by Jeremy A. Sabloff and

C. C. Lamberg-Karlovsky (Albuquerque: University of New Mexico Press, 1975), pp. 227–83.

2. On this point, see J. C. van Leur, *Indonesian Trade and Society* (The Hague and Bandung: W. van Hoeve, 1955) and O. W. Wolters, *Early Indonesian Commerce* (Ithaca, N.Y.: Cornell University Press, 1967).

3. See George Coedès, *The Indianized States of Southeast Asia*, tr. by Susan Brown Cowing and edited by Walter F. Vella (Honolulu: East-West Center Press, 1968), pp. 37–38; and L. P. Briggs, *The Ancient Khmer Empire* (Philadelphia, Pa.: American Philosophical Society Transactions, No. 41, Part 1, 1951), pp. 26–27.

4. See S. J. Tambiah, *Buddhism and the Spirit Cults in North-East Thailand* (Cambridge: Cambridge University Press, 1970), pp. 296–98; and C. F. Keyes, "A Note on the Ancient Towns and Cities of Northeastern Thailand," *Tonan Ajia Kenkyu* [The Southeast Asian Studies], XI, 4 (1974), pp. 498–500.

5. Coedès, *op. cit.*, p. 48.

6. *Ibid.*, p. 98.

7. George Coedès, *Angkor: An Introduction*, tr. and edited by Emily Floyd Gardiner (Hong Kong: Oxford University Press, 1963), p. 30.

8. *Ibid.*, p. 31.

9. Robert Heine-Geldern, "Weltbïld und Bauform in Südostasien," in *Wiener Beitrage zur Kunst und Kultur Asiens* (1930) as quoted in Codès, *Angkor*, p. 40.

10. *Ibid.*, p. 96.

11. Gordon H. Luce, *Old Burma-Early Pagan* (3 vols., Locust Valley, N.Y.: J. J Augustin, *Artibus Asiae* Supplementum 25, 1969–1970), I, p. 4.

12. The major source of this legend is the early nineteenth-century chronical, the *Hmannan Yazawin*, which has been partially translated under the title of *The Glass Palace Chronicle of the Kings of Burma* (London: Oxford University Press, 1923). It has also been used as the major source by G. E. Harvey, in his *History of Burma* (London: Longmans Green, 1925, reprinted, London: Frank Cass, 1967). For the story of Anorahta, see Harvey, *op. cit.*, pp. 23–34.

13. Luce, *Old Burma-Early Pagan*, p. 33.

14. Harvey, *op. cit.*, p. 33.

15. Luce, *op. cit.*, p. 73.

16. Clifford Geertz, *Islam Observed* (Chicago, Ill.: Chicago University Press, 1968), p. 39.

17. See H. G. Quaritch Wales, *Siamese State Ceremonies* (London: Bernard Quaritch, 1931), p. 302.

18. Charles F. Keyes, "Buddhist Pilgrimage and the Twelve Year Cycle: Northern Thai Moral Orders in Space and Time," *History of Religions*, XV (1975), pp. 71–89.

19. George Coedès, *The Making of South East Asia*, tr. by H. M. Wright (Berkeley and Los Angeles: University of California Press, 1966), p. 126.

20. Coedès, *Indianized States, op. cit.*, p. 189.

21. Cf. Kachorn Sukhanbanij, "The Thai Beach-Head States in the eleventh–twelfth centuries," *Sinlapakon* (Bangkok), I (1957), pp. 1–22. I have also drawn on an

M.A. Thesis, " Early Political Institutions of the Thai: Synthesis and Symbiosis," by Barry M. Broman (University of Washington, 1968).

22. G. Coedès, " Documents sur l'histoire politique du Laos occidental," *Bull. de l'Ecole Française d'Extrême-Orient*, XXV (1925), pp. 31–32; 92ff.

23. A. B. Griswold, *Towards a History of Sukhodaya Art* (Bangkok: The Fine Arts Department, 1967), p. 2.

24. There have been considerable advances in knowledge of the history and culture of Sukhothai, most of which has not yet been incorporated into standard histories of Southeast Asia. See, especially, Griswold's *Towards a History of Sukhodaya Art, op. cit.*, and the studies of Sukhodayan epigraphy by A. B. Griswold and Prasert na Nagara that have appeared in the *Journal of the Siam Society*, LVI, 2 (1968), pp. 207–50; LVII, 1 (1969), pp. 29–148; LVIII, 1(1970), pp. 89–114; LIX, 1 (1971), pp. 153–208; LIX, 2 (1971), pp. 179–228; LX, 1 (1972), pp. 21–152; LXI, 1 (1973), pp. 71–182; LXI, 2 (1973), pp. 91–128; LXII (1974), pp. 89–142.

25. See Griswold, *op. cit.*, pp. 15–16 and Prince Dhani Nivat, *A History of Buddhism in Siam* (Bangkok: The Siam Society, 1965), pp. 5–6.

26. See O. W. Wolters, " A Western Teacher and the History of Early Ayudhya," *Sangkhomsat Pǫrithat* [Social Science Review] (Bangkok), Special Issue No. 3 (1966), pp. 88–97.

27. Michael D. Coe, " Social Typology and the Tropical Forest Civilizations," *Comparative Studies in Society and History*, IV (1961), pp. 83–84.

28. Chou Ta-kuan, *Notes on the Customs of Cambodia*, tr. from French translation of Paul Pelliot by J. Gilman D'arcy Paul (Bangkok: Social Science Association Press, 1976), p. 25.

29. Pierre-Bernard Lafont, " Introduction du Bouddhisme au Laos," *France-Asie*, CLIII–CLVII (1959), pp. 889–92.

30. Theravada Buddhist tradition places the death of the Buddha in 547 B.C., but historical scholarship has established that his death was in 483 B.C. In Theravada Buddhist societies today, the Buddhist Era is calculated to have begun in 547 (or 648) B.C.

31. Luce, in *Old Burma-Early Pagan, op. cit.*, pp. 39–40, summarizes the evidence on this exchange between Vijaya-Bahu and Anoratha.

32. Richard F. Gombrich, *Precept and Practice: Traditional Buddhism in the Rural Highlands of Ceylon* (Oxford: Clarendon Press, 1971), pp. 29–30.

33. See Harvey, *op. cit.*, pp. 55–56.

34. See Luce, *Old Burma-Early Pagan, op. cit.*, pp. 127–28.

35. Coedès, *Indianized States, op. cit.*, p. 178.

36. *Loc. cit.*

37. *Nirvana* is the Sanskrit form of the word used by Buddhists for ultimate salvation. The Pali form is *Nibbana*. Since the Sanskritic forms of Buddhist terms are better known in Western literature, I will employ them rather than Pali forms.

38. The scriptural sources is *Samyutta Nikaya* V. The English translation used here is from *Sources of the Indian Tradition*, compiled by William Theodore de Bary, *et al.* (New York: Columbia University Press, 1958), p. 102. I have changed the

translation of *dukkha* used in this text from "sorrow" to "suffering" as the latter term is in more common usage.

39. Edward Conze, *Buddhism: Its Essence and Development* (New York: Harper and Brothers, 1959 [orig. 1951]), p. 22.

40. For the purposes of the present argument I am ignoring recent changes in the interpretation of Therevada Buddhism, which have occurred in all Theravada Buddhist societies, although as yet affecting only a minority of the populations of these countries. Some of the more important works on "popular" religion in Therevada Buddhist societies include the following: *Theravada Buddhism generally:* Heinz Bechert, *Buddhismus, Staat und Gesellschaft in den Landern des Theravada Buddhismus*, 3 volumes, (Wiesbaden: Otto Harrassowitz, 1966–1967); Heinz Bechert, "Theravada Buddhist Sangha; Some General Observations on Historical and Political Factors in Its Development," *J. Asian Studies*, XXIX (1970), pp. 761–78; Hans-Dieter Evers, "The Buddhist Sangha in Ceylon and Thailand," *Sociologus*, n.s., XXVIII (1968), pp. 20–35; Manning Nash, *et al.*, *Anthropological Studies in Theravada Buddhism* (New Haven: Yale University Southeast Asia Studies, Cultural Report Series No. 13, 1966); Gananath Obeyesekere, "Theodicy, Sin and Salvation in a Sociology of Buddhism," in *Dialectic in Practical Religion*, ed. by E. R. Leach (Cambridge: Cambridge University Press, 1968), pp. 7–40. *Sri Lanka (Ceylon):* Michael M. Ames, "Magical-Animism and Buddhism: A Structural Analysis of the Sinhalese Religious System," in *Aspects of Religion in South Asia*, ed. by Edward B. Harper, in *Journal of Asian Studies*, XXIII (1964), pp. 61–76; Richard F. Gombrich, *Precept and Practice: Traditional Buddhism in the Rural Highlands of Ceylon* (Oxford: Oxford University Press, 1971); G. Obeyesekere, "The Great Tradition and the Little in the Perspective of Sinhalese Buddhism" *J. Asian Studies*, XXII (1963), pp. 139–54. *Burma:* Winston L. King, *A Thousand Lives Away: Buddhism in Contemporary Burma* (Cambridge, Mass.: Harvard University Press, 1965); E. M. Mendelson, "Initiation and Paradox of Power: A Sociological Approach," in *Initiation*, ed. by C. J. Bleeker (Leiden: E. J. Brill, Studies in the History of Religions, Vol. X, 1965), pp. 214–22; Mendelson, *Sangha and State in Burma*, ed. by John P. Ferguson (Ithaca, N.Y.; Cornell University Press, 1975); Manning Nash, "Burmese Buddhism in Everyday Life," *Am. Anthropologist*, LXV (1963), pp. 285–95; Melford E. Spiro, "Buddhism and Economic Action in Burma," *Am. Anthrop.*, LXVIII (1966), pp. 1163–73; M. E. Spiro, *Burmese Supernaturalism* (Englewood Cliffs, N. J.: Prentice-Hall, 1967); M. E. Spiro, *Buddhism and Society* (New York: Harper and Row, 1970). *Thailand:* Jane Bunnag, *Buddhist Monk, Buddhist Layman* (Cambridge: Cambridge University Press, 1973); Richard Davis, "Tolerance and Intolerance of Ambiguity in Northern Thai Myth and Ritual," *Ethnology*, XIII (1974), pp. 1–24; Lucien M. Hanks, Jr., "Merit and Power in the Thai Social Order," *Am. Anthrop.*, LXIV (1962), pp. 1247–61; A. T. Kirsch, "Phu Thai Religious Syncretism" (Ph.D. Dissertation, Harvard University, 1967); Kirsch, "The Thai Buddhist Quest for Merit," in *Southeast Asia: The Politics of National Integration*, ed. by John McAlister (New York: Random House, 1973), pp. 188–201; Kirsch, "Economy, Polity, and Religion in Thailand," in *Change and Persistence in Thai Society: Essays in Honor of Lauriston Sharp*, ed. by G. William Skinner and A. Thomas Kirsch (Ithaca, N.Y.: Cornell University Press, 1975), pp. 172–196; Kirsch, "Modernizing Implications of 19th Century Reforms in the Thai Sangha," in

Contributions to Asian Studies, VIII (1975), pp. 8–23; C. F. Keyes, " Buddhism and National Integration in Thailand," *J. Asian Studies*, XXX (1971), pp. 551–68; Keyes, " Buddhism in a Secular City: A View from Chiang Mai," *Visakha Puja 2518* (Bangkok: Buddhist Association of Thailand, 1975), pp. 62–72; Keyes, " Tug-of-War for Merit: Cremation of a Senior Monk," *J. Siam Society*, XXIII (1975), pp. 44–62; Keyes, " Buddhist Pilgrimage Centers and the Twelve Year Cycle: Northern Thai Moral Orders in Space and Time," *History of Religions*, XV (1975), pp. 71–89; S. J. Tambiah, " The Ideology of Merit and the Social Correlates of Buddhism in a Thai Village," in *Dialectic in Practical Religion*, ed. by E. R. Leach (Cambridge: Cambridge University Press, 1969), pp. 41–121; Tambiah, " *Buddhism and Spirit Cults in Northeastern Thailand* (Cambridge: Cambridge University Press, 1970); Andrew Turton, " Matrilineal Descent Groups and Spirit Cults of the Thai-Yuan in Northern Thailand," *J. Siam Society*, LX, 2 (1972), pp. 217–56; K. E. Wells, *Thai Buddhism: Its Rites and Activities* (Bangkok: Police Press, 1960). *Laos:* C. Archaimbault, " Religious Structures in Laos," *J. Siam Society*, LII (1964), pp. 57–74; Archaimbault, *Structures réligieuses Lao (rites et mythes)* (Vientiane: Vithanga, 1973); George Condominas, " Notes sur le bouddhisme populaire en milieu rural Lao," *Archives de Sociologie de Religions*, XXV (1968), pp. 80–150; Condominas, " Phibān Cults in Rural Laos," in *Change and Persistence in Thai Society*, ed. by Skinner and Kirsch, pp. 252–78; Pierre-Bernard Lafont, " Introduction du Bouddhism au Laos," *France-Asie*, CLIII–CLVII (1959), pp. 889–92; Marcel Zago, *Rites et cérémonies en milieu bouddhiste Lao* (Roma: Universita Gregoriana Editrice, 1972). *Cambodia:* Etienne Aymonier, *Le Cambodge* (3 vols. and index volume, Paris: Leroux, 1900–1904); Adhémard Leclère, *Le Buddhisme au Cambodge* (Paris: Ernest Leroux, 1899); Eveline Porée-Maspero, *Etude sur les rites agraires des Cambodgiens* (3 vols., Paris and the Hague: 1962, 1964, 1969).

41. For a recent statement of this argument, see M. E. Spiro, *Burmese Supernaturalism*, *op. cit.*, pp. 4, 286.

42. Tambiah, *Buddhism and Spirit Cults . . .*, p. 41.

43. Gombrich, *op. cit.*, p. 145.

44. See *Les Trois Mondes* (*Traibhumi Brah R'van*) by G. Coedès and C. Archaimbault (Paris: Publ. de l'Ecole Française d'Extrême-Orient, LXXXIX, 1973). An English translation by Mani and Frank Reynolds is forthcoming.

45. See Keyes, " Buddhism Pilgrimage Centers. . . ."

46. Cf. Kitsiri Melalgoda, "Millennialism in Relation toBuddhism," *Comp. Studies in Society and History*, XII (1970), pp. 424–41; E. Michael Mendelson, " A Messianic Buddhist Association in Upper Burma," *Bull. School Oriental and African Studies*, XXIV (1961), pp. 560–80; E. Sarkisyanz, *Buddhist Backgrounds of the Burmese Revolution* (The Hauge: Martinus Mijhoff, 1965); C. F. Keyes, " The Power of Merit," *Visakha Puja BE 2516* (Bangkok: The Buddhist Association of Thailand, 1973), pp. 95–102; Keyes, "Millennialism, Theravada Buddhism, and Thai Society," *J. Asian Studies*, forthcoming.

47. There are only a few studies of traditional Southeast Asian Buddhist societies for the period between the thirteenth and nineteenth centuries. The standard sources for this period for Burma are G. E. Harvey, *History of Burma*, Arthur Phayre, History of Burma (London: Trübner, 1883). For Thailand, see H. G. Quaritch

Wales, *Ancient Siamese Government and Administration* (London: Bernard Quaritch, Ltd., 1934) and Akin Rabibhadana, *The Organization of Thai Society in the Early Bangkok Period* (Ithaca, N.Y.: Cornell University Southeast Asia Program, Data Paper, No. 74, 1969). For Cambodia, see J. Moura, *Le Royaume du Cambodge* (2 vols., Paris: E. Leroux, 1883) and Adhémard Leclère, *Histoire du Cambodge* (Paris: Paul Guenther, 1914). For Laos, see Paul Le Boulanger, *Histoire du Laos Français* (Paris: Librairie Plon, 1931). *In Search of Southeast Asia: A Modern History*, ed. by David Joel Steinberg (New York: Praeger, 1971), Parts one and two, provides the best overall summary of the social history of traditional Southeast Asian societies. Also see the relevant sections of *A History of South East Asia* by D. G. E. Hall 3rd ed., (London: Macmillan, 1968).

48. Here we will be concerned primarily with French expansion in Cambodia and Laos; in Chapter 4 French expansion in Vietnam will be discussed in more detail.

49. The rationalization of bureaucracy in Burma has been examined by James Guyot in " Bureaucratic Transformation in Burma " in *Asian Bureaucratic Systems Emergent from the British Imperial Tradition* ed. by Ralph Braibanti (Durham, N.C.: Duke University Press, 1966), pp. 354–443. Also see F. S. V. Donnison, *Public Administration in Burma* (London: Royal Institute of International Affairs, 1953) and J. S. Furnivall, *The Governance of Modern Burma*, 2nd ed. (New York: Institute of Pacific Relations, 1960). Donnison and Furnivall had both served as officials in British Burma. The best studies of the bureaucratic and administrative transformations in Thailand are William J. Siffin, *The Thai Bureaucracy* (Honolulu: East-West Center Press, 1966) and Tej Bunnag, " The Provincial Administration of Siam from 1892 to 1915 " (D. Phil. Thesis, Oxford, 1968). On colonial administration in Cambodia, see René Morizon, Monographie du Cambodge (Hanoi: Impr. d'Extrême-Orient, 1931) and A. Silvestre, *Le Cambodge administratif* (Phnom Penh, 1924). For Laos, see Katay D. Sasorith, *Le Laos: son évolution politique, sa place dans l'union Française* (Paris: Editions Berger-Levrault, 1953).

50. Josef Silverstein, " Burma," in *Governments and Politics of Southeast Asia*, ed. by George McT. Kahin, 2nd ed. (Ithaca, N.Y.: Cornell University Press, 1964), p. 79. The best study of the economic impact of British rule on the rural Burmese of lower Burma is *The Burma Delta* by Michael Adas (Madison: University of Wisconsin Press, 1974). Also see Cheng Siok-Hwa, *The Rice Industry of Burma 1852–1940* (Kuala-Lumpur-Singapore: University of Malaya Press, 1968). For Thailand, see James C. Ingram, *Economic Change in Thailand, 1850–1970* (Stanford: Standord University Press, 1971).

51. See J. S. Furnivall, *Netherlands India* (Cambridge: Cambridge University Press 1939), esp. Ch. XII and Furnivall, *Colonial Policy and Practice* (New York: New York University Press, 1956 [first published, 1948]). In the latter book Furnivall discusses Burma, which he knew first hand as a colonial official, and compares it with the Netherlands Indies. On the Chinese in Thailand, see G. William Skinner, *Chinese Society in Thailand* (Ithaca, N.Y.: Cornell University Press, 1957).

52. These figures are based on data discussed by T. G. McGee in the *Southeast Asian City* (London: G. Bell and Sons, 1969).

53. Roger Smith, " Cambodia," in Kahin, *op. cit.*, p. 602.

54. The major source on the economic development of all of the countries of Indo-

china under French rule is *The Economic Development of French Indo-China* by Charles Robequain (London: Oxford University Press, 1944).

55. On the postconquest resistance in Burma, see C. Crossthwaite, *The Pacification of Burma* (London: Longmans, Green and Co., 1912). On the Saya San rebellion, see Donald Eugene Smith, *Religion and Politics in Burma* (Princeton: Princeton University Press, 1965), pp. 107–109; and E. Sarkisyanz, *Buddhist Backgrounds of the Burmese Revolution* (The Hague: Martinus Nijhoff, 1965), pp. 160–65.

56. On the uprisings in Thailand, see Charles F. Keyes, " The Power of Merit," Keyes, " Buddhism and National Integration in Thailand," Keyes, "Millennialism, Theravada Buddhism, and Thai Society," *J. Asian Studies*, forthcoming; and John B. Murdoch, " The 1901–1902 ' Holy Man's Rebellion'," *J. Siam Society*, LXII, 1 (1974), pp. 47–66. This latter source also contains a discussion of the uprising in Laos.

57. Milton E. Osborne, *The French Presence in Cochinchina and Cambodia* (Ithaca, N.Y.: Cornell University Press, 1969), pp. 206–30.

58. See Michael E. Mendelson, " A Messianic Buddhist Association in Upper Burma," *Bull. School of Oriental and African Studies*, XXIV, 3 (1961), pp. 560–80; Mendelson, " Buddhism and Politics in Burma," *New Society*, I, 38 (1963), pp. 8–10; Mendelson, " Buddhism and the Burmese Establishment," *Archives de Sociologie de Religions*, IX, 17 (1964), pp. 85–95; T. Stern, " Ariya and the Golden Book: A Millennary Buddhist Sect among the Karen," *J. Asian Studies*, XXVIII (1968), pp. 297–328; Kitsiri Malalgoda, "Millennialism in Relation to Buddhism, "*Comp. Studies in Society and History*, XII (1970), pp. 424–41.

59. See John S. Furnivall, *Educational Progress in Southeast Asia* (New York: Institute of Pacific Relations, 1943) and Guyot, *op. cit.*

60. Smith, " Laos," in Kahin, *op. cit.*, p. 533.

61. Smith, " Cambodia," in Kahin, *op. cit.*, p. 602–603. Smith bases his statistics for both Laos and Cambodia on Charles Bilondeau, Somlith Pathammavong, and Le Quang Hong, *Compulsory Education in Cambodia, Laos, and Viet-Nam* (Studies on Compulsory Education, no. XIV, Paris: UNESCO, 1955).

62. On the educational reforms of Thailand, see David K. Wyatt, *The Politics of Reform in Thailand: Education in the Reign of King Chulalongkorn* (New Haven: Yale University Press, 1969).

63. On the changes in Buddhism in Burma during the colonial period, see Sarkisyanz, *op cit.*, Donald E. Smith, *op. cit.*, and Mendelson, *Sangha and State in Burma*. Some of my information on the Burmese Buddhist meditation tradition is drawn from interviews with several knowledgable Burmese laymen carried out in March 1973 in Rangoon and Taunggyi.

64. Damrong's observations are from his biography (in Thai) of Mongkut and are quoted (in English translation) in " State and Society in the Reign of Mongkut, 1851–1868," by Constance M. Wilson (Ph.D. Thesis, Cornell University, 1970, p. 260.

65. Craig Reynolds, " The Buddhist Monkhood in Nineteenth Century Thailand," (Ph.D. Thesis, Cornell University, 1973), pp. 82, 113.

66. *Ibid.*, pp. 125–37.

CHAPTER 3
RURAL LIFE IN THE THERAVADA
BUDDHIST SOCIETIES

Between 80 and 85 per cent of the people of Burma, Thailand, Laos, and Cambodia live today—as the vast majority of these populations have always lived—in rural communities (for percentages by country, see Appendix B). The study of life in these villages is of relatively recent vintage, having developed from the colonial period on. The first studies of rural conditions in the region were usually reports on the socioeconomic conditions of some particular part based on surveys made in a large number of villages. A few studies of rural folklore were also carried out, although these usually did not focus on a particular locality. Not until after World War II was something approaching a systematic effort made to study the rural society and culture of the Theravada Buddhist societies. Particularly valuable to this effort were " village studies," that is, accounts of particular local communities by those who had personally lived in them for extended periods of time and who based their writings on observations and interviews made within these communities.

In this chapter, I propose to compare the findings on several different aspects of rural life as reported in studies made in the 1950s and 1960s in lower Burma,[1] upper Burma,[2] central Thailand,[3] northern Thailand,[4] northeastern Thailand,[5] central Laos,[6] and central Cambodia.[7] These comparisons will be interpreted with reference to the history of the region. Although the political and economic contexts to which villagers in the region have adapted have varied considerably, what is striking are the common patterns of rural life that pertain throughout this part of mainland Southeast Asia.

CULTURAL KNOWLEDGE OF THERAVADA BUDDHIST VILLAGERS

Traditional World View

The modes of adaptation adopted by the villagers in Theravada Buddhist Southeast Asia to the natural and social environments in which they live can be understood only with reference to the fundamental nature of reality as it is conceived of by these villagers. As was argued in Chapter 2, Theravada Buddhist beliefs were adopted as the basis of the world views of the peoples throughout the region in the period between about the thirteenth and fifteenth centuries. With only rare exceptions, most villagers today continue to hold to concepts of ultimate reality that are orthodox Theravada Buddhist in nature.

Although the terms are different in the various languages used in the region, all Theravada Buddhist villagers believe that sentient existence is in constant flux, that sentient beings have no enduring essence, and that life is suffering. Absolute reality is the Law of Karma, the impersonal cosmic balance that ensures that every evil action brings an increase in suffering and that every good action brings a decrease. Villagers further believe that karmic causation operates across the boundaries of death and rebirth. Only after many lives of diligent effort can one hope to achieve that successful combination of wisdom, morality, and concentration that results in the transcendence of reality itself, that is, in the attainment of Nirvana.

At birth, one is born into one of the thirty-one planes of existence recognized in the Buddhist cosmology. For Theravada Buddhist villagers the only relevant planes are those of humans, the subhuman realms of spirits, animals, and Hell, and the superhuman realm of Heaven.[8] Each plane has its own characteristics, including what might be called natural laws. Thus, for example, those who live in the heavenly realm do not have to produce food in order to maintain life, whereas those who live in the human realm do. Successful production involves compliance with these natural laws, which regulate the rains, determine how rice should be planted, affect the ripening of the rice plants, and so on. Traditionally, these " natural " laws were conceived of by the peoples of the region in terms of spirits and gods and the " spirit essence " of rice.[9] Today, some few villagers have come to understand these natural laws in terms of modern agricultural technology.

In more general terms, the various theories of causation, including beliefs in spirits, in " vital essence," in gods, in the influences of the stars as well as more modern beliefs such as the germ theory of disease, are to be understood, as Tambiah has argued, in terms of a " total field " of belief that is cosmologically constructed.[10] The Law of Karma provides the ultimate constraints for the systems of beliefs held by most peasants in Theravada Buddhist Southeast Asia. Western writers of an older generation often did not understand how peoples in this region could believe both in the teachings of the Buddha and in the innumerable spirits, the *nats* and *phi*, which were claimed to be the source of the slings and arrows of outrageous fortune. Many such writers thus agreed with LeMay who argued with reference to the people of northern Thailand that Buddhism was merely a decoration, while the true popular religion remained animistic:

> Yet, in spite of the vast number of temples built, the innumerable images of the Lord Buddha fashioned and venerated, the endless pilgrimages to the more famous shrines, the countless store of money spent on gold leaf and incense, and the armies of priests that have been ordained during all these

past centuries, the Lao people remain at heart what they have been from time immemorial, from the earliest days in their ancestral homes in China— animists.[11]

Even modern writers have found it difficult to understand how Buddhism and other " religious " beliefs could belong to a single religious system. Spiro, in writing of upper Burma, thus argues that the Burmese are adherents of two distinctive religions, the one Buddhism and the other supernaturalism. Moreover, he also argues that these two religions are often contradictory.[12]

To posit such a contradiction leads to a distorted understanding of religion in societies in this region. Rather, I agree with Tambiah who argues that Buddhism and animism belong to a single religious system, albeit a system within which a tension between Buddhist and animistic beliefs may sometimes exist.[13] Such a tension is not unique to the Theravada Buddhist world, however. It can be found in any culture in which ambiguity exists about whether particular events have been caused directly by some ultimate cause (e.g., cosmic, or divine law, or, in deistic religions, the " Will of God ") or indirectly through the operation of some proximate cause (e.g., natural law). The various manifestations of this tension are of great interest for the comparative study of religion.

Villagers in Theravada Buddhist Southeast Asia recognize several types of proximate causation. To subsume all of these under the rubric of " supernaturalism " or " animism " or " spirit cults " is to obscure the different forms of causation recognized. There are, to be sure, a variety of supernatural beings in which people of the region believe. The spirits and gods believed in by peoples in this part of mainland Southeast Asia provide explanations for the proximate causes of some types of illnesses and accidents, for the abundance or scarcity of the wild plants and animals they eat, for the fertility of the land in which crops are grown, for the fertility of women, and so on. In addition, as we shall see, spirits serve as cultural projections for certain social groups and are believed by villagers to have the power to enforce compliance with the customs of these groups. According to the cosmology of Theravada Buddhism as it is believed in by villagers, spirits belong to planes of existence below that of humans, whereas gods belong to planes of existence above them.

On occasion certain events can be explained by villagers either as due to a proximate cause, conceived of in terms of spirits or gods, or an ultimate cause, conceived of in terms of the Law of Karma. For example, in a northeastern Thai village a married woman who has been unable to conceive may explain her condition either as a function of low fertility—a condition which can be bettered by seeing the help of the *thewada* (Hindu-derived gods)—or as a function of her karmic heritage about which she can do nothing. Such a woman obviously finds it psychologically more satisfying to continue to perform ritual offerings to the *thewada* in the hopes of becoming fertile than to resign herself to her condition. Only after many years of barrenness will a woman finally accept that Karma is the cause of her condition, not the lack of attention by the gods.

In addition to spirits and gods, all Therevada Buddhists also believe that every human being, rice, and certain animals (e.g., buffaloes and elephants) have a "vital essence," called *leikpya* in Burmese, *khwan* or *khuan* in the various Tai languages, and *pralu'n* in Khmer. In theory, this "vital essence" exists in plural forms, occupying 32 parts of the human body, according to the Thai belief or 19 parts of the body of humans and rice in the Khmer belief.[14] In practice, villagers throughout the region think of the "vital essence" as a unity. The "vital essence" must be in the body of the human, the rice, or the animal lest the human or animal suffer misfortune and eventually die or the rice be deprived of its nutrient quality and its fertility. Thus, periodic rites are performed in order to secure the "vital essence" to the body, such rites for humans occurring on such occasions as a radical change in status, a shift of residence, or a serious accident, or disease. Spiro has said that the Burmese with whom he studied believed the *leikpya* to have an enduring essence, to be able to survive death, and to be reborn again.[15] If this is truly the case, then the Burmese do hold to a belief directly contrary to a basic tenet of Buddhism, namely that beings have no permanent essence. In northeastern Thailand, as among all Tai-speaking peoples, this is not the case. At death, the *khwan* ceases to exist and a new *khwan* is formed at conception. Northeastern Thai villagers believe, instead, that it is "consciousness" (*winyan*; Pali *viññāṇa*) that survives.[16] Such a belief is orthodox Buddhist, as can be seen from the following interpretation of doctrine in the Vissuddhi-Magga, the work of the great systematic Theravada theologian, Buddhaghosa, who lived in the fifth century A.D.:

> For when, in any existence, one arrives at the gate of death either in the natural course of things or through violence; and when, by a concourse of intolerable, death-dealing pains, all the members, both great and small, are loosened and wrenched apart in every joint and ligament; and the body, like a green palm-leaf exposed to the sun, dries up by degrees; and the eye-sight and the other senses fail; and the power of feeling, and the power of thinking, and vitality are making the last stand in the heart—then consciousness residing in that last refuge, the heart, continues to exist by virtue of karma, otherwise called the predispositions. . . .[17]

If the "vital essence" disappears at death, as is the belief in Thailand and Laos, and I suspect, Spiro notwithstanding, in Burma as well,[18] then this belief poses no contradiction with Buddhist belief.

Other beliefs found throughout the region might be subsumed under the label *fate*. By *fate* is meant those fixed cosmic elements—notably the heavenly bodies, the directions, the topography of the land, the elements of the body, the oscillation of day and night, and so on—whose juxtaposition can influence the course of events. In Burma, one's orientation to the cosmic elements, summarized in a horoscope called *sadā*, is determined shortly after birth and is consulted thereafter throughout life whenever any important changes in regular patterns have occurred or are contemplated.[19] In northern Thailand, similar attention is shown to the orientations toward the cosmic elements, an orientation subsumed under the term *cata*, a word cognate to the Burmese word.[20] Throughout Thailand, and in Laos, ill fate, which can be corrected through ritual action, is known under the term *khrọ* or *khọ* (from the Sanskrit *gṛha*). The ritual action involves the reorientation of an individual to the cosmic elements.[21]

The concept of fate is less easily rationalized in terms of Buddhist cosmology than are other concepts held by peoples in the Theravada Buddhist societies. *Fate* implies a causation that operates irrespective of the moral actions of people, whereas the Buddhist concept of Karma relates all causation ultimately to moral action. Yet, despite the apparent contradiction, most people in the Theravada Buddhist world, since about the fifteenth century at least, have conceived of fate as a proximate, not an ultimate form of causation. Human beings are subject to the influences of fate, because they have been born in the human realm. However, even in this realm these influences are limited to the vicissitudes of living and not to ultimate concerns. Any fundamental aspect of suffering, including death itself, is caused by Karma not fate.[22]

Karma, as we have already seen, provides an explanation for the cosmo-logical divisions of samsaric existence and for some of the fundamental divisions within each cosmological plane as well. In other words, it is because of actions performed in a previous existence that one is born as an animal, a spirit, a human, or a god, and, if one is born a human, these previous actions also determine whether one is born a man or woman, whether one is born rich or poor, powerful or powerless, beautiful/handsome or ugly and deformed. But, one is not absolutely fixed in a hierarchy of relative suffering because of past actions. One's place in this hierarchy may change during the course of a lifetime because the Karma that determined the previous position has " burnt itself out." Moreover, one has a considerable freedom of choice in regard to one's actions, one's choices determining the Karma that will in turn have consequences in this or a subsequent existence.

Traditional Ethos

The ideas of Karma and of the cosmological structure of existence that comprise the traditional world view of villagers in Burma, Thailand, Laos, and Cambodia serve not only to make the world meaningful but also to define ways of acting in the world. In other words, the world view of Theravada Buddhist villagers is associated with a distinctive ethos. Great emphasis is given in this ethos to the actions that can effect alterations in relative suffering. All students of popular religion in Theravada Buddhist Southeast Asia agree that the salvation goal of almost all Buddhists is not Nirvana, at least not in the next lifetime, but a better rebirth. To achieve this goal it is necessary to avoid demeritorious actions (Pali *pappa*) and to perform acts of merit (Pali *puñña*).

All people in the region agree that the major acts of demerit to be avoided include the actions proscribed in the five precepts:

In undertake the precept to abstain from taking life.
In undertake the precept to abstain from taking what is not given.
I undertake the precept to abstain from improper sexual acts.
I undertake the precept to abstain from telling lies.

I undertake the precept to abstain from imbibing or ingesting substances which cause heedlessness.

In addition to transgressions of the precepts, people throughout the region also conceive of action that results in demerit as being that which entails giving vent to one of the three cardinal vices of *lobha* (" greed "), *dosa* (" anger "), or *moha* (" delusion "). The vice of greed includes being stingy, selfish, avaricious, and lustful after wealth one did not inherit. Those whose behavior could be characterized as *dosa* are people who give vent to passionate expression of temper, to aggressiveness, and to lust for power over others. Those who do not avail themselves of the opportunity to learn the teachings of Buddhism and who ignore the advice of those who are learned may be described as being deluded. It is widely believed that those whose behavior reveals attachments to one of the three vices will be reborn in an appropriate subhuman state in the next life. Those who are afflicted by delusion may be reborn as animals whose dumbness makes it impossible for them to learn. Those who are afflicted by anger may be reborn as vengeful ghosts, condemned to continue actions that make it almost impossible (but not totally) to make merit. And those who are afflicted by greed might be reborn as *preta*, ghosts who have enormous stomachs, but extremely small mouths and find, thus, that they never can eat enough to satisfy their appetites.

As a good Buddhist, one should undertake to keep the precepts and avoid the three vices; one should also seek to perform acts that result in merit. Meritorious acts include those that are the positive inversions of the three vices. Instead of being greedy, one should be compassionate, charitable, and merciful (Pali *mettā* and *karuṇā*); instead of being angry and aggressive, one should maintain equanimity (*upekkhā*). And instead of being deluded, one should seek wisdom (*paññā*). Through the practice of these three virtues in the course of everyday life, one will gain merit.

In traditional thought, the most marked method for gaining merit was through the performance of certain ritual acts, among the more important being various acts of charity (*dāna*) whereby a lay person makes an offering, ranging from a simple meal to monks to the expenditure of large amounts of wealth for the construction of a major religious edifice. Another major ritual act of merit making is the ordination of a person into the Buddhist Sangha. Ordinations are also considered acts of *dāna*, since the parents of the person ordained sacrifice their son to the order and the person ordained sacrifices the pleasures of the world in order to become a mendicant. Yet other ritual acts include the giving (by members of the Sangha) and listening to (by the laity) of sermons on Dharmic subjects and the performing of acts of veneration to the Three Gems (the Buddha, the Dharma, and the Sangha). Such veneration may be conducted on a regular basis at the local temple or undertaken at some important shrine that can only be reached after a pilgrimage of perhaps as much as several hundred kilometers. Yet another form of merit making is meditation (*bhāvanā*). Although meditation is usually interpreted by students of Buddhism to be action appropriate for those intent on achieving Nirvana, it is conceived of by peoples throughout the region as one important means for acquiring merit. Meditation, as an act of merit making, is performed particularly by those who in their old age have begun to prepare themselves for their approaching death.

Throughout the region, villagers believe that merit can be made not only for oneself, through ritual and ethical acts, but that it can also be shared with others. Such sharing of merit (which in Thai, for example, is called *caek bun,* " to distribute merit ") occurs regularly at the end of every ritual act of merit making when the merit maker pours a libation of water and asks the Goddess of the Earth to carry the merit to all sentient beings. More important acts of sharing merit take place at funerals, when relatives of the deceased make merit in order to ensure that the departed relative will have a good rebirth. Those who " have merit," that is, those who have a store of good Karma from previous existences, may also share their merit with others, thereby effecting immediate reduction of suffering in the lives of those who receive the merit. Monks who are renowned for their virtuosity in meditation or for their learning may be believed to " have merit," which can be tapped by those who suffer from an affliction. As we shall see, those who hold legitimate power are also believed to be persons who " have merit," which they can share with others.

Merit is sought by villagers in the region, because it is believed that such merit, the consequence of moral acts, will effect a reduction in suffering either in this life or the next. Demerit, on the other hand, will bring about an increase in suffering. In traditional thought, it is believed that relative degrees of suffering are associated with a hierarchy of states into which one is born because of the Karma, the balance of merit and demerit, inherited from previous existences. Depending on the state into which one is born, one has more or less freedom to act, that is, to undertake actions that will change one's Karma.

Communication of the Cultural Tradition

Villagers in the region acquire their understanding of the traditional world view and ethos through a variety of processes of enculturation. One of the more important processes, and one that has received some attention in studies made in the region, is early infancy socialization.[23] Piker, who studied socialization in a rural community in central Thailand, has argued that early infancy socialization provides the " general content and structure both to definitions of mundane, interpersonal situations and to orientation to the world of the supernatural."[24] The Burmese, according to Spiro, who has studied the same process in a village in upper Burma, hold to their beliefs, because early childhood socialization has provided them with the experiences that made these beliefs meaningful.[25] Rather than assigning to childhood socialization the *cause* for *why* certain beliefs are adopted, it is more useful to think of experience, including childhood experience, and beliefs as belonging to a circuit wherein the one serves to reinforce the other. From their beliefs, parents derive the values that inform their action in socializing children; the experience of children (including infancy experience) in turn makes the beliefs offered to them in the process of postinfancy education meaningful. Although not formulated precisely in this way, Phillips has recognized the importance of both the experience of childhood and the values, which he argues are " cultural derivatives of Buddhist doctrine," that inform interpersonal relations.[26]

Although the importance of early socialization cannot be denied, it is not the only process by which villagers acquire their cultural tradition. From their earliest years, villagers learn meanings through their traffic in public symbols. The village temple monastery often contains paintings that portray themes from the life of the Buddha, from the Jataka tales (the stories of former lives of the Buddha), or from Buddhist cosmology. Invariably, several images of the Buddha will be found in the various buildings of the temple monastery and images of the Buddha are often found in private homes as well. Each image provides a condensation of religious ideas. The most common image of the Buddha to be found in village temple monasteries is one in which the Buddha sits in the pose known as " calling the earth to witness." This pose recalls when the Buddha was engaged in the meditation that would lead him to enlightenment. He is tempted to many worldly pleasures and comforts by Mara, the Buddhist equivalent of the Devil, but he resists these temptations and calls on the earth (depicted in paintings as a Goddess) to witness his steadfastness of purpose. For villagers the image carries the meaning that whatever temptations the world may pose, true reality can be found only through emulation of the Buddha.

The organization of space in the temple monastery and even the organization of space in village houses also carry meanings for those who live in rural communities in the region. The use of space in the temple monastery retains something of the quality of a microcosm of the cosmos, which in former times was expressed in much more elaborate form in the architecture of Pagan and Angkor. Tambiah has also shown how the structure of space in a village house in northeastern Thai villages serves to reiterate messages about the structure of social relations and the ordering of the classifications of animals.[27]

One of the more important processes whereby villagers obtain cultural knowledge, today as in the past, is their participation in or witnessing of rituals performed during the year. Every village has its ritual cycle consisting of collective rites that mark changes in the seasons and in the organization of labor. Other rites, such as those associated with the ordination of a boy or man into the Buddhist monastery or with the construction of a new edifice at a temple monastery, signify that someone in the village has achieved religious virtue. Only rites of affliction, that is, those rites whose purpose is to effect a cure, and some rites of passage (notably those associated with birth), are private. Even these rites are performed sufficiently often to be a common source of cultural knowledge for most villagers. Rituals present the participants and the observers with condensed and highly repetitive summaries of their belief systems. As Tambiah has demonstrated with reference to rituals in a northeastern Thai village, " cosmological and supernatural categories are embedded in the rituals " of the village.[28] The same can be said of rituals in villages in all parts of the region.[29]

Dance dramatization of the myth of the Salween butterfly performed by Shans in Mae Sariang, northern Thailand. (*C. F. Keyes photograph*)

Burmese dancer and orchestra in Mae Sariang, northern Thailand. (*C. F. Keyes photograph*)

Rather closely related to ritual as a medium of cultural communication are the traditional forms of drama and folk opera found throughout the region. Whether it be the shadow puppet plays so popular in southern Thailand, the troubadour singing found in northern and northeastern Thailand, in Laos, and in Cambodia, the dance dramatizations of myth found among the Shans, the folk dramas of central Thailand and Burma, or the folk operas of northeastern Thailand, some form of popular entertainment accompanies any major festival. The themes of these performances, based often on texts kept in the monasteries, may be drawn from the Jataka tales of the Buddhist tradition, from other legends of Indian origin, or from local myths, legends, and courting lore.[30]

In order to use traditional texts, whether in the performance of folk operas, folk dramas, or rituals, in the presentation of sermons, or for some other purpose, it is necessary to be literate.[31] Traditionally, formal instruction in language was conducted by monks at temple monasteries in the majority of villages in the region. The texts used for language instruction often presented in didactic form the themes presented symbolically in other forms. For example, traditional Thai school primers laid great emphasis on the respect that should be shown to the Buddha, to the Sangha, to one's parents, and to one's political superiors. Also stressed were basic Buddhist moral values, that is, that one should keep the Five Precepts, avoid the Three Vices, and display the Three Virtues, especially that of equanimity.

It was the traditional expectation that every boy would receive at least some rudimentary degree of educational instruction in order to prepare for entrance into the Sangha. Since girls were barred by their sex from entering the order, they never attended the traditional monastic schools. Some of the boys who began as " temple boys " or " disciples of the temple " became members of the Sangha and continued their studies. They might travel to a center, usually at a monastery in another village, where more advanced instruction was offered than was available in their home village. Monks would offer instruction in Pali language (the sacred language of Theravada Buddhism) and in the interpretation of sacred texts. Those who showed particular aptitude might then go on to a center of higher education in the capital of the country. Traditionally, the kings of Burma and Siam, and perhaps of other Theravada Buddhist countries as well, witnessed the examinations given to the most advanced religious scholars in their domains. Today, in Thailand, Laos, and Cambodia, monks who pass the basic examinations in the Pali language set by the Sangha and taught at designated local centers receive the title of *mahā* (" great "), a title they carry with them even if they leave the order. A monk who achieves even higher levels of educational attainment receives successively more advanced " degrees."

Those who chose to continue their studies beyond the level of basic literacy were not limited in the past, nor are they today, to the field of sacred Buddhist knowledge. Almost every village monastery still has a library of non-Buddhist texts containing knowledge in such fields as customary law, herbal medicine, astrology, love magic, " vital essence " calling and securing, and spirit exorcism.

Larger libraries may also contain works of poetry, local history, and legend. Traditionally, some texts also circulated outside the temple monasteries. Texts on sorcery, for example, were passed from hand to hand and would rarely be found in a monastic library except when a local monk might be a specialist in countersorcery. Today, many traditional texts have been printed and even more copies are in private circulation than are found in monastery libraries.

These who devoted themselves to the acquisition of knowledge that could be put to practical uses such as curing, divination or the retelling of myths or legends (usually as a troubadour or in some other entertainment form), received in the past and still receive today in much of the area recognition as a specialist by their fellow villagers. In northeastern Thailand, for example, such specialists are designated by the general status title, *mọ*, a title that today is usually transated as " doctor." In Burma, similar specialists are called *saya*, a title indicating he possession of a skill learned through the study of texts.

Traditional education still exists in parts of the region, although it is rarely the only form available. Nash reports that in upper Burma a traditional monastic school existed side by side with a modern government school in the village of Nondwin and that a few boys there received only a monastic and no secular education.[32] More commonly, only those boys who actually enter the Sangha as novices receive a monastic education. As modern secular education has spread throughout the region, traditional education—and traditional knowledge gained from sources other than monastic schools—has come to be challenged by new types of cultural knowledge.

Modern Education and Cultural Change

In Burma and Thailand today, most village children, male and female alike, receive a basic secular education, limited in most cases to no more than four years of training. By 1970, secular schools had also been established in most of the villages of Cambodia, although the war brought instruction in much of Cambodia to a virtual standstill. In Laos, extension of secular education to the rural areas has been slower than in other parts of the region; nevertheless, by 1975, some efforts were being made to establish schools in rural areas.

The governments of all the countries in the region have seen the inculcation in students of a sense of national identity as one of the major purposes of secular education.[33] This theme is given curricular expression not only in the teaching of such subjects as history and geography but also in the constant and repetitive use of national symbols in a variety of contexts. In Thailand, for example, each school day opens with the raising of the national flag and the singing of the national song. A second objective of modern secular education is the attainment of literacy by the populace. In some cases, for example, among the Shans of Burma and the northern and northeastern Thai, the literacy inculcated through modern secular education is in a language or dialect different from that spoken by the local people. Thus, those who wish to become literate in the national language, or conversely those who wish to acquire a knowledge of traditional texts, may have to study two languages. Modern secular education also seeks to instruct the citizens of the country in the rudiments of modern science, geography, arithmetic, and the like. Insofar as my own observations from northeastern Thailand can be generalized, instruction in modern curricular subjects at the primary level has been too limited to become fully absorbed without additional reinforcement outside the school context.

Such reinforcement has sometimes been provided by what might be termed " extension " education. For example, a government may send community development workers to villages to teach sanitation or agricultural techniques. Village leaders may be brought together by a government agency for a seminar on agricultural credit. Traditional village practitioners may be given instruction by government health teams in the fundamentals of modern health care delivery. Village women may (as I observed in northeastern Thailand) receive instruction in clothes-making provided by the store that had sold them a sewing machine, and so on.

A rather different form of " extension " education found in Thailand today is that provided by monks who have been sent to villages to conduct what might be termed moral rearmament campaigns.[34] In a similar vein, Communist cadres in Laos, Cambodia, and, to a lesser extent, in Thailand and Burma have gone into villages to teach rural people interpretations of the nature of the social order that are radically different from those associated with the Buddhist cosmological world view.

Yet another source of cultural change in rural communities in the area is to be found in the new mass media. Radios are nearly ubiquitous in the villages of rural Thailand and are not uncommon in other rural areas of the region. Thai villagers also have regular opportunities to see films, and not a few have access to television. Films and TV are rarely seen, however, by villagers elsewhere in the region.

The radio programs listened to by villagers also communicate certain aspects of traditional culture. For example, Thai villagers have the opportunity to listen to performances of traditional folk opera and troubadour singing on the radio. Traditional forms may also be employed on the radio to communicate new messages. In Laos, for example, both the Royal Lao Government and Pathet Lao radio stations carried programs in which interpretations of contemporary events were presented in the context of troubadour singing. A similar form was used in northeastern Thailand to present the essentials of a government community development program. Yet other programming is new in both form and content. Villagers who have access to radios may listen to programs from official government stations, from " liberation " stations, from Radio Peking, the BBC, VOA, and so on. They may listen to the news, or interpretations thereof, to modern popular music, quasi-educational programs (e.g., foreign language teaching), soap operas, religious programming, or a variety of advertisements. How much such programming is actually listened to in the villages is not known except in the case of Thailand. There, it would appear, villagers tend to listen mainly to programming in traditional forms, whether or not the messages are new.

New messages have also been introduced into villages in printed form. Although villagers purchase few books or periodicals, posters and booklets printed by government agencies are a common phenomena in the rural areas. Posters, and other literature with graphic illustrations, have been somewhat effective in promoting government-sponsored messages, or rather in communicating those symbols that villagers recognize their government wishes them to know.

With the creation of modern systems of transportation, it has become increasingly possible for villagers to travel from their homes to the cities and to return again. They bring back to their homes their impressions of Bangkok, Vientiane, Rangoon, or Phnom Penh and discuss them with those villagers who have not had the opportunity to visit these cities. Whatever the nature of these impressions, they undoubtedly involve a recognition of the disparities that exist between the world of the village and the world of the city. We shall return to a consideration of the implications of this recognition in the last chapter. For the moment, we shall restrict our attention to the fact that these impressions also serve to reinforce messages the villagers receive from other sources and that together these impressions pose a challenge to the traditional knowledge held by rural people.

Some villagers are beginning to put forward explanations for the ways in which they adapt to the natural, psychological, and social environments in which they live in terms other than those derived from traditional culture. It is not uncommon today in central Thailand, for example, to meet villagers who no longer see the rice cycle as subject to influences by fate or by the *devas*, but rather as subject to the influences of chemical inputs, water management, and so on. Spiro found that a significant number of village men who he interviewed in a village in upper Burma expressed skepticism about the existence of *nats*, or spirits. Such skepticism was rare, however, among village women.[35] Throughout the region, villagers have become increasingly willing to receive modern medical treatment, even though they see this as an addition to rather than a substitute for traditional medical practices. How widespread the rejection of traditional ideas and the adoption of modern ones by villagers in the region really is has yet to be fully assessed, however. It would appear that villagers in central Thailand have probably abandoned more of their traditional beliefs than villagers anywhere else in the region, whereas villagers lying in the more remote areas of Laos would be likely to retain many traditional patterns of life.

No matter what the degree of modernization, traditional ideas, nonetheless, still continue to be widely held. Moreover, few villagers who have adopted new ideas reject the fundamental concepts of the traditional system. Ideas concerning merit and demerit involved in the conception of Karma, together with the derivative idea that although one's situation in life is both affected by past Karma one is also free to create new Karma, continue to provide the grounding for the cultural meanings that villagers throughout the region use in adapting to the world as they experience it.

POPULATION AND SOCIAL STRUCTURE

Demography and Health

During the course of the past century or so, the rural populations of Theravada Buddhist Southeast Asia have increased at rates unparalleled in their previous histories. The various countries of the region experienced some degree of population growth during the latter half of the nineteenth century, yet even greater growth, on the average of about 2 per cent per year, between the turn of the century and World War II, and between $2\frac{1}{2}$ and $3\frac{1}{2}$ per cent per year since the war, with Thailand apparently experiencing the most rapid overall population growth in the region.[36] One of the more important factors in bringing about high population growth rates has been the reduction in the death rate, particularly in infant mortality rate. The decline in death and infant mortality rates has continued to the present. For example, between 1962 and 1970 the crude annual death rate in Burma declined from 18.9 to 10.2 per thousand, whereas in Thailand the rate declined from 7.9 to 6.5 per thousand in the same period. The annual infant mortality rate in Thailand declined from 44.7 in 1962 to 25.5 per thousand in 1970, and in Burma the decline was even more dramatic, dropping from 139.3 per thousand in 1962 to 62.8 per thousand in 1970.[37] Although statistics are not available for Laos, there has also probably been a decline in death and infant mortality rates there too. In Cambodia, however, the war most certainly resulted in an increase in both rates for the period between 1970 and 1975. Cambodia's recent experience notwithstanding, the overall direction of death and infant mortality rates has been markedly downward throughout the region since at least the latter part of the nineteenth century. In order to explain these dramatic declines in mortality rates, it is necessary to examine changes in nutrition and health care delivery.

The staple food in all Southeast Asian villages is rice, of which as many as thirty different types are recognized. The Burmese, central Thai, and Khmer all eat, as their basic staple, varieties of rice that are variants of the white rice commonly known to Westerners. The northern and northeastern Thai and the Lao eat as their staple those varieties of rice usually termed " glutinous " or " sticky " in English. Glutinous rice is also known to other peoples of the region but is only used for making desserts.

What villagers in the region eat with their rice varies to some degree according to cultural tradition and to the relative wealth of the villagers. Nonetheless, there is a family relationship in the diet of all villagers throughout the region. The most important source of protein for Theravada Buddhist Southeast Asians is fish in one form or another. Although some fish is fried or toasted over charcoal fires and some is eaten cooked in " soups " or " stews " (sometimes misleadingly referred to as " curries "), the most common form in which fish (and shrimp) is found at the meals of Southeast Asian villagers is that in which the fish has been fermented in brine.[38] The *ngapi* of the Burmese, *kapi* and *pla ra* of the central Thai, *pa daek* of the northeastern Thai and Lao, and *prahoc* of the Khmer are found in one form or another at almost every meal. Fish soya (best known in the West under the Vietnamese term *nuoc mam*) is also often used for seasoning in the preparation of many dishes.

Villagers in the region eat very little meat compared to Westerners. Among the Burmese, the Buddhist injunction against the taking of life is interpreted as a proscription of the slaughter of any animals for food or other purposes. Although some villagers slaughter some animals (particularly fowl), those who do so are likely to be looked on as having transgressed Buddhist moral principles. In contrast, throughout Thailand, Laos, and Cambodia, the slaughter of chickens, particularly for feasts or for serving to honored guests, is quite common and elicits little moral censure. The slaughter of larger animals, however, is looked on as bringing demerit to the one who performs the act, although not to those who consume the meat thus produced. Since someone, in some cases a Muslim or a Chinese, can almost always be found to slaughter animals, the rarity of beef or pork in the diet of Thai, Khmer, and Lao villagers is more a function of economics than of morality.

In addition to rice and fish in some form, the villagers of the region also eat a variety of vegetables, including cucumbers, squashes, certain types of aquatic plants, cabbages, cauliflower, beans, and some root vegetables such as yams. Often foods are prepared with peppers and are thus spicy hot. Fruits are sometimes eaten as vegetables, (for example, papaya and jack fruit) and sometimes as sweets. When eaten as sweets, fruits such as mangoes, oranges, pineapples, bananas, and, for those who can afford it, the pungent durian are often eaten between meals rather than with them. In recent years, cheap manufactured sweets (candies and cookies, the latter often made of cassava flour) have found their way into even remote villages in the region.

Among the beverages consumed by villagers in the region, the most evident are the rice beer and whiskey the villagers often make themselves. Only in Burma has the Buddhist injunction against ingesting those things that cause one to lose control of one's senses been interpreted (by some, but not all) as proscribing the consumption of alcoholic beverages. Although village men throughout Thailand, Laos, Cambodia, and often Burma as well drink rice beer and whiskey on festivel occasions (and sometimes more often), women rarely consume these beverages. In some parts of the region, tea is a regular beverage, but it is not consumed much in the villages of northeastern Thailand or Laos. In northern Thailand and the Shan States, tea is fermented and chewed for its slight narcotic effect. Elsewhere in the region, betel nut is prepared and chewed for the same purpose. Coffee is almost unknown in the villages, although villagers will visit coffee houses when they go to town. Traditionally, the only sweet drink taken by villagers was the liquid from inside a coconut; in recent years, commercially produced colored sweetened water and soft drinks have found their way into villages and are commonly consumed on feast days.

Although somewhat dated, one of the best studies on nutrition that takes into account the cultural attitudes toward food held by villagers in a specific community is that made by Hazel M. Hauck and her associates in the central Thai village of Bang Chan in 1952–1954.[39] Hauck reports that vegetables are introduced rather late in the diet of the infant in Bang Chan, apparently because villagers believe vegetables to be " hot " foods, that is, foods believed to excite one both physiologically and emotionally.[40] The findings of Hauck and her associates that nutritional deficiencies existed in the diet of rural Thai villagers were confirmed by a national nutritional survey in Thailand in 1960. The survey found deficiencies in total caloric intake, in thiamine, and in riboflavin. There was also evidence of protein malnutrition and vitamin A deficiencies in infants and children. Goiter was also found to be common in the northern and northeastern parts of the country.[41]

Although there have been some improvements in diet in certain parts of rural Thailand in the fifteen years since the nutrition study, the findings of the survey still remain true for much of rural Thailand and are indicative of the state of nutrition among all populations in the region. In general, it would appear that villagers in rural Theravada Buddhist Southeast Asia have not seen marked improvements in nutrition during the past century. This being the case, the decline in mortality rates throughout the region is explainable in reference to the improvements in health care delivery.

As we have already observed, traditional theories of disease and health care are still strongly held by villagers in the region.[42] Some illnesses are believed to be caused by spirits against whom some offense has been committed. In such cases, mediums may be called on to contact (often through possession) the relevant spirit in order to ascertain from the spirit the act that caused offense and the action (often including an offering to the spirit) that should be taken in order to persuade the spirit to cease its malevolence. Some illnesses are believed to be caused by a malevolent spirit possessing the individual and consuming the person's vital essence, an act that if not arrested will result in the death of the individual. In such a case, an exorcist must be called in to rid the host of the unwanted spirit possessing him or her.

Witchcraft, which looms so importantly in African theories of illness, holds a very minor place in the medical theories held by villagers in Theravada Buddhist Southeast Asia. Beliefs in witches appear to be more prevalent in Burma than they are in other parts of the region.[43] Although most people I knew in Thailand could relate well-known witch tales, very few were able to recall any actual incidence of witchcraft. In short, my observations confirm those of Tambiah who found witchcraft in northeastern Thai villages to be a " peripheral " phenomenon.[44]

Some illnesses are believed by villagers in all parts of the region to be caused by the loss of the " vital essence " of the individual. When loss of " vital essence " is suspected as the cause of an illness, a specialist will be called in, who through enticements of words and magical offerings is able to recall the vital essence and " tie it " to the body.

Other illnesses are believed to be caused when one is in disharmony with the cosmic elements, that is, when the elementary composition of one's body and the directions taken by one's acts are out of tune with the astrological constellations and the basic elements of fire, wind, earth, and water. When cosmic disharmony is diagnosed as the cause of an illness, another type of specialist is called in. This specialist will attempt through ritual acts and the prescription of certain appropriate " medicines " to effect a reorientation of the individual and the individual's elements such that harmony with the cosmic elements is once again achieved. Associated with this aspect of the traditional theory of medicine is the belief, held by people throughout the region, that some foods are inherently " hot " and some " cold"' and that, depending on the state of the individual, " hot " foods may or may not be eaten. " Hot " foods not only include some that because of their spiciness would lead Westerners to think of them that way but also foods such as certain fruits (e.g., lychees, durian, and so on) that have no apparent connection with the category, " hot," to the Westerner.

Throughout the region, villagers also employ herbal remedies, some, if not most, of which are conceived of fundamentally in terms of cosmic harmonies. Almost every adult will know of the curative qualities of salt, of certain leaves, of some kinds of juices, and so on. In addition, in most villages there may also be someone who has a rather more specialized knowledge of herbal medicines. This specialist is usually one who is also skilled in one or other of the curing arts.

In addition to using traditional medical practices, villagers have also been provided with certain modern health care services. The more successful of these services have been those directed at bringing communicable diseases under control. One of the more widespread diseases in the area has been malaria. Since World War II, all the countries of the region have attempted to bring malaria under control through programs, sponsored in part by WHO, which have involved the spraying of domiciles and other breeding grounds of mosquitoes with DDT. The accomplishments of this program have been negated to some extent in recent years by the emergence of a DDT-resistant strain of mosquito and by the disruption of the programs by the war in Cambodia and Laos. Some success has also been achieved in the control of other diseases such as smallpox, cholera, and leprosy. In contrast, there has been little success in controlling the ingestion of parasites commonly found among the rural peoples of the region, since such control involves radical changes in diet.

Where delivery of modern health care depends on consistent attention by a person skilled in modern health care techniques, the rural areas of the region have not benefited greatly. Even Thailand, which has the largest number of trained modern medical personnel of any country in the region, has few trained persons at centers accessible to villagers. Doctors and nurses in Thailand have preferred to remain in towns and cities, where they can gain additional income through private practice and can maintain a higher standard of living than they could in the rural areas. Delivery of modern health care has also been greatly restricted in Burma by a severe lack of medicines. In Laos and particularly in Cambodia, the war has brought efforts to extend modern health care delivery to the countryside to almost a complete standstill. Although there would be some resistance, for cultural reasons, on the part of rural people to accepting certain aspects of modern health care, such resistance is a very minor factor compared to the difficulties of getting modern health care into the countryside.

Despite the fact that great improvements in rural health care delivery remain to be accomplished, there is still no question but that health standards in rural Theravada Buddhist Southeast Asia today are qualitatively different from those in premodern times. It is primarily due to improvements in the control of illness that significant declines in mortality rates have occurred throughout the region.

Although death and infant mortality rates have declined, fertility, particularly in the rural areas, has remained high in Burma, Thailand, Laos, and Cambodia. A study of fertility made in Thailand in 1968/9 and 1969/70 found that the fertility level in the population of rural Thai women " fits well within the range of . . . values characterizing populations where the absence of deliberate fertility limitation has been fairly well established."[45] Although the level of fertility in Thailand may be higher than that of other countries of Theravada Buddhist Southeast Asia—data are not available to make such a comparison— it is more probable that the conclusion drawn above in regard to fertility levels in Thailand could also be applied to Burma, Laos, and Cambodia. The significant contrast in fertility lies not among the rural populations in the different countries of the region, but between rural and urban populations. The same study carried out in Thailand found that

> Among the most important differences in fertility levels within the Thai population, are those found between rural and urban sectors of the society. . . . Rural women experience the highest fertility and women residing in Bangkok-Thonburi, the only truly metropolitan area in the country, experience the lowest fertility. Provincial urban women are characterized by an intermediate fertility level which is closer, however, to the experience of women in the capital than to their counterparts in the countryside.[46]

Comparable statistics are not available for Burma, Laos, and Cambodia, but there is strong impressionistic evidence to suggest that similar contrasts between the fertility of rural and urban women exist in these countries.

It is sometimes said that rural people have large families because they are ignorant of any means to control birth. For rural people in this part of mainland Southeast Asia, such a conclusion is only partially true. Jane Hanks found in the central Thai village of Bang Chan that although Buddhist villagers did not talk openly of traditional abortifacients and contraceptives, they certainly knew of their existence.[47] M. Nash reports that in the village of Yadaw in upper Burma there was no knowledge of contraception (including the rhythm method), but several methods of abortion were known. These methods were used solely by women who became pregnant out of wedlock.[48] In general, it can be said that villagers in all parts of the region have knowledge of ways of either controlling birth or of effecting abortions that are not dependent on exposure to modern ideas of birth control. The limited use to which such practices appear to have been put can be explained, I believe, by the fact that until quite recently infant mortality was high and most villagers wished to have enough children to carry out the economic and religious functions that in Theravada Buddhist Southeast Asia are organized with reference to kinship ties.

In Burma, Cambodia, and Laos little effort has been made to introduce modern methods of contraception into the rural communities. In Thailand, however, such efforts have been going on since the early 1960s and have recently been very much intensified. Despite these efforts, women still appear to be continuing to have large numbers of children. A study of fertility in Thailand reports that as of the early 1970s " rural women, who constitute the vast majority of Thai women, . . . average over six live births by the time they reach the end of their childbearing years."[49]

This statistic may be somewhat misleading, however, as the introduction of birth control methods and devices into rural Thailand is still so recent that a full assessment of the degree of their acceptance and utilization cannot yet be made. It is likely that the knowledge of contraception has not yet been widely disseminated in Thailand and that many rural women still do not have easy access to inexpensive birth control methods and devices. Moreover, the study just cited also reports that rural women desire an average of four children, not six. Finally, as we shall now see, rural people in Thailand, as in the rest of the region, no longer feel impelled to have large families because not all important aspects of social action are structured with reference to kinship.

Fundamental Bases of Social Structure

The kinship structures of the Theravada Buddhist societies have been generally characterized as " bilateral," " cognatic," or " nonunilineal."[50] By this is meant that these structures are not based on a principle of descent that stresses either the male or the female side. Such a characterization is, in fact, not entirely valid, and the inappropriateness of such a generalization reflects the problem of forcing the social patterns of all peoples who live within state societies into a single mold. The ruling elites of several of the Therevada Buddhist societies have long recognized a principle of patrilineal descent in connection with the allocation of power. Even today, when hereditary rights to power have been eliminated in most parts of the region, a patrilineal principle remains in force for determining succession to the thrones of Thailand and Laos. Moreover, the king of Thailand is the chief officiant of a cult of his patrilineal ancestors. As we shall see below, the idea that power is allocated through a male line of descent finds some reflection in the rural parts of the region. Matrilineal descent is also given some recognition in parts of the region, especially in connection with the allocation of responsibility for attending to the demands of certain categories of spirits. Although stress is placed on both patrilineal and matrilineal descent for some purposes, it remains true that unilineality is far less important in the kinship systems of the peoples of the Theravada Buddhist societies than it is, for example, in the societies of the Vietnamese or some of the neighboring hill tribes.

The kinship terminologies of all the rural peoples of the region stress the same principles, those of sex, relative age, and generation. None of these kinship terminologies reveal any unilineal skewing, although it might be noted that in textual sources dealing with the Thai royal family terminologies derived from Indian sources are used and do reveal a patrilineal emphasis.[51]

The distinction between masculinity and femininity is fundamental to social life in the rural communities of Therevada Buddhist Southeast Asia. An inherent link is believed to obtain between women and the forces associated with the earth. Although the names are different, the Burmese, the various Tai-speaking groups, and the Khmer all conceive of the divinities associated with the earth and with rice as feminine. Women, as also the earth and rice, are deemed to have nurturing qualities, such nurturance serving not only to ensure the physical well being of individuals, but their spiritual well-being as well. Thus, for example, it is believed that the *khwan*, the vital essence of human beings as it is conceived of by the central Thai, is nourished first by the body of the mother, then after birth by mother's milk, and finally by rice, all three being conceived of as inherently the same:

> Thus the *khwan* is sustained by, and its incarnation grows from, the physical nourishment of a woman's body. What is to sustain it after a woman's milk gives out? Rice, because rice, too, is nourishment from a maternal figure. " Every grain is part of the body of Mother Rice (*Maeae Posop*) and contains a bit of her *khwan*." When weaning is to rice, there is no break in female nurture for body and *khwan*.[52]

Whereas the essence of femininity is nurturance, the essence of masculinity is potency. The power to fertilize the earth and to fertilize women, the power to govern others, and the power to reject the world are masculine qualities. For the Burmese, this quality is given expression under the rubric of *pon*:

> Pon, in the sense of a glory, a religious essence, is limited mostly to men. Women may have a bit (on this informants are unclear), but, if they do, it is so little that it does not really count. Pon is part of the male principle and is derived from the Buddhist understanding that men, and men alone, can reach the final state of " blowing out " of desire . . . *Nibbana* [Nirvana]. Pon places men in a higher spiritual state than women.[53]

As will be recalled from the discussion of the myth of the Naga Princess in the last chapter, the dualism that links women with the earth and with nurturance and men with the supramundane and with potency is a very old idea in Theravada Buddhist Southeast Asia. It remains a powerful conception in the social life of most of the villagers of the region today.[54]

The villagers of Theravada Buddhist Southeast Asia use criteria of age not only to separate people of different generations but also to separate people in the same generation who are of different ages. Among the Thai peoples as among the Khmer, siblings are distinguished by relative age, but not fundamentally by sex. The Burmese distinguish siblings by relative age and by sex. The status distinction between older sibling and younger sibling is used in structuring many nonkin relationships in all these societies.

Kin Groups and Marriage Patterns

The basic kin group of the rural peoples of the region is the group that lives together in a single household and shares a common hearth. Such a " household " group usually consists of either a nuclear family (parents and unmarried children) or a stem family (parents, unmarried children, and one married child and spouse and, perhaps, the children of this couple). Almost nowhere does the household include more than two married couples, and usually the couples in question are of different generations, although in some cases two couples related through sibling ties may live in the same household. The inclusion of a married child and child-in-law in a household does not reflect any principle of unilineal descent; rather it is a function of a rule of postmarital residence. The most common pattern of postmarital residence is one that leads a husband to settle with his wife's family, at least for a short period following marriage. The rural peoples of northeastern Thailand, Laos, and northern Thailand almost invariably follow this pattern, whereas in Cambodia and Burma the pattern is followed by a majority, but not all of the people.[55]

Only among the central Thai does there appear to be no pattern of initial matrilocal residence following marriage.[56] However, the central Thai pattern whereby a newly married couple may just as likely be found living with the parents of the husband as with the parents of the wife is apparently of recent vintage. Young, writing at the end of the nineteenth century, reports that after the marriage of a young couple at that period, it was the pattern for them to live with the parents of the wife until after the birth of a first child.[57]

Beyond the " household," one finds in some of the rural communities of Theravada Buddhist Southeast Asia a larger kin group made up of those who live in several " households " in the same " compound." " Compounds " are reported from upper Burma, northern and northeastern Thailand, and Laos and may also exist elsewhere. Where " compounds " are found, the principle of inclusion is again based partially on the pattern of postmarital residence. Since this pattern is generally one of matrilocality, " compounds " generally consist of a parental household (perhaps with a married daughter and her husband living with the parents) and one or more daughter households.

From northern Thailand matrilineal descent groups whose membership is defined in terms of descent alone have been reported.[58] Although no such matrilineages are reported from other parts of the region, the fact that matrilineally related kinsmen also share responsibility for specific spirits in upper Burma and perhaps also in Cambodia suggests that matrilineages (albeit ones with very limited functions) may also exist in these other areas as well.[59]

Although patrilineages are not reported anywhere in the region, patrilineal descent is recognized by some peoples in rural Theravada Buddhist Southeast Asia as the basis for some types of social action. For example, Spiro has noted that for the village in upper Burma in which he carried out research, the headmanship had been inherited patrilineally for as far back as people could remember.[60] I also found in the northeastern Thai village in which I worked that patrilineal descent was important in determining access to headmanship, although the principle had not always been followed. When surnames were introduced into Thailand, Laos, and Cambodia earlier in this century, they were allocated in much the same way as they are in the West; that is, at birth one takes the same surname of one's father and women change their surname on marriage to that of their husband. As in the West, patrilineal inheritance of surnames does not create patrilineal descent groups.

The personal kindred, that is, a set of relatives defined in terms of their relationship to an individual, is recognized in all rural communities in Theravada Buddhist Southeast Asia. Although almost everyone living within the same community is related to almost everyone else through either consanguineal or affinal ties, not everyone in a community will belong to the personal kindred of each individual member of the community. Rather, inclusion in a kindred is determined by whether a connection is cultivated or not. M. Nash has described this process as follows: " A person has the option of building a structure of reciprocity between himself and a kinsman or the alternative of ignoring the relationship."[61] Similar " optional variety " kindreds are found throughout the region.

Throughout the region, there are no prescriptive marriage rules other than that which prohibits marriage between those who are living or have lived together in the same household. This rule not only applies to kinsmen with whom marriage would lead to incestuous relations but also to more distant kinsmen and nonkinsmen such as servants who may live in the same household. Parents attempt to exert some influence over their children's choices of mates and in some instances are successful. However, all sources on village life in the region attest to the great elaboration given to courting customs associated with the forming of unions by the parties themselves. Associated with feast days, with cooperative labor parties, and often with ordinary nights during the dry season, the young unmarried people in the villages throughout the region engage in what the French have called with regard to Laos, the " courts of love." In northeastern Thailand, groups of young men gather of an evening at one or the other of their homes, at least one in each such group having a *khaen*, or polyphonic mouth organ. The group then strolls to the house of a young girl where the admirer of the girl serenades her to the accompaniment of the *khaen* and the joking of his friends. Sometimes the group moves on to the next house without one of the companions who remains seated in quiet conversation with his girl friend. In northern Thailand at almost every feast day there are song competitions between maidens and unmarried young men in which the men make sexual overtures and the girls rebuff them through clever word play. While these public competitions are taking place, some young couples may wander off quietly to the nearby forest for more serious love play.

Wedding in a village in northeastern Thailand at which the "vital essences" of the couple are linked. (*C. F. Keyes photograph*).

Although courting sometimes leads to sexual intimacy between unmarried couples in villages throughout the region, such actions are everywhere condemned as offenses against certain spirits. If a girl should become pregnant, the man responsible is supposed not only to marry the girl but also to pay a fine to the offended spirit. Fines are also levied against couples who establish unions without ceremony and particularly without the permission of the girl's parents. The spirits who are thus offended can be seen as cultural projections of the rights of parents (and especially the parents of girls) in the determination of marriages. Yet, these rights are nowhere in the region held to preempt the rights of young people themselves to choose their partners.

Except when there has been an elopement, a marriage is preceded by negotiations between representatives of both families over wealth to be spent in connection with the wedding. Among the Lao, northeastern Thai, northern Thai, and central Thai this wealth takes the form of a bridewealth paid by the family of the groom to the family of the bride, some of this being used to defray the costs of the wedding. In return, the family of the bride is expected to give a large wedding gift to the young people. Among the Khmer, the negotiations determine the amount to be spent at the wedding and the amount to be received by the couple, all wealth to come from the groom's family. Among the Burmese, both families determine the amount of wealth they can afford to spend on the wedding and to give the couple. Throughout the region, all those who are invited to participate in the wedding—the guests being mainly those belonging to the kindreds of the parents of the couple and of the couple themselves—will make small gifts to the couple.

Marriages are not necessarily permanent, and divorces can occur without the serious social disruptions caused by divorces in those societies in which unilineal descent groups are important.[62] Nevertheless, there are strong social pressures for maintaining a marriage, since the family has important economic functions. This point will become clearer, after we have examined the economic organization of rural society.

ECOLOGICAL ADAPTATION AND ECONOMIC ORGANIZATION

Ecological Adaptation and Production

Studies of ecological adaptation of rural people in Thearvada Buddhist Southeast Asia have tended to concentrate on agricultural communities. Although some attention has been given to patterns of ecological adaptation in fishing villages—of which there are considerable number in the region[63]—and in villages in which craft specialization is the dominant form of production,[64] systematic inquiry into patterns of ecological adaptation in the region has been carried out only with reference to agricultural communities. The overwhelming majority of agricultural communities, perhaps as many as 75 per cent of the rural communities in the region, are primarily rice-producing villages. The remaining agricultural communities are based on mixed crop or garden crop production.[65] The ecological adaptation of rice-producing villages can be said to be the basic pattern of adaptation and the other types considered variant forms.

In his study, *Rice and Man: Agricultural Ecology in Southeast Asia*, Lucien Hanks has summarized research findings to date on the ecological adaptation of rice-cultivating villages in Southeast Asia and has discussed in some detail the patterns of ecological adaptation as he studied them in the village of Bang Chan in central Thailand.[66] With some additional attention to the variant forms of agriculture that are not focused on rice, we can use Hanks' study as the basis for a discussion of patterns of ecological adaptation in the agricultural communities in this part of mainland Southeast Asia. Hanks identifies four different modes of ecological adaptation associated with rice production: gathering, shifting cultivation, broadcasting, and transplanting. Gathering of wild rice was part of the mode of ecological adaptation of some prehistoric peoples in the region and was probably engaged in for centuries before rice was finally domesticated. Gathering of wild rice continues to be practiced to this day, but it is no longer a major form of production.

Basic to shifting cultivation, as to any other form of agriculture, is the conversion of land from its natural or wild state into land that is put to uses determined by humans. Shifting cultivation involves the growing of rice " in dry fields watered only by the rains. This work must be timed like a dance to fit the rhythms set mainly by the composition and decomposition of soils, by the seasons, and by the cycles of vegetational growth."[67] Shifting cultivation is a mode of ecological adaptation mainly associated, as we have already seen, with the tribal peoples of Southeast Asia. However, some of the civilized peoples of Theravada Buddhist societies have also adapted themselves to this mode.[68]

As Condominas has observed of the villagers in the Vientiane Plain of Laos, initial cultivation of land often begins with the conversion of natural land into swidden fields even when the ultimate purpose is to use the land in other ways.[69] Some land originally cleared by swiddening methods has been converted in almost every village into garden plots, planted with fruit trees or such garden crops as vegetables. With rare exceptions, garden farming is not a dominant mode of agricultural production among Theravada Buddhist Southeast Asians and in those rare cases where it is, as among the *neak chamcar* of Cambodia, it appears to be a recent innovation practiced by immigrant Chinese or borrowed from them.[70] In northeastern Thailand, the villagers with whom I worked classified all agricultural land that had not been made into paddy rice fields or that was not planted to garden crops under a rubric (*hai*), which also included swidden fields. This classification suggests the marginal place the cultivation of crops other than paddy rice has for most of the people of Therevada Buddhist Southeast Asia. Villages such as Nondwin in upper Burma where paddy rice cultivation has been subordinated to the production of other crops[71] are also rare, although they may represent the vanguard of the future. For the present, the vast majority of agriculturalists in the region devote themselves primarily to the growing of wet rice.

Broadcasting and transplanting modes of adaptation are both associated with the growing of rice in permanent fields flooded by water. Whereas the shifting cultivators' crops draw their water directly from rainfall, the wet-rice agriculturalists must obtain water for their crops from floods that follow monsoonal rains, from rivers or canals filled by the rains, or from reservoirs of water kept after the end of the rainy season. The waters bring not only themselves but also nutrients that are left on the soil, thus making possible the use of the same fields year after year. Broadcasting, as defined by Hanks, " refers to a complex of agricultural techniques associated with particular terrains and conditions of watering the crop."[72] The rice producer who follows the broadcasting patterns employs animal power—in the form of either oxen or water buffalo—for plowing and harrowing his fields. He shares this practice with the producer who follows the transplanting patterns, and both differ in this from the shifting cultivator who prepares his fields by using a stick to poke holes in the ground. The broadcaster constructs dikes in his fields only as necessary to control the flow of flood waters; otherwise he leaves his fields open. After plowing his fields, he will cast the seed abroad on them, sometimes even before the rains come. The plants, grown rather irregularly, are often interspersed among weeds.

Transplanting, again a term that stands for a complex of activities, is much more labor intensive than broadcasting. The transplanter attempts to construct dikes around his fields to assure that each plot will receive the same amount of water, thus preventing crop loss through the starvation or through the drowning of the plants. These dikes must be prepared at the beginning of each season and

Transplanting rice in northeastern Thailand. (*Jane Keyes photograph*)

kept in repair throughout the growing season. The transplanter may depend only on the natural flow of waters at the end of the rainy season, guiding these waters by means of dikes, or he may depend on some form of irrigation works. If irrigation works exist, then these too will require labor to build them and to keep them in repair.

The transplanter plants rice in two stages. First he prepares a nursery bed, where germinated rice seeds are planted broadcast. While these are growing, he then prepares his other fields. After the rice has grown for a few weeks, the farmer and his family and in some cases extra labor will pull up the seedlings and replant them in even rows in the main fields. Both the transplanter and the broadcaster harvest their rice in much the same way as does the shifting cultivator. They use a small sickle with which they cut off the rice by hand.

In some areas of Southeast Asia, where there are permanent supplies of water—as for example from the streams in northern Thailand or the Shan states or near the Tonlé Sap in Cambodia—rural people have planted more than one rice crop per year. Those who engage in double cropping employ, almost of necessity, the techniques associated with transplanting. In some of the same areas, multiple cropping has involved the alternation of rice cultivation with the cultivation of other crops. For example, in parts of northern Thailand, tobacco and groundnuts are planted in the off season in the same fields that contain rice during the rainy season. Multiple cropping is relatively rare in the Theravada Buddhist societies, a fact that contrasts markedly with the well-developed pattern of multiple cropping in the Tonkin Delta of northern Vietnam.

In recent years, certain innovations in the technology of rice cultivation have been introduced into parts of the region. Mechanized water pumps, tractors, fertilizers, insecticides, new strains of rice, and so on have been adopted very readily by those villagers who have geared their production to the market, although those who still produce goods primarily for home consumption have usually found such innovations to be uneconomical.[73] In addition to the technological innovations adopted by villagers themselves, government agencies have also effected certain changes in the ecology of the rural areas through the introduction of such developments as irrigation and hydroelectric schemes. These last, although existing only to a very limited extent in Cambodia and Laos, have been developed on a wide scale in Thailand during the last couple of decades.

Although rice cultivation, by either broadcasting or transplanting methods, is the dominant form of production for most villagers in the region, it is not the only form used. Almost all villagers will use land unsuitable for rice cultivation for raising vegetables, bananas, mangoes, peppers, or some other garden crop. Today, it is also common for villagers to use land not planted in rice for the cultivation of cotton, sesame, peanuts, kenaf, or some other crop that can be sold. In addition to agriculture, villagers throughout the region also add to their diet through fishing and through the collection of snails, fresh water shrimp, frogs, and other small animals that live in the flooded paddies and streams of the region. Villagers may also hunt small animals such as birds, lizards, or squirrels, although they only rarely hunt large animals. Almost every household will also own a few domestic animals, including chickens, cattle, and buffaloes. In recent years, some villagers have taken up animal husbandry for additional income. The most common animals raised for the market are pigs, ducks, cattle, and horses.

Whenever villagers are not working in the fields or fishing and hunting, they are likely to be engaged in some form of craft production. In many parts of the region, village women still prepare cloth from raw cotton and silk, which is raised locally or obtained from neighboring villages. Men cut down bamboo, cut it into long strips, and use these strips to weave walls, mats, and a variety of baskets and utensils. Rattan is also widely used by villagers for making baskets, fish creels, bird traps, and the like. In short, the mode of ecological adaptation found in villages in which rice cultivation is the main form of productive activity is one that involves more than simply the growing of rice.

Some villagers in areas concentrating primarily on rice production specialize, sometimes full time but more often part time, in the production of tools and utensils used in rice-growing communities. In northeastern Thailand, for example, in the village in which I worked, there were four part-time blacksmiths who made plowshares, machetes, axes, and knives for people from surrounding villages. Throughout the region, there are entire villages whose inhabitants specialize in the production of pottery. In northeastern Thailand, potting skills are transmitted from mother to daughter, the latter continuing to live in the household or compound of her mother after marriage. The men marrying into the family take on the roles of firing and marketing the pots.[74] In

Villager using bamboo strips to
weave a wall for a house, northeastern
Thailand. (*Jane Keyes photograph*)

some parts of the region, there are villages that specialize in the manufacture of
cloth, of bark paper used for traditional manuscripts and umbrellas, of utensils
made out of teak, and so on. Those engaged in specialized craft production
have never comprised a very large part of the rural population of the area, and
their economic position has often been threatened in modern times by the
intrusion of competitive products manufactured in the cities or even in foreign
countries.

Agricultural products raised for local consumption have generally been
processed by those who grow them. The only major exception occurs in relation
to rice milling. Rice millers, operating mechanized mills, have, of course, long
existed in the cities of mainland Southeast Asia, but they have only recently
been found in villages, and then almost exclusively in Thailand. From about
the early 1950s, small motor-driven commercially operated mills began to
proliferate throughout rural Thailand, extending to the more underdeveloped
parts of the country. By 1963, a study made in one province in northeastern
Thailand, the poorest area of the country, found that there was a small mill in
almost every village of any size and that about 80 per cent of the rice consumed
by the villagers themselves was milled in these small mills.[75]

The existence of mechanized rice mills at the village level is indicative of
fundamental changes in the economy of these villages. Traditional methods of

milling rice in the villages, although involving much tedious labor in pounding the rice with mortar and pestle, did not necessitate the expenditure of any cash or the loss of any of the milled rice to pay for the costs of milling. Milling by mechanized mills requires not only that someone have sufficient capital to buy the necessary equipment but also that a sufficient number of farmers be willing to pay, in cash or kind, for the costs of milling. Those who own and operate these mills are often villagers who have accumulated the necessary capital for investment in a mill through work outside the village or through loans from dealers selling mill equipment. Once established, village-based entrepreneurs may accumulate yet further capital, which they often invest in land, thereby contributing to a process of change in land tenure patterns that began during the colonial period.

Land Tenure, Taxes, and Rents

For most people in the region, even today, access to land is a function, in part, of membership in a kin group. The kin group that controls agricultural land may be the " household," or in some instances the " compound," that is, the collection of households bound together by proximity and by kinship. Productive land may be divided among heirs on the occasion of the establishment of a new household or it may be divided on the death of the surviving parent of the senior couple in a compound. Among the rural peoples of central Thailand and Cambodia, as well as in other parts of the region, land is divided equally among all children regardless of sex and regardless of where these children live after marriage. That is, such a division is made if there is sufficient property to make it feasible. Among most of the other peoples in the region, land is divided among only those children who are still residing with or near their parents after marriage. Since a pattern of matrilocal residence is general in these areas, land is usually inherited by daughters and their husbands. Such a transmission of property is associated with a continuity through women, an idea that finds strong mythical support, as we have already noted, in the connection between women and the earth.[76]

Even traditionally, not all villagers in Theravada Buddhist Southeast Asia gained rights of access to productive land by virtue of kinship alone. Where a family held land that could not be divided among all legitimate claimants so that all who inherited would have sufficient land for their needs, it was common for one or more claimant, usually an elder child and her or his spouse, to waive their rights to inheritance and to go in search of new land that could be homesteaded. The quest for new lands was greatly stimulated by the dramatic population growth and by the commercialization of rice agriculture, which took place during the colonial period. Access to new land has always been a right conferred by the state, although in many cases mediated through local authorities. In Burma, during the period of the Konbaung dynasty, the state recognized the right of local *myothugyi*, " lords of circles," that is, local authorities who usually controlled a number of villages, to allocate unused land in their territory. The *myothugyi*, in turn, would allow those who requested it to open new lands, with the understanding that the rights to such lands would be conferred on those who continued to cultivate them.[77] Similar patterns apparently existed throughout the region and are still followed in Laos. Condominas found that in the Vientiane Plain of Laos, local village headman (*nay ban*) provided the authorization to those who wished to open new lands. Rights in such land were further established by the act of continuous cultivation.[78]

In return for the right to cultivate lands within the domain of one of the traditional rulers of Theravada Buddhist Southeast Asia, the villager had to pay a tax and/or provide his labor for service to the ruler. In Burma, at the end of the Konbaung period, a tax of 6 per cent of the produce is reported to have obtained, and village men were also subject to corvée service.[79] In premodern Thailand there was, as in Burma, a tax on produce and also a corvée, the amount of service required varying greatly according to social and geographical proximity to one of the centers of authority. In addition, a head tax was also placed on adult males. In northeastern Thailand, and perhaps elsewhere as well, this head tax varied according to whether a man was married or not and whether or not he had reached old age.

During the colonial period, patterns of both land tenure and taxation were changed throughout the region, excepting, possibly, in parts of Laos. The colonial powers in both Burma and Cambodia introduced land laws whereby the governments of these countries reserved to themselves the right to determine the distribution of unopened land and the right of eminent domain over all lands under their political control. Similar land laws were promulgated in Thailand by King Chulalongkorn, who modeled his programs on those of British Burma. Today, any villager in Burma, Thailand, or Cambodia who wishes to acquire previously uncultivated land must, by law, obtain a land grant or purchase such land from the government. All cultivated land in which rights are well established should, according to present land laws, be recognized in titles issued by the relevant government. In fact, given that much cultivated land in these countries has not been measured or recorded, many rural people continue to cultivate their land without benefit of full title.

The institution of land laws in Burma, Cambodia, and Thailand occurred in connection with a growing recognition of the importance of land as revenue-generating property, a transformation that came about mainly as a function of the commercialization of rice agriculture. The idea of land being a commodity that could be transferred from one legal party to another was not only one that became incorporated into the legal codes of Thailand, Burma, and Cambodia during the colonial period, but also one that from that period on has gradually begun to be accepted by the peasants themselves, and especially by those peasants living in areas where the production of rice for the market was undergoing major development, most notably in lower Burma and central Thailand. Once accepted, the idea made possible the alienation of land, that is, the transfer of land from one party to another by sale rather than through inheritance.

The changes in land laws connected with the idea that land had a revenue-generating value were associated with changes in the taxes that governments in the region imposed upon the rural populace. During British rule in Burma, the traditional corvée system was abolished, but other traditional taxes, including those on produce, were retained.[80] In addition, the British imposed a property tax that " was assessed on villages at a fixed rate per household and distributed among the people according to their means by village assessors."[81] Direct taxes, mainly on produce, were continued in Burma after independence, at least up till the time of the coup by General Ne Win in 1962.[82]

In Thailand, under King Chulalongkorn, the taxation system was changed, with the corvée being eliminated and land taxes raised in direct emulation of the pattern in Burma. However, quite to the contrary of the trend in Burma, the Thai government reduced taxes on the rural people in the succeeding years and in 1938 eliminated the land and capitation taxes altogether.[83] Although a nominal land tax was later introduced (averaging about 1 baht or 5c per *rai*, the equivalent of 13c an acre, in the late 1950s and early 1960s), it has never attained the importance of the direct taxes levied on land in Burma. This is not to say that rural people in Thailand pay no taxes, however. The main tax levied on Thai farmers between World War II and 1975 has been an indirect tax in the form of a rice premium, or a tax paid to the government by exporters on all rice exported. The rice premium had the effect of depressing the price of rice within Thailand relative to the price of rice on the world market. Thus, farmers who sell their rice receive less income than they would if the rice premium did not exist. As Ingram has said, the institution of the rice premium " has been to *reverse* the prewar policy of reducing the tax on the farmer, who now bears an extremely heavy tax."[84]

French policy in Laos and Cambodia tended to give greater emphasis to indirect taxes than to direct taxes and this tendency was continued by the post-colonial governments. In recent years, Cambodian peasants have been reported to pay few taxes and Lao peasants apparently pay no taxes at all.[85]

The differences in tax policies in the countries of Theravada Buddhist Southeast Asia during the colonial period reflect differences in the importance of commercial rice production in these countries. Where commercial rice production was important, as in lower Burma and central Thailand, land alienation was widespread and land rents of greater significance. Land sales, which became increasingly important in lower Burma and central Thailand in the latter part of the nineteenth and the first part of the twentieth century, initiated a process that transformed many peasants in these areas from land owners into tenant farmers and wage laborers. This process was exacerbated by the fact that land that could be obtained through homesteading was becoming increasingly scarce at the same time. By the 1930s land available for homesteading was all but nonexistent in lower Burma and central Thailand. A further factor was that the commercialization of rice was associated with a growth of rural indebtedness. Many farmers in both lower Burma and central Thailand adopted the practice of borrowing against their future crop in order to meet immediate expenses.

With the collapse of the rice market in the early years of the Great Depression, many agriculturalists in lower Burma were suddenly faced with recalls of loans they could not pay. Their only choice was to give up their land, which they had used as collateral to obtain credit. " The amount of the total occupied area in Lower Burma held by nonagriculturalists rose from 31 per cent in 1929–1930 to nearly 50 per cent by 1934–1935."[86] Those who were forced to give up their land became tenants or wage laborers instead. Widespread tenancy continued to exist in Burma until the end of the colonial period. One of the first acts of the government of an independent Burma was the passage of the Land Nationalization Act of 1948. However, it was not until the institution of land reform in the late 1950s and early 1960s that rents were actually abolished in Burma.[87]

During the first part of the Depression, land alienation and tenancy also increased markedly in those parts of central Thailand where commercialized rice agriculture had developed. This pattern was reversed during World War II and the immediate postwar period, only to reemerge again in the 1960s.[88] By 1967, 38 per cent of the farmers living in 26 provinces of central Thailand—this is, in the area most involved in production for the market—were fully or partially tenant farmers.[89] Moreover, newspaper accounts suggest that this process of alienation of land in central Thailand has continued to increase.

In contrast to the situation in lower Burma and central Thailand, almost all farmers in Cambodia own their own land. Delvert has concluded from his study of rural life in Cambodia that: " Farm tenancy is practically unknown."[90] Although data from Laos are more limited, Halpern's assertion that " for Vientiane province (in Laos) over 80 per cent of the rural households own their own fields "[91] could probably be generalized to much of rural Laos. With the changes in governments in both Cambodia and Laos, it is probable that radically new conceptions of land tenure, those embedded in programs of collectivized agriculture, will be introduced.

Trade, the Market Economy, and Economic Change

A picture of traditional trade in Theravada Buddhist Southeast Asia is somewhat difficult to construct since little scholarly attention has been given to the subject. However, some general features can be discerned.

Currency is known to have existed in Southeast Asia since at least the early centuries of the Christian era, but until modern times its circulation has been very limited. Accounts of those who traveled through the region in the nineteenth century reveal that the value of currency used for trade (as distinct from the currency used for tribute or for religious offerings) varied from locality to locality. Traditionally, villagers had little use for currency, because most of what they did not produce themselves could be obtained through barter with others who lived in the vicinity. Some commodities, however, had to be purchased, among them pottery, salt, iron, religious objects made of bronze, and paper for manuscripts. These commodities were usually carried to villages by peddlers who traveled from village to village until they had sold whatever they brought with them. Peddlers from bronze-working villages in the Shan states might travel thousands of miles before selling their supply of bronze gongs or

Five-day market in Yawnghwe, Shan State, Burma. (*C. F. Keyes photograph*)

images; they would then drive back cattle purchased with the proceeds of their sales. In contrast, peddlers selling (or bartering) pots might travel only a few dozen miles to neighboring villages and would use their proceeds to buy (or exchange for) rice and other foodstuffs. Regular periodic markets that drew peasants from the surrounding countryside are reported for upper Burma, northern Thailand, and upper Laos, but they apparently did not exist elsewhere in the region. Larger towns and cities would have some permanent shops, but such shops were rarely patronized by villagers.

During the colonial period, patterns of trade and marketing in the region underwent radical changes; these changes occurred first in the areas of lower Burma and central Thailand in which villagers began to produce rice for sale. Commercialization of rice agriculture in these areas led to a decline in the varied supplementary productive practices traditionally engaged in by villagers. Thus, they wished not only to sell their rice, but also to buy foodstuffs, cloth, tools, and so on, which they might previously have produced themselves. The same patterns involving a shift to production for the market (at least as part of productive activity) and of an increase in demand for goods not produced locally spread throughout the region, until prior to about 1970 there were few villages where these patterns did not exist. Since 1970, the spread of these patterns has continued in Thailand, but it has been retarded by the economic situation in Burma and by the war in Laos and Cambodia.

With the spread of the market economy, there has been a proliferation of market centers. Such centers tended to emerge first at administrative capitals located along the major routes of communication. Thus, the first major market centers outside the primate cities in the region were to be found at provincial capitals located at strategic points along the waterways or railways. As highways were built, new centers were founded in other provincial capitals, in some district capitals, and even in certain villages. Some villagers living in close proximity to these centers produce foodstuffs for the daily fresh markets that are almost invariably found in the centers. Throughout the region, those who sell foodstuffs in these fresh markets are predominantly women.[92] Bulk commodities produced by villagers are more often sold to middlemen (or, in Burma since 1962, to representatives of government trade corporations) in the villages rather than transported by villagers to the center to sell. Villagers who have nothing to sell may still travel to market centers in order to buy goods offered by permanent shops located in these centers.

Throughout the region, middlemen have played an essential role in the economic life of villagers. Until quite recently, middlemen in all the countries of the region were typically ethnically different from the rural population. In the main, middlemen have been Chinese, but in Burma they have sometimes been Indians. Other ethnic minorities, such as the Mon in Thailand or the Vietnamese in Cambodia, have also played middlemen roles.[93] Such ethnic specialization in middlemen roles has begun to break down throughout the region. In Burma, it was directly attacked by the Ne Win government, which took power in 1962. Since 1962, all trade in Burma has been nationalized and organized through government trade corporations, administered in the main by Burmans coopted from the military who today fill the middlemen roles formerly held by those of minority ethnic groups. It would appear that the new governments of Cambodia and Laos will seek to end the ethnic specialization of middlemen roles through nationalization of the economy. In Thailand, middlemen positions have multiplied, but increasingly they are coming to be filled by native Thai rather than by the Chinese who filled them traditionally. Today even Thai villagers are becoming middlemen.

Concomitant with the development of middlemen roles, which serve to facilitate the flow of rural produce into the wider market, there has been a development of shopkeeper rôles, which serve to facilitate the flow of manufactured goods into the villages. Shops are found today not only in the market centers associated with administrative capitals, but also in a number of villages. Village shopkeepers may sometimes be ethnically different from villagers, such people representing an extension of the minority-dominated shopkeeping roles in the towns. It is, however, probably more typical today to find shopkeepers who are from the same ethnic and rural background as the villagers they serve. Many shops in Thailand are run on a part-time basis by villagers, who may as often be women as men.

The existence of shopkeepers and middlemen in villages is indicative of the marked changes in rural economy that have come about as a consequence of the spread of the market economy. Traditionally, it was difficult for one villager to acquire more wealth than other villagers. Sufficient land was generally available through inheritance or homesteading for those who needed it; even if a villager were to become the owner of a sizable land holding, he would probably have had difficulty in finding a large enough labor force to work the land for him, since all labor was committed either to family enterprises or to fulfilling corvée obligations imposed by the rulers of the country. Trade offered some villagers an opportunity to increase their wealth vis-à-vis other villagers. In northeastern Thailand and Laos, for example, a man could demonstrate his economic prowess by becoming a successful cattle or buffalo trader, his success being recognized in the term *hǫi*, which villagers would then use to address him.[94] The size of a man's herd was proof of his wealth, but although it might enable him to sponsor a more lavish feast on the occasion of a son's ordination or a daughter's marriage, given the underdeveloped state of the monetary system in traditional times, the successful livestock trader would find it difficult to transform his wealth into other forms.

With the opening of the region to the world market in the latter half of the nineteenth century, it became increasingly possible for certain villagers to acquire more wealth than their fellow villagers. Those villagers who began to produce goods for the market found they were able to earn income in cash generated outside the rural economy itself. Cash income became important in the region, first in lower Burma and central Thailand where commercialized rice agriculture was initially developed, and then in other parts of the region as well. In a survey made in Thailand in 1934–1935, for example, it was found that the average cash income of farmers in the central plains, which was then about $82 per year, was six times greater than cash income in northeastern Thailand, where cash cropping had only begun to develop and where the average annual cash income was about $13.50.[95]

Today, villagers throughout the region generally have some cash income, but there still remains a disparity in this regard between villagers from those regions that have long been involved in the cash economy and villagers from those that have only more recently become thus involved. Data on cash income among villagers are really not adequate except for Thailand, but some rough comparisons can be made on the basis of the information which is available. In Table 1, estimates are given for average annual per capita income for each country in the region. These figures provide some idea of the relative overall

Table 1. Comparison of average per capita annual income in Burma, Thailand, Laos, and Cambodia

Country	1959*	ca.1965†
Burma	$ 48	$121
Thailand	102	202
Laos	—	104
Cambodia	88	155

* Charles A. Fisher, *South-East Asia* (London: Methuen, 1964), p. 190.
† Keith Buchanan, *The Southeast Asian World* (Garden City, N.Y.: Doubleday Anchor, 1968), pp. 170-73
Buchanan does not give a date for his figures, but from the context it would appear to be about 1965.

differences in income between the countries, but they are not very useful for distinguishing income differences between the rural peoples of the different countries of the region.

On the basis of data given by M. Nash on cash expenditures for 1959–1960 in the two upper Burmese villages of Yadaw and Nondwin, some estimates of cash income for rural upper Burma can be made. In Yadaw, which is described as a typical rice-producing village, the average per capita annual income was about $62, whereas in Nondwin, where production is based on mixed cropping, the per capita annual income ranged from about $33 per year for poor families to about $235 per year for rich families.[96] In a demographic survey made in Cambodia in 1958, it was found that the average per capita annual income of agriculturalists was 1700 riels, that is, $48 at the official rate of exchange of 35 riels to the dollar or $34 at the more realistic rate for the time of 50 riels to the dollar.[97] Average per capita annual income for agriculturalists producing rice range from $30 to $90 at the official rate of exchange or from $22 to $65 at the more realistic rate of exchange. Data on income for rural Laos are practically nonexistent. Halpern estimated on the basis of unspecified sources " that a typical rural Lao family in central Laos spends about $150 a year or approximately $35 per family member."[98] Although no date is attached to this estimate, it would appear to be from the 1950s. Such an estimate would certainly be too high for some of the more remote rural areas in northern and eastern Laos.

I have calculated, on the basis of data collected in a government-sponsored survey in Thailand in 1963, that the average per capita income of farmers in northeastern Thailand was about $25 per year, that of farmers in central Thailand was $71, and that of farmers elsewhere in the country was between these two figures.[99] By 1968–1969, average per capita cash income in rural Thailand had risen significantly (probably far more so than in other countries in the region), but the relative position of the rural areas remained the same. Average per capita income in northeastern Thailand in 1968–1969 was about $50 per year, in the north $73 per year, in the south $83 per year, and in the central plains, $153 per year.[100]

Although much of the cash income earned by villagers in all parts of the region is expended for consumption, some has been used for capital investment. Throughout the region, the main form of capital investment made by villagers has been investment in land, since land today, in contrast to traditional times, is now seen to have income-generating value. While the demand for land has been increasing, the amount of land relative to the existing population has been declining sharply. Those who have bought land have, thus, acquired their holdings at the expense of fellow villagers, and villagers who no longer own land often become laborers employed by those who do own land. What M. Nash found for villages in upper Burma in 1959–1960, namely that villagers conceived of wealth in terms of the size of land holdings owned,[101] also obtains in much of the rest of the region. Even land reform as carried out in Burma does not appear to have eliminated all differences in the sizes of land holdings owned by villagers.

In Thailand, and much more rarely in Burma, Cambodia, and Laos, a certain amount of wealth generated by villagers and some capital made available to them through credit extended by middlemen and dealers has been invested in nonagricultural enterprises. There now exists in rural Thailand a significant number of local entrepreneurs who have invested in rice mills, in the construction and stocking of shops, in trucks or motorized boats used to transport village produce to the market, and so on. Village entrepreneurship has not yet been studied sufficiently to enable one to generalize about the subject to any major extent. However, the fact that village entrepreneurs not only exist but are expanding in numbers and in the scope of their operations renders questionable the widely held view that the culture of villagers in Theravada Buddhist Southeast Asia serves to inhibit economic development.

Buddhism and Economic Development

Perhaps the most extended debate regarding the relationship between religious belief and social action in Theravada Buddhist Southeast Asia has been over whether beliefs held by people in this region are a stimulus, a hindrance, or irrelevant to economic development. This debate has started, in some cases, with the " Weber Thesis," that is, with the argument of Max Weber that capital accumulation essential for economic development depends not only on ecological and economic conditions that make the production of " surplus " capital possible but also on an ideological motivation that leads people to work to accumulate capital. Weber found such an ideological motivation in " the Protestant ethic " and did not find it in other cultural traditions in other societies. He specifically did not find it in Buddhism, although he did argue that Buddhism more closely approximated Protestant Christianity than any other religious tradition he examined.[102]

The " Weber Thesis " has been examined by students of every Theravada Buddhist society.[103] Spiro has shown for Burma, and the same interpretation can be applied generally, that the strong motivation that villagers have to make merit in order to achieve their salvation goals leads them to work to gain sufficient wealth to expend on merit-making activities. This argument must be qualified somewhat, since in one's effort to accumulate wealth, even if one's purpose is to use the wealth in merit making, one must not do so in such a way that one falls into the vice of greed. In other words, one's wealth should not be accumulated at the expense of others. In modern times, when the various countries of the region have experienced, to a greater or lesser degree, periods of economic expansion, it has been possible for villagers to engage in entrepreneurial activities without endangering their relationship with their fellow villagers. In such situations, Spiro's argument holds.

Spiro argues further that since accumulated wealth is " invested " in merit making—that is, is spent for nonproductive purposes—rather than saved or invested in capitalist enterprises, Buddhist beliefs still hinder economic development. This argument must also be modified, perhaps somewhat more severely than the other half of the argument. One needs to examine rather closely what effects wealth expended for merit making actually does have. First, some wealth may be invested in edifices—such as *cetiya*—with little or no function other than a religious one. However, other wealth is donated for the construction of such buildings as monastic residences and assembly halls, which are used not only for religious purposes but also as dormitories for members of the Sangha and for lay boys living at the monasteries or as schools, village meeting halls and the such like. A part of the wealth expended at merit-making activities is also used to support the members of the Sangha. Although the Sangha live in reasonably comfortable surroundings, their consumption level is certainly below that of wealthy peasants or moderately well-off urbanites. Yet other wealth expended for merit making is actually redistributed. I have observed in both northern and northeastern Thailand that the surplus food given on major feast days is used to feed poorer members of the society (and also village cats and dogs). Some wealth is used to purchase goods for the temple or monastery. A few such goods, such as images, have only a religious function, but others, such as chairs, cooking utensils, dishes, and movie projectors, may be treated as communal property that can be borrowed for home use or for community functions. Finally, some wealth donated in conjunction with merit making is used for the support of students; that is, it has the function of fellowships or scholarships. This function is particularly important in urban temples, which support large numbers of boys and young men, a number of whom are members of the Sangha and others of whom are simply residents of the temple monastery, who come from poor rural backgrounds.

In short, the wealth spent on merit-making activities is not necessarily non-productive wealth. Even the wealth used for the construction of religious edifices or for the purchase of religious goods supports some labor and some who have specialized skills. Some wealth thus expended may help provide for communal facilities, whereas other wealth so used actually supports those who are in the process of acquiring a modern education.

Yet another qualification needs to be made to Spiro's argument. The data from villages throughout the region suggest that the wealthier a person becomes the less wealth relative to his or her income is spent on merit making. Although Buddhist ideology, as translated into social values, serves to motivate people to use some of their wealth for merit making, this ideology does not, except for those who become members of the Sangha, enjoin poverty as a virtue. Rather, to be wealthy and to enjoy the comforts that wealth can obtain is indicative of previous good Karma whose consequences are now being manifest.

This interpretation of Buddhist ideas has come under attack in all countries of the region by those who advocate that wealth should be equitably distributed. In some cases, mainly in Burma and to some extent also in Thailand, those who have advanced such arguments have grounded them in a reinterpretation of Buddhist doctrine. Others have used other ideologies, notably secular Socialism in the case of Burma and Communism in Laos and Cambodia, as grounds from which to base their attacks. While some form of Socialist ideas regarding the distribution of wealth may inform official policy in some or all of the countries of the region, the idea that wealth should be used by the individual and the individual's family who have gained it remains widely held by villagers in the region. For villagers, the pursuit of wealth, which can be used for personal ends including those of merit making and investment, continues to inform their economic endeavors. The limitation to this pursuit lies not in the cultural ideas held by villagers but in the economic conditions within which they must work.

LOCAL COMMUNITIES AND THE POLITICAL ORGANIZATION OF RURAL LIFE

Local Communities

Rural people throughout the region have formed basically three types of settlements. Some settlements consist of households strung out along the bank of a river or a stream or, in more recent times, along a roadway. These " linear " settlements contrast with " nucleated " settlements in which households are collected together, usually on a knoll or a high ground surrounded by fields. In some areas, notably in central Thailand, households are " dispersed " among the fields in a manner quite similar to that of rural America.

The size of the settlements vary considerably. Settlements in the densely populated parts of Cambodia averaged in the 1950s between 100 and 200 persons per settlement.[104] In 1956–1957, Kaufman found settlements in the Vientiane Plain of Laos ranging in size from 50 to over 1,000 inhabitants with the average being 350.[105] Manning Nash reports two nucleated villages in upper Burma had over 550 inhabitants each in 1960 and were in the modal group of settlements in the area.[106] I found that the village of Ban Nọng Tụn in northeastern Thailand with a population of 709 in 1963 was about average in population size for settlements in the central Chi River valley. The village of Bang Chan in central Thailand had a population of 1,608 in 1949, but it is important to note that Bang Chan was divided into seven hamlets and that the settlement pattern of this area is very dispersed.[107] As the case of Bang Chan demonstrates, the settlement defined in ecological terms is not everywhere the same as the " village " defined in social terms.

Rural people throughout the region view their local communities as social contexts within which moral and political actions take place. With perhaps the exception of some villages in modern-day central Thailand, rural peoples believe themselves subject to the power of locality spirits. These spirits are credited with controlling events within their domains and with guarding local custom. In upper Burma, for example, every village has its *ywa-saun nat* or *ywa-dawshin*, that is, its " village guardian *nat* " or its " Lord of the village as a royal domain."[108] In northeastern Thailand, villagers believe themselves subject to three different types of locality spirits. There is a village spirit, *phi pu ta* (lit., " father's father/mother's father spirit "), with a shrine on the outskirts of the village; a spirit of the temple monastery, known as *cao phọ pha khao* (" Lord Father of the White Robes "), with its shrine in the precincts of the temple monastery; and the *phi ban* (" village spirits ") with their shrine at the " navel of the village " (*buban*).[109]

Villagers also see themselves as members of congregations of particular local temple monasteries. Although in many parts of the region, adherents of the cult of specific locality spirits may also be the members of the same congregation of a local temple monastery, it is not uncommon to find cases where spirit-cult members belong to two temple monastery congregations or vice-versa. Traditionally, the temple monastery was also the school, but with the implementation of modern systems of education, schools have been functionally separated from the religious system. Generally school districts are coterminous with religious congregations, but there are cases where this is no longer true. In theory, the school district could provide another basis for defining local communities, but in practice the school has come to be seen by rural people as a specialized institution of the state.

From the point of view of rural people, the state is relevant to the defining of local communities by virtue of the demarcating boundaries the state chooses to recognize for local administrative units. Traditionally, it may have been general practice for state authorities to recognize those boundaries defined in terms of peasant practice, that is, in terms of the domains of locality spirits and the extent of temple monastery congregations. Laws instituted during the colonial period in the various countries of the region, however, introduced new criteria for defining units of local administration. In 1887–1889, following the conquest of upper Burma, the British Commissioner promulgated two regulations that redefined " villages " to suit governmental rather than peasant purposes. Furnivall has described the consequences of these acts:

> [The new regulations issued by Sir Charles Crosthwaite, the British Commissioner] abolished self-government over any unit larger than the village and, by converting the village from a social and residential unit into an administrative unit, cut at the roots of organic social life within the village.[110]

King Chulalongkorn and his advisers in Thailand made an effort to copy directly the new system of local administration implemented in Burma. This administrative reorganization of the countryside was carried out most systematically in central Thailand, where a dispersed settlement pattern obtained. As a consequence, the resultant administrative units had almost no connection whatsoever with the " natural " village as conceived of by the peasantry. For example, as we have already noted, the central Thai village of Bang Chan consists of seven administrative " villages " (*mu*), divided between two administrative " communes " (*tambon*), located in two different " districts " (*amphoe*).[111] In Cambodia, two ordinances were proclaimed in 1908 and 1919, during the period of the French Protectorate, which had similar effects of confounding peasant and legal definitions of the " village." The peasant *phum*, which was conceived of in terms of a populace settled together in one place, became in the eyes of the government a local population under a headman appointed by the government. *Phum*, in turn, became " hamlets " in a larger administrative unit, the *khum* or "commune." As Delvert has stated, the boundaries of the *khum* are artificial and "do not correspond to any human reality."[112] Only in Laos, apparently, has the village remained as the unit of local administration recognized by the state.

Both the local community defined as a unit of local administration within the state and the local community defined as a domain of a locality spirit are contexts within which political action takes place. We shall turn here to a consideration of the political organization of rural life, beginning with the roles played by those whose authority is believed to derive from locality spirits.

The power attributed to village spirits is wielded by those who serve as their intermediaries and/or administrators. In the upper Burmese village of Yeigyi, the cult of the village *nat*, centered on a shrine located at the entrance to the village, is officiated at by "a committee appointed by the village elders and consisting of three women and one man . . . Known as caretakers of the shrine . . . , the women are shamans (*nat kadaw*), while the status of the man . . . is unknown. . . ."[113] The women shamans qualify for appointment to the office by being possessed by the village *nats*. In northern Thailand, I also found that locality spirits had intermediaries who attained their offices as a consequence of possession. In northeastern Thailand and Laos, as in Burma, the officiants of the cult of the village spirits are chosen by the villagers. In both areas, as reported by Condominas and Tambiah and observed by myself, the normal method for selecting a new officiant of a village spirit cult is selection by the village headman in consultation with villagers. As Tambiah reports, the incumbent officiant may also nominate the person actually chosen. It is noteworthy that the selection is made by the village headman, since this makes the role of officiant of the cult of the village spirits subordinate to that of headman. The possibility of conflict in authority may be reflected in the situation in one Lao village, discussed by Condominas, in which the headman had made himself officiant of the cult.[114]

The role of the locality spirits in rural life has come under attack as customary law, which villagers traditionally believed was enforced by locality spirits, has given way to laws enforced by agents of the state, including village headmen in their capacity as local representatives of the state's authority.[115] In more general terms, as the authority of the state has been widened, the authority of locality spirits has been narrowed.

The tension between locally derived power and power emanating from the state is particularly evident in the role of the headman. Traditionally, in at least some parts of the region, the role of headman was inherited. For example, Spiro has reported that in a village in upper Burma, headmanship "had descended patrilineally in one family line. Even after the office became elective, it was the traditional heir—usually the only candidate—who was always elected."[116] Whether or not headmanship was inherited, it was often associated as much with the authority believed to emanate from locality spirits as it was with the authority of the state.

The reforms introduced in local administration during the colonial period changed the role of headman throughout much of the area. Today, headmen in all parts of the region are supposed, by law, to be elected by the people. Although such elections are held, in many places they serve to confirm, in ritual fashion, the right to office of a person whose claim may, in fact, be based on kinship or may be a function of the fact that he (and headmen are always male) is the preferred choice of a government official under whom he will serve.

Reforms in local administration have also placed increased demands on the headmen in the region. A headman is expected by officials of the state to transmit and implement those directives that serve the purposes of local administration. With improved communications and expanded administrative bureaucracies, the directives sent to headmen have multiplied. At the same time, a headman is still expected by his fellow villagers to mediate their disputes and to represent their interests even when those interests are in conflict with the interests of the state. A headman might well have to choose between reporting a crime (such as cattle rustling or bodily injury) to the state authorities, as the latter expect him to do, and not reporting such a crime because of pressures exerted on him by fellow villagers. A headman may also be ordered directly by state officials to recruit labor for the construction of some project such as road improvement or bridge building and simultaneously be faced by the unwillingness of his fellow villagers to participate in the project. Such conflicts have made the performance of the role difficult in many cases and have led, at least in some villages, to a situation in which it is difficult to find men who wish to become headmen.[117]

Not all villagers who aspire to power become village headmen. Some men are able through their actions, which are independent of office, to inspire fear and awe in others. Such actions may include bullying, success in flouting such laws of the state as those proscribing the manufacture of alcohol or the organization of gambling parties, and perhaps engaging in more serious crimes such as murder or robbery. Obviously there is only a thin line between the village " strongman " who in Thailand is called a *nakleng*, " a specialist in boldness," and a *dacoit* or outlaw. Being a dacoit holds an appeal to not a small number in the rural society of the region. During the period of British rule in Burma when local life was seriously disrupted by economic and political changes, many men, particularly in lower Burma, turned to dacoity.[118] A similar development occurred in Thailand, particularly in central Thailand, during the period of development of commercialized rice agriculture.[119] It can also be plausibly argued that the appeal that becoming soldiers has had for many villagers in Laos and Cambodia, irrespective of the sides on which they have fought, has some connection with efforts to acquire locally recognized power.

Although a " strongman " may gather a following who admire him for his boldness, other men may acquire followings because they are believed to be endowed with charisma, that is, what the Thai call *iddhi* and the Burmese *pon*. This charisma enables a man to influence events for the betterment of himself and his followers.

Both " strongmen " and charismatic individuals are expected to serve as patrons for their followers. Patronage is the more possible if the patron holds an office, and for this reason " strongmen " and charismatic individuals often compete for the office of headman within the village context. Even more effective patrons, from the point of view of villagers, are those " strongmen " or charismatic individuals who hold office in the bureaucracy, who are successful politicians, or who may even be managers of large business enterprises. Although few villagers become patrons of note, the " entourages ", to use Lucien Hanks' term, of these patrons often consist primarily of villagers.[120] Clients may call their patron by some title; for example, in Thailand, a patron may be referred to as a *phọ liang* or " nourishing father." In turn, clients may be referred to as " children " or " younger siblings " or some other term indicating inferior relationship vis-à-vis the patron.

Larger Communities and the Legitimacy of the State

Rural people throughout the region recognize that they belong to communities that are more inclusive than those found at the local level. Some spirits, for example, are considered to exercise authority over a region larger than a single village. Such is the case in upper Burma, where some well-known *nats* serve as the tutelary spirits of certain villages and also as regional spirits. In such cases, the shamans who serve these spirits are ranked in a hierarchy conceptualized in terms of the relationship between shaman and *nat*.[121] In northeastern Thailand, there is also a regional cult, one associated with the worship of generalized *devas* who are believed to be responsible for fertility. These *devas* are the object of an annual celebration, known as *bun bọng fai*, the " fire-rocket " festival, at which congregations of a group of neighboring temple monasteries compete in the sending off of rockets that are believed to inform the *devas* that it is time to send the rains and bring fertility to the land.[122] There is no special officiant for this cult; it is organized cooperatively by the religious and political leaders of the participating communities. Buddhist shrines throughout the region are also associated with regionally defined moral communities.[123] One of the politically more significant regional communities is that which encompasses peoples living in the whole of northeastern Thailand. This regional community, known under the label of *Isan*, a Sanskrit-derived word meaning " northeast," has been an important factor in contemporary Thai politics.[124]

Ethnically defined communities are also found in some parts of rural Theravada Buddhist Southeast Asia. For example, there are rural communities in northern Thailand and in Laos whose members identify themselves as " Lue," an identity that links them with a cultural tradition originally associated with Tai-speaking people living in an area of south China and northeastern Burma known as the Sipsọng panna.[125] Near the old Burmese capital of Pagan are communities of lacquer makers who identify themselves as " Yon," an identity that links them with the cultural tradition of the Tai-speaking people of northern Thailand. There are also " Lao " communities in central Thailand, " Phu Thai " communities in northeastern Thailand, " Khmer " communities in eastern Thailand, " Siamese " communities in western Cambodia, and so on. Some low-

and rural people are also of tribal background, and they too are often ethnically distinctive.

Closely related to ethnic distinctions are those distinctions based on caste. Caste groups differ from ethnic groups in that they are (theoretically) totally closed, with recruitment being exclusively through birth. Caste groups are also ranked hierarchically, whereas ethnic groups may or may not be. Although the cultural traditions of Theravada Buddhist Southeast Asia owe much to India, concepts of caste have never held much meaning for the rural peoples of these societies. Rural society is nowhere in this region divided into caste groupings. The only manifestation of caste to be found in the ideas held by rural people is in connection with the distinction between royalty and nonroyalty. In Cambodia and among the Tai-speaking peoples, kings are sometimes referred to by a term derived from the Indian term *ksatriya*, a term that in India proper refers to the caste that includes warriors and rulers. In Therevada Buddhist Southeast Asia, royalty has traditionally constituted a group apart, having its own *dharma* or tradition, albeit a group that unlike its Indian counterpart is not necessarily endogamous. Other caste-designating terms, most notably that of " brahmin," are known to people in the region, but they are not used to distinguish between caste groupings. " Brahmin " may be ritual specialists found at the courts of Southeast Asia rulers or, in northeastern Thailand and Laos, for example, local ritual specialists whose status is acquired, not inherited.

The most inclusive community most villagers would recognize is that of the state. For Burmese villagers, at least, the state is also associated with a national spirit. Min Mahagiri, who is said to reside at Mt. Popa near the old capital of Pagan, remains a powerful influence in the lives of villagers, although this influence is probably due mainly to the fact that Min Mahagiri is not only the national *nat*, but also the household *nat*.[126] For most villagers, Burmese included, the power of the state is a function not of its association with a national spirit but with the Buddhist merit of the ruler.

Legitimate power[127] throughout the region was traditionally believed by villagers to be vested in those who " have merit," that is, in persons whose status was determined by previous Karma. This idea contains an inherent problem, since it can only be demonstrated that one's Karma entitles one to rule if one is, in fact, ruling. So long as power was vested in kings belonging to a caste-like royal status group, this problem was not critical, at least not so from the point of view of the populace at large. It only became so during periods of inter-regnums, when there were several competitors seeking to establish their right to rule. In modern times, that is, since the onset of the colonial period, the problem has become endemic. The modern form of the problem can be stated in the following way. If power is not inherited but has to be competed for, then those who involve themselves in such competition run the danger of being immoral since they have to be aggressive (a quality subsumed under the cardinal vice of anger). In other words, the successful claimant to power may prove himself to have good past Karma by virtue of having gained power, but he may also have created bad Karma in the process.

In Thailand, this legitimacy problem has been ameliorated in part by the continued existence of a monarchy, albeit since 1932 a constitutional monarchy. The king, who is regarded as being above politics but who in the villagers' eyes embodies the merit believed to be necessary in one who rules, confers, albeit in only a symbolic fashion, the right to rule on his ministers. Yet even in Thailand the problem has not been fully resolved, as can be seen by the fact that corrupt ministers may rule in the king's name. In Cambodia, Prince Sihanouk was regarded by villagers as having the right to rule in view of his inherited position and the widely held belief that he too was a man who had merit. His deposition produced a severe crisis of legitimacy that has yet, even with the triumph of the Khmer Rouge, to be resolved fully. In Laos, the legitimacy of power has involved a complicated set of relationships between members of the various royal families of Luang Prabang, central Laos, and southern Laos. Although the King of Luang Prabang was officially recognized at the end of the period of French rule as King of all Laos, much of the populace of the country outside the traditional domains of Luang Prabang never came to view the throne at Luang Prabang as the source of legitimate power for all Laos. The Lao monarchy was eliminated altogether from the framework of political authority in late 1975 when a People's Republic was proclaimed. It is likely to be some years, however, before any new concept of legitimate power can be widely disseminated and understood by the Lao people as a whole.

In Burma, U Nu attempted to build a basis for legitimate power by publicly identifying himself with the cause of Buddhism in Burmese society. Not only did he put himself forward as a virtuous man, a man who was karmically endowed with the qualities of a ruler, but also as one who could lead others to salvation goals while working out his own salvation. This latter claim was to be carried out in form of socialist programs. As Smith has argued,

> Socialist Nu, by working to replace a capitalist economic structure based on acquisitiveness and competition with a cooperative socialist society, could help the common man toward the ultimate goal . . . U Nu could thus justify his socialism by associating it with Buddhism. But of equal importance is the fact that he could in this way rationalize his own deep involvement in politics as a *means* for the attainment by vast numbers of the ultimate spiritual goal.[128]

This effort to make good a claim to be a Bodhisattva, a future Buddha helping others to attain salvation, floundered on practical problems of political action. Yet, whatever pragmatic justification there may have been for Ne Win's successful coup in 1962, which brought U Nu's Prime Ministership to an end, this coup did create problems of legitimacy the Ne Win government has yet to resolve. U Nu had a large popular following because of his ability to link his leadership to Buddhist values. The Ne Win government has rejected such efforts and has attempted to base its political action on secular ideas. However, secular socialist ideology has not yet been adopted by the populace at large and cannot, thus, serve as a source of legitimating values for political rule. Although the crisis of legitimacy is perhaps most extreme in Burma (and, perhaps, equally as extreme in Cambodia), it is present everywhere in the region. The resolution (or resolutions) to this crisis will determine not only the future of political action but also the role of Buddhism within the societies of Therevada Buddhist Southeast Asia.

RELIGION, SOCIAL STRUCTURE, AND RURAL LIFE

Acquisition of Religious Virtue

Villagers throughout Theravada Buddhist Southeast Asia act not only in terms of the ecological, economic, and political contexts within which they live but also with reference to their ideas of salvation. As noted earlier in this chapter, salvation is conceived of by villagers to involve the acquisition of religious merit that will be translated into a reduction of suffering. The quest for merit or virtue in a person's life should begin with maturation.

Maturation is not only a matter of biological development; for villagers in this part of Southeast Asia, it also requires that people take part in acts of ritual transformation. Such a transformation will divide the " raw " from the " ripe," to use the terms employed by people in Thailand. The " raw " person is believed to be morally untempered and to be tempted more easily to commit socially irresponsible acts. For women, ripening involves the bearing of a child after marriage. In addition, in all parts of the region except northern Thailand, it also calls for the woman who has borne a child to " lie by the fire " for a number of days, and, in some instances, for as much as three weeks. Immediately after the birth of the child, the mother is made to rest on a plank bed placed next to a fire, which is kept going for the entire period involved. During this period, the woman can consume only a broth made of herbs and perhaps a limited number of bland foods. One basic purpose of " lying by the fire " is curative; villagers believe that the fire will dry the uterus, rid the woman of the bad blood of childbirth, heal the wounds, and bring the milk necessary for nursing. But more is involved than a cure; as Jane Hanks has written of Bang Chan:

> The fire rest was one of the series of rites of the life cycle which marked the course of an individual from birth to death. . . . Through the consecrated fire a woman formally achieved full maturity: she became *suk* (cooked, ripe, mature). Maturity did not come just by bearing a child. The fire brought about the transformation.[129]

Moreover, not every woman attains this maturity. In northeastern Thailand women who had never borne a child and, thus, never laid by the fire, were considered to be women who either had bad *Karma* and were to be pitied or who chose to create bad Karma (e.g., prostitutes) and were to be criticized.[130] Villagers also recognized that the practice of lying by the fire was not followed by many women living in towns. They saw the practice of having babies in hospitals as being functionally equivalent to the lying by the fire.

Village woman "lying by the fire" in a northeastern Thai village. This woman had just given birth to her first child. (*Jane Keyes photograph*)

Ordination of a young man into the Buddhist Sangha, northern Thailand. (*C. F. Keyes photograph*)

For males, the ritual transformation equivalent to the " lying by the fire " for women is that of ordination into the Buddhist Sangha. Men, unlike women, are born with the karmic possibility of becoming members of the Sangha, thereby acquiring a great store of " merit." Moreover, it is not required, as it is in Christian monasticism, that those who become members of the Sangha take on vows for life. The merit acquired for even a temporary sojourn in the Sangha is believed to be more efficacious in reducing suffering than is the merit acquired by almost any other act. In addition, it can also be shared with those who sponsor the act of ordination, such sponsors most usually being the parents of those ordained. Not only does entrance into the Order bring religious rewards, but it also serves to effect a moral transformation of a person. A former member of the Order is believed to be one who is less tempted to commit demeritorious acts. In addition, the symbolism of the rite of ordination reinforces the popular belief that those who have been members of the Order have become sexually potent.[131] Finally, it is believed by many people throughout the region that ordination for men and " lying by the fire " for women is a prerequisite for those who would acquire certain magical skills. Again, to quote Jane Hanks regarding Bang Chan in central Thailand,

> Only the ritually mature could be counted on to be compassionate, strong, responsible adults, and so were permitted access to occult powers. Whether by ordination or the fire-rest, to be *suk* [" ripe "] was an absolute prerequisite to magical knowledge.[132]

The age at which ordination normally takes place varies throughout the region. In Burma, it is the ideal that boys between about the ages of 8 and 13 (and sometimes boys of an even younger age) should be ordained novices in the order. A similar ideal formerly obtained in northern Thailand, but it was modified in about the 1930s when Thai Sangha authorities began to insist that the candidates first be literate. Today, those who are ordained as novices have already finished the four years of compulsory primary education. Thus, boys in northern Thailand are rarely ordained novices before the age of about 11 or 12. In northeastern Thailand, Laos, and Cambodia, it is not uncommon for boys to be ordained novices, but whether they have been or not, it is the ideal that all men should have been ordained monks. In central Thailand, ordination as a novice is less common and the ideal is that men should be ordained monks. Since ordination as a monk cannot take place until a man has reached 20 years of age, those who fulfill the ideal by becoming monks are fully adult.

Whereas in Burma it appears that almost every village boy will be ordained a novice, there are a significant number of men in Thailand, Laos, and Cambodia who have never been members of the Order. In these countries, those who have been members of the Order are distinguished by title from those who have not. In Laos and northeastern Thailand, the ex-novice is called a *siang*, in central Thailand, a *chiang*, in northern Thailand a *nọi*. In Laos, northeastern and central Thailand, a man who has been a monk carries the title of *thit*, whereas in northern Thailand such a man carries the title of *nan*.

In northeastern Thailand and in Laos, the ordination ritual is not the only ritual connected with the Sangha that effects a ritual transformation in status. Villagers themselves may organize a ritual, the central act of which involves the pouring of water over a monk, and the function of which is to honor a monk for his piety and virtue. After this ritual has been performed, the monk has a new title, a title moreover that he retains if he leaves the monkhood. In the past this ritual may have been performed for a single monk as many as eight times, each time resulting in a change in status, but today it is performed no more than three or four times. After the first performance of the ritual, the monk attains the title of *somdet*, or *can* when he leaves the order; after the second, he becomes known as *sa*, or *can sa* on becoming a layman; after the the third, he receives the title of *nja khu*, or *can khu* on leaving the order; and (according to my informants) after the fourth, he attains the title of *atchanja than*, or *can than* on leaving the order.[133] These set of ranks serve as incentives, I suggest, to keep a man in the monkhood for more than just a brief period. The longer the stay in the Order, the more virtue the man acquires.

Becoming a member of the Buddhist order is not the only way one can enhance one's virtue. In Laos, and perhaps elsewhere as well, a man who has sponsored the ordination of his son will be known as " father-of-novice-so-and-so " or " father-of-monk-so-and-so." Even where such a title does not exist, those who sponsor ordinations are believed to acquire great merit. Yet another significant way to gain religious virtue is to donate wealth sufficient for the construction of major religious edifices. In Burma, a person who sponsors the construction of a new monastery or a new reliquary (*cetiya*) will gain a title. The donor of a monastery henceforth will be known as *kyaung taga*, whereas the donor of a *cetiya* will be known as *paya taga*.[134]

Lesser acts of charity are also recognized as being indicative of virtue and the recognition accorded a " pious person," that is, one who regularly undertakes merit making, is aspired to by some, especially women. Piety can also be demonstrated in another way; one may become a lay devotee, a role taken up mainly by the elderly. In Thailand, and perhaps elsewhere, such lay devotees are sometimes referred to as *upāsaka* and *upāsikā*, terms that in their original context in the Pali literature meant simply lay male supporter and lay female supporter. The lay devotee is one who keeps eight rather than five precepts, who spends Buddhist holy days, at least during the lenten period, at the monastery or temple monastery, and who undertakes meditation at least on such holy days.

Taking into consideration all social roles and the structural bases whereby these roles are distributed, we can now construct something of a general picture of rural society in Theravada Buddhist Southeast Asia. Of fundamental importance is the ascriptive distinction between the sexes. Women are regarded as inherently lower in religious status than men, and women are barred by sex from aspiring to the roles to which the greatest virtue attaches, namely the roles associated with the Buddhist Sangha. On the other hand, women in most rural communities in the region provide the continuity of domestic groups and control the transmission of the most important means of production, land. Although a woman's role is often confined to the domestic context, those who have undergone the ritual transformation of " lying by the fire " can aspire to the authority that derives from being a spirit medium or shaman. Mature women, can, and, perhaps more often than men, do play entrepreneurial roles. Traditionally because women did not have access to the education provided at temple monasteries, they could not acquire most of the specialized roles found in the villages. Today, in those parts of the region where women have been given access to modern secular education, they can aspire to, and occasionally attain, such roles as those of village school teacher, midwife, or nurse.

Men today, as in the past, have a greater range of possible roles to which they can aspire. For the most part such aspirations are not conditioned by membership in kin groups, an exception being those cases in which access to the role of headman is determined by inheritance. A few men may seek to maximize the qualities of virtue, or power, or wealth to the total exclusion of other qualities. Thus, some men become and remain monks for life. Some men become outlaws, the leaders of dacoit bands. And others orient themselves entirely to the pursuit of wealth. It should be noted, however, that although those who become monks for life are greatly respected, those who devote themselves totally to the pursuit and use of power or wealth are considered to be immoral; we will discuss the reason for this in the next section. Within the village context, the " ideal " man is one who has acquired virtue through entrance into the Buddhist Sangha and, thus matured, has gone on as a layman to acquire another role such as headman, ritual specialist, entrepreneur.[135]

Even traditionally, villagers could aspire to roles in contexts other than those provided by the village in which they were born or into which they had married. For most mobile villagers in the past, however, the shift was still from one village context to another, often made in the search for better land. Nonetheless, there have probably always been some villagers who have succeeded in moving upward from the village via the Buddhist Sangha; in modern times, this form of social mobility has become very significant, at least in Thailand.[136] Modern formal education has also provided a channel of social mobility, although only a very small number of villagers anywhere in the region have advanced upward through this channel. In addition, those villagers who have been physically mobile in modern times have much more commonly moved from villages to towns and cities than from village to village. In instances in which villagers move to towns and cities, they are usually constrained to accept unskilled proletarian jobs. However, not a few villagers—particularly in Thailand—have been able to apprentice themselves to those holding more skilled jobs. Such villagers may move up into skilled positions and thereby transcend not only the traditional village pattern whereby apprenticeship was a relationship established between kinsmen but also the wider social pattern of the ethnic division of labor, which we shall examine in more detail when we focus our attention on urban life. Some villagers have also succeeded through entrepreneurial activities in attaining roles in social contexts other than that of the village.

Although physical and social mobility appear to be more characteristic of Theravada Buddhist societies in the modern period than they were traditionally, most born in villages still remain members of village society for their whole lives. For some purposes, the peasantry of these countries may be conceived of as belonging to a distinctive class segment,[137] although the boundaries that divide peasants from other segments of the society may also be those of ethnicity, of regionalism, or, even, in the case of royalty vis-à-vis the rest of society, peasants included, something approaching caste.

Within the rural communities themselves, society is not stratified, but roles are ranked. Those with the highest prestige within rural society are the members of the Sangha, that is, those men who have demonstrated that they have acquired great virtue. Elaborate codes of deference are used in all Theravada Buddhist societies by laymen and laywomen in their relationships with monks. Below the monks come the men who have been " ripened " through the ritual transformation of ordination into the Sangha, and below them are the " raw " but still moral men and the " mature " women, that is those women who have married, born children, and (except where the custom does not exist) passed through the ritual transformation of " laying by the fire." Immature but moral women are considered to be of roughly the same rank as children, the latter being those who are too young to have reached ritually marked maturity. The people held in lowest regard in the countryside are those whose immoral and/or criminal acts have placed them literally beneath society, roughly on a par with animals and malevolent spirits.

"Loosely Structured" Social Systems

Whether one examines the social life of peasants in the region from the perspective of local communities or the total social system, it can be seen that nonascriptive criteria are of equal if not greater importance than ascriptive criteria in the distribution of social roles and in the determination of the hierarchical positioning of these roles. This fact has been taken by some interpreters as evidence that these societies are " loosely structured." The concept of the " loosely structured social system " was first advanced by John F. Embree in an article published in 1950 and based on rather unsystematic observations made in Thailand.[138] Embree's characterization of Thai society, it should be noted, was formed partially on the basis of contrasts with society in Japan, where Embree had undertaken anthropological researches prior to World War II.

In his article, Embree examined the behavior of the Thai within a number of social contexts such as the family, the village, the military, and games. On the basis of his observations, Embree concluded that Thai behavior is " loosely structured," that is, within these contexts there is " considerable variation of individual behavior."[139] He further argued that his analysis was applicable to those neighboring societies with whom the Thai share many of the same cultural patterns, including (especially?) Indian influences.

Embree's rather impressionistic analysis has been the subject of considerable subsequent debate by anthropologists and other social scientists.[140] This debate has sometimes focused on the wrong issues. For example, some have argued as though they regard social structure and the organization of social roles to be irrelevant to an understanding of behavior in the rural areas of Theravada Buddhist Southeast Asia. For example, H. P. Phillips has maintained that the concern of those who study Thai rural society " is not and should not be structural analysis but rather the study of the behavior of Thai peasants."[141] In a similar vein, Piker has argued that " individuals in Thai society as a rule either behave independently of the formal groups to which they nominally belong . . . or find membership in these groups does not yield unequivocal prescriptions and proscriptions for their behavior in many situations that arise from their capacity as group members."[142] As the survey of rural society we have undertaken here shows, social structural and social organizational factors provide frameworks within which behavior takes place. The study of social structure and social organization and the study of behavior are not alternative research strategies, the one valid the other invalid. Rather, they are complementary strategies, both needed if a full picture of life in any society is to be comprehended.

The real issue at stake in the debate over the utility of the characterization of " loosely structured " as applied to social systems in Theravada Buddhist Southeast Asia is how one is to explain why there is at least equal emphasis in these societies on the individual's " making " himself or herself as there is on learning and carrying out roles assigned on the basis of ascribed status. Embree's original interpretation, albeit impressionistic, provided an important insight into this question. It is to Thai culture, and the values derived from this culture, Embree argued, that one is to look for an explanation of what he termed " individualistic behavior."[143]

The fact that in all Theravada Buddhist societies nonascriptive criteria are at least as important as ascriptive criteria in the allocation of social roles can be explained, I believe, with reference to the Buddhist ideas that Karma not only determines one's place along the hierarchy of relative suffering but also that human beings create their own Karma. This granted, it does not follow, as a number of observers have argued, that people in these societies are highly individualistic. This position has been especially developed by Phillips in his interpretation of personality as found in the central Thai village of Bang Chan. Phillips argues that Buddhist belief emphasizes " the primacy of individual action and individual responsibility." According to Phillips, " the principal tenet of Hinayana Buddhism is the complete psychological freedom, isolation, and responsibility of every person."[144] Phillips then argues that although these Buddhist beliefs " translate and function on the level of workaday behavior in an extremely subtle manner," they do " impart a fundamental legitimacy to the pursuit of individualistic self-concern."[145]

Although Phillips' argument has some plausibility, it has two major difficulties that preclude its application generally in this part of Southeast Asia. First, as reported by a number of different observers, villagers in other parts of the region do not exhibit individualistic behavioral patterns, at least not to the degree that Phillips has reported in Bang Chan. That this is the case does not, of course, necessarily negate the argument that values derived from Buddhism provide a meaningful basis for individualistic behavior. Rather, it means that Buddhist belief cannot be claimed as the only cause of individualistic behavior.[146] The second problem with Phillips' argument is that he reduces the religious world view of Theravada Buddhist villagers to an interpretation of the Law of Karma, which includes the actions undertaken to affect future salvation, but excludes the consequences of actions committed in previous lifetimes. In other words, he does not recognize that karmic theory sanctions not only freedom of action (i.e., " loose structure ") so that humans can work out their own destiny, but also prescriptive constraints on such action as rationalized in terms of karmic heritage. Moreover, he also tends to discount those merit making actions that require the individual to operate not in isolation but as a member of social groups. As a number of observers have reported, many of the rituals associated with merit making are collective rituals, and, even when they are privately sponsored, they are often occasions for promoting social solidarity.[147] In addition, ethical interpretations of making merit emphasize being generous and charitable toward others as well as maintaining equanimity and avoiding entanglements that might lead to outbreaks of anger. He also does not take into account the idea that merit can be shared with others, an idea that may appear to Westerners as unorthodox, but, in fact, has been a part of Theravada Buddhist doctrine since at least the fifth century A.D. and is to be found in every local tradition of Theravada Buddhism. In sum, Phillips was quite right in attempting to connect religious derived values and social action. However, a fuller picture necessitates taking into account the whole panoply of social action as well as the total field of religious belief found in particular communities.

In Bang Chan, as elsewhere in central Thailand and in lower Burma, practically the only inalterable social attribute determined by birth is one's sex. Even one's kinship status is potentially changeable. In at least some central Thai villages, adoption and fosterage are well-developed patterns; even if one is raised within the same family through childhood, one eventually will establish a totally independent family. Phillips has characterized these kinship patterns as " centripetal."[148] Such centripetal patterns can be rationalized by reference to beliefs that stress the impermanence of all things and the ever-changing nature of experience. In contrast to these patterns, however, observers of village life in northern and northeastern Thailand and in Laos have reported patterns of enduring kinship relationships that last throughout the lifetime of the individual. These patterns too can be rationalized by reference to Buddhist beliefs as one's ascriptive kinship position is seen as a consequence of past Karma. However, nowhere in the region do we find social action constrained by kinship patterns to the degree that it is in either India or China. Although one may have certain responsibilities to one's kinsmen because of an ascriptive status determined by past Karma, one also has the responsibility to oneself in determining what actions one will undertake since these actions will have consequences for oneself. It should also be noted in this connection that even in those areas where kinship structure has been relatively strongly emphasized, religious beliefs have still tended to preclude any significant development of ancestor worship, such worship being almost invariably associated with unilineal kinship. The idea of the dissolution of the " vital essence " at death or within a short period of time thereafter and the belief in rebirth are ill suited to any well-developed system of ancestor worship. Although some forms of ancestor worship are found in parts of the region, the belief in the continued existence of ancestors in the spirit state also entails believing that these ancestors are living in a plane of existence lower than that of the human. This is certainly not a very adequate belief on which to posit the continued presence of revered ancestors in spirit form.

In sum, some ascriptive characteristics of social life are recognized by all peoples throughout Therevada Buddhist Southeast Asia and rationalized in all cases by reference to the effects of Karma acquired in previous existences. These prescriptive characteristics vary to some extent from area to area, although villagers everywhere continue to recognize a basic ascriptive division between the sexes. Yet even where ascriptive characteristics are relatively strongly emphasized, villagers in the region nowhere belong to worlds whose social parameters are absolutely and unchangeably defined. All people in the region believe that they have some significant degree of freedom of action whereby they generate the Karma whose consequences will determine their position on the hierarchy of suffering. This dual orientation of Buddhist belief, one to past Karma whose consequences are apparent in the present state of the social world and the other to present Karma whose consequences will determine future freedom from suffering, stands in marked contrast to the traditional world view of the other civilized people of the region, the Vietnamese.

NOTES

Chapter 3

1. For lower Burma, the main sources on which I have drawn are those by Pfanner based on research carried out in 1959–1960 in a village located eight miles north of Pegu. See David E. Pfanner, *Rice and Religion in a Burmese Village* (Ph.D. Thesis, Cornell University, 1962); Pfanner, " The Buddhist Monk in Rural Burmese Society," in *Anthropological Studies in Theravada Buddhism*, by Manning Nash, *et al.* (New Haven: Yale University Southeast Asia Studies, Cultural Report Series No. 13, 1966), pp. 77–96; Pfanner and Ingersoll, " Theravada Buddhism and Village Economic Behavior," *J. of Asian Studies*, III (1962), pp. 341–61.

2. For upper Burma, I have used as my primary sources the various studies based on research in 1959–1961 carried out by June Nash, Manning Nash, and Melford E. Spiro. See June Nash, " Living with Nats: An Analysis of Animism in Burman Village Social Relations," in Manning Nash, *et al.*, *op. cit.*, pp. 117–36; Nash, " Education in a New Nation ": "The Village School in Upper Burma," *Inter-*

national *Journal of Comparative Sociology*, II (1961), pp. 135–43; Nash, " Burmese
Buddhism in Everyday Life," *American Anthropologist*, LXV (1963), pp. 285–95;
Nash, *The Golden Road to Modernity* (New York: John Wiley and Sons, 1965);
Nash, " Ritual and Ceremonial Cycle in Upper Burma," in M. Nash, *et al.*,
op. cit., pp. 97–116; June Nash and Manning Nash, " Marriage, Family and
Population Growth in Upper Burma," *Southwestern Journal of Anthropology*,
XIX (1963), pp. 251–66; M. E. Spiro, " Religious Systems as Culturally Con-
stituted Defense Mechanisms," in *Context and Meaning in Cultural Anthropology*,
ed. by M. E. Spiro (New York: Free Press, 1965), pp. 100–113; Spiro, " Buddhism
and Economic Saving in Burma," *American Anthropologist*, LXVIII (1966), pp.
1163–73; Spiro, *Burmese Supernaturalism* (Englewood Cliffs, N.J.: Prentice-Hall,
1967); Spiro, " Religion, Personality, and Behavior in Burma," *American
Anthropologist*, LXX (1968), pp. 359–63; Spiro, " Factionalism and Politics in
Rural Burma," in *Local-Level Politics*, ed. by Marc J. Swartz (Chicago: Aldine,
1968), pp. 401–21; Spiro, " The Psychological Functions of Witchcraft Belief:
The Burmese Case," in *Mental Health Research in Asia and the Pacific*,
ed. by William Caudill and Tsung-Yi Lin (Honolulu: East-West Center Press,
1969); Spiro, *Buddhism and Society* (New York: Harper and Row, 1970);
Spiro, " Some Psychodynamic Determinants of Household Composition in
Village Burma," in *The Psychological Study of Theravada Societies*, ed. by Steven
Piker (Leiden: E. J. Brill, Contributions to Asian Studies, Vol. 8, 1975), pp.
126–38; Spiro, " Marriage Payments: A Paradigm from the Burmese Perspective,'
J. Anthropological Research, XXXI (1975), pp. 89–115.

3. The most intensive research on a particular rural community anywhere in main-
land Southeast Asia was the research carried out between 1948 and 1958 by
Sharp, Hanks, and associates in Bang Chan, a community located 31 kilometers
northeast of Bangkok. The published literature on Bang Chan is quite extensive.
Among the more important are the following: R. K. Goldsen and Max Ralis,
Factors Related to Acceptance of Innovations in Bang Chan Thailand (Ithaca,
N.Y.: Cornell University Southeast Asia Program, Data Paper No. 25, 1957);
Jane R. Hanks, " Reflections on the Ontology of Rice," in *Culture in History:
Essays in Honor of Paul Radin*, ed. by Stanley Diamond (New York: Columbia
University Press, 1961), pp. 298–301; Hanks, *Maternity and Its Rituals in Bang
Chan* (Ithaca, N.Y.: Cornell University, Southeast Asia Program, Data Paper
No. 51, 1963); Lucien M. Hanks, Jr., " Indifference to Modern Education in a
Thai Farming Community," *Practical Anthropology*, VII (1960), pp. 18–29;
Hanks, " Bang Chan and Bangkok: Five Perspectives on the Relation of Local
to National History," *Journal of Southeast Asian History*, VIII, 2 (1967), pp.
250–56; Hanks, *Rice and Man: Agricultural Ecology in Southeast Asia* (Chicago:
Aldine, 1972); L. M. Hanks, Jr., and H. P. Phillips, " A Young Thai from the
Countryside: A Psychosocial Analysis," in *Studying Personality Cross-Culturally*,
ed. by Bert Kaplan (Evanston, Ill.: Row, Peterson and Company, 1961); Hazel M.
Hauck, and others, *Aspects of Health, Sanitation and Nutritional Status in a
Siamese Rice Village* (Ithaca, N.Y.: Cornell University Southeast Asia Program
Data Paper No. 22, 1956); H. M. Hauck, Saovanee Sudsaneh, Jane R. Hanks,
and others, *Food Habits and Nutrient Intakes in a Siamese Rice Village* (Ithaca,
N.Y.: Cornell University Southeast Asia Program, Data Paper No. 29, 1958);
H. M. Hauck, and others, *Maternal and Child Health in a Siamese Rice Village:*

Nutritional Aspects (Ithaca, N.Y.: Cornell University Southeast Asia Program, Data Paper, No. 39, 1959); Kamol Odd Janlehka, *A Study of the Economy of a Rice Growing Village in Central Thailand* (Bangkok: Division of Agricultural Economics, Office of the Under-Secretary of State, Ministry of Agriculture, n.d. [Orig., Ph.D. Thesis, Cornell University, 1955]); Herbert P. Phillips, "The Election Ritual in a Thai Village," *Journal of Social Issues*, XIV, 4 (1958), pp. 36–50; Phillips, "Relationships between Personality and Social Structure in a Siamese Peasant Community," *Human Organization*, XXII, 2 (1963), pp. 105–108; Phillips, *Thai Peasant Personality* (Berkeley and Los Angeles: University of California Press, 1965); Lauriston Sharp, "Peasants and Politics in Thailand," *Far Eastern Survey*, XIX (1950), pp. 157–61; Lauriston Sharp, Hazel M. Hauck, and Robert B. Textor, *Siamese Rice Village: A Preliminary Study of Bang Chan 1948–1949* (Bangkok: Cornell Research Center, 1953); Robert B. Textor, *An Inventory of Non-Buddhist Supernatural Objects in a Central Thai Village* (Ph.D. Thesis, Cornell University, 1960); David A. Wilson and Herbert P. Phillips, "Elections and Parties in Thailand," *Far Eastern Survey*, XXVII (1958), pp. 113–19. For central Thailand, I also draw on the work of Howard Kaufman who carried out research in 1953 in the community of Bangkhuad, also located near Bangkok. See Howard K. Kaufman, *Bangkhuad: A Community Study in Thailand* (Locust Valley, N.Y.: J. J. Augustin, 1960).

4. For northern Thailand, I have used the studies of Kingshill, Potter, and Wijeye-wardene on rural life in the Chiang Mai Valley, of Moerman and Turton on rural life in Chiang Rai province, and of Davis on a village in Nan province. See Konrad Kingshill, *Ku Daeng—The Red Tomb: A Village Study in Northern Thailand*, 2nd rev. ed. (Bangkok: Bangkok Christian College, 1965); Jack M. Potter, *Thai Peasant Social Structure* (Chicago: University of Chicago Press, forthcoming); Gehan Wijeyewardene, "Address, Abuse and Animal Categories in Northern Thailand," *Man*, n.s. III (1968), pp. 76–93; Wijeyewardene, "The Language of Courtship in Chiang Mai," *J. Siam Society*, LIX (1968), pp. 211–31; Wijeyewardene, "The Still Point and the Turning World; Toward the Structure of Northern Thai Religion," *Mankind*, VII (1970), pp. 247–55; Wijeyewardene, "Patrons and *Pau Liang*," *J. Siam Society*, II (1971), pp. 229–34; Michael Moerman, "Ethnic Identification in a Complex Civilization: Who Are the Lue?" *Am. Anthropologist*, LXVII (1965), pp. 1215–30; Moerman, "Ban Ping's Temple: The Center of a 'Loosely Structured' Society," in *Anthropological Studies in Theravada Buddhism* by Manning Nash, *et al.* (New Haven: Yale University Southeast Asia Studies, Cultural Report Series No. 13, 1965), pp. 137–74; Moerman, "Kinship and Commerce in a Thai-Lue Village," *Ethnology*, V (1966), pp. 360–64; Moerman, "A Minority and Its Government: The Thai-Lue of Northern Thailand," in *Southeast Asian Tribes, Minorities and Nations*, ed. by Peter Kunstadter (Princeton, N.J.: Princeton University Press, 1967), pp. 401–24; Moerman, *Agricultural Change and Peasant Choice in a Thai Village* (Berkeley and Los Angeles: University of California Press, 1968); "Being Lue: Uses and Abuses of Ethnicity," in *Essays on the Problem of Tribe*, ed. by June Helm (Seattle: University of Washington Press, Proceedings of the American Ethnological Society, 1967 Spring Conference, 1968), pp. 153–69; Moerman, "A Thai Village Headman as Synaptic Leader," *J. of Asian Studies*, XXVIII (1969), pp. 535–49; Andrew Turton, "Matrilineal Descent Groups and Spirit Cults of

the Thai-Yuan in Northern Thailand," *J. Siam Society*, LX (1972), pp. 217–56; Richard Davis, " Muang Matrifocality," *J. Siam Society*, LXI (1973), pp. 53–62; Davis, " Tolerance and Intolerance of Ambiguity in Northern Thai Myth and Ritual," *Ethnology*, XIII, 1 (1974), pp. 1–24.

5. For northeastern Thailand I have drawn on my own research, carried out primarily in 1962–1964 with some additional data collected in 1967–1968 and 1972–1974 and focused on the village of Ban Nong Tun in the central part of the region. I have also drawn on the work of S. J. Tambiah who made a study of a village in the northern part of the region in 1961–1962 with additional data being collected in 1965 and 1966. See Charles F. Keyes, " Ethnic Identity and Loyalty of Villagers in Northeastern Thailand, *Asian Survey*, VI, 7 (1966), pp. 362–70; Keyes, " Peasant and Nation: A Thai-Lao Village in a Thai State " (Ph.D. Dissertation, Cornell University, 1967); Keyes, *Isan: Regionalism in Northeastern Thailand* (Ithaca, N.Y.: Cornell Southeast Asia Program, Data Paper No. 65, 1967); Keyes, " Local Leadership in Rural Thailand," in *Modern Thai Politics*, ed. by Clark Neher (Cambridge, Mass.: Schenkman, 1976); Keyes, " The Northeastern Thai Village: Stable Order and Changing World," *Journal of the Siam Society*, LXIII, 1 (1975), pp. 177–207; Keyes, " Kin Groups in a Thai-Lao Village," in *Change and Persistence in Thai Society: Homage to Lauriston Sharp*, *II*, ed. by G. William Skinner and A. Thomas Kirsch (Ithaca, N.Y.: Cornell University Press, 1975), pp. 275–97; Keyes, " In Search of Land: Village Formation in the Central Chi River Valley, Northeastern Thailand," *Contributions to Asian Studies*, IX (1976), pp. 45–63; S. J. Tambiah, " Literacy in a Buddhist Village in North-East Thailand," in *Literacy in Traditional Societies*, ed. by Jack Goody (Cambridge: Cambridge University Press, 1968), pp. 86–131; Tambiah, " The Ideology of Merit and the Social Correlates of Buddhism in a Thai Village," in *Dialectic in Practical Religion*, ed. by E. R. Leach (Cambridge: Cambridge University Press, 1968), pp. 41–121; Tambiah, " Animals are Good to Think and Good to Prohibit," *Ethnology*, VII1 (1969), pp. 423–59; Tambiah, *Buddhism and the Spirit Cults in North-East Thailand* (Cambridge: Cambridge University Press, 1970).

6. For Laos, I have drawn on studies made in the rural area of the Vientiane Plain by Ayabe in 1959, Kaufman in 1956–1957, and Condominas and associates in 1959 and 1960–1961. See Tsuneo Ayabe, *The Village of Ban Pha Khao, Vientiane Province*, ed. by Joel M. Halpern (Los Angeles: University of California, Department of Anthropology, Laos Project Paper No. 14, 1961); Howard K. Kaufman, Village Life in Vientiane Province (1955–1957), ed. by Joel M. Halpern (Los Angeles: University of California, Department of Anthropology, Laos Project Paper No. 12, 1961); C. Gaudillot and G. Condominas, *La Plaine de Vientiane*, *Rapport d'étude* (3 vols., Paris: Bureau pour le développement de la production agricole, 1959); Condominas, *Essai sur la société rurale Lao de la région de Vientiane* (Vientiane: Commissariat aux affaires rurales, 1962); Condominas, " Notes sur le Bouddhisme populaire en milieu rural Lao," *Archives de Sociologie de Religions*, XXV (1968), pp. 80–110; XXV (1968), pp. 111–150; Condominas, " Notes sur le droit foncier lao en milieu rural dans la plaine de Vientiane," in *Felicitation Volume Presented to George Coedès*, ed. by A. B. Griswold and Jean Boisselier (Ascona, Switzerland: Artibus Asiae, Special Number of *Artibus Asiae*, Vol. XXIV, 3/4, 1961), pp. 255–62.

7. For Cambodia, I have drawn on the work of Delvert and Ebihara, the former having carried out survey research in the rural areas between 1951 and 1956 and the latter an anthropologist who made a study in 1959–1960 of life in Village Kong, a village located 30 kilometers southwest of Phnom Penh. See Jean Delvert, *Le Paysan Cambodgien* (Paris: Mouton, 1961); May Ebihara, " Inter-relations between Buddhism and Social Systems in Cambodian Peasant Culture," in *Anthropological Studies in Theravada Buddhism* by Manning Nash, *et al.*, pp. 175–96; Ebihara, " Khmer " in *Ethnic Groups in Mainland Southeast Asia*, by Frank M. LeBar, Gerald C. Hickey, John K. Musgrave, and others (New Haven: HRAF Press, 1964), pp. 98–105.

8. Full descriptions of Buddhist cosmology are contained in texts that could probably be found in most village-monastery libraries. It is unlikely, however, that many villagers would be able to give any more elaborate description of the cosmological classifications than I have given here. These subdivisions are also the only ones to figure prominently in the Buddhist art found in local temples. For a discussion of the cosmological tradition as it is found in Burma, see Shway Yoe, [Sir James George Scott], *The Burman* (New York: W. W. Norton, 1963 [orig. 1910]), pp. 88–106. For Thailand, see " La Naissance du Monde selon le Bouddhisme Siamois," by Charles Archaimbault, in *La Naissance du Monde* (Paris: Ed. Seuil, Sources Orientales I, 1959), pp. 368–81; and Tambiah, *Buddhism and Spirit Cults . . .* , pp. 32–52. The same tradition as that found in Thailand is also found in Laos and Cambodia.

9. On the cultural conceptions related to agriculture in Laos, see Charles Archaimbault, " Les rites agraires dans le Moyen-Laos," in *Structures Religieuses Lao* by Charles Archaimbault (Vientiane: Vithagna, 1973), pp. 219–42.

10. Tambiah, *Buddhism and Spirit Cults . . .* , p. 41.

11. Reginald LeMay, *An Asian Arcady: The Land and Peoples of Northern Siam* (Cambridge: Heffer, 1926), p. 135. In the older literature on northern Thailand, the people of the region are often called " Lao."

12. Spiro, *Burmese Supernaturalism*, pp. 247–80.

13. Tambiah, *Buddhism and Spirit Cults . . .* , p. 41.

14. Tambiah, *Buddhism and Spirit Cults . . .* , p. 58; E. Porée-Maspero, *op. cit.*, I, p. 19. One of the best studies of the concept of the " vital essence," with particular reference to the Tai peoples, but also with comparisons with beliefs of neighboring peoples, is the work in Thai, *Khwan lae prapheni tham khwan* (" The *Khwan* and Customs Connected with the *Khwan* ") by Sathian Koset (Phya Anuman Rajadhon) (Bangkok: Kaona, 1963). An abbreviated English version of this work has appeared as " The Khwan and Its Ceremonies," by Phya Anuman Rajadhon, *Journal of the Siam Society*, L, 2 (1962), pp. 119–64.

15. Spiro, *Burmese Supernaturalism*, pp. 69–70.

16. Cf. Tambiah, *Buddhism and Spirit Cults . . .* , pp. 57–59. My observation is based on my own interviews in Ban Nọng Tụn.

17. *Vissuddhi-Magga*, chap. xvii, from the translation in *Buddhism in Translations* by Henry Clarke Warren (Cambridge: Harvard University Press, 1953), p. 238.

18. Spiro reports that many villagers interviewed did not know the concept of *leikbya* or professed they did not believe in it; rather they used the terms *winyin*

(i.e., *viññāna*) or *nāma* instead. Spiro appears to have missed the point, recognized by Tambiah, that " vital essence " and " consciousness " are complementary not synonomous concepts. See Spiro, *op. cit.*, p. 69n; Tambiah, *Buddhism and Spirit Cults* . . . , pp. 57–59.

19. See Shway Yoe, *op. cit.*, pp. 4–13. Spiro, in his compendia volumes on Burmese religion gives scant mention to astrology and related topics.

20. See C. F. Keyes, " Buddhist Pilgrimage Centers and the Twelve-Year Cycle," *History of Religions*, XV (1975), pp. 44-62.

21. Tambiah (*Buddhism and The Spirit Cults* . . . , pp. 272–75) only briefly touches on the subject of fate and does not mention the concept of *khọ*.

22. See Keyes, " Buddhist Pilgrimage Centers and the Twelve-Year Cycle . . .", for a case (in northern Thailand) in which the concept of fate comes close to posing an alternative definition of ultimate reality to that offered by Buddhist thought.

23. Spiro's discussion of socialization is to be found interspersed throughout his various writings based on his researches in Burma. Steven Piker's research focused on a village in central Thailand and has been reported on in the following: Piker, *Character and Socialization in a Thai Peasant Community* (Ph.D. Thesis, University of Washington, 1964); Piker, " ' The Image of Limited Good ': Comments on an Exercise in Description and Interpretation," *American Anthropologist*, LXVIII, 5 (1966), pp. 1202–11; Piker, " Friendship to the Death in Rural Thai Society," *Human Organization*, XXVII, 3 (1968), pp. 200–204; Piker, " The Relationship of Belief Systems to Behavior in Rural Thailand," *Asian Survey*, V (1968), pp. 384–99; Piker, " Sources of Stability and Instability in Rural Thai Society," *J. of Asian Studies*, XXVII (1968), pp. 777–90; Piker, " The Post-Peasant Village in Central Plain [sic] Thai Society," in *Change and Persistence in Thai Society: Essays in Honor of Lauriston Sharp*, ed. by G. William Skinner and A. Thomas Kirsch (Ithaca: Cornell University Press, 1975), pp. 298–323; Piker, " Introduction," *Contributions to Asian Studies*, VIII (1975), pp. 1–7; Piker and E. Hollis Mentzer, " Personality Profiles for Two Central Thai Villages," *Contributions to Asian Studies*, VIII (1975), pp. 24–40; and Piker, " Changing Child Rearing Practices in Central Thailand," *Contributions to Asian Studies*, VIII (1975), pp. 90–108; Piker, " The Closing of the Frontier: Land Pressures and Their Implications for Rural Social Organization in the Thai Central Plain," *Contributions to Asian Studies*, IX (1976), pp. 7–26. Also see Lucien M. Hanks, Jr., " The Quest for Individual Autonomy in the Burmese Personality," *Psychiatry*, XIX (1949), pp. 285–330; Hazel M. Hitson, *Family Patterns and Paranoidal Personality Structure in Boston and Burma* (Ph.D. Thesis, Radcliffe College, 1959); and Lucien Pye, *Politics, Personality and Nation Building: Burma's Search for Identity* (New Haven: Yale University Press, 1962).

24. Piker, " The Relationship of Belief Systems. . . ," p. 384.

25. Spiro, *Buddhism and Society*, pp. 131f.

26. See Herbert P. Phillips, " Social Contract vs. Social Promise in a Siamese Village," in *Peasant Society: A Reader*, ed. by Jack M. Potter, May N. Diaz, and George M. Foster (Boston: Little Brown, 1967), pp. 346–67. This article is a revised version of ch. II in Phillips' book, *Thai Peasant Personality*.

27. See Tambiah, " Animals are Good to Think. . . ."

28. Tambiah, *Buddhism and the Spirit Cults* . . . , p. 35.

29. For Cambodia, see *Cérémonies privées des Cambodgiens* by Eveline Porée-Maspero, Chap-pin, Pich-sal, Chek-prak, Luy-sean, and Nhem-Khem (Phnom Penh: Editions de l'Institut Bouddhique, 1958); and Eveline Porée-Maspero, *Etudes sur les rites agraires des Cambodgiens*. For Laos, see Condominas, " Le Bouddhisme au Laos . . . "; Marcel Zago, *Rites et Cérémonies en Milieu Bouddhiste Lao* (Roma: Università Gregoriana Editrice, 1972); and Charles Archaimbault, *Structures Religieuses Lao*. For Thailand, in addition to the work of Tambiah, see also Richard Davis, " Tolerance and Intolerance of Ambiguity in Northern Thai Myth and Ritual." Spiro provides considerable information on ritual in his studies of Burmese religion, but does not focus specifically on ritual as a process of communication. Shway Yoe's *The Burman* still remains an excellent source on this subject.

30. See James R. Brandon, *Theatre in Southeast Asia* (Cambridge: Harvard University Press, 1967); Michael Smithies, " *Likay:* A Note on the Origin, Form and Future of Siamese Folk Opera." *Journal of the Siam Society*, LIX, 1 (1971), pp. 33–64; H. Marchal, " Joux, divertissements, et chants populaires au Cambodge," *Sud-Est Asiatique* (August 1950), pp. 20–27; U Htin Aung, *Burmese Drama* (Oxford: Oxford University Press, 1937).

31. By far the best study of traditional education is S. J. Tambiah's " Literacy in a Buddhist Village. . . . "

32. M. Nash *Golden Road* . . . , p. 95.

33. Some further discussion of modern education, from the perspective of the role that cities in the region play as centers for the dissemination of new knowledge can be found in Chapter 5, pp. 291–97.

34. A forthcoming thesis by Roger Harmon at the University of Washington contains a very detailed description of the Thammathut program. Also see Donald K. Swearer, " Community Development and Thai Buddhism: the Dynamics of Tradition and Change," *Visakha Puja B.E. 2516* (Bangkok: The Buddhist Association of Thailand, 1973), pp. 59–68; and C. F. Keyes, " Buddhism and National Integration in Thailand," *J. Asian Studies*, XXX (1971), pp. 551–68.

35. Spiro, *Burmese Supernaturalism*, pp. 55–63; also see pp. 30–32 and 36–39 for Spiro's discussion of the degree of acceptance of some supernatural beliefs by Burmese villagers. Spiro is almost unique among those who have carried out research on popular religion in Therevada Buddhist Southeast Asia in his effort to measure and interpret the degree of acceptance of beliefs.

36. For a discussion of population growth in the Theravada Buddhist societies see Charles A. Fisher, South-East Asia (London: Methuen, 1964), pp. 172–75; Keith Buchanan, The Southeast Asian World (Garden City, N.Y.: Doubleday Anchor, 1968), ch. 7; J. C. Caldwell, " The Demographic Structure," in *Thailand: Social and Economic Studies in Development*, ed. by T. H. Silcock (Canberra: Australian National University Press, 1967), pp. 27–64; Harvey H. Smith, and others, *Area Handbook for Thailand* (Washington, D.C.: U.S. Govt. Printing Office, DA Pam 550–53, 1968), pp. 61, 63–64; Joel M. Halpern, *Economy and Society of Laos* (New Haven: Yale University, Southeast Asia Studies, Monograph No. 5, 1964), pp. 2–4; Donald P. Whitaker, and others, *Area Handbook for Laos* (Washington, D.C.: U.S. Govt. Printing Office, DA Pam 550–58, 1972),

p. 20; David J. Steinberg and others and revised by Herbert H. Vreeland, *Cambodia: Its People, Its Society, Its Culture* (New Haven: HRAF Press, 1959), pp. 28–32; Donald P. Whitaker, and others, *Area Handbook for the Khmer Republic (Cambodia)* (Washington, D.C.: U.S. Govt. Printing Office, DA Pam 550–50, 1973), p. 17; John W. Henderson, and others, *Area Handbook for Burma* (Washington, D.C.: U.S. Govt. Printing Office, DA Pam 550–61, 1971), pp. 18–19.

37. United Nations. Economic Commission for Asia and the Far East, *Statistical Yearbook for Asia and the Pacific* (Bangkok, 1973). Comparable statistics are not available for Cambodia and Laos.

38. For an excellent description of the making of various types of fermented fish (and shrimp) in brine which are eaten by the Burmese, see Shway Yoe [Sir James George Scott], *The Burman* (New York: W. W. Norton, 1963 [orig. 1910]), pp. 280–85.

39. The findings of this study are reported in a number of publications, the most comprehensive of which include the following: Hazel M. Hauck and others, *Aspects of Health, Sanitation and Nutritional Status in a Siamese Rice Village*; Hazel M. Hauck, Saovanee Sudsaneh, Jane R. Hanks, and others, *Food Habits and Nutrient Intakes in a Siamese Rice Village*; and Hazel M. Hauck and others, *Maternal and Child Health in a Siamese Rice Village: Nutritional Aspects.*

40. Hauck, *Maternal and Child Health . . .*, p. 29.

41. United States. Interdepartmental Committee on Nutrition for National Defense. *The Kingdom of Thailand Nutrition Survey, October–December 1960* ([Washington, D.C.: Government Printing Office], 1961). The relationship between malnutrition, disease, fertility, and life expectancy in a population of urban poor in Chiang Mai, Thailand is explored in a forthcoming dissertation by Marjorie Muecke at the University of Washington.

42. For an overview of traditional medical theory in Southeast Asia, see M. A. Jaspan, *Traditional Medical Theory in South-East Asia* (Hull: University of Hull, 1969). Among the best studied traditional medical systems in Theravada Buddhist societies is that found in Laos. See Joel M. Halpern, "Traditional Medicine and the Role of the Phi in Laos," *The Eastern Anthropologist*, XVI, 3 (1963), pp. 191–200; Khamsome Sassady, *Contribution à l'étude de la médicine laotienne* (Thèse pour le Doctorat en Médicine, Faculté de Médicine de Paris, 1962); Jules E. Vidal, "Manuscrits de médicine populaire lao et leur intérêt ethno-linguistique," en *Langue et Techniques; Nature et Société; II. Approche Ethnologique, Approche Naturaliste*, ed. par Jacqueline M. C. Thomas et Lucien Bernot (Paris: Editions Klincksieck, 1972), pp. 249–59.

43. See M. Nash, *Golden Road . . .*, pp. 177–82; Spiro, *Burmese Supernaturalism.*

44. Tambiah, *Buddhism and Spirit Cults . . .*, p. 332.

45. John Knodel and Visid Prachuabmoh, *The Fertility of Thai Women* (Bangkok: Chulalongkorn University, Institute of Population Studies, Research Report No. 10, 1973), p. 11.

46. *Ibid.*, p. 79.

47. Jane R. Hanks, *Maternity and Its Rituals in Bang Chan*, pp. 16–17.

48. M. Nash, *The Golden Road . . .*, pp. 256–57.

49. John Knodel and Visid Prachuabmoh, "Demographic Aspects of Fertility in Thailand," *Population Studies*, XXVIII, 3 (1974), p. 448.

50. See George Peter Murdock, "Introduction," in *Social Structure in Southeast Asia*, ed. by George Peter Murdock (Chicago: Quadrangle Books, Viking Fund Publications in Anthropology, No. 29, 1960).

51. See R. B. Jones, *Thai Titles and Ranks* (Ithaca, N.Y.: Cornell University Southeast Asia Program, Data Paper No. 81, 1971). For discussions of nonroyal kinship terminology, see Paul K. Benedict, "Studies in Thai Kinship Terminology," *J. Am. Oriental Society*, LXIII (1943), pp. 168–75; M. Nash, *The Golden Road...*, pp. 70–73; May Ebihara, "Khmer," pp. 101–102.

52. Jane R. N. Hanks, "Reflections on the Ontology of Rice," p. 299.

53. M. Nash, *The Golden Road...*, p. 52.

54. The most extended treatment of this dualism, a treatment that focuses on Cambodia but also discusses other parts of Theravada Buddhist Southeast Asia, is Eveline Porée-Maspero's *Etude sur les rites agraires des cambodgiens* (3 vols, Paris: Mouton, 1962, 1964, 1969).

55. Ebihara (in "Khmer", pp. 102–103) reports that for Village Kong near Phnom Penh, the preferred mode of postmarital residence was neolocality, that is, the immediate establishment of a separate household. However, she further reports that circumstances were such that in practice a pattern of initial matrilocal residence following marriage was observed in most cases. In partial contradistinction to Ebihara, Delvert (*op. cit.*, p. 180) asserts that the rule recognized and usually followed by the Khmer is one whereby the husband lives near the parents of his wife. M. Nash reports that, in Upper Burma, those from rich families chose to "follow wealth" in deciding where to live after marriage. This choice was often with the husband's family. However, for most of the people, a pattern of initial matrilocal residence was also observed (M. Nash, *Golden Road...*, pp. 44–45, 50–51).

56. See, for example, Kamol Janlehka, *op. cit.*, p. 38.

57. Ernest Young, *The Kingdom of the Yellow Robe*, 3rd ed. (London: Archibald Constable, 1907), pp. 92, 96, 98. This change is, I suspect, a consequence of the readjustments made in central Thai rural society following the commercialization of agriculture. In this connection, see Steven Piker, "The Closing of the Frontier..."; David B. Johnston, "Opening a Frontier: The Expansion of Rice Cultivation in Central Thailand in the 1890's," *Contributions to Asian Studies*, IX (1976), pp. 27–44; and Johnston, "Rural Society and the Rice Economy in Thailand, 1880–1930" (Ph.D. Dissertation, Yale University, 1975).

58. Turton, *op. cit.*; Davis, "Muang Matrifocality."

59. Although Spiro argues, on the basis of rather ambiguous data, that the Burmese spirits in question are inherited patrilineally (Spiro, *Burmese Supernaturalism*, pp. 104–105), June Nash makes a convincing case that the *mizaing-hpazaing* spirit(s) is matrilineally inherited and it is a matrilineally defined group that perpetuates the cult of this spirit (J. Nash, *op. cit.*, p. 120). Ebihara notes the existence in Cambodia of an ancestral spirit called *meba*; although she suggests that this spirit is the concern of bilaterally related kinsmen, other evidence (such as the residence rule and the fact that women are the main persons responsible

for propitiation of this spirit) suggests that it may also be the focus of a matri-lineally defined unit.

60. Spiro, " Factionalism and Politics in Village Burma," p. 402.

61. M. Nash, *The Golden Road* . . . , p. 59.

62. In this connection, see the discussion regarding the causes for fissioning of families among the central Thai given in Phillips, *Thai Peasant Personality*, pp. 29–32. Also see Spiro's discussion of intrafamilial tensions in " Some Psycho-dynamic Determinants of Household Composition in Village Burma."

63. The best studies of fishing villages in the region are those of Malay villages in southern Thailand and northern Malaya. See Raymond Firth, *Malay Fisherman: Their Peasant Economy*, 2nd ed. (London: Routledge and Kegan Paul, 1966); Thomas M. Fraser, Jr., *Rusembilan; A Malay Fishing Village in Southern Thailand* (Ithaca, N.Y.: Cornell University Press, 1960); and Fraser, *Fishermen of South Thailand: The Malay Villagers* (New York: Holt, Rinehart and Winston, 1966).

64. See Wilhelm G. Solheim II, " Pottery Manufacture in Sting Mor and Ban Nong Sua Kin Ma, Thailand," *J. Siam Society*, LII, 2 (1964), pp. 151–62; Solheim, " Notes on Pottery Manufacture near Luang Prabang, Laos," *J. Siam Society*, LV, 1 (1967), pp. 81–86.

65. One of the villages studied by Nash (*The Golden Road* . . .) is a mixed crop village. Although Delvert devotes most of his study to rice-producing villages, he also discusses (*op. cit.*, pp. 371–424) the *neak chamcar*, the Khmer rural people who devote themselves to garden production.

66. Lucien M. Hanks, *Rice and Man*.

67. *Ibid.*, pp. 28–29.

68. See, for example, Laurence C. Judd, *Dry Rice Agriculture in Northern Thailand* (Ithaca, N.Y.: Cornell University Southeast Asia Program, Data Paper No. 52, 1964).

69. Condominas, " Notes sur le droit foncier lao. . . ."

70. Delvert, *loc. cit.*

71. M. Nash, *The Golden Road* . . . , pp. 15–28.

72. Hanks, *Rice and Man*, p. 35.

73. By far the best study of peasant decision making regarding the adoption of technological innovations is that by Moerman concerning a village in northern Thailand. See Moerman, *Agricultural Change and Peasant Choice in a Thai Village*.

74. Solheim, " Pottery Manufacture in Sting Mor . . . " pp. 156–61.

75. Jancis F. Long, Millard F. Long, Kamphol Adulavidhaya, and Sawart Pongsu-wanna, *Economic and Social Conditions among Farmers in Changwad Khonkaen* (Bangkok: Kasetsart University, Faculty of Economics and Cooperative Science, September, 1963), p. 66.

76. Compare, M. Nash, *The Golden Road* . . . , pp. 49–52; Eveline Porée-Maspero, *op. cit.*

77. See J. S. Furnivall, " Land as a Free Gift of Nature," *Economic Journal*, XIX

(1909), pp. 552–62; Furnivall, *Colonial Policy and Practice* (New York: New York University Press, 1956 [orig. 1948]), pp. 109–110; Adas, *op. cit.*, p. 28.

78. Condominas, *Droit foncier lao* . . . , pp. 256, 262.

79. Furnivall, *Colonial Policy and Practice*, p. 34.

80. *Loc. cit.*

81. J. S. Furnivall, *Colonial Policy and Practice*, p. 107; also see pp. 33–35.

82. M. Nash, *The Golden Road* . . . , p. 93.

83. James C. Ingram, *Economic Change in Thailand, 1850–1970* (Stanford: Stanford University Press, 1971), p. 184.

84. *Ibid.*, p. 92; also see pp. 243–61.

85. Frederick P. Munson, *et al.*, *Area Handbook for Cambodia* (Washington, D.C.: Government Printing Office, DA Pam 550–50, 1968), p. 288. Frank M. LeBar and Adrienne Suddard, ed., *Laos: Its People, Its Society, Its Culture* (New Haven: HRAF Press, 1960), p. 196.

86. Adas, *op. cit.*, p. 188.

87. Frank M. Golay, Ralph Anspach, M. Ruth Pfanner, and Eliezar B. Ayal, *Underdevelopment and Economic Nationalism in Southeast Asia* (Ithaca, N.Y.: Cornell University Press, 1969), pp. 224–25.

88. Ingram, *op. cit.*, p. 267.

89. *Ibid.*, p. 267.

90. See Delvert, *op. cit.*, pp. 496f, 502.

91. Halpern, *Economy and Society of Laos*, p. 100.

92. See A. Thomas Kirsch, " Economy, Polity, and Religion in Thailand," in *Change and Persistence in Thai Society*, ed. by G. William Skinner and A. Thomas Kirsch, pp. 172–96.

93. See Furnivall, *Colonial Policy and Practice*, pp. 46–47; 95–99, 117–19; 189; G. William Skinner, *Chinese Society in Thailand* (Ithaca, N.Y.: Cornell University Press, 1957), pp. 108, 221–23; William E. Willmott, *The Chinese in Cambodia* (Vancouver, B. C.: University of British Columbia Publications Centre, 1967), pp. 52–60; Joel M. Halpern, *The Role of The Chinese in Lao Society* (Santa Monica: Rand Corporation, P-2161, 1960); Brian L. Foster, " Ethnicity and Commerce," *Am. Ethnologist*, I, 3 (1974), pp. 437–48.

94. This observation is based on my own research in northeastern Thailand.

95. Data from J. M. Andrews, *Siam: 2nd Rural Economic Survey, 1934–1935* (Bangkok: Bangkok Times Press, 1935), p. 372. The rate of exchange for the period was taken to be $1.00 = Baht 2.25.

96. M. Nash gives expenditure figures by families, not by individuals. To reach a per capita figure, I have used the figure of 5.9 persons per economically independent kin group for Nondwin and 4.8 persons per unit for Yadaw. I also assumed an exchange rate of $1.00 = 4.29 kyats, the official rate for the period. See M. Nash, *The Golden Road* . . . , pp. 39, 244.

97. Delvert, *op. cit.*, p. 520; Delvert says that 1,700 riels was equivalent " theoretically to 17,000 francs, [but] in fact to around 12,000 francs."

98. Halpern, *Economy and Society of Laos*, p. 112.

99. Data from the *Household Expenditure Survey, B.E. 2508*, prepared by the National Statistical Office of Thailand (Bangkok, 1964).

100. Figures calculated on the basis of data reported in *Report: Socio-Economic Survey B.E. 2511–2512* by the National Statistical Office of Bangkok (Bangkok, n.d.).

101. M. Nash, *The Golden Road* . . . , pp. 28–33. Yadaw differed from Nondwin in that prior to independence most of its residents were tenants, not land owners.

102. Weber's argument regarding the rise of capitalism and its association with Protestantism is developed in *The Protestant Ethic and the Spirit of Capitalism* (tr. by Talcott Parsons, N.Y.: Scribners, 1958). His fullest discussion of Buddhism is presented in *The Religion of India*, Tr. and ed. by Hans H. Gerth and Don Martindale (New York: The Free Press, 1958).

103. On Burma, see M. E. Spiro, " Buddhism and Economic Action in Burma "; David E. Pfanner and Jasper Ingersoll, " Therevada Buddhism and Village Economic Behavior "; Mya Maung, " Cultural Value and Economic Change in Burma," *Asian Survey*, IV (1964), pp. 757–64. On Thailand, see Pfanner and Ingersoll, *op. cit.*; and Eliezar Ayal, " Value Systems and Economic Development in Japan and Thailand," *J. Social Issues*, XIX (1963), pp. 35–51. On Laos, see Arthur Niehoff, " Therevada Buddhism: A Vehicle for Technical Change," *Human Organization*, XXIII, 2 (1964), pp. 108–112. On Cambodia, see May Ebihara, " Interrelations between Buddhism and Social Systems in Cambodian Peasant Culture ".

104. Delvert, *op. cit.*, pp. 308–309.

105. Kaufman, *Village Life in Vientiane Province*, p. 1.

106. M. Nash, *The Golden Road* . . . , pp. 14, 212.

107. Sharp, *et al.*, *op. cit.*, pp. 18, 24.

108. Spiro, *Burmese Supernaturalism*, p. 95.

109. Compare Tambiah, *Buddhism and Spirit Cults* . . . , pp. 263–291.

110. Furnivall, *Colonial Policy and Practice*, p. 74.

111. Sharp, *et al.*, *op. cit.*, pp. 17–18.

112. Delvert, *op. cit.*, p. 201; my translation.

113. Spiro, *Burmese Supernaturalism*, pp. 109–110n.

114. Condominas, " Le bouddhisme au Laos . . . ," p. 134.

115. See Keyes, " The Northeastern Thai Village . . . ," p. 205.

116. M. E. Spiro, " Fractionalism and Politics in Village Burma," p. 402.

117. See, in this connection, Moerman, " The Village Headman as Synaptic Leader," and Keyes, " Local Leadership in Rural Thailand."

118. See Furnivall, *Colonial Policy and Practice*, pp. 137–41.

119. This assertion is based on information collected by David Johnston, who carried out research on the concomitants of the development of commercial rice production in central Thailand. See Johnston, " Rural Society and the Rice Economy in Thailand, 1880–1930."

178   *The Golden Peninsula*

120. Lucien M. Hanks, Jr., " The Corporation and the Entourage: A Comparison of Thai and American Social Organization," *Catalyst*, II (1966), pp. 55–63; Hanks, " Entourage and Circle in Burma," *The Bennington Review*, II 1 (1968), pp. 32–36, 41–46; Hanks, " The Thai Social Order as Entourage and Circle," in *Change and Persistence in Thai Society*, ed. by G. William Skinner and A. Thomas Kirsch, pp. 197–218. On the subject of patron-client relationships in Theravada Buddhist Southeast Asia, also see the following: James Mosel, " Thai Administrative Behavior," in *Toward the Comparative Study of Public Administration*, ed. by William J. Siffin (Bloomington: Indiana University, Department of Government, 1957), pp. 278–331; Gehan Wijeyewardere, " Patrons and *Pau Liang*; James C. Scott, " Patron-Client Politics and Political Change," in *The Political Economy of Development*, ed. by Norman T. Uphoof and Warren F. Ilchman (Berkeley and Los Angeles: University of California Press, 1972).

121. J. Nash, *op. cit.*, pp. 124–27; Spiro, *Burmese Supernaturalism*, pp. 109–112.

122. See C. F. Keyes, " A Note on the Ancient Towns and Cities of Northeastern Thailand," *Tonan Ajia Kenkyu* (The Southeast Asian Studies), XI, 4 (1974), pp. 498–99; Tambiah, *Buddhism and Spirit Cults . . .*, pp. 285–311.

123. See Keyes, " Buddhist Pilgrimage Centers and the Twelve-Year Cycle; Northern Thai Moral Orders in Space and Time," *History of Religions*, XV, 1 (1975), pp. 71–89; and James B. Pruess, " Veneration and Merit-Seeking at Sacred Places: Buddhist Pilgrimage in Contemporary Thailand " (Ph.D. Dissertation, University of Washington, 1974).

124. Keyes, *Isan: Regionalism in Northeastern Thailand.*

125. Moerman, " Ethnic Identification in a Complex Civilization . . ."; Moerman, " Being Lue . . ."; Karl Gustav Izikowitz, " Notes about the Tai," *Bull. of the Museum of Far Eastern Antiquities*, XXXIV (1962), pp. 73–91.

126. Spiro, *Burmese Supernaturalism*, p. 54. Also see E. Michael Mendelson, " Observations on a Tour in the Region of Mount Popa, Central Burma," *France-Asie*, XIX, 179 (1963), pp. 780–807.

127. For a discussion on the relationship between Buddhist belief and political legitimacy, see Keyes, " The Power of Merit"; Keyes, " Millennialism, Theravada Buddhism, and Thai Society," *J. Asian Studies*, forthcoming; E. Michael Mendelson, " Buddhism and Politics in Burma," *New Society*, I, 38 (1963), pp. 8–10; Mendelson, " Buddhism and the Burmese Establishment," *Archives de Sociologie de Religions*, IX, 17 (1964), pp. 85–95; E. Sarkisyanz, *Buddhist Backgrounds of the Burmese Revolution* (The Hague: Martinus Nijhoff, 1965); and Donald Eigene Smith, *Religion and Politics in Burma* (Princeton: Princeton University Press, 1965).

128. Smith, *op. cit.*, p. 316.

129. Jane R. Hanks, *Maternity and Its Rituals in Bang Chan*, p. 71.

130. It is worth noting, in this connection, that the Lao of the Vientiane Plain call the custom of lying by the fire, *yu kam*, " residing in Karma." See Kaufman, *Village Life . . .*, pp. 42–43.

131. On the ordination ritual, see Tambiah, *Buddhism and Spirit Cults . . .*, pp. 103–108; Spiro, *Buddhism and Society*, pp. 234–47; 290–92; Paul Levy, *Buddhism: A " Mystery Religion " ?* (London: University of London Press, 1957). Levy's book deals with ordination in Laos.

132. Jane R. Hanks, *Maternity and Its Rituals in Bang Chan*, p. 78.

133. Condominas, " Le Bouddhisme au Laos . . .", pp. 105–106; Tambiah, *Buddhism and the Spirit Cults* . . . , pp. 109–115; Keyes, " The Northeastern Thai Village . . .", pp. 186–87. In Ban Nong Tun, the village where I carried out field work, the title of *somdet* was no longer used because of a ruling, I was told, by Thai Sangha authorities. In the Thai Sangha, *somdet* is used for high-ranking monks in the hierarchy, not for monks honored by local congregations.

134. See Spiro, *Buddhism and Society*, pp. 454–56.

135. For a discussion of the " ideal villager," see William Klausner, *Reflections in a Log Pond* (Bangkok: Suksit Siam, 1972), Klausner is writing of a village in northeastern Thailand, Ban Nong Khon, " the village of the log pond."

136. See David K. Wyatt, " The Buddhist Monkhood as an Avenue of Social Mobility in Traditional Thai Society," *Sinlapakon* (Bangkok), X, 1 (1966), pp. 41–52. Also see Keyes, " The Northeastern Thai Village . . . ," p. 188.

137. In this connection see Boonsanong Punyadyana, " Social Structure, Social System, and Two Levels of Analysis: A Thai View," in *Loosely Structured Social Systems: Thailand in Comparative Perspective*, ed. by Hans-Dieter Evers (New Haven: Yale University Southeast Asia Studies, Cultural Report Series No. 17, 1969), pp. 77–105.

138. John F. Embree, " Thailand—A Loosely Structured Social System," *Am. Anthropologist*, LII (1950), pp. 181–93. The article has been republished in *Loosely Structured Social Systems*, ed. by Evers, pp. 3–15.

139. Embree in *Am. Anthropologist*, p. 182.

140. See, especially, the essays in Evers, *op. cit.*

141. Herbert P. Phillips, " The Scope and Limits of the ' Loose Structure ' Concept," in Evers, *op. cit.*, p. 26.

142. Steven Piker, " ' Loose Structure ' and the Analysis of Thai Social Organization," in Evers, *op. cit.*, p. 67.

143. The following argument has been stimulated, in part, by the insightful essay by Lucien Hanks, " Merit and Power in the Thai Social Order," *Am. Anthropoligist*, LXIV (1962), pp. 1247–61. Some villages in Cambodia and Laos may provide important exceptions to the generalizations made here. However, at present, hard data on the cultural views of villagers long under Communist control are almost nonexistent. The cultural transformation being attempted in these countries has become one of the most intriguing of all problems for students of Therevada Buddhist societies.

144. Phillips, *Thai Peasant Personality* . . . , p. 88.

145. *Ibid.*, p. 89.

146. In a recent paper, Steven Piker (" The Post-Peasant Village in Central Plain [sic] Thai Society "), who previously took a similar position to that of Phillips, has argued that the individualistic behavior observed in villages in central Thailand can be traced in part to socioeconomic factors associated first with settlement on a frontier and subsequently with the impact of commercialization of rice agriculture. A similar case can be made for villages in lower Burma; see Furnivall, *Colonial Policy and Practice*.

147. See, for example, Jane Bunnag, *Buddhist Monk, Buddhist Layman* (Cambridge: Cambridge University Press, 1973), pp. 180–87.

148. Phillips, *Thai Peasant Personality* . . . , pp. 21–38; Also compare the studies of Piker, cited above, which provide supporting evidence for the conclusions reached by Phillips about life in central Thai villages.

CHAPTER 4
TRADITION AND REVOLUTION IN VIETNAM

The course of cultural development followed by the Vietnamese has been markedly different from that of their neighbors in mainland Southeast Asia. Whereas the other civilizations of Southeast Asia drew their inspiration from India, the Vietnamese have drawn theirs from the great tradition of China. Yet, while belonging culturally to the East Asian rather than the Southeast Asian world, the Vietnamese have adapted themselves to a Southeast Asian environment—not only the natural one with its tropical and monsoonal features, but also a social one. Over the centuries, the Vietnamese have had intensive relations with Southeast Asian hill peoples, with the Chams and the Khmer, and with various Tai peoples. It is the adaptation of a Chinese-derived cultural tradition to a Southeast Asian environment that has given the Vietnamese tradition its distinctive cast.

During the course of Vietnamese history, the forms that this mode of adaptation assumed differed as the Chinese cultural tradition on which the Vietnamese drew underwent changes and as the Vietnamese developed new relationships in the Southeast Asian world in which they lived. In the latter half of the nineteenth century, the basic parameters of Vietnamese life were themselves radically changed. The establishment of French colonial domination over Vietnam shattered the cultural consensus that had previously existed and also brought about a fundamental restructuring of Vietnamese society.

French rule itself never provided a reasonable alternative to the traditional order. It did, however, serve as the context within which a radical reorientation of Vietnamese life was worked out. During the colonial period and the post-colonial period (which, for South Vietnam, lasted until 1975), the Vietnamese experimented with a number of different cultural systems in their efforts to find years to adapt to the radically changed world in which they lived. For many ways several systems appeared to be viable candidates for providing the basis for a new Vietnamese order, but it is now clear that this order will, throughout Vietnam, be based on the Western-derived ideology of Communism.

In this chapter, discussion will focus on some aspects of traditional Vietnamese society and culture as they existed prior to the establishment of

French rule and on the impact of French rule on Vietnam. In both cases attention will be given to the majority of the Vietnamese people, or those who have lived in the countryside. In the final sections of this chapter, rural life in contemporary Vietnam will be discussed, with particular attention being given to the conditions of life or rural people in northern Vietnam, since that is the area of the country in which efforts to adapt a Communist ideology to the exigencies of the local environment have been of longest duration. Urban life in Vietnam will not be discussed in this chapter, but will be dealt with in Chapter 5 in the context of a wider treatment of urban life in mainland Southeast Asia in general.

TRADITIONAL SOCIETY IN VIETNAM

Formation of the Vietnamese Tradition

The prehistoric culture of the ancestors of the Vietnamese who lived in what is today northern Vietnam was quite similar to other prehistoric cultures in mainland Southeast Asia. Indeed, Southeast Asian prehistory has been divided into periods whose names are derived from the type sites of Hoa-binh, Bac-son, and Dong-son all found in northern Vietnam. Beginning in the third century B.C., however, the people of this region, later to be known as the Yueh, were launched on a path of cultural development that was quite different from that followed by their neighbors. In 214 B.C. the Chinese established a military outpost in the area just north of the Tonkin Delta. From this beachhead, the Han Chinese expanded their control over the region, until by 111 B.C. much of the area of what is today northern Vietnam had been organized into the Chinese province of Giao Chi. From this time until 939 A.D., the Vietnamese were, with a few minor periods of independence, a population within the Chinese Empire.[1]

During the first millennium A.D., a period during which the Vietnamese were confined to an area consisting mainly of the Tonkin Delta in northern Vietnam, the Vietnamese underwent a process of Sinification. The Vietnamese peasantry began to use Chinese methods of irrigation and agricultural terracing.[2] The Vietnamese elite, like its Chinese counterpart, came to support Mahayana Buddhism, and Mahayana monasteries in Tonkin developed into important centers that attracted Chinese pilgrims on their way to and from the Buddhist holy land in India.[3] Buddhism never, however, became the exclusive religion of Vietnam any more than it did of China. The elite were also educated in the Confucian tradition, whereas the populace continued to worship a multitude of spirits and gods, many of them non-Chinese in origin.

The efforts of the Chinese administrators and their Vietnamese emulators to " civilize " the peoples of what is today northern Vietnam were not wholly successful. The populace continued to perpetuate certain aspects of its own pre-Sinitic Southeast Asian tradition, among the most important of these being the emphasis it placed on the cultural and social distinctiveness of the village. Moreover, although the Vietnamese, elite and peasant alike, adopted Chinese cultural patterns, they did not come to view themselves as Chinese. Rather, they saw themselves as a separate people who had the right to control their own political destiny. This conception of the right to independence prompted the numerous Vietnamese uprisings against their Chinese rulers, which took place during the millennium of Chinese domination and which prompted the Vietnamese to undertake the struggle that ultimately led to their gaining independence in 939 A.D. The tension felt by a people who recognize Chinese culture as the wellspring of their civilization while also viewing their own tradition as distinctive from the Chinese has provided one of the dominant motifs in Vietnamese history.

Even after achieving independence, the Vietnamese continued to look to China for cultural inspiration. Under the Ly dynasty (1009–1224 A.D.), the state in Vietnam as in China continued to recognize Mahayana Buddhism as the dominant religion. When Mahayana Buddhism underwent a decline in China, and Confucianism emerged as the preeminent state religion, so too, did the strength of Mahayana Buddhism decline in importance and Confucianism rise in Vietnam. From the thirteenth century until the middle of the nineteenth century, the Vietnamese rulers attempted to emulate Confucian-based Chinese tradition as closely as they could, and there were no more zealous promoters of this tradition in Vietnam than the first three emperors of the Nguyen dynasty who ruled Vietnam from 1802–1847.[4]

While continuing to look to China for cultural models, the Vietnamese in the period following their independence from China also were engaged in increasingly intensive contact with other peoples in Southeast Asia. To a large extent, this contact was structured with reference to what is known as the Vietnamese " push to the South." During the millennium of Chinese rule, population pressure in the area of the Tonkin Delta rose to proportions unequaled anywhere else in premodern Southeast Asia. Partially to relieve these pressures and partially to carry forward a policy of cultural imperialism toward the surrounding " barbarians," Vietnamese rulers from the time of the Tran dynasty (1225–1407 A.D.) up to the time the French arrived undertook to promote an expansion of Vietnamese culture and society into what is today central and southern Vietnam. This expansion brought the Vietnamese into violent contact first with the Chams, an Austronesian-speaking people who had long established an Indianized state in what is today central Vietnam. The wars between the Vietnamese and Chams reached a climax in the fifteenth century, and by the end of that century the kingdom of Champa had ceased to exist.

With the collapse of Champa, the Vietnamese next confronted the Khmer, whose kingdom at that time still included all of what is today southern Vietnam. Gradually, the Khmer were forced to concede their former territories to the Vietnamese, until by the middle of the eighteenth century the Vietnamese had completed their conquest of the Mekong Delta. In the nineteenth century, the Nguyen rulers attempted to continue their expansion into Cambodia proper. This expansion was resisted, however, not only by the Khmer but also by the Siamese, and there followed a long struggle between the Vietnamese and Siamese for control of Cambodia, which ended only with the arrival of the French.

Once the various territories had been conquered, Vietnamese migrants would move into and settle these areas. Here, they often intermarried with Chams and Khmer, and, even when they did not, they were exposed to the different social and cultural patterns of these Indianized peoples. These contacts tended to result in some compromising of the dominant Chinese-derived tradition, at least among the peasantry. Many of the cultural differences between northern and southern Vietnamese can be traced to such compromises.

The push to the south tended to promote instability within traditional Vietnamese society. As a consequence of migration, the clusters of population were strung out over a distance of 1,500 miles with only poor communications linking them. Moreover, the push to the south led to the incorporation into Vietnamese society of peoples who were culturally quite different from the Vietnamese. Given the poor communications and the differences in contexts to which the Vietnamese had to adapt, they came to develop distinctive patterns that varied from region to region. These factors, together with the tension inherent in the effort to model Vietnamese culture on Chinese culture, help to explain why political unity was so rare in traditional Vietnam. For most of the period during which Vietnam was independent of China, it was divided into two or more polities. Even the political unity effected under the Nguyen in the first half of the nineteenth century proved tenuous and short lived, although " the memory of this fragile unity . . . became an important symbol and force in Vietnamese politics after French colonialists had administratively dismembered the country."[5] Not only was power in traditional Vietnam often divided between competing rulers, but it was also challenged periodically by peasant uprisings.

Peasant rebellions appear to have been far more common in traditional Vietnam than they were in any other traditional state in mainland Southeast Asia. Most of the uprisings of the Vietnamese peasantry were short lived and brutally suppressed. However, one led by the Tay-son brothers at the end of the eighteenth century resulted in the establishment of a new regime, albeit one replaced in 1802 by that ruled by the Nguyen emperor Gia-long. Although the Tay-son rebellion did not result in the creation of a new and lasting political order in Vietnam, in retrospect it can be seen to have foreshadowed developments that were later to change Vietnamese political life radically. The Tay-son rebellion was a popular rebellion, drawing its support from a peasantry that keenly felt the demands levied on it by state officials. The Tay-son rebels protested not only the privileged position of the political elite but also the privileged position of the commercial elite; in 1782 Tay-son rebels massacred thousands of Chinese traders living in southern Vietnam. Gia-long and his followers ultimately succeeded in defeating the Tay-son armies, but only through the support of a number of Westerners. The involvement of these Westerners, the first to be directly concerned with political events in Vietnam, proved to be one of the factors leading to ultimate French control of the area. In short, one can agree with Woodside who has argued that the Tay-son rebellion " inaugurates modern Vietnamese history."[6]

Production and the Division of Labor in Traditional Vietnam

With the dynamics of traditional Vietnam in mind, let us consider some of the salient characteristics of the Vietnamese traditional order, beginning with the types of production and the division of labor that obtained in premodern

times. The basic adaptation of the Vietnamese to the natural world and the dominant system of production in which most Vietnamese were engaged had first
been developed in the Tonkin Delta.[7] Like their counterparts in other lowland
areas of mainland Southeast Asia, the Tonkinese peasants have long been
cultivators of wet rice and have used water buffaloes as a source of power. However, in contrast to the other cultivators of the region, the Tonkinese adopted
the Chinese pattern of irrigation. The system of dikes found in the Tonkin delta
resulted in better water control there than in any other region of mainland
Southeast Asia in premodern times. These irrigation works, operated by the
peasantry themselves and supervised by local officials, have permitted the
Tonkin Delta Vietnamese to produce two crops of rice per year for centuries.
Elsewhere in mainland Southeast Asia, double cropping has only been introduced in very recent years. The intensive cultivation of rice in the Tonkin Delta
permitted a concentration of population there that has yet to be equaled in the
region.

   Although most of the Vietnamese who settled in central and southern
Vietnam were also rice farmers, they only rarely attempted to build a diking
system comparable to that found in Tonkin in the new lands where they settled.
Double cropping was rare in Vietnam outside the Tonkin Delta until after
World War II[8] when efforts were made to introduce the pattern.

   Although the overwhelming majority of the " common people " in traditional Vietnam were engaged in rice agriculture, some of these people also
engaged in other forms of production. Next to rice agriculture, fishing was the
most important productive activity traditionally engaged in by the Vietnamese.
Most fishing was carried out by rice farmers who used their spare time to fish in
fresh-water streams and rivers. In central Vietnam, however, there was some
specialized production in salt-water fishing. In this region also, production of
nuoc mam, the fish soy used as a basic ingredient in Vietnamese cooking, was
most developed.

   Artisan crafts were also mainly part-time specialization practice by those
whose primary occupation was rice farming. Only those who were too poor to
make a living at rice farming turned to full-time production of craft items:

> A map of the traditional Vietnamese economy would reveal that it was the
> villages with poor agricultural potential—villages with meagre or infertile
> land—that specialized in crafts like pottery, copperware, weaving, and hat
> making.[9]

Some full-time artisans were also to be found in the urban centers, where they
produced to fill the requests of the upper classes. Vietnamese craft industry
never developed to the extent that it did in China, in part because Vietnamese
artisans had to compete with Chinese craftsmen whose products were available
in Vietnamese cities. Moreover,

> Because of Vietnam's smallness, the Vietnamese court, far more than the
> Chinese court, had the means to control Vietnamese guilds and tax their
> artisans out of business. The fate of clever artisans in nineteenth-century
> Vietnam was a kind of labor slavery rather than an opportunity to accumu-
> late profits and capital.[10]

Local trade in the bazaars of traditional Vietnamese cities and villages appears to have been in the hands of women much as it was in other mainland Southeast Asian societies. John Crawfurd, who visited Vietnam in 1822, observed in Saigon (then a small town) that " women alone attended in the shops."[11] Occupational specialization in commerce, that is, in inter-regional and international trade, was limited almost totally to Chinese who formed a powerful and alien merchant class.[12] Chinese entrepreneurs also managed the mining of iron, silver, and gold in northern Vietnam, and Chinese also served as the labor in these mines.[13]

The power holders in traditional Vietnam were dominated by the emperor and members of the royal family who held their positions by hereditary right or by virtue of marriage. The administrators were the scholar officials, the mandarins, that is, those who had passed state-determined examinations and had then been appointed to office. At the local level there was also a class of gentry, consisting of scholars who had passed the examinations but had not been appointed to office, scholars who had not passed the examinations, retired mandarins, and local notables who controlled extensive property either in their own name or in the name of lineages or of the village.

A final occupational category that was, it appears, more important in traditional Vietnam than in China was that of religious specialists. Although many practitioners of magical arts were farmers who engaged in these practices in their spare time, some—notably Buddhist monks and, of far less importance, Taoist priests—were full-time specialists.

The Vietnamese had adopted the Chinese conception of society consisting of four hierarchically ordered classes: scholars, peasants, artisans, and merchants. As Woodside has observed, " these theories matched realities even more poorly in Vietnam than they did in China."[14] The fact that an alien minority dominated the merchant class and the fact that this merchant class was most certainly not at the bottom of the hierarchy more closely paralleled the situation found in neighboring mainland Southeast Asian societies than that in China. Again, like in neighboring Southeast Asian societies, artisans did not make up a highly significant segment of the population. Yet for all the deviations from the ideal, the Chinese conceptions of the occupational divisions of society continued to be " ideologically necessary " for the Vietnamese—at least for the elite—until the time of French rule.[15]

Kinship in Traditional Vietnam

For all classes in traditional Vietnam, the basis of social life was the family.[16] The ideal model of the traditional Vietnamese kinship system was constructed with reference to Chinese prototypes. The Gia Long code, promulgated in 1812, reproduced almost word for word the provisions of the Ching code and went even further in copying Chinese ideals than did the Hong Duc Code, a fifteenth-century code that the Gia Long code replaced. According to this ideal system, the basis of Vietnamese family life was the patrilineal extended family. Several such families, being the descendants of a common ancestor, comprised the patrilineage (Sino-Vietnamese, *toc*; Vietnamese, *ho*). Each lineage had a ritual head, the *truong toc*, who, according to the law, was the senior male in the direct line of descent from the focal ancestor. Revenues necessary for maintenance of the lineage ancestral cult were derived from lineage property, known as *huong hoa* (lit., " incense and fire "), which was controlled by the *truong toc*. The *truong toc* was also responsible for maintaining the lineage hall and the tombs of ancestors and for making entries in the genealogies (*gia pha*).

In this androcentric world, as defined by the official code, women had few rights and little status outside their relationship with their husbands, their fathers, or their sons. They had no legal right to own personal property or to inherit anything from their parents.[17] At marriage they were expected to transfer their loyalties from their own families to that of their husbands. The ideal role for males in the system was that of the dutiful son; the ideal for women was that of the dutiful daughter-in-law.[18]

The actual kinship practices of the Vietnamese diverged in several significant ways from the Chinese ideal delineated in the Gia Long code. The adaptation of Chinese ideals to the Vietnamese context may have been constrained, in part, by differing demographic conditions in Vietnam and China. It has been suggested that the Vietnamese suffered a higher mortality rate than the Chinese because of tropical diseases and relatively greater loss of life in wars. As a consequence, the argument goes, many nominal kinship positions in the Vietnamese family and lineage had to remain unfilled.[19] Another possible factor, as yet undocumented, may be that more Vietnamese than Chinese relative to their respective overall populations engaged in migration and resettlement.

Perhaps the most striking contrast between the Vietnamese and Chinese systems (or between the actual Vietnamese system and the ideal system based on the Chinese model) was the fact that in Vietnam women, as well as men, inherited land. This practice was first given legal recognition under the fifteenth-century Hong Duc code, and although it was specifically forbidden in the Gia Long code drawn up in the early nineteenth century, the practice continued to be followed throughout the Nguyen period and on through the colonial and postcolonial periods as well.[20] A number of legal-minded French officials attempted to enforce the provisions of the Gia Long code regarding inheritance through the male line, but their efforts only succeeded in creating confusion.[21] Not only did women inherit land along with their brothers, but in some areas they also exerted considerable influence in the administration of the *huong hoa*, the lineage property whose revenues provided the support for the maintenance of the ancestral cult. The fact that women inherited property may also help to explain why households (*gia*) were sometimes reported as including sons-in-law in contrast to the ideal wherein all the members of a household would be agnatically related.[22]

As in China, the depth of the patrilineage varied according to class, with peasant lineages fissioning much sooner than those of the elite. Only among the elite were there some who were greatly concerned with keeping extended genealogies. Among the peasantry in the north, the normative depth of lineage was apparently four generations, whereas among the peasantry in the south lineage depth was rarely extended to more than three generations.[23] The patrilineage was nowhere as elaborate a structure in Vietnam as it was in the neighboring area of southeastern China.[24] Although surname villages (*ho*) have been reported as existing in Tonkin, they were not common. In a study made in the 1930s in Bac Ninh province in the Tonkin Delta, Gourou discovered 50 surname villages out of a total of 610 villages in the province. Moreover, all but one of these surname villages was associated with the name Nguyen, which accounted for 54 per cent of all surnames in the province.[25] As we shall see, village structure was quite independent of kinship considerations.

Some evidence suggests that traditionally the lineage head (*truong toc*) was not everywhere the senior male in the senior line of descent.[26] Lustéguy reports that traditionally lineage leadership in southern Vietnam was divided between two men, the *truong toc*, or ritual head, and the *ton-truong*, or secular head. The former was the eldest male in the direct line, whereas the latter was the most respectable, influential, and experienced of the older males of the lineage.[27] Hickey found that in the village of Khanh Hau in contemporary south Vietnam, the *truong toc* was chosen by a council of adult male *and female* members of the lineage rather than being the eldest male in the direct line.[28]

The kinship idiom was used for many social relations involving people who were not actual kinsmen. Nonetheless, kinship and society were not, even ideally, isomorphic. Of equal importance to kinship in traditional Vietnamese society was the village.

The Traditional Vietnamese Village

The traditional village (Sino-Vietnamese *xa*) was not simply a collection of patrilineages, but was structured according to a number of nonkinship principles.[29] Marked differences obtained between villages within traditional Vietnam, such differences reflecting adaptations to the differing regional contexts in the country.

Villages in Tonkin were well-defined physical entities, being surrounded by hedges that defined the borders of the communities.[30] Villages (*xa*) in the Tonkin Delta usually comprised smaller " hamlets " (*thon*), of which there were two to five per village.[31] How many people inhabited the *thon* and the *xa* in traditional times is not known, but the number would most likely have been less than the mean population of 940 inhabitants per village, which Gourou reports for Tonkin in the 1930s.[32]

Many of the villages of central Vietnam were oriented toward fishing, and even the rice-growing villages do not seem to have been characterized by the well-defined hedge boundaries of the Tonkinese villages.[33] Moreover, some evidence suggests that the hamlet was less commonly found in the central Vietnamese village than it was in the Tonkin area.

Villages in southern Vietnam, and particularly those in the Mekong Delta were significantly different from villages in both Tonkin and central Vietnam.[34] Vietnamese settlement in the Mekong Delta only began in the first part of the eighteenth century. In contrast to Tonkin or central Vietnam, the settlement pattern in this area was far more dispersed, with isolated homesteads scattered about the countryside.[35] As the population in the area grew, these homesteads were consolidated, by order of the Emperor, into villages. This pattern of consolidation continued into the modern period, giving rise today to communities of considerably larger populations than were to be found in the Red River Delta. Hendry notes that the village of Khanh Hau, which he studied in 1958–1959, with a population of 3,241 was " probably slightly smaller than other villages which surround it."[36] These large villages today are divided into a number of hamlets; Khanh Hau, for example, comprises six separate hamlets of which two were formerly centers of totally separate villages.[37] It is likely that villages in the Mekong Delta in the nineteenth century were considerably smaller than are villages found there today. Nonetheless, the dispersed settlement pattern and lack of well-defined boundaries most likely characterized villages of that period as they do villages of the present day.

The component social groups of the Vietnamese village included kinship groups, although the patrilineal extended families and localized lineages were apparently relatively less important in the determination of community policy in Vietnam than they were in China.[38] More important were the " hamlets " (*thon*). Of particular importance in the north of Vietnam were mutual-aid societies (*giap*), which seem to have had some of the characteristics of an age set.[39]

Leadership in the villages in traditional Vietnam was vested in men (never women) who belonged to the council of notables (*hoi dong hao muc*).[40] This council consisted of " a heterogeneous group of men—true elders, retired officials, lesser degree holders, and former village chiefs."[41] In some areas, wealth, that is to say extensive land holdings, also qualified a man for membership. The council of notables was headed by the *tien-chi*, the man among them with the highest status. The *tien-chi* was not the same as the village headman or " mayor," the *ly truong*, the latter being the man elected by the council to represent the village in its dealings with the state.[42]

The responsibilities of the traditional village headman (*ly truong*) in dealing with the state derived from the fact that the village, and not the individual, was defined by law and practice as the fundamental constituent of the state. Taxes were collected and corvée levied with reference to villages rather than to peasants or to feudal lords.

> [T]he Vietnamese *xa* was not the property of any private individual or family, in the way that the English or French manor belong to its manorial lord. It paid taxes, furnished men for the army, or performed corvée labour services, entirely by virtue of its obligations to the emperor; and if at a particular time the actual recipient of these dues was someone other than the emperor himself, that person derived his position entirely from an imperial grant.[43]

The village headman had to keep registries of land holdings and men eligible for military or corvée service in order that the demands of the state could be met.

A *dinh* or shrine of the tutelary spirit of a Vietnamese village (building in left center, Mekong Delta, southern Vietnam. (Photo from Gerald C. Hickey, *Village in Vietnam* [New Haven: Yale University Press, 1964, first plate.]

In addition to being a unit of local administration, the Vietnamese village was also a religious congregation. Gourou reports that in every village in the Tonkin Delta there was a *dinh*, a shrine dedicated to the cult of the village guardian spirit, the shrine also being used as a communal meeting hall, and a *chua*, a Buddhist pagoda.[44] In some villages, such other shrines as temples of letters (dedicated to Confucius) and temples of war were also to be found, but these were not so common as the *dinh* and the *chua*. The Buddhist pagoda was not comparable to the temple monasteries found in villages in Theravada Buddhist societies, since these *chua* served religious functions that were neither exclusive nor dominant in Vietnamese culture.[45] In other words, the *chua* and its resident clergy provided access to only one among several equally important sources of supernatural power. Only a few older women in any village were constant devotees of Buddhism. The real religious focus of the village was the *dinh*. As Nguyen Van Khoan has said:

> In the village, the notables officiate in the *dinh*, and the old women in the *chua*. These men come to perform the *lay* before the Buddha, and the women before the guardian spirits, only on the days of major sacrifices.[46]

The guardian spirit of a village could be a heavenly divinity who had become a patron of a particular village or a human spirit who in life had had some particular connection with the village of which it later became the patron. The spirit who became a patron could have been a man of virtue, a mandarin who had performed a service for the village, a man who had founded the community, or a man who had died a violent death at a time deemed to have been a " sacred hour."[47] Only when the Emperor had conferred a patent upon the patron spirit of a village was the spirit believed to assume his office:

> When a new settlement became self-sufficient, it achieved the status of a *xa* (village) by receiving a name from the emperor who also appointed a guardian spirit or spirits to watch over the village and bring it peace and prosperity. On its part, the village was expected to construct a *dinh* or communal temple as a repository for the imperial document naming the guardian spirit. The *dinh* also housed the altars honoring the guardian spirit and, in effect, it is a symbolic bond between the village and the emperor.[48]

Guardian spirits could also be raised or lowered in rank by the emperor, depending on the actions ascribed to the spirits over the course of the year. Each year, mandarins were required to review the actions of the spirits and to determine, for example, whether the *dinh* had been used as an asylum for wrongdoers, whether rebellion had been plotted in a *dinh*, whether a village had suffered from some calamity, and so on. After reviewing the reports of the mandarins, the emperor would then confer one of three ranks on the spirits.[49]

The Council of Notables had the responsibility for maintaining the cult of the guardian spirit. The main officiant of the cult was the ranking member of the Council of Notables. In addition to his ritual responsibilities, this person was also the main leader in all internal secular affairs of the community. In other words, his role was complementary to that of the *ly truong* who represented the village in its relations with the state. Like the lineage head who held title to the ancestral property (*huong hoa*), the ritual head of the cult of the village guardian spirit also controlled the property associated with the *dinh*. During his tenure in office, the main officiant was expected to give up living with his wife; in other words, he was expected to live a less worldly life than he normally led.[50]

The main rituals that were performed at the *dinh* and that served to draw the whole village together were those connected with the agricultural cycle. In the 1960s in the South Vietnamese village of Khanh Hau, three annual celebrations were held at the *dinh* connected with " descent to the fields," " ascent from the fields," and the end of the harvest. In addition, an annual ceremony was also held at the Khanh Hau *dinh* " to request peace and prosperity from the Guardian Spirit of the village," to honor the ancestral spirits of village members, and to exorcise evil spirits.[51] A number of other minor festivals were also held at the *dinh* during the course of the year.

The major festivals, as well as the construction and maintenance of the *dinh*, required considerable support. For major festivals, each household was expected to make a contribution. Other revenues were raised, at least in Tonkin, through taxes on weddings and registration of changes of titles.[52] Perhaps the most important source of revenue came from the renting of communal lands. In Tonkin, significant tracts of communal land were held by each village. Some of these, namely those not earmarked for support of the *dinh*, were periodically distributed among the registered members of the community, the decision on distribution being made by the Council of Notables. Lands assigned to the *dinh* (and to other cults) were not distributed, but were rented so that the revenue generated could be used to support the cult.[53]

The Council of Notables constituted the most important group of men within village society, but some others were distinguished from their neighbors. Traditionally, almost every village, at least in northern Vietnam, had one or more resident Buddhist monks, and many villages also had a resident Taoist priest. Both Buddhist monks and Taoist priests performed rituals primarily for individual clients rather than for collectivities. Functionally, and sometimes terminologically, Buddhist monks and Taoist priests were similar to yet another type of specialist, the *thay*. In the village, most *thay* were soothsayers, sorcerers, and others who held specialized knowledge that could be used in performing services for members of the community.[54]

The State in Traditional Vietnam

The Vietnamese village, although it enjoyed considerable autonomy, was embedded in a larger social entity, the state. The traditional Vietnamese state was modeled on the Chinese state with an Emperor holding supreme power and a mandarin bureaucracy administering the system. As Woodside has argued most persuasively, the mandarins and the emperors of traditional Vietnam under the Nguyen in the first half of the nineteenth century " saw themselves as Chinese players on a Chinese historical stage."

> On such a stage, the Vietnamese ruler's own part had to be dramatically convincing. His own life and style of power had to be interchangeable with the Chinese emperor's, any Chinese emperor's.[55]

Yet for all the efforts of emperor and mandarins to order events according to a Chinese script, the Southeast Asian context in which these events took place often made such efforts impossible.

According to Chinese theory, all power in the state resided in the emperor. Succession to this office was determined, except for periodic usurpation, by membership in the royal family. However, as in other countries in mainland Southeast Asia, the absence of a fixed order of succession provided a basis for internal dissension in the royal family.[56] Moreover, Vietnamese history is filled with stories of challenges to the power of emperors by feudal lords, locally powerful bureaucrats, recalcitrant vassals, and disgruntled peasants. Even under the Nguyen rulers who had brought a unity heretofore unknown to Vietnam, there was almost always a rebellion or two somewhere within the state. It has been estimated that there were over 300 rebellions during the reigns of Gia Long and Minh Mang, that is, during the period between 1802 and 1840.[57] This degree of political instability was unequaled elsewhere in traditional Southeast Asia.

Where the emperor's authority was unchallenged, it was exercised by bureaucrats who were mandarins, or " superior men " (*quan tu*). One became a mandarin by successfully passing a succession of state examinations based on studies of the Confucian classics.[58] The Confucian content of the education required for becoming a mandarin had not always been as emphasized in Vietnam as it was under the Nguyen in the nineteenth century. Under the Ly dynasty (1009–1225), a knowledge of Mahayana Buddhism had been included in the curriculum preparing those who aspired to become Mandarins. However, from at least the beginning of the fourteenth century on, Buddhism was de-emphasized and finally eliminated as as relevant subject for those who became Mandarins.[59] Buddhism, however, continued to be an important element in cultural tradition of the populace. Whereas Confucianism became the dominant element in elite culture, it assumed only a secondary importance in the popular tradition. In other words, the Mandarins were not only differentiated from the peasantry by virtue of social status, but also by culture. As Parsons has said with reference to China: " The Mandarins . . . became a broad governing class whose status was defined in cultural terms. This was something entirely new in societal evolution."[60] This innovation was copied in meticulous detail by the Vietnamese.

Although some mandarins held specifically cultural roles, serving as teachers and as ritual officiants, the vast majority held occupations as bureaucrats. Civil mandarins were given provincial administrative posts in the provinces (*tran*) and districts (*phu* or *huyen*), but not in the villages, although, as noted above, resident scholars or retired mandarins might be made members of the Council of Notables in the village in which they lived. There was always a surfeit of qualified scholars and an even larger number of failed scholars or scholars still attempting to pass the examinations. Such educational " wastage," to employ a modern term, followed from the application of the principle that there must be a much larger pool of applicants, for examinations and jobs, than actual positions so that only the best would succeed. Although some had passed the examinations but had not been given bureaucratic positions and some who had failed the examinations found compensatory employment, there was always a rather large population of unemployed literati. This population was the source of potential trouble for the state. As Smith has noted, the leadership of secret societies within which rebellion was sometimes plotted included a number of ambitious literati who had not succeeded in obtaining positions as mandarins.[61]

Those who did become members of the bureaucracy were " generalists " rather than functional specialists. This said, it must also be added that bureaucratic action in traditional Vietnam was more rationalized than was the action of the officials of traditional Burma, Thailand, Laos, and Cambodia. The latter were bound to their superiors and inferiors by feudal-like patterns of patronage, whereas the former were expected to act in accord with more universalistic principles. Under the Nguyen, mandarin bureaucrats were salaried in order " to nourish incorruptibility," whereas the officials of the Theravada Buddhist states were given domains " to eat " (to use both the Burmese and Thai metaphor).[62]

The Emperors and mandarins of traditional Vietnam saw themselves as " the cultural cynosures of a society surrounded by subversive ' barbarians '."[63] Such " barbarians " were, in theory, to be made into tutelaries of culturally superior Vietnam and, eventually, to be civilized. However, the sinified rulers of Vietnam were not sufficiently powerful relative to all their neighbors nor sufficiently in control of their own society to force all their neighbors to assume subordinate places and to submit to the Vietnamese version of a civilizing mission. By attempting to act on the belief that Vietnam was the center of civilization in Southeast Asia, as was the case with regard to Cambodia in the nineteenth century prior to the arrival of the French, the rulers of Vietnam created further political instability in the area.[64]

The endemic political crisis that plagued the rulers of traditional Vietnam was a consequence, in part, of unsuccessful efforts to impose a Confucian-derived ideal order on a world very different from that in which the order had originally been developed. Of equal, if not more importance, was the vast gulf that separated the cultural tradition of the elite from the cultural traditions of the people. This was true even in northern Vietnam where the peasantry had long been exposed to Sinitic influences. It was even more true in southern Vietnam which " was more Cambodian, more Buddhist, less Confucian, less Sino-Vietnamese than the center and the north."[65] The elite and popular traditions did articulate, but the tensions that also obtained between them were more acute than was the case in the Theravada Buddhist societies of mainland Southeast Asia.

CULTURAL TRADITIONS AND CULTURAL CONFLICT IN TRADITIONAL VIETNAM

Cosmic Harmony and the Political Order

Smith has observed that in traditional Vietnam, the Vietnamese " distinguished . . . between two levels of the supernatural, Heaven and the spirits. Personality was an attribute not of Heaven but of the spirits, which were legion."[66] The popular tradition emphasized the legion of spirits, whereas the elite tradition stressed the idea of " Heaven." For the elite, Heaven was an " impersonal moral force—the source of infinite harmony, uniting in itself both the positive and negative elements of the universe."[67] It was the responsibility of the elite to attune the human world to the cosmic forces through performance of proper rituals and through constant attention to ethical action. Neither the mandarins nor the Emperor could resolve the injustices (apparent as well as real) and contradictions of the world. Such were resolved only in Heaven. Humans could accept these as their fate knowing that they were subject to forces that transcended human powers. In the concept of Heaven, one finds both the concept of the Tao, universal harmony, and the Buddhist concept of Karma, an impersonal force that determined the fate of humans.[68]

Unlike Theravada Buddhists, Vietnamese conceived of no escape from the dictates of fate, from the consequences of disharmony; there was no ultimate salvation for the Vietnamese, at least for the Vietnamese elite. The Confucian elite of Vietnam, as their counterpart in China, did not see this world as undesirable, a world that should be rejected in favor of an infinitely more desirable other world. This world was not the best of all possible worlds; it was the only world. Religious action was not focused on a salvation quest, but on the achievement of harmony in this world.[69]

The Vietnamese Emperor had a special role in assuring that the state was in harmony with Heaven; he held the " mandate of Heaven "; he was the " Son of Heaven." He did not claim divinity, however, as did the rulers of the classical Indianized states. Nor was he a man believed to be endowed uniquely with virtue as was the case with the rulers of the Theravada Buddhist states. Rather, he was the high priest, the pope of the cult of Heaven and Earth. He carried out the duties of his role primarily in the annual rites of *nam giao*, the " sacrifice to Heaven and Earth." This ceremony, whose chief officiant was the Emperor or his personally chosen substitute, culminated in the sacrifice of young buffaloes, pigs, and she-goats to the celestial powers.[70] The proper performance of these rites ensured the stability and the prosperity of the state. However, harmony with the cosmic forces might not be achieved. In such as case, ill fortune would befall the nation.

> Floods, droughts, and other catastrophes are indicative of disharmony and the disapproval of heaven. This is the time for " change of mandate," the literal Vietnamese expression for revolution.[71]

Concerns with harmony and social equilibrium were held by mandarins as well as by the Emperor. For the mandarins, the attainment of harmony was accomplished not through performance of rites of sacrifice to Heaven (such was the sole prerogative of the Emperor) but through ethical action. As the Emperor's right to rule was legitimated by his position as the " Son of Heaven," the mandarins' right to exercise their authority was derived from their being " superior men " (Sino-Vietnamese, *quan-tu*; Chinese *chun-tzu*) who acted in accord with Confucian ideals.

The most important of these ideals included the promotion of the five fundamental relationships of society and the evincing of the five basic virtues.[72] The five fundamental relationships included the relationships between ruler and his subjects, between father and son, between husband and wife, between elder brother and younger brother, and between friend and friend. The first three were known as the three basic elements of social ethics (*tam cuong*). The five basic virtues (*ngu thuong*) were human heartedness (*nhan*), righteousness (*nghia*), proper ritual conduct (*le*), wisdom (*tri*), and good faith (*tin*). These virtues were given a variety of expressions, one of the more important in late traditional Vietnam being the ten maxims proclaimed by Emperor Minh-mang in 1834.[73]

The five relationships define a society based on personalistic connections rather than on universalistic premises. Fundamental to these personalistic connections was kinship and the kinship idiom was used in defining relationships among those who were not actual kinsmen. In particular, the Emperor was conceived of and regarded as a superior father, whereas his subjects were viewed as children. As in China, no religious priesthood could appeal to general principles that were as applicable to rulers as to the ruled.

In addition to attempting to observe various rules of ethical conduct, the mandarins also undertook certain ritual acts at temples and altars dedicated to Confucius, the Master of Wisdom, found at each bureaucratic center.[74] These rites were held for the mandarins alone; the general populace did not participate in them. Each August, a Festival of Confucius was celebrated at the capital and in each provincial center. In this ceremony, the solidarity of the ruling elite was manifest:

> The high mandarins and the university members of all ranks, followed by the lower officials and the people, go in a procession to the temple of literature. In the capital, it is the Emperor himself who officiates; in the provinces, it is the governor . . . or, in his absence, the provincial inspector of instruction. . . . The principal person officiating is assisted at Hué by the members of the Academy . . . , in the provinces by the inspectors of the first and second degree.[75]

In ritual action, as in moral action, the mandarins were concerned to demonstrate that they were " superior men," that is, men set apart from the populace in general. Although this division was very great, certain cultural beliefs were shared by elite and the people alike, although they interpreted these beliefs rather differently. The most important beliefs held in common by all members of traditional Vietnamese society were those connected with the ancestral cult.

The Ancestral Cult and Popular Religion

The ancestral cult was predicated on the belief that after one's physical death, a person is survived by what Cadière terms " vital principles."[76] Every person is vitiated by three major vital principles (*hon*) and by seven, if one is a male, or nine, if one is a female, minor vital principles (*via*).[77] Although some of these vital principles stay with the corpse after death, of main concern are those that become attached to the ancestral tablets. These latter, which become the ancestral spirits, remain involved in the lives of the family to which they belonged. Their needs, which are very human, must be met. They attempt to influence the lives of their relatives for good and to judge and punish those relatives whose acts are offensive or who do not fulfill the duties imposed by filial piety.

For the populace generally, the ancestral spirits possessed an unquestioned reality. The elite in Vietnam, as in China, tended to be more skeptical about the actual existence of the spirits. Nevertheless, they were motivated to support the ancestral cult, since Confucian writings stressed the way in which the cult served to bind kinsmen together. The rites of propitiation of ancestral spirits functioned to reinforce kinship ties that formed the basis of traditional Vietnamese society.

In addition to the cult of the ancestral spirits, the cult of communal spirits also derived support from the elite as well as from the populace. Like the ancestral spirits, the communal spirits were believed to play active roles in the everyday lives of the people. The community religion functioned not only to promote social solidarity among residents of the same communities, but also to

An old Vietnamese man offers joss sticks, flowers, and drink to the spirits of his ancestors. [Photo from David C. Cooke, *Vietnam: The Country, the People* (New York: W. W. Norton, 1968), p. 31.]

tie peasants to the state. As already noted, communal spirits received their mandate from the emperor and were raised or lowered in rank by the emperor according to the actions ascribed to the spirits in the course of a year. Given the sociological importance of the village in traditional Vietnamese society, the elite found it useful to support and coopt the communal religion even if, as with the ancestral spirits, they were skeptical about the actual existence of the communal spirits.

The popular religion of the Vietnamese villagers included more than the ancestral and village guardian spirits.[78] Villagers also believed that their fortunes and misfortunes were influenced by innumerable other spirits that populated the Vietnamese countryside and by cosmic forces that they interpreted rather differently from the elite. Vietnamese popular religion was extremely eclectic. In traditional times, beliefs were derived from local customs, which varied from region to region, from Mahayana Buddhism, and from Taoism. In addition, some of the southern Vietnamese also borrowed beliefs from the Indianized or Theravada Buddhist cultures with which they had contact. By late traditional times (i.e., early nineteenth century), Christianity had also become an important element in the religious life of many Vietnamese, having had an impact beyond those who were actually converted.[79]

The spirits of the Vietnamese pantheon varied so much from region to region that it is possible to see some truth in Langrand's statement that " in a certain way . . . religion in Annam is a geographical fact ".[80] Even within regions, there were differences in spirit beliefs between those who were mainly rice farmers and those who followed such other occupations as fishing. Such diversity of spirit beliefs notwithstanding, the Vietnamese did believe that some supernatural power derived from the Buddha, from certain Bodhisattvas, and from the Taoist Jade Emperor.

The social organization of the popular religion, other than the cults associated with ancestral and communal spirits, was predicated in most cases on a relationship between a religious practitioner (i.e., one who could communicate with the spirits or who could calculate geomantic formulas) and a client. Some religious practitioners were attached to such institutions as Buddhist pagodas or spirit shrines, but many had no base of operations. Some, like Buddhist monks, were full-time religious specialists, whereas many others engaged in their practices as a supplementary occupation. Periodically, sectarian associations would emerge among adherents to a specific body of beliefs. Such sects were looked on with grave misgivings by the Emperor and the mandarins for they saw in them the potential loci of political rebellion. These fears were not unfounded. As Smith has said: " It was not easy to draw a hard and fast line between secret societies whose character was fundamentally religious, and others whose main concern was with politics or with banditry and crime."[81] As discussed above, peasant uprisings, many of which were religious in nature, were very common in traditional Vietnam.

The assigning of Buddhism to the popular religion may appear somewhat strange; however, Buddhism in Vietnam traditionally (as well as in recent times) has had a significance quite different from that it has for the Theravada Buddhist neighbors of the Vietnamese. This contrast was evident to the English envoy, John Crawfurd, in his report of a trip made in Southeast Asia in 1821–1822:

> Coming from countries like Hindostan and Siam, where systematic and national forms of worship are established and where religion exerts so powerful a sway over society, we were surprised at the contrast which Cochin-China presented in this respect. . . . The ministers of religion, instead of being honoured, reverenced, and powerful, as in Buddhist and Brahminical countries, are few in number and the meanest orders, and little respected. They seem, in short, to be looked upon as little better than a kind of fortune-teller.[82]

Such had not always been the case. Buddhism had been introduced in Vietnam from both India and China in the early years of the Christian era. By the time of the Ly dynasty (1009–1224), Buddhism was flourishing with the rulers providing patronage and the clergy having great influence.[83] However, from the thirteenth century on, Buddhism declined in importance, eventually becoming, as in China, socially marginal.

Traditionally, the Buddhist monk was called on to chant some parts of the *sutras* (Buddhist scriptures) on occasions such as weddings or funerals. In return for these services, which helped to sanctify the events in question, the people gave the monks gifts. As already noted regarding the village *chua*, or Buddhist shrine, most patrons of Buddhism in traditional times were women, and most of these women were elderly. Beside these women, few Vietnamese ever undertook to perform acts of Buddhist piety.[84] Moreover, few, if any, Vietnamese, other than some monks, would have had any fundamental understanding of the dogmas of Buddhism. The Buddha, Quan Am, the Buddhist Goddess of Mercy, and other Bodhisattvas and Arahats, were, for the Vietnamese, particularly powerful and benevolent spirits.

Taoist beliefs, unlike Buddhist beliefs, were rarely recognized by Vietnamese as deriving from a distinct religious tradition.[85] The belief in the Tao itself had been assimilated to broader conceptions of cosmic destiny. The beliefs in Taoist divinities, and especially the Jade Emperor, were often associated with other spirits. An idol of the Jade Emperor might be found in the *dinh*, whereas Taoist rites could be performed in Buddhist temples.[86]

Beyond the Buddhist and Taoist divinities, each community had its own pantheon of spirits. Among these were such malevolent spirits as *ma* (" phantoms," " ghosts "), *yeu* (" demons "), or *tinh* (" soul-stealing ghosts "). There was also a class of benevolent spirits (*tien*) and such named supernaturals as the " Thunder Spirit " (*thien loi*) and " Water Goddess " (*ba thuy*), which might have special rituals performed for them.[87] Practioners associated with the popular religion were mainly those who gained power through the patronage of a specific spirit. For example, in the southern Vietnamese village of Khanh Hau, one " master of sorcery " (*ong thay phap*) derived his special powers from his supernatural patron, Ong Thay Thuong (" the supreme being "). With this power he was able to combat with evil spirits and to exorcise them when they were causing illnesses.[88]

Concern with orienting one's actions with reference to cosmic forces found expression in the popular religion, although this expression was sometimes different from that found in the elite religion. Astrologers and geomancers were consulted to interpret omens about one's future. Rites of passage could not be undertaken until proper orientation of the involved parties had been accomplished. Geomantic and astrological skills were often the prerogative of the *thay phap*, the " sorcerers."[89] Although most of the expression of beliefs in the popular religion connected with cosmic orientations were grounded in very pragmatic concerns, the idea of " Heaven," that is, of an impersonal order, provided the ultimate grounding for religious belief among the villagers as it did for the religion of the elite.

Cultural Tensions and Social Conflict in Traditional Vietnam

Ultimately it was the belief in Heaven, a " Heaven that was simply ' there,' transcending all conflicts and activity, the source of infinite harmony, uniting in itself both the positive and negative elements of the universe,"[90] on which the traditional order in Vietnam rested. Human action was not directed toward any other worldly salvation, but toward the achievement of more perfect harmony between earth and Heaven, or, alternatively, toward the acceptance of a fate dictated by cosmic forces over which humans had no control.[91] By reading the omens and by employing geomantic calculations, it was possible to determine what fate dictated and to act accordingly. Such fortune telling was found at all levels of society. Through ritual action it was possible to " orient " the individual, the lineage, the community, and the state with reference to the cosmic verities. Ritual action reached its climax in the *nam giao*, the sacrifice to Heaven and Earth performed by the Emperor himself. Under the assumption that the omens were right and that the Emperor performed this ritual correctly, his right to rule was accepted as legitimate in the eyes of the people. Harmony with the cosmos was achieved not only through ritual action but also through ethical action. Virtuous action included the fulfillment of obligations to those who were one's superiors: the Emperor, one's father, one's lineage elders, the village notables, one's teachers, officials, and so on. Although virtuous action was incumbent upon all humans, such was the special responsibility of the literati whose learning had led them to a more acute understanding of their obligations than was held by their less-educated country men. By becoming *quan-tu*, the mandarins established their right to administer the powers vested in them by the Emperor.

In traditional Vietnamese society, power was theoretically totally unrelated to wealth. Wealth was considered to be a fortunate consequence of one's fate, but it carried none of the positive connotations of the virtue achieved by the study of the Confucian classics. Insofar as actions were directed toward the accumulation of wealth, they preempted actions that might have been devoted to the demonstration of virtue. Moreover, the pursuit of wealth might necessitate nonvirtuous acts; for example, selling one's product to a mandarin at a " fair price " rather than giving him a " special price " in deference to his status, renting one's land rather than lending it to poor lineage mates, and so on. Merchants were denigrated by the political elite in part because Confucian orthodoxy so dictated and perhaps more importantly because of the fear that those with great wealth in a poor society would wield too great an influence. As with other societies in Southeast Asia, the most successful merchants in traditional Vietnam were alien Chinese rather than indigenous Vietnamese. Limited by the resources of their country and discouraged by official attitudes, Vietnamese did not readily turn to entrepreneurship and, as a consequence, the economy of their country tended to stagnate.[92] Yet for all the barriers to the acquisition of wealth through trade that existed in traditional Vietnam, a small wealth-defined class did emerge. Moreover, in times when central authority was weak—which was often—a few could even use wealth to gain access to power.

That central authority was often weak in traditional Vietnamese society reflects the fact that ritual and virtuous actions were believed to effect harmony in the society yet did not preclude the eruption of conflict. The death of an emperor often precipitated a succession crisis. Natural and human-made disasters were quite often interpreted as meaning that the emperor had lost his " Mandate of Heaven " and that rebellion was in order. Conflict also arose through the actions of overly ambitious mandarins who stood on its head the premise that virtuous men have the right to rule by maintaining that those who rule are *ipso facto* virtuous men.

Yet another source of conflict in traditional Vietnamese society had its roots in the emphasis given in the popular religion to the beliefs in the powers of spirits and gods. Whereas theistic beliefs were heterodox insofar as the Confucian-educated elite was concerned, they had to be tolerated since they legitimated the important institutions of kinship and community (*gia-dinh*), which formed the basis of the traditional society. The rulers thus supported beliefs in ancestral spirits and community guardian spirits and attempted to manipulate them for their own purposes. Insofar as theistic beliefs and belief in an impersonal Heaven were functionally separated and associated with different institutions, the potential contradiction between them posed no threat. However, when conditions—economic, political, or demographic—became un-bearable in some area of traditional Vietnam, it was quite common for a move-ment to challenge the authority of the state by accepting the power of a spirit or god, such as a Bodhisattva, as being greater than the power of Heaven that legitimated the emperor. Insofar as such movements, with their strongly millennarian character, gained any significant support, they could pose serious threats to the society. The rulers thus undertook to suppress ruthlessly, if necessary, such movements and the secret societies in which they were often born.[93] The fact that the state was triumphant proved that the greater power resided in Heaven rather than with spirits and gods.

The reassertion of the state's power in areas in which it had been challenged by peasants holding millennarian ideas was never accomplished once and for all. There was a constant tension between cultural concepts of power grounded in theistic beliefs on the one hand and in an impersonal Heaven on the other. This tension proved to be an Achilles heel in Vietnamese culture, when it was forced to confront the challenge of Western colonialism. It seems clear that the success of Catholic missionaries in Vietnam in late traditional times was in part a function of the prediliction of the peasantry to find power in spirits and gods. The Vietnamese elite responded to the success of Catholic missionization much as they had responded to the success of other movements in gaining adherents to the belief in the power of particular spirits. Emperor Minh-mang and his mandarins began a persecution of the missionaries and a suppression of in-digenous Christians, because they saw in both a potential threat to their own power. Yet, despite the persecutions, the Catholic population continued to grow in Vietnam during the first half of the nineteenth century. Moreover, the persecutions of Western missionaries became the pretext, the legitimating reason for French intervention. The establishment of French colonial control over Vietnam, the preservation of the forms of the monarchy notwithstanding, provided the *coup de grace* to the traditional religious system based on belief in the ultimate power of an impersonal Heaven.

VIETNAM AS A COLONIAL SOCIETY

Colonial History of Vietnam

French rule in Vietnam began in the late 1850s, when the French established footholds in the southern part of the country. It came to an end with the Geneva agreement of 1954. Although French rule lasted only a relatively short period of time—only 70 years in the northern part of the country, and from 90 to 95 years in the Mekong Delta region—it radically changed the course of Vietnamese history. French rule led to changes in the very foundations of Vietnamese society and precipitated a cultural crisis that has continued to the present time.

French intervention in Vietnam had its roots in events of the late eighteenth century, but it was not until the middle of the nineteenth century that a concerted effort was made to establish French influence in the country.[94] A French force had attacked Danang in 1847 in order to punish the Vietnamese for their mistreatment of Catholic missionaries. After Napoleon III came to power in France, support was found for further action in Vietnam. This action began in 1857 with yet another attack on Danang and was followed by the capture of Saigon in 1859. The French were not, however, immediately successful in establishing their presence in Vietnam, and it was not until 1861 that they finally gained a firm foothold in southern Vietnam. In 1867 the French took over the whole of the territory, which became the French colony of Cochin China.

Although the French had been a factor in the Vietnamese political scene since at least 1847, it was not until 1867 that a colonial order began to be established in Vietnam. As Marr has observed,

> Until 1867 only a handful of educated people had collaborated with the French. They had been on the psychological defensive, cowed and apologetic before their peers. After 1867 more coherent, positive arguments were being advanced, for example, in favor of accepting a subordinate role under a foreign master in the " higher interests " of economic and technical development.[95]

While French officials began to establish their control over Cochin-China, the situation in the territories still under the control of Emperor Tu Duc at Hué was deteriorating. The situation was particularly grave in the Tonkin area where trouble was being caused by bands of Chinese rebels who had fled into the area following the end of the Taiping Rebellion. These bands attracted some dissidents in the local population. In 1872–1873 a small French party under the leadership of Francis Garnier was sent to Tonkin to see what advantage could be taken of the situation. Garnier exceeded his orders by capturing the citadel at Hanoi and was killed shortly thereafter as he tried to achieve yet other military successes. His actions were repudiated by the French authorities in Saigon. However, the French advance was only postponed, not brought to a halt.

In 1874 the French and Vietnamese concluded a treaty wherein Emperor Tu Duc recognized French sovereignty over Cochin China and granted the French considerable control over his own domains. Although the Vietnamese attempted to subvert this treaty subsequently and tried also to gain Chinese support in resisting the French advance, the final take over by the French was inevitable. In 1882 the French launched an attack on Tonkin, and Hanoi was taken again. Then the French turned to attack Hué itself. This attack on Hué coincided with the death of Emperor Tu Duc and the almost inevitable crisis over succession. The Vietnamese had little choice but to negotiate away their freedom, making Vietnam (other than Cochin China which was already under French rule), a protectorate of France. This agreement notwithstanding, the French still had to establish actual control over the territories that continued to be in turmoil from the almost free movement of bandit and dissident groups. In 1884 a new treaty with the court at Hué established a protectorate over central Vietnam (which the French called Annam) and a separate administration, also nominally a protectorate, over northern Vietnam (Tonkin).

The 1884 treaty did not secure French interests in Vietnam. The Chinese found the treaty unacceptable and for almost a year following the treaty with Hué, the French and the Chinese engaged in a series of battles, several of which took place in northern Vietnam. Finally, a treaty was concluded between France and China whereby the Chinese recognized French sovereignty over Vietnam. In the meantime, political change in Vietnam stimulated a continuing crisis over who should occupy the throne. The man who replaced Tu Duc and who was forced to sign away Vietnamese sovereignty to the French was killed. His successor was on the throne only a few months when he too was deposed, by Ham Nghi. Ham Nghi remained on the throne about a year, but then he fled Hué to lead a resistance movement against the French. He was captured in 1888 and sent into exile. In the meantime, the French placed a man of their own choosing on the throne.

Marr has argued that " there should be no hesitation in marking July 5, 1885, the date of Ham Nghi's flight from the capital, as the turning point in the history of Vietnam's response to foreign intervention."[96] Although the French continued to maintain the form of the traditional monarchy, Ham Nghi's act had seriously undermined any legitimacy that might be claimed for that monarchy. Moreover, the actuality of French power was but ill-disguised behind the facade of the indigenous monarchy. From 1885 on, politically conscious Vietnamese, save for a very small minority who accepted the right of the French to rule, sought ways to return power to the Vietnamese. Although the anticolonialist Vietnamese were divided about the party that should wield legitimate power, they were united in their desire to deny the French the right to rule their country.

By the mid 1890s the French felt that they had completed their " pacifica-tion " of Vietnam and could now institute a new colonial order throughout the country. Vietnam was divided into three political units, the colony of Cochin China, which was administered directly by Frenchmen, and the two protectorates of Annam and Tonkin, which were administered by Vietnamese officials who must clear all important actions with French counterparts. These three polities, together with Cambodia and Laos, were included within the Union Indochinoise whose Governor General was the ultimate source of power in the French domains. The evolution of the colonial structure of Indochina, and of Vietnam in particular, reached its climax during the administration of Paul Doumer, who was Governor General between 1897 and 1902.

> Doumer left on the country an imprint sufficiently strong for his pro-consulate to be considered as the beginnings of a new stage in the history of the Vietnamese nation itself. He it was who caused the colonial regime to pass from an empirical—so to speak " handicraft "—stage, to a stage of systematic organization. He it was who set up the co-ordinated apparatus of financial exploitation and political domination which was to remain practically intact until 1945.[97]

Although Indochina was later to have Governor Generals who were liberal in tendency and even one who was a socialist, the structure created by Doumer was never fundamentally altered until after World War II.

French rule in Vietnam, as in the rest of Indochina, was not seriously challenged until the end of World War II. At the outset of the War, the Japanese recognized the authority of the Vichy government in Indochina in return for the right to station troops in the country and to use it as a staging area for attacks on neighboring areas. Only as the War drew to a close, and the French in Indo-china became more openly pro-Allied, did the Japanese decide to bring French rule to an end. In March 1945, the Japanese staged a *coup de force* against the French administration in Indochina. They then recognized Vietnam, with the Emperor Bao Dai as its head of state, as an independent country, albeit within the Japanese sphere of influence.

Bao Dai was not long to remain head of state. In mid-August when the Japanese surrendered, they handed over administrative authority to a repre-sentative of Bao Dai. By this time, however, the Viet Minh, the Vietnamese revolutionary movement led by Ho Chi Minh, had succeeded in establishing its control over much of Vietnam. Following the Japanese surrender, the Viet Minh assumed control of the government and their authority gained legitimacy on August 23, 1945 when Bao Dai abdicated and handed over to the Viet Minh the symbolic emblems of the state. Although the French did not recognize the trans-fer of power that had occurred between the Japanese and the government of Bao Dai and then between Bao Dai and the Viet Minh government under Ho Chi Minh, the Democratic Republic of Vietnam continues to this day to trace its legitimacy to these acts of transfer of power.

After World War II, the French attempted to reestablish authority over Vietnam and the rest of Indochina. World War II had done little to temper French colonial policy. The fundamental principle of postwar policy, laid down in a conference in 1944, stressed that: " the aims of the work of civilization which France is accomplishing in her possessions exclude any idea of autonomy and any possibility of development outside the French Empire bloc. The attainment of ' self government ' in the colonies, even in the most distant future, must be excluded."[98] The efforts of the French to act in accord with this principle in a Vietnam where it was believed independence had already been attained led to the bitter conflict that ended with the French defeat at Dien Bien Phu. In 1954, the French finally recognized in the agreements signed at Geneva that their colonial rule in Vietnam and Indochina had come to an end.

French Rule and the Vietnamese Village

French colonial policy in Vietnam, as in all French territories, was predicated to the very end on the premise that French rule was beneficial for the colonized. More specifically, French rule was predicated on the idea that the French had a " civilizing mission " (*mission civilisatrice*) in Asia and Africa. Through education, the Vietnamese, and other colonial peoples, could become Frenchmen and thereby partake of all of the advantages accruing to those who were French. The converse of this premise was that those who did not become French were accorded a distinctly less privileged place within the French colonial system. Such a place was filled by the vast majority of Vietnamese until the end of French rule.

In political terms, French policy implied that only Frenchmen could hold real power in Vietnam. This was in fact very much the case, although the debate about whether French rule should be one of " assimilation " or " association " somewhat obscured this fact. " Broadly, the terms were supposed to reflect the contrast between colonial policies that emphasized the introduction of forms of government approximating those used in France and an indirect form of government that built upon existing institutions."[99] In Cochin China there was no question but that French rule aimed at " assimilation " as Frenchmen filled not only the highest positions in the colonial administration, but also many of the lower levels as well. Tonkin and Annam, however, appeared to be administered in terms of a policy of " association," since they were protectorates in which an indigenous bureaucracy continued to exist. Yet, even in these areas, French power was never compromised. Ultimate power lay with the Governor General of Indochina and was implemented in Tonkin and Annam by French *résident superieurs*. Moreover, every important bureaucratic position filled by a Vietnamese official was linked with a French advisor who determined what the Vietnamese official could and could not do. What the maintenance of the forms of indirect rule in Tonkin and Annam actually accomplished was that French rule was less visible in northern and central Vietnam than it was in Cochin China.

The institutional restructuring effected by the French was not limited to the state level. It was also carried down into the villages themselves. The impact was felt first in Cochin China, where French rule had been established longest and where there was no pretence of indirect rule.[100] The village councils, made up of notables, and the village leaders who had been chosen by the councils, were subjected to a succession of demands that they carry out administrative functions for the colonial authorities. Those who sought positions on the councils tended to be those who were more concerned with their personal fortunes than with promoting communal interests. This state of affairs was not lost even on the French. In 1902, the Lieutenant Governor of Cochin China said the following in a report before a meeting of the Superior Council of Indochina:

> The recruitment of notables becomes, unfortunately, more and more difficult in some provinces; the prosperous and honorable families show a certain repugnance for these perilous functions, which thus too often fall into the hands of those who are unskilled, and even, sometimes, dishonest.[101]

Yet, despite their recognition that the village social organization was deteriorating, the French implemented yet other policies that had the effect of causing further disintegration of communal life.

In 1904 a decree reduced the number of notables in the councils and defined the functions of these members in terms of the requirements of colonial local administration rather than the needs of the local community.[102] By another decree in 1921, recruitment to the Council of Notables was made subject to election by members of the villages in which the council was found. The French saw this reform as a step toward the establishment of democratic institutions at the local level, but it actually had the effect of undermining the authority of the councils in the eyes of villagers:

> The village showed no willingness to introduce new values, along with the men who stood for them, into its own affairs. As for the notables, who were the customary leaders of the rural population, they had too much to lose financially by the change. They therefore withdrew from participation and saw to it that rather unrepresentative men were elected. Without coming forward themselves, the notables maneuvered other men into position and then conducted a veiled opposition to all the measures recommended by the colonial administration.[103]

All the reforms the French attempted to introduce at the local level simply confirmed further the fact that local institutions no longer served local needs.

Village leaders were made responsible by the colonial government for the collection of taxes, such taxes having increased severalfold over what they had been in traditional times. They were responsible for implementing the laws of the colonial government, including the highly unpopular law against local production of alcoholic beverages. They were responsible for controlling banditry and preventing rebellion in their local communities. The village that supported or harbored a rebellion was severely punished. Among the possible penalties were the dissolution of the village and its annexation to neighboring villages, the confiscation of property belonging to villagers, and the levying of fines against the leaders and notables of the village.[104] Rather than serve as agents of the

French government for which they received little or no benefits and for which they made themselves vulnerable to the wrath of both villagers and government, many qualified men withdrew from participation in village councils or in village leadership positions.

Local institutions were not only altered by the direct actions of the colonial government; they also underwent radical changes as a consequence of the socioeconomic impact of colonialization in Vietnam. French rule opened Vietnam to capitalist economic development, and this development had profound effects on rural life in Vietnam.

Economic Development in Colonial Vietnam

From the very first, the French government in Indochina took as a primary function the responsibility for the economic development of the colony. Initially, such development necessitated the investment of public funds from France, but after the beginning of World War I public investment declined substantially and revenues used for meeting the budgets of the Indochinese Government and the governments of the five constituent states were generated locally. Prior to World War I, Indochina had attracted little private investment, but after the War, and particularly during the 1920s, private investment reached very high levels:

> Altogether some 2,870 million francs were invested in the colony in one form or another between 1924 and 1930—Indochina's most prosperous post-war years—From 1924 on, therefore, Indochina drained off a good deal of French capital. The abundance of inflation-born currency resources facilitated investment while the franc's depreciation made money seek the security offered by the piastre.[105]

Capital investment by the government of Indochina was mainly in infrastructure, that is, in railways, port facilities, roadways, and the like. Some investment, such as that in the canal system in the Mekong Delta, was more specifically directed at the promotion of certain types of production, commercial agriculture in this case. Although direct investment by government in productive enterprises was limited, the government encouraged the development of such enterprises by instituting laws that facilitated the flow of capital into the country.

Private investment was predominantly in commercial agriculture and specifically in commercial production of rice and rubber. Nonagricultural investment was mainly in the production of such raw materials as metal ores and coal[106] and in trade and transportation.[107] Although Vietnam produced raw materials, it imported manufactured goods. In other words, Vietnam (and the rest of Indochina) became a classic colonial dependency, producing raw materials for export and importing manufactured goods from metropolitan France and (to a much lesser extent) from other developed countries.

By far the most significant amount of capital invested in Vietnam was in agriculture, and the larger percentage of this went into the promotion of the commercial production of rice. As with the development of commercial rice agriculture in Burma and Thailand, there was little investment in technological improvements in rice cultivation in Vietnam. Some monies were invested, by the colonial government itself, in hydraulic works (canals and dikes), mainly in the Mekong Delta, but these did not represent any radical change from the type of hydraulic works that had long existed in northern Vietnam. In Vietnam, as in Burma and Thailand, the increased production of rice for the world market was accomplished mainly through the intensification of labor.

The French also introduced some new cash crops into Vietnam, the most important being rubber, and also including coffee, tea, and tobacco. The planting of these crops necessitated certain changes in the modes of ecological adaptation traditionally found in Vietnam. Rubber, for example, was planted in upland fields, which had previously been cultivated, if at all, almost exclusively by swiddening methods by tribal peoples.

The limited industrial development of Vietnam occurred primarily in the extraction of natural resources. Mining of coal and metal ores, mainly in northern Vietnam (and Laos), was the most important of such industries. There was some development of the lumber industry, but this development was quite minor in comparison with the development of the same industry in Burma or even in Thailand. There was also some development of processing and manufacturing industries, but such development was minimal as both governmental and private interests favored the import of manufactured goods from France rather than their production locally.

Given the importance of trade in the colonial economy, it is hardly surprising that the most significant changes in the environment effected during French rule were in transportation and port facilities. During the French period, nearly 3,000 kilometers of rail-line, over 35,000 kilometers of road ways, expanded facilities at the three major ports of Haiphong, Hon Gay, and Saigon, as well as at some of the minor ports such as Danang (Tourane) and Cam Ranh, airports, and other communication and transportation facilities were constructed.[108] For the most part, these facilities were used by the French, by Chinese traders, and by the small number of Vietnamese involved in trade or administration. Most Vietnamese peasants continued to get about by ox or pony cart or, more commonly, by foot.

Land Tenure and Agriculture in Colonial Vietnam

Although only a small number of Vietnamese peasants adopted new modes of production during the colonial period, few peasants did not have their lives radically changed as a result of the type of political economy created during the period of French rule. The greatest impact occurred in the development of commercial rice production. Whereas in Thailand, and to a great extent, also, in Burma, expansion of rice production to meet world market demand had been undertaken by the peasants themselves on the small holdings they owned, in Vietnam this expansion was promoted by large land owners, mainly in the Mekong Delta. As large land holdings had not been significant in precolonial times, commercialization of rice agriculture in Vietnam was associated with significant changes in land tenure.

In precolonial Vietnam, two main types of tenure were to be found in the countryside. A majority of the land was owned and operated by kin groups in much the same way as land was an extension of kin-group membership in the Theravada Buddhist countries. In addition to this form of tenure, a form of communal tenure (*cong dien*), unknown in Theravada Buddhist societies, was also very important in Vietnam. Land owned by villages or by lineages and controlled by village or lineage leaders was redistributed or rented out according to the needs of village or lineage members. Although some large-scale land owners did emerge in traditional Vietnam, they were rare. Moreover, the Vietnamese court instituted policies to prevent the emergence of a landed aristocracy since such proved, during those periods when it had emerged, to be a threat to the throne.

The French introduced very different ideas of land tenure in Vietnam. After they had established their control over Cochin China, the French colonial government confiscated lands belonging to former Vietnamese officials who had fled or who had resisted the French. These lands were then given to Frenchmen or Vietnamese collaboraters. With full control over Vietnam, the government also instituted the policy of granting land concessions, usually involving tracts of land of considerable size, to the French *colons* or to Vietnamese capitalists. Such concessions were more common in southern Vietnam, but they were also to be found to a lesser extent in Annam and Tonkin.[109]

Shifts in land tenure were by far the most dramatic in Cochin China. By 1930, only 2.5 per cent of the cultivated land of this colony was held under communal land tenure. Of the privately held property, 45 per cent was held in estates of over 50 hectares (124 acres), 43 per cent held as properties of 5–50 hectares (12–124 acres), and only 12 per cent in properties of less than 5 hectares (12 acres). The vast majority of the farmers in Cochin China by this year were tenants or sharecroppers. Communal property still accounted in 1930 for 20 per cent of cultivated land in Tonkin and 25–26 per cent of cultivated land in Annam. Moreover, the majority of the peasants in these areas continued to be owner-operators, although the amount of land owned was very small. Y. Henry, a French economist who made a study of conditions in Tonkin in 1930, found that 62 per cent of the owners held land of less than one *mau* (0.36 hectare) in size, and that an additional 30 per cent held land in properties of from one to five *mau* in size. Gourou, who made a study in the Tonkin delta at about the same time, estimated that the number of taxpayers in the area who were landless or who held less than 5 *sao* (0.18 hectare, or 0.45 acre) of land was 63 per cent. In contrast, by using figures from both Henry and Gourou, it can be calculated that 17 per cent of the land in Tonkin was held by 1,100 landowners or about 0.1 per cent of the total number of landowners.[110] The situation was basically the same in Annam as in Tonkin. In short, most land owners in the Tonkin delta were peasants who held only enough land to eke out a bare subsistence. The number of large capitalist landowners were few, but they controlled a disproportionate amount of the cultivated area of the region.

Most of the large tracts of land (properties of 10 hectares or about 25 acres, or more) were rented out to or worked through sharecropping by nonowners.

However, some of the large properties, particularly those in the Red Land areas of the southern Vietnamese highlands, were worked as plantations on which such crops as rubber, coffee, and tea were planted. Whether he be a tenant, a sharecropper, or a wage laborer, the Vietnamese who worked land that he did not own was a product of the colonial period. Such roles had been all but non-existent in precolonial times.

Although the large landowners who promoted the expansion of rice production were interested in the yields obtained, they were not willing to invest in new techniques that would have increased the yields on the properties they owned. Rather, they permitted their tenants and agricultural laborers to work the land with the same techniques as before. Given the increased pressures placed on the land through intensification of agriculture to meet the demands of both landowners and the people who consumed part of what they grew, rice yields in Vietnam underwent a marked decline during the colonial period. A number of students of the impact of colonialism on the peasantry in Vietnam have argued that this decline resulted in yields lower than those of any other country in the region and that the decline was directly attributable to the system of land tenure in Vietnam.[111] Such conclusions are misleading.

By the 1930s, according to estimates made by Gourou, the average yield of rice in Tonkin was about 1.4 metric tons per hectare in Tonkin and 1.34 metric tons per hectare in Cochin China.[112] How great the decline had been is uncertain, although there is no question but that significant declines had taken place. Ngo Vinh Long, citing some scattered evidence, suggests that average yields in the late 1890s were as high as 2.5 to 3 metric tons per hectare.[113] However, these figures probably represent exceptional rather than average yields. Assertions by Long and others notwithstanding, Vietnam had not experienced declines in yields greater than all neighboring countries. Rice yields had declined commensurately in Thailand, for example, where most land was worked by owners rather than by tenants and sharecroppers as in much of Vietnam. Translating figures provided by Ingram into ones comparable to those given in sources on Vietnam, we find that rice yields in Thailand had suffered a decline from an average of 1.83 metric tons per hectare in 1907–1909 to 1.17 metric tons per hectare in 1940–1944.[114] If anything, the decline had been greater in Thailand than in Vietnam; moreover, the decline was even greater within Thailand in those areas least touched by commercialized rice production.

In short, although the peasantry in Vietnam unquestionably suffered from a decline in rice yields during the colonial period, the reason for this decline cannot be said to be a function of changes in land tenure. Rather, the cause of the decline must be laid to a combination of increasing population and increased demands for rice for the market, both of which led to an intensification of land use. This said, the French can be blamed for not introducing any improvements in technology to offset the declines in rice yields. Moreover, from the peasantry's point of view, their deteriorating economic situation was directly connected with the changed political economic situation of colonial Vietnam. Most importantly, the land-tenure system in Vietnam also functioned to leave the peasantry with a declining proportion of the yields realized, since the demands for rents and shares of the crop did not decline commensurately with the decline in yields.

Rents, Taxes, and Indebtedness in Rural Vietnam During the Colonial Period

According to data collected and analyzed by Gourou, tenants in Vietnam paid, either in kind or cash (the cash being realized through sale of rice) the equivalent of between one-third and one-half of the yield realized.[115] But share-cropping arrangements varied considerably, and the amount expropriated could be as high as 70 per cent of the yield.[116] While increasing numbers of country people in Vietnam, and especially in Cochin China, were losing part of their product through rents and sharecropping dues, the whole of the rural population was also forced to bear heavier taxes. Chesneaux estimates that by 1879 the taxes levied on the rural populace of Cochin China were ten times what they had been in pre-French times.[117] Comparable increases in taxes were experienced in Tonkin and Annam after their annexation.[118]

The major tax levied was the " head tax " (or " body tax " as it was called by the Vietnamese), which was calculated independently of the income earned by adult males who had to pay it. The taxes were calculated in terms of numbers of men listed on rolls kept by village leaders, and these same leaders were responsible for the collection of taxes. The demand for increased taxes to be collected by village leaders was a major factor, if not the major factor, in the disintegration of traditional village structures:

> [P]olemicists have a good chance to point out how the framework of village life was struck a body blow by the French conception of taxes, payable in money and levied on a scale that must have seemed exorbitant to the villagers. The traditional village could not survive. . . . [I]t became an empty shell, void of the social substance it had once had which had kept life constantly renewed.[119]

Even the dry prose of a French economist reveals the plight of the Vietnamese peasantry given the tax load they were expected to carry:

> As a matter of fact, the direct taxes on Asiatics were so inelastic that, during the depression, they had to be reduced in order to take account of the natives' shrunken resources.[120]

Not only did the peasants have to pay head taxes, but they were also subject to corvée labor demands. Moreover, those who owned land were also subject to a land tax. In other words, it was the Vietnamese peasantry on whom the responsibility was placed for making the colony " pay for itself," that is, produce its own revenues for its budgets.[121]

Vietnamese peasants who could not meet both the tax and rent demands levied against them and also provide for their own needs were often forced to borrow. Although financial institutions such as banks and government credit organizations provided loans for investors in Indochina, few agriculturalists had the security necessary to obtain loans from these institutions. Traditionally, peasant society had a number of different types of credit associations, but these too were unable to provide the necessary funds for the increasing needs of the peasants. Thus, the peasant who had to borrow was forced to turn to Vietnamese, Indian *chettiar*, or Chinese money lenders who charged extremely high rates of interest. These rates were not rarely over 100 per cent per year. During the depression, Vietnamese peasants, like their counterparts in Burma, were forced into such extreme indebtedness that it became impossible for many of them to extricate themselves without government aid. The government aid provided in the late 1930s did ameliorate the situation, but it did not eradicate peasant indebtedness.[122]

Some of the peasantry in Vietnam left their traditional agricultural pursuits and became laborers on rubber plantations, in the mines, or in one of the small number of industries that developed in the cities. The exact number of Vietnamese who became laborers during the colonial period is unknown; however, all sources agree that they never comprised more than a small percentage of the total labor force. Marr has reviewed the various estimates and has concluded that even if those involved in cottage industry and artisan trades were classified as laborers, " it is apparent that during the 1920s the laboring class in Vietnam made up no more than 2 per cent of the population."[123]

Pluralism and Welfare in Colonial Vietnam

As in Burma, the colonial economy in Vietnam was characterized by an ethnic division of labor. The peasantry, including small owner-operators, tenants, sharecroppers, and agricultural laborers, were almost exclusively Vietnamese. The laboring class consisted primarily of Vietnamese with some montagnards (who worked on the plantations in the highlands) and some Chinese who worked in such trades as stevedoring and mining. The owners and managers of the large land estates and of the various industrial enterprises were predominantly French, but a few Chinese and Vietnamese were also to be found among this class. It is worth noting that such Vietnamese were often those who had received a French education and had in some cases even become French citizens. Administrative positions were also filled primarily by Frenchmen, although there were some Vietnamese in fairly high positions, albeit holding only nominal authority, in the " protectorates " of Tonkin and Annam.

Although the French dominated both the economy and the polity in Vietnam, and throughout Indochina as a whole, the number of Frenchmen in the colony was never great. According to figures obtained in the 1937 census, the only systematic census made in Indochina, there were 42,345 " Europeans and Assimilated " living in Indochina, of whom 39,237 were living in the three parts of Indochina that made up Vietnam. Robequain estimates that less than three-fourths of the total number in the category were " pure white," the rest being " naturalized Frenchmen " (2,746) and other Asians or *métis*. Of the total number of " Europeans and Assimilated," (i.e., Europeans and those Asians who had acquired French citizenship) 3,873 were employed as government officials (including members of the constabulary), 10,779 were in the military,

1,795 were doctors, lawyers, and educators, and 4,062 were in private business and trade. The remainder were women, children, and others " without profession." The total population of Indochina in 1937 was 23,030,000 of whom 18,972,000 lived in the three parts of Vietnam. The percentage of " Europeans and Assimilated " in the total population of Indochina was 0.18 per cent, with the biggest percentage being found in Cochin China.[124]

The number of Chinese in Vietnam in the same year was nearly eight times the number of Frenchmen. In 1937, 326,000 Chinese were to be found throughout Indochina, with 217,000 of these being in Vietnam. The largest percentage of Chinese in the total population was in Cochin China (3.7 per cent), with the next highest percentage being found in Cambodia (3.48 per cent). The Chinese of Indochina, like the Chinese in other parts of Southeast Asia, were predominantly urban dwellers (see next chapter for further discussion). When Chinese migrants did take up agricultural pursuits, they tended to become market farmers. Many Chinese were also to be found in the laboring class, especially in construction occupations. Chinese were also very conspicuous in trade. Although the Chinese competed with the French in large-scale trade, they had an almost total monopoly on small-scale trade, because they operated on margins of profit that were unthinkable to Europeans.[125]

The ethnic division of labor was also associated with an ethnic division in the living standard of the peoples in Vietnam. While French officials, colons, temporary residents, and a small number of Vietnamese and Chinese enjoyed the luxuries of colonial life, the vast majority of the Vietnamese lived in what an official British handbook termed a " wretched condition."[126] Modern healthcare facilities, for example, were available only to the French and the wealthy indigenous peoples. The rest of the population was left to treat its illnesses, which included malaria, tuberculosis, and trachoma among others, by rather ineffective traditional means.[127]

By far the most significant difference between the vast majority of the Vietnamese population, on the one hand, and the small number of Frenchmen and wealthy Vietnamese and Chinese on the other, was in nutritional intake. With the demands levied in the form of taxes, rents, share dues, and interest rates, the Vietnamese peasants found themselves with decreasing amounts of rice for their own consumption. Chesneaux cites one calculation that the consumption of rice per capita has fallen from 262 kilograms per annum in 1900 to 182 kilograms per annum in 1937.[128] This latter rate might not have been of concern had the consumption of rice been replaced by the consumption of alternative foodstuffs, but this did not occur. During World War II, demands placed on the peasantry by both the French and the Japanese led to a serious depletion in the rice reserves of the country. When rice production suffered from droughts in 1943 and 1944, the amount of food available to the peasantry dropped significantly below the amount needed to maintain minimal nutrition. The result was the great famine of 1944–1945, during which between 400,000 and 2 million people died. This famine is still regarded by many Vietnamese as the culmination of the disaster French rule brought Vietnam.

VIETNAM IN CULTURAL CRISIS

Loss of Harmony and the Confucianist Response

The impact of colonial rule in Vietnam was not only manifest in extreme economic hardships, in the deterioration of such traditional social institutions as the village, and in the emergence of new social patterns that sharply divided the ruled from the rulers. Colonial rule also precipitated a cultural crisis experienced by a large segment of the population. The quest for a resolution to this crisis provided the cultural basis for the Vietnamese revolution.

Paul Mus has characterized Vietnam during the cultural crisis produced by colonial rule as a " nation off balance ":

> Viet Nam's lack of balance . . . comes from the irreparable loss of that ancient harmony which gave its life its sense of being natural.[129]

This loss of harmony was not experienced in the same way or in the same degree of intensity by all Vietnamese. Some, living mainly in isolated backwaters, never experienced it all. However, the vast majority of Vietnamese came to realize that a great gulf lay between the actual conditions of life they experienced during the colonial period and the life they would expect to have if efforts at harmonizing themselves with cosmic forces had succeeded.

Throughout the colonial period, efforts were made by both intellectuals and the populace at large to build bridges across this gulf; to, in other words, find a resolution to the cultural crisis. Some Vietnamese, mainly those who had been traditionally educated, sought a resolution to the crisis by reasserting the meaningfulness of the Confucian system. For this solution to succeed, it was necessary that French rule be ended and that the monarchy and the mandarinate be returned to power. In 1885, shortly after the French had established their protectorate in northern and central Vietnam, a royalist rebellion was instigated by the flight of Emperor Ham Nghi from Hué and his subsequent call to arms in the Cam Vuong (Loyalty to the Emperor) edict. Ham Nghi was captured in 1888 and sent into exile by the French, but the Cam Vuong rebellion continued until 1897.[130] The crushing of the Cam Vuong rebellion did not stop efforts to restore the monarchy and with it to reestablish the traditional Confucian ideology. Subsequently, another royalist movement, centered on Prince Cuong De, attempted to gather support within the country. However, Cuong De never inspired the loyalty that Ham Nghi had done. When the Japanese, who were Cuong De's nominal patrons, took power during World War II, they ignored Cuong De in favor of Bao Dai, the Vietnamese " Emperor " maintained by the French. Bao Dai, the last " Emperor," perpetuated the outward forms of the office, but few, if any, Vietnamese ever had any doubt that the French held the real power. The final demise of Vietnamese conservatism as a viable ideological solution to the cultural crisis of Vietnam came in 1945 when Bao Dai abdicated and transferred the seals of state to Ho Chi Minh. Later attempts by the French to reestablish Bao Dai as Emperor were but futile gestures. As Paul Mus has said of more recent advocates of a return to the Confucian world of traditional Vietnam:

> The lost Confucian equilibrium was a whole, in a vanished world; it cannot be brought back piecemeal, and that world will not return.[131]

French Education and Catholicism

In some senses, the polar opposite to the conservative solution offered by those who continued to work for the reestablishment of an independent Confucian Vietnam were those who totally accepted the French order to the point of becoming Frenchmen. It was a basic tenet of the *mission civilisatrice* policy of French colonialism that " assimilation " of the natives would result in their ultimate betterment. The instrument for effecting " assimilation " was education. From the early years of colonial control in Cochin China, the French worked to institute a French-oriented system of education.[132] This system was predicated on initial education being not in Chinese characters as had been the case traditionally, but in the romanized alphabet *quoc ngu*, which had originally been devised by Catholic missionaries in the seventeenth century. By the end of the colonial period, *quoc ngu* had become almost the exclusive medium for literacy in Vietnam, and Chinese characters were learned only by a small number of traditionalists and scholars. However, beyond this, French educational policy was not notably successful, at least if the numbers of those who were educated under the French curriculum are any indication of such success. In 1939, only 16 per cent of the children of school age in the whole of Indochina were enrolled in school.[133] This percentage would appear to be an increase over previous years. In 1925, only about 10 per cent of eligible children were in school.[134] Moreover, very few went beyond primary schooling; in 1937 there was a total of 4,611 students in all secondary schools in Indochina.[135] Although those who did finish at the *lycées* were regarded as having had an education in no way inferior to that offered to children in France itself, they were extremely few. In short, French educational policy did not succeed in transforming very many Vietnamese into Frenchmen. It would appear that whereas colonial leaders paid lip service to " assimilation," they were actually not very interested in promoting education among the Vietnamese populace:

> Another cardinal feature of French policy is that the mass of the population shall receive only simple instruction on subjects associated with their daily life, and that education beyond the primary stage shall be restricted to those who are not likely to abuse such privileges by fomenting political troubles and creating social unrest.[136]

Although government-sponsored education did not succeed in " assimilating " Vietnamese to French civilization, it might appear that Catholic missionization succeeded in the same task to a much greater extent. Catholic missions had been established in Vietnam from the seventeenth century on and from the very beginning had been successful in converting significant numbers of Vietnamese, although rarely the Vietnamese elite. Those who converted to Catholicism in the eighteenth and nineteenth centuries, prior to the establishment of French rule, could well be seen to be in the tradition of those who turned to millennarian ideologies as a basis for challenging the Vietnamese throne.[137] Since Catholics, like adherents of other popular religious movements in traditional Vietnam, created divisiveness within the society, the rulers sought to eliminate them, often by means of bloody persecutions. These persecutions reached a crescendo in the period just prior to French intrusion into the country, for Catholics then came to be seen as a type of fifth column for the French. Despite the persecutions, or, perhaps, because of them, Vietnamese continued to convert to Catholicism in large numbers:

> Despite the persecutions . . . which had given to the Church some 130,000 martyrs—of whom 125 were beatified by various successive popes—Catholics never ceased increasing in number: 310,000 in 1800, with 20 European priests and 119 native; 420,000 in 1840, with 24 European priests and 144 native; 708,000 in 1890, with 270 European priests and 398 native (in 1890 there were 10 vicars apostolic and one vicar coadjutor, 2,886 churches or chapels).[138]

The persecutions were used as justification for French intervention in Vietnam. After the establishment of French control, the Church was given a freedom it had not enjoyed under the traditional rulers. During the colonial period, the Church continued to grow; in 1933 the baptized numbered 1,365,000 and by 1941 there were 1,638,000.[139] By the end of the colonial period, about 10 per cent of the Vietnamese population was Catholic.

Yet, although the Church grew during the colonial period and came to be viewed by many non-Catholic Vietnamese as a " foreign " body within Vietnamese society, it did not actually enjoy the support of the French colonial leadership:

> France . . . always followed the policy of assisting the local religions as a means of subduing the native: in Vietnam the chief support of the government and the colonial functionaries—for the most part Freemasons and anticlericals—went always to Buddhism which was considered to be the only organized religion in the country. In 1932, at a meeting of the International Colonial Institute, Gourdon, the French delegate, in speaking of the colonial policy in Indochina, stated: " It is impossible to count on Christianity, whatever its intrinsic value, to give these populations a morality or an effective rule of life. Christianity says nothing to them. Therefore the government policy consists in ignoring the Catholic mission and intensely favoring Buddhism which has great intrinsic value, and is furthermore perfectly adapted to the native mentality and tradition."[140]

Vietnamese Catholics found themselves in the impossible position of being considered allies of the French by their fellow Vietnamese, whereas in fact the French officials were often at odds with missionaries and with Catholic leaders.

Although Catholicism originally came to Vietnam as a foreign religion, over the three centuries it was established there it became adapted to the Vietnamese context. This adaptation was spurred by the fact that Catholicism in Vietnam has always been a religion of the people rather than a religion of the elite. Take, for example, the following description of the domestic shrine in Catholic homes in the southern Vietnamese village of Khanh Hau:

> On entering a Catholic home in Khanh Hau, one may at first easily mistake the Catholic shrine for a Buddhist or a Cao Daist altar. It is in the same place and contains the same incense burner, candles, and flowers. Upon closer scrutiny, however, it becomes clear that the stylized figures are Christian deities.[141]

Such adaptation notwithstanding, Catholicism has remained the religion of only a minority in Vietnam.

The Buddhist Revival and the Emergence of New Religions

Whereas Catholicism was one alternative open to those Vietnamese who found their traditional culture had lost meaning, a number of other alternatives, while representing departures from the tradition, were still much closer to it than was Catholicism. Among the most important of these " indigenous " alternatives was a revitalized Buddhism. Buddhism had long been an element within the popular religion of traditional Vietnamese culture, but it had not been a dominant world view for any who lived in Vietnam, save the Khmer minority, since about the fourteenth century. The revitalization of Buddhism in Vietnam began in the 1930s and was manifest in the emergence of such organizations as the Cochin China Buddhist Study Society, the Annam Buddhist Study Society, and the Vietnamese Buddhist Association, each associated with one of the three divisions of Vietnam. The Venerable Thich Nhat Hanh, a Thien (Zen) monk who has gained fame in recent years because of his efforts to promote peace in Vietnam, acknowledges that the support the colonial officials gave to Buddhism provided an important stimulus for the development of a revitalized Buddhism in Vietnam. He says that the French colonial government supported this development for the following reasons:

> [I]nstead of leaving the initiative of establishing their own associations to the natives, who might use them against the administration, the government would take them over, install its own men among the ranks, and thus control them. Furthermore, this magnanimous religious policy would win the gratitude and good will of the Vietnamese. Another great advantage of this clever policy was that the people would then be occupied with religious observances and thus be distracted from patriotic agitation.[142]

Yet, although such support may have provided the initial impetus, the various Buddhist movements eventually developed a dynamic that reflected Vietnamese rather than French concepts. Moreover, the cultural sources for the Buddhist revitalization were Asian not French. Thich Nhat Hanh points, for example, to the impact on Vietnam of the Buddhist revitalization movement led by the monk Tai Hsu in China.[143] Other sources were to be found in developments in Japanese Buddhism and, closer to home, in the Theravada Buddhism of the Khmer and the Thai.[144]

In the years just prior to the war, " Buddhism experienced a widespread renewal and above all became aware of its being a real, organized religion and not merely a moral philosophy, like Confucianism or a superstitious and magic practice like Taoism."[145] Given that Buddhism does not insist on its exclusivity, it is difficult to determine how many adherents the revitalized Buddhist movements actually attracted. However, there is no question but that by World War II, Buddhism had emerged as a viable solution for many Vietnamese to the cultural crisis the colonial experience had precipitated.

The Buddhist revival movements in Vietnam had difficulty in extricating themselves from the magical connotations that Buddhism had long had in the popular religion. Whereas popular Buddhism was centered on the magical manipulation of Buddhist sacra in order to attain some immediate desired goal, the revitalized Buddhism of the late colonial period laid stress on the illusion and impermanence of the world of everyday experience. The Thien (Zen) monks who have been at the forefront of the Buddhist revival have stressed the attaining of a true *awareness* of the situation in which people actually live. As Thich Nhat Hanh says: " *What we lack is awareness of what we are, of what our true situation really is.* Through this awakening we will rediscover our human sovereignty."[146] It is the purpose of Buddhism to provide a guide to the achievement of such awareness.

The emergence of a fundamental Buddhism promoted by Zen monks was not the only form that revitalized Buddhism took during the colonial period. In terms of its political implications, the " reform " Buddhism usually discussed under the rubric of the " Hoa Hao sect " was probably more important than the more orthodox movements. *Phat Giao Hoa Hao* or Hoa Hao Buddhism was founded in 1939 by one Huynh Phu So who was born in the village of Hoa Hao (thus the name). Bernard Fall has described the emergence of So as a prophet in the following terms:

> [So was] the son of a small notable, his childhood was not remarkable; he was lackadaisical, sickly, and graduated from junior high school only through the influence of his father. His father then sent him to a sorcerer at Nui Cam, in the Seven Mountains, where So learned magic tricks, acupuncture and also the teaching of Phat Thay [Buddha-master]. Still in ill health, he returned to his native village upon the death of his master in 1939. One evening, after a period of extreme nervousness, he walked out of the house, meditated in front of the family altar, and then returned to his family, apparently completely healed, and began to explain to the startled family members the teachings of Buddha as he saw them. Neighbors gathered, listened, and marveled at his recovery. A new prophet was born.[147]

So apparently had the charismatic ability, a function as much of his verbal abilities as of his reputed powers, that made it possible for him to convince others of his interpretation of Buddhism. By the early 1940s he had a following of 100,000, and by 1954, at the end of the colonial period, adherents of the Hoa Hao sect were reported to number 1,500,000.[148] So's teachings strongly de-emphasized the traditional rituals associated with popular Buddhism and other folk practices. In his own words, he described the religion he promoted as follows: " The cult must stem much more from internal faith than from a pompous appearance. It is better to pray with a pure heart before the family altar than to perform gaudy ceremonies in a pagoda, clad in the robes of an unworthy bonze."[149] His teachings also emphasized moral reform and specifically proscribed such practices as the taking of child brides, the arranging of marriages, gambling, the drinking of alcohol or the smoking of opium. His following grew as the French attempted to restrict it. Every time the French forced So to move to a different place, this place of exile became a place of pilgrimage. The followers were organized by lieutenants of So into quasi-military units, such organization ultimately making the Hoa Hao a movement to contend with in the political life of late colonial and postcolonial Vietnam.

Although Hoa Hao remained a Buddhist movement, albeit a rather heterodox one, a number of other religious movements that emerged during the colonial period were more eclectic, drawing on elements of both Vietnamese and French/European cultures for their symbolism. By far the most important of the new syncretic religions in Vietnam during the colonial period was *Dai-Dao Tam-Ky Pho-Do*, the " Third Amnesty of God," which is better known as Cao-Dai (" High Palace," a synonym for God). [150] The Cao Dai God is believed by followers to have first revealed himself to a southern Vietnamese low-level mandarin-trained administrator by the name of Nguyen Van Chieu in 1919. Chieu's revelation did not make any great impact until 1924, when, in the context of a seance, God again revealed himself. One man present at the seance was Le Van Trung, " an intelligent but dissolute merchant on the verge of total ruin ":

> Told by a spirit to change his ways of living and become an instrument of God, he became a fervent believer in the new faith. Chieu, a scholarly and timid man, unwilling to engage in large-scale proselytism, retired and thus Le Van Trung became, in April 1926, the first Great Master of the Cao-Dai.[151]

Caodaism recognizes the major world religious figures—Buddha, Moses, Laotze, Confucius, Jesus Christ, Mohammed, and a number of Vietnamese cultural heroes—as the instruments of God in the past. All the diverse religious traditions, which began when people were divided, are believed to have come together in the one tradition of Cao-Dai.

Although Caodaists believe in the Law of Karma, Caodaism is not a heterodox form of Buddhism as is Hoa Hao. Above the Law of Karma is God. Moreover, this transcendent being, who is represented in Cao Dai art as the all-seeing eye, actively intervenes in human affairs. Through proper ritual and moral action, which is enjoined by God and enforced by his earthly representatives, one can, according to Cao Dai belief, attain greater freedom from suffering not only in this life but also in future lives.

The rituals practiced by Cao Daists are very similar in form to those practiced by Buddhists and by other Vietnamese in the course of ancestor worship. The organization of the Cao Dai religion, on the other hand, has been

The Cao Dai Great Divine Temple, Tay Ninh, Vietnam. [*Marjorie Muecke, photograph; with permission*].

strongly influenced by Catholicism. At the head of the religion is the Giao-Tong or " Pope," this office being filled not by a man but by a long dead saint, Ly Tai Pe. During his lifetime, Le Van Trung was " temporary " Pope, but since his death in 1934, this office has not been filled, even " temporarily," by a person now in the world. Since 1934, the head of the religion has been the person occupying the office of Ho Phap (" the protector of the law "). Below him are a large number of hierarchically ordered offices whose Western titles are translated by such terms as " cardinal " and " archbishop."

Caodaism spread quite rapidly, particularly in southern Vietnam. By the end of the colonial period, Caodaists numbered upward of two million. Moreover, its power was greater than its numbers, since many Caodaists had been organized into quasi-military units whose function was to protect the faith. Yet despite its size and influence, Cao Dai never attained the potential for being a " national " religion, a religion that could serve to bring a resolution to the cultural crisis for the whole of the Vietnamese people. On the other hand, its size and influence have precluded the possibility of its being ignored as an aberration that will eventually be absorbed by more dynamic cultural movements.

The religious ferment of modern Vietnamese history gave birth not only to a number of well-organized religious movements, but also to smaller movements that emerged briefly and then disappeared. Unlike those movements that had but a brief existence, the revitalized Buddhist movements, the Hoa Hao and the Cao Dai, all offered the Vietnamese populace new cultural moorings to replace those destroyed during the colonial period.

Communism as a Popular Ideology

Although Catholicism, Buddhism, including the heterodox Buddhism of Hoa Hao, and the new religion of Cao Dai have provided new meanings for many millions of Vietnamese whose world was shattered by the colonial experience, the cultural system that eventually emerged as the dominant culture in postcolonial Vietnam was Communism. It is important at the outset to stress that although Communism, like Catholicism, was borrowed by the Vietnamese from the West, it has been adapted over a period of nearly half a century to the social and cultural context found in Vietnam itself. To put this in other words, Communism in Vietnam became not simply the ideology of a small number of Western-educated Vietnamese but a popular ideology with strong resonance within the folk tradition of the Vietnamese peasantry.

Vietnamese Communism has incorporated many of the themes first developed in the early, non-Communist, nationalist movements. As David Marr has shown in his excellent study of early nationalism in Vietnam, a dominant concern of these early nationalists was *mat-nuoc*, a loss of country and ethnicity that had been effected by French colonial domination.[152] Such an interpretation distinguished the colonial situation from previous troubled periods. It was not enough merely to support a new Emperor who could restore the harmony of Heaven and Earth; an entirely new basis for Vietnamese society had to be sought if Vietnam were to regain its national identity. Although the belief in *mat-nuoc* was limited mainly to the educated, it had wider importance, because it led a number of nationalist leaders to search for new ideologies to provide the means for regaining national identity.

The early nationalist movements also gave birth to a type of figure that was to become increasingly common in the Vietnamese countryside during the colonial period. This was the " partisan," known in Vietnamese as *nghia quan*, " the righteous warrior."[153] Here was a figure who opposed the *quan tu*, the " superior man " as mandarins were known in traditional Vietnam. Whereas the mandarin sought to effect a harmony in society, the *nghia quan* sought to remake society. That society could be remade was an idea almost inconceivable in traditional times to mandarins and peasants alike.

Certain important early nationalist leaders contributed importantly to the search for an ideology that could serve as a basis for remaking Vietnamese society. The most outstanding and most influential leader was Pham Boi Chau (1867–1940). Pham had been born to a mandarin family and had received a traditional classical education in the waning years of an independent Vietnam and the early years of the colonial period. He had been marginally involved in Cam Vuong movement, but had not been forced into exile or underground when this movement was being suppressed by the French. Not until about 1900–1904 did he begin the career of anti-French resistance for which he would become famous.[154] From this period until 1925, when he was captured and tried by the French, he was the towering figure in the anticolonialist movement.

The anticolonialist ideology of Pham Boi Chau underwent several transformations while he dominated the nationalist movement. His early efforts, expressed in his widely read pamphlet, *Viet-Nam Vong Quoc Su* ("History of the Loss of Vietnam"), stressed the need to rid Vietnam of the French. In post-colonial Vietnam, he looked to the reestablishment of the monarchy and of something resembling the *ancien régime*. Subsequently, influenced by Chinese reformist writings and by the Chinese Revolution of 1911, Pham came to lay increasing stress on the welfare and involvement of the populace at large in the new order to be constructed. Although Pham was too much a product of traditional Vietnam to be able to conceive fully of a radical new world, he did serve as a bridge between the early anticolonialist movement and the later Communist-led movement.

The man who was to succeed and eventually surpass Pham Boi Chau as the pre-eminent figure of Vietnamese nationalism was Ho Chi Minh. Ho was born in 1890 as Nguyen Sinh Cung, the son of a traditional scholar. Although Ho received a smattering of classical education in his childhood, his father was not convinced that such education had any future and so did not insist that Ho receive it. When Ho was 15, he was sent by his father to undertake French studies in Hué. As Marr has said: "This was a turning point for the fifteen-year-old boy. Among other things, it tended to focus his attention straight toward Europe instead of on Japan and China as cultural and political intermediaries."[155]

After six years in Hué, Ho moved to Saigon where he signed on as a crewman on a French merchant ship. His two plus years on this ship may well have served to create in Ho his sense of belonging to the working class despite his origins. Just prior to World War I, Ho left his job with the merchant ship in Europe and made his way to London. Toward the end of the war, he moved to Paris. In Paris Ho became a Communist, thus setting himself on a different path from that pursued by the older generation of Vietnamese nationalists. His Communist affiliation led him to travel first to Moscow and later to China in the company of Borodin. Once in China, Ho set about the task of organizing the more radical of the Vietnamese expatriate nationalists as well as establishing a network of agents in Vietnam itself. This organizational activity reached a climax in 1930, the year in which the Indochinese Communist Party was founded.

Initially, the Indochinese Communist Party was considerably smaller than a number of the other Vietnamese nationalist organizations. Moreover, given the Western source of its ideology and the fact that it had attracted mainly those who were expatriates, the party did not have the roots in the Vietnamese countryside that the other parties had. During the period between 1930 and the end of World War II, members of the Party worked arduously to create those roots. At the same time, they also worked, sometimes in a violent way, to emerge as the dominant element in the anti-French movement.

By the end of World War II, Ho Chi Minh was the undisputed leader of the nationalist movement that has come to be referred to as the Viet Minh, and he headed the government that took power in August 1945. Ho Chi Minh also led the resistance when the French attempted to reassert their control over

Indochina during the French-Indochina War of 1946–1954. Between 1945 and 1951, the Indochinese Communist Party was officially disbanded, although those who had been members continued to dominate the Viet Minh. In 1951, the Communist Party was resurrected, this time under the name of the Lao Dong or Workers' Party.

Vietnamese Communism is often presented in Western writings as a unified ideology derived totally from alien Marxist-Leninist writings. In fact, Vietnamese Communism has long had two major divisions: the one being " doctrinaire " and the other being what might be termed " adaptionist." Adherents of the former have attempted to force events in Vietnam to fit the framework laid down by non-Vietnamese. Such doctrinaire advocates as Tran Van Giau in southern Vietnam brooked no deviation and ordered his associates to eliminate any advocates of nationalist ideologies that were not in accord with orthodox international Communist ideas. On the other hand, the " adaptionists," best represented by Ho Chi Minh himself, have sought to preserve the essence of Marxist-Leninism, while also maintaining and incorporating those aspects of the Vietnamese cultural tradition and other nationalist ideologies that give locally meaningful expression to Communist principles.

The adaptionist form of Communist ideology made Communism a popular ideology in Vietnam, an ideology that could offer to more than a small number of the educated few a solution to the cultural crisis created by the colonial experience. The terms used by Communist cadres (*can bo*) to present their message often carried traditional meanings of great significance to the Vietnamese peasantry. " In the traditional language of politics, Communism has seemed more a fulfillment than a break with the past."[156] For example, the idea of socializing landed property was presented to the Vietnamese peasants under the rubric of *xa hoi hoa*. *Xa*, as Paul Mus has noted, connotes " the traditional village with all its spiritual and social connotations."[157] Together with the term *hoi*, *xa* carries the meaning of society as it is and as it was known by the Vietnamese peasant:

> The verb *hoa* completes this Confucian imagery. Far from denoting an anarchic convulsion, it applies specifically to the action in depth by which the " mandate of heaven," through its trustees the imperial rulers, civilizes a country. This action brings out what man's social nature potentially contains everywhere in Viet Nam: a patriarchal organization at least partially collectivized ... and based on the ancient model in accordance with the decrees of heaven.[158]

The images chosen for the presentation of the Communist message were often familiar ones to the Vietnamese peasantry. For example, the exemplary behavior of the Trung sisters, the legendary first-century Vietnamese leaders of the resistance against Chinese domination, was recommended by Ho Chi Minh as a model for contemporary Vietnamese women to emulate in their efforts to resist colonial domination.[159] The resonance the Communist message found in Vietnamese culture went even deeper than the rhetoric and images employed to communicate the message. One of the fundamental tenets of Communism, and one that involves a commitment comparable to religious faith, is that of historical determinism, that is a belief in the inevitable evolution of one form of society following from the resolution of the inherent contradictions of the previous form. For the Vietnamese, such a conception of the ultimate determinism of human existence was not a radically new idea:

> For there is a sense in which Communism might be said to strengthen rather than to undermine belief in [the traditional Vietnamese conception of] Fate. In day-to-day policy decisions, the Marxist idea of *praxis* demands a study of concrete conditions and a determination to change the world instead of being dominated by it; but when it comes to the dialectics of history there is room for a less practical view. The historical process itself is the guarantee of eventual success: in this, History has taken on the role of Heaven. Just as the Mandate of Heaven could in the old days pass from one dynasty to another, now the Mandate of History is held to be passing from one class to another . . . [F]or the ordinary peasant, does he make any sharp distinction in his mind between the " sorcerer " or " bonze " who once claimed to know the future decreed by Heaven, and the party cadre who now insists that he knows what has been decreed by History?[160]

The Vietnamese Communists interpreted the tenet regarding class conflict in Leninist rather than Marxist terms. That is, Ho Chi Minh and his associates were concerned with the conflict inherent in the relationship between the Vietnamese as the ruled and the French as the rulers more than they were with the conflict inherent in the relationship between capitalists and workers. In this connection, it can be seen that the common assertion that the Vietnamese Communists disguised their Communism beneath a veneer of nationalism is nonsensical; Vietnamese Communism was intrinsically nationalistic. However, the Vietnamese Communists did offer the peoples of Vietnam a different version of nationalism from that offered by other groups who were also involved in efforts to free Vietnam of French rule. The Communists claimed to have the force of History on their side and that by working in harmony with this force they would be able to create a new world in which all would be materially better off. Before the task of creating a brave new world could be pursued through the total commitment of the human and natural resources of Vietnam, it was first necessary for the Communists to gain full power in Vietnam.

WAR AND THE TWO VIETNAMS

The War with France, the Geneva Agreements, and the Emergence of Two Vietnams

In perhaps no other country of the world has the ending of the colonial era been so prolonged and so costly in human life as it has been in Vietnam. At the outset of what is often referred to as the first Indochina War, that is, the war that ended with the Geneva Agreements of 1954, the Viet Minh enjoyed wide support among the local Vietnamese populace.[161] However, a number of segments of the populace did not wish to see postcolonial Vietnamese society structured according to Communist ideals. As the war dragged on, these segments began to coalesce around what has been called the " Bao Dai solution," that is, around the goal of creating an independent and non-Communist Vietnam under Emperor Bao Dai as head of state. The French government came to support and to promote this solution, after it realized that it would be impossible to maintain Vietnam (and Indochina) as a colony. The French goal became the creation of a Vietnamese client state that would be a member of the French Union, a collectivity of French colonies that still remained politically and economically dependent on France. In June 1948, an agreement was signed whereby " France solemnly recognizes the independence of Viet-Nam," while Vietnam under Bao Dai proclaimed " its adherence to the French Union as a state associated with France."[162]

The agreement did not bring an end to the war; nor did it lead to large-scale disaffection by Vietnamese from the Viet Minh cause. However, it did create the basis for the emergence of two Vietnams: one Communist and the other non-Communist. The American government, owing to its extreme anti-Communist position during this period, began to provide considerable financial and military support to the French and Vietnamese forces fighting against the Viet Minh. Yet, despite this support, the Viet Minh were not defeated. Quite the contrary: in 1954 the Viet Minh inflicted a decisive defeat on French-led forces at the fortress of Dien Bien Phu in northwestern Vietnam.

By the time of the fall of Dien Bien Phu, the French had become war weary and were no longer implacably opposed to recognizing a Viet Minh led government as an independent government in Vietnam. In 1953 Soviet foreign minister Molotov had called for a five-power conference consisting of the Soviet Union, the United States, France, Great Britain, and the People's Republic of China to consider the questions of both Korea and Indochina. The conference, which was convened in 1954, became, in effect, two conferences: one dealt with the Korean question and the other with the problem of Indochina.

In addition to the five powers, the conference was attended by representatives of the Viet Minh, of the State of Vietnam headed by Bao Dai, and of the two " associated " states of Cambodia and Laos whose independence as part of the French Union had also been previously recognized. During the negotiations, Bao Dai appointed Ngo Dinh Diem as Prime Minister of the State of Vietnam, a move that was to have fateful consequences.

The conference ended with an agreement to partition Vietnam at the seventeenth parallel pending elections that would lead to a reunification of the country. However, the State of Vietnam never signed this agreement; nor did the United States, whose representative was only prepared to make a unilateral declaration " that the government of the United States took note of the Agreements and declared that it would refrain from the threat or the use of force to disturb them, and ' would view any renewal of aggression in violation of the aforesaid Agreements with grave concern, and as seriously threatening international peace and security'."[163]

Under the Geneva Agreements, the Viet Minh under Ho Chi Minh was recognized as the government exercising power in the area of Vietnam lying north of the seventeenth parallel. This government gave the name, the Democratic Republic of Vietnam, to the state that now existed in North Vietnam. In the South, power was vested in the government of the State of Vietnam, whose head of state was Bao Dai and whose Prime Minister was Ngo Dinh Diem.

As the government of the Democratic Republic of Vietnam (DRV) began to solidify its control of the North, it ran into opposition from certain segments of the population. This opposition was strongest among the Catholics, whose leaders (notably the bishops of Bui Chu and Phat Diem) did not believe that they had any future in the new Communist order of North Vietnam. Of the upward of a million people who migrated from North Vietnam to South Vietnam following partition, the vast majority were Catholics.[164] Some peasants also resisted the land reform policies instituted by the new DRV government. In November 1956, a popular uprising against the regime occurred in Nghe-An province. The uprising was repressed by the army and " allegedly, close to 6,000 farmers were deported or executed."[165] In 1956 and 1957 a number of North Vietnamese intellectuals launched an attack in print on various government practices. This expression of dissent was tolerated only briefly by the government before the dissident intellectuals were sent to the countryside to learn " socialist realism " at first hand.[166] By 1957, the government of the DRV had succeeded in establishing its control throughout northern Vietnam and was well underway in implementing policies designed to build a socialist society.

The government of the State of Vietnam faced more serious problems than had the government of the DRV in establishing control over its territory. At the time of the Geneva Agreements, the government of the State of Vietnam had no real base of popular support. Real power over the people living in South Vietnam was held by the French commanders of combined Franco-Vietnamese forces and by the " warlords " associated with the Cao Dai and Hoa Hao sects and with the Binh Xuyen, which might be described as a brotherhood of bandits. Viet Minh influence was strong in parts of South Vietnam, especially in the Mekong delta areas that had been under Viet Minh control for years prior to the Geneva Agreements. Many of the montagnards of the South Vietnamese highlands also supported the Viet Minh or, where this was not the case, enjoyed considerable local autonomy.

Ngo Dinh Diem took as his mission the creation of an anti-Communist Vietnam. He began by moving to eliminate all opposition to his authority. With the support of both the French and the Americans, he was able to succeed in gaining the upper hand over the " warlords." His hand was also considerably strengthened with the arrival of the Catholic refugees from North Vietnam. Diem, who was himself a Catholic and brother to an influential Catholic bishop, and who was implacably opposed to any compromise with the Communists, was a natural leader for these refugees.

Once embarked upon his career as the creator of an independent anti-Communist Vietnam, Diem came to see Bao Dai as a potential threat to his position. In October 1955, an election was held in order to determine whether

South Vietnam should continue as a monarchy or become a republic. Although circumstances surrounding the election rendered it a farce, its decision was upheld, the monarchy was abolished, and South Vietnam became the Republic of Vietnam with Diem as its first President.

Viet Minh elements continued to exist in South Vietnam following the signing of the Geneva Agreements, but they did not mount a serious challenge to Diem's rule while they waited for elections as specified by the Agreements to be held. However, when it became apparent that elections would not be held to effect the reunification of Vietnam and when the government of the DRV became secure in its control of northern Vietnam, the stage was set for a confrontation between those who supported the Communist cause in Vietnam and those whose goal it was to build a non-Communist Vietnamese society. This confrontation evolved into what subsequently came to be called the second Indochina war.

The Two Vietnams and the Second Indochina War

By early 1957, Communist-led elements in South Vietnam had begun to wage a guerilla war against the government of the Republic of Vietnam. By late 1958, the Communists had established a military command and in 1959 the National Liberation Front (NLF) for South Vietnam came into existence. The NLF was headed by members of the Communist Party, the Party first being known as the Vietnamese Workers Party of South Vietnam and later as the People's Revolutionary Party. The complex that included the People's Liberation Armed Forces, the NLF, and the Communist Party in South Vietnam collectively came to be known as the " Viet Cong."[167] From the outset, the Viet Cong was given material support and military guidance by the DRV. However, it was not until the mid-1960s that units of the North Vietnamese army, the People's Army of Vietnam, were sent to fight in the South. The Soviet Union, China, and, to a lesser extent, other Communist countries supported the Viet Cong through the supply of weapons and through diplomacy.

The war against the Viet Cong was carried out by the government of the Republic of Vietnam through its local political representatives and through the Army of the Republic of Vietnam. From its very beginnings, this government received significant support and advice from the United States. By the early 1960s Americans were actively involved in the fighting and by the late 1960s the war became an American as well as a Vietnamese war.

Although the military strength deployed by both side was very important, the outcome of the war depended on the leadership provided for the two causes. The highly disciplined Communist leaders of both North and South Vietnam gave unqualified loyalty to Ho Chi Minh. Even after President Ho died in 1969, the Communist leaders continued to present a strong image of solidarity, despite any disagreements they may have had. The situation was very different for the leadership of the government of the Republic of Vietnam.

After Diem succeeded in becoming the undisputed ruler of the Republic of Vietnam, he became increasingly autocratic and remote from the populace. By 1962, there was growing sentiment in the officer corps that Diem's leadership was hindering rather than helping the war effort. The United States government became increasingly disillusioned with Diem as he resisted American pressures to effect significant reforms and to grant more political freedom to the non-Communist opposition in the country. Popular dissent against Diem began to be expressed more openly, particularly by student groups and by Buddhist organizations. Popular feeling against Diem reached a climax in May 1963 when troops in Hué killed and wounded a number of people involved in a Buddhist demonstration. In protest against the repressive acts of the Diem government, Thich Quang Duc, a Buddhist monk, sat down in the middle of a street in Saigon, poured gasoline over himself, and set fire to himself. Thich Quang Duc's human-torch suicide, which was emulated by several others in the following weeks, became a powerful symbol of protest against Diem.

Growing popular opposition to Diem together with concern about the military situation finally prompted a number of high-ranking officers to organize a *coup* in November 1963. This *coup*, which was staged with at least the tacit support of the American government, resulted in the assassination of Diem and his brother, Ngo Dinh Nhu.

After Diem's downfall, the Republic of Vietnam had a succession of leaders, none of whom were successful in forging a stable coalition of Buddhists, Catholics, Coadaists, and other non-Communist elements. Lacking someone who could provide a political basis for the war with the Communists, leadership of the government of the Republic of Vietnam went, almost by default, to the military. In 1967, General Nguyen van Thieu succeeded in gaining supremacy over his military competitors. Thieu, served as President of the Republic of Vietnam from 1967 until just before the fall of Saigon in 1975. Prompted in no small part by pressures from American advisors, Thieu made an effort through the institution of land reform and other programs aimed at the peasantry to obtain the support of the rural populace. These efforts were ineffective, because the rural people by this time were more concerned with survival in a war-torn world than with putative rights of land ownership.[168]

From 1963 on, the war increased in intensity, as the United States and the DRV began to play more active roles. From about 1964 on, units of the People's Army of Vietnam were sent from the North to fight in the South.[169] In 1964 President Johnson used a battle between North Vietnamese and American naval forces in the Gulf of Tonkin as the pretext to ask the United States Congress for a resolution to permit the commitment of American troops to direct involvement in the war in Vietnam. From the Gulf of Tonkin Resolution until early in 1969, the number of American military personnel in Vietnam increased steadily, reaching over a half million just before President Nixon ordered the gradual withdrawal of troops in May 1969.

Although most American ground action was confined to South Vietnam, the bombing undertaken by American forces brought the war to North Vietnam as well. Beginning in 1965, American bombing missions were sent against NLF held territories in the South and against various targets in North Vietnam. The last of the bombing missions were ordered by President Nixon at Christmas in 1972. Even before this last bombing took place, the statistics on the bombing of Vietnam were staggering. Close to six million tons of bombs had been dropped on Indochina, most of it on Vietnam. This total was about triple the tonnage of bombs dropped by Americans during World War II.[170] In addition to the bombs, defoliants were sprayed over wide areas of South Vietnam. One estimate made in 1972 placed the amount of defoliated land in South Vietnam at one seventh the total land area of the country.[171]

From 1965 on, war became the overwhelming condition of life for both North and South Vietnamese. The South Vietnamese economy became heavily dependent on American aid and on the jobs and money that American involvement brought into the country. In North Vietnam, the populace had to not only work to produce supplies needed by the forces in the South but also to cope with the effects of the constant bombing raids made by American planes. In order to prevent the total destruction of Vietnamese industry, a program of radical decentralization was put into effect. Almost every family in both North and South Vietnam had at least one member fighting on one side or the other in the war, and in some cases families had members on opposing sides. Those who were not actually engaged in fighting were often made homeless by bombing attacks, destruction of their villages, or forced migration on order from differing authorities. Frances Fitzgerald, writing in 1972, summarized the effects of the war in South Vietnam in saying that it had brought the destruction of an entire society:

> Out of a population of seventeen million there are now five million refugees. Perhaps 40 or 50 per cent of the population, as opposed to the 15 per cent before the war, live in and around the cities and towns. The distribution is that of a highly industrialized country, but there is almost no industry in South Vietnam. And the word " city " and even " town " is misleading. What was even in 1965 a nation of villages and landed estates is now a nation of *bidonvilles*, refugee camps, and army bases. South Vietnam is a country shattered so that no two pieces fit together.[172]

The total number of casualties is difficult to comprehend. " The official numbers," as of 1972, " 858,641 ' enemy,' over 165,268 ARVN soldiers and about 380,000 civilians killed—only begin to tell the toll of death this war has taken."[173] The demographic implications of the death of so many young men (and many young women as well) between the ages of 15 and 35 will be felt in Vietnam for years to come.

There is now general agreement that the turning point in the war was the offensive launched by the Communists at the time of Tet, the traditional New Year, in January–February 1968. NLF forces, with the support of the North Vietnamese army, launched an all out attack throughout the South, temporarily captured Hué, and attacked Saigon itself. Initially, the assessment made by many observers was that the Tet offensive had resulted in a serious setback for the Communist side. A " general uprising," which had been the apparent goal, had not occurred. The Communist suffered massive casualties and they actually lost some territory to the Saigon forces after the latter launched a counterattack. Moreover, the brutality shown by NLF forces, particularly in Hué, alienated some who had previously been neutral. For example, Pond reports that neutralist-oriented Buddhists, " shocked by the Communist massacre even of anti-government Buddhist cadres during the Hué occupation, did recoil from flirtation with the communists."[174] Yet despite their losses in personnel and in territory and despite the alienating effects of their action, the Tet offensive proved in the end to alter the direction of the war in the favor of the Communists:

> The 1968 Tet Offensive was a sharp blow to America's solar plexus. It effectively knocked out American determination to keep fighting and thereafter the U.S. government moved rapidly to seek an end to the war and a disengagement of its forces. The much vaunted rural pacification program was set back . . . [The Tet offensive] effectively toppled a number of prominent non-Communist fence-sitters into the NFL's camp.[175]

In brief, the Tet offensive destroyed the American belief that a military victory by the non-Communist side in Vietnam could be achieved. It is noteworthy that, within a very short time after the Tet offensive, the United States began direct peace talks with representatives of the DRV. The Tet offensive also succeeded in convincing many South Vietnamese that the NLF was a political force in South Vietnamese life that had to be reckoned with.

In June 1969 the NLF set up the Provisional Revolutionary Government (PRG), which was presented as an alternative government to that of the Republic of Vietnam led by General Thieu. Although dominated by members of the Communist Party, the PRG also included a number of non-Communists who had been persuaded by the results of the Tet offensive to support the Communist side. Despite strong protests by the government of the Republic of Vietnam, the PRG as well as the Thieu government were represented at the Paris peace negotiations opened by the DRV and the United States in 1968.

The negotiations were prolonged and often acrimonious. The U.S. negotiating position was determined, in great part, by the fact that the war had become extremely unpopular in America. The more negotiations dragged on, the more the pressure built up within the United States, including within Congress, for America to end its direct involvement in Vietnam. Finally, in January 1973, following a final bombing of North Vietnam over the Christmas period, the " Paris Agreement on Ending the War and Restoring Peace in Vietnam " was signed by all parties. With this accord, President Nixon had the justification to complete the withdrawal of American forces, which had been going on since 1969. Although the agreement resulted in the *de facto* recognition by the United States of the existence of the PRG, the United States also received the assurance that American POW's would be released and returned to the United States. It is clear from the public statements made by Le Duc Tho, head of the DRV delegation, and President Thieu following the accord that neither side considered the struggle for political dominance in South Vietnam to have ended with the Paris accord.[176]

The outcome of the struggle was not decided until two years after the Paris agreement had been signed. During this period, the military position of the Republic of Vietnam was seriously eroded, in no small part owing to the withdrawal of American forces. On the other hand, the Communist side had rebuilt its strength following the serious losses suffered in the Tet offensive of 1968.

Early in 1975 the Communists began a new offensive that picked up momentum as first the towns in the northern highlands of Vietnam fell and then the northern cities of Danang and Hué were captured. By mid-April effective resistance by the armed forces of the Republic of Vietnam had all but ended. The final climax came not in a battle for Saigon but in the mad rush of the remaining Americans and of Vietnamese most closely associated with the American cause to flee the country. In late April, the war in Vietnam finally ended as Communist forces occupied Saigon.

After the capture of Saigon, the PRG transformed itself into a government and began to institute changes that would make possible the articulation of the political economy of South Vietnam with that of the North. In November 1975, it was announced that elections would be held in the near future to effect the reunification of Vietnam. Following elections held in Spring 1976, the first assembly with representatives from the whole of Vietnam was convened in Hanoi in June 1976. Although Ho Chi Minh had died in 1969 and, thus, did not live to see his country reunified, it is, nevertheless, his vision of a unified, independent, and Communist Vietnam, structured in terms of Communist ideals, that is finally being realized.

RURAL LIFE IN COMMUNIST VIETNAM

Land Reform and the Restructuring of Vietnamese Society

Although parts of southern Vietnam have been under Communist control almost continuously since 1945 and although many other parts have been under Communist rule for varying periods of time, prior to April 1975, the war in Vietnam prevented any permanent Communist transformation of rural life in southern Vietnam.[177] The problems faced by the present rulers of South Vietnam in bringing about such a transformation are immense, not the least of which is the necessity of coping with the tremendous dislocation of people in South Vietnam as a consequence of the war. Pike, writing in 1969, reported that

> Perhaps one quarter of the South Vietnamese have moved their place of residence since 1960 . . . About 1.5 million villagers have been registered on GVN refugee relief rolls. An additional estimated million are the so-called hidden refugees, middle-class persons who leave the village to resettle in the cities, but with enough money to support themselves while finding new jobs and thus never appear on relief rolls.[178]

Although the restructuring of South Vietnamese society with reference to Communist ideas will be forced to take into account the particular ecological, demographic, and socioeconomic conditions of South Vietnam, it seems clear that the future shape of South Vietnamese society will be modeled as closely as possible on the Communist society that has evolved in North Vietnam since 1954. For an understanding of rural life in Communist Vietnam, then, we must examine what is known about rural life in the Democratic Republic of Vietnam.[179]

The course of " socialist " development in the Democratic Republic of

Vietnam can be divided into three phases. During the first phase, from 1954 to 1958, various programs, notably the land-reform program, were implemented with the purpose of effecting a radical break with traditional social, economic, and political practices. Then, between 1958 and 1965, the government instituted new programs, the most notable of which was the establishment of cooperatives, which sought to institutionalize socialist practice and to instill a sense of socialist consciousness. These efforts were curtailed from 1965 on, because of the increasing demands of the war effort and the necessity of coping with the United States bombing.

The first major program the Communist government in North Vietnam put into effect was land reform. This program was actually begun in 1953 in areas firmly under Viet Minh control, and it was extended throughout northern Vietnam in 1954–1956 following the establishment of the Democratic Republic of Vietnam. To understand the significance of the program, one must look at the agricultural conditions that prevailed in the countryside in the period prior to the establishment of Communist control. It is also important to understand that the DRV leaders saw land reform as a method for effecting a radical break with the patterns of the past.

During the colonial period, the French had done very little to stimulate developmental change in the rural society of Vietnam. They had " no desire to foster modern village organizations of any kind " and they introduced no new methods of technology.[180] As has already been observed, the lot of the peasantry under the colonial system was hard and had culminated in the tragedy of 1944–1945 when between 400,000 and 2 million Vietnamese died of famine. As Woodside observes, the process of reform in the countryside " began against the background of the disastrous socially demoralizing famine of 1944–1945."[181]

The elimination of French power was the first step toward a radical alteration of the political economy of Vietnam, which was believed necessary if such a tragedy was to be prevented from occurring again. By 1953, the Viet Minh had sufficient power to begin eliminating local indigenous bases of control over access to land and its products and the unequal distribution of rice and other agricultural produce. After the Communist assumption of power, following on the Geneva Agreements, the land-reform program was greatly expanded and extended in the countryside of North Vietnam. The land-reform program, as outlined in a decree of March 1953, entailed the classification of the rural populace into the categories used in the land-reform program in China. Tran has paraphrased the classification as contained in the decree as follows:

> *Landlords* are those who own land, but who do not engage in labour or only engage in supplementary labour, and who depend on exploitation by land rent for the main source of livelihood. Also classified as landlords are those who lend out money for interests [*sic*], [hire] labour, or [carry] on . . . industrial or commercial enterprises. But the exploitation of the peasants by exacting land rent is the major form of exploitation.
>
> *Rich peasants* are those who own land, means of production, and engage in labour, and at the same time exploit the peasants by hiring labourers.

Middle peasants are those who, generally speaking, own the land which they cultivate. But there are people who possess only a portion of the land while the remainder is rented. Some of them possess no land and rent all their land from others. In general, they have land, farming implements, cattle and they engage in the cultivation themselves or mainly depend upon their own labour for their living. Some middle peasants were exploited to a certain extent by others in the form of land rent and loan interest. But generally, they do not sell their labour power nor exploit others.

Poor peasants are those who own little and inadequate farm implements. Some have no land, own only some inadequate farm implements and rent the land from others to cultivate. Having little land, poor peasants have to sell their labour power for their living, and generally they were exploited in the form of land rent, loan interests and hired labour.

Workers (including farm labourers . . .) generally speaking are those who have neither land nor farm implements, and have to sell their labour power for their living.[182]

This classification was accomplished by local committees consisting of poor peasants and workers under the guidance of party cadres. The classification provided the basis for expropriating land (and such other elements of production such as buffaloes) from the " exploiting " classes and for reallocating this land and other elements of production to the " exploited." A redistribution of the elements of production was not, however, the only purpose of the land-reform program. In addition, local power previously vested in councils of notables whose members were often landlords was now vested in elected people's councils whose members were drawn mainly from the poor peasants and workers. Landlords were not eligible to become members of these new councils. Furthermore, the local committees were also empowered to try landlords for exploitation. During these trials, considerations other than economic ones were often allowed to influence judgments. Landlords who had resisted the Viet Minh found themselves particularly suspect, whereas those who had fought for and/or become members of the Communist Party were supposed to be treated more leniently. This was not always the case, however. In certain instances the Party used the land-reform trials to purge " undesirable " elements from it. The trials frequently proved to be occasions for personal vendettas, and over-zealous cadres demonstrated their Party loyalty by trying and punishing people who could be classified as " landlords " only by considerable stretching of the definition of this category.

Those who were found guilty of being landlords were subjected to punishment. For the really " evil " landlord, this could be death; more often, it meant prison for the man and social isolation for his family. Even when no specific punishment was prescribed, those whe were classified as " landlords " were deprived of many of the rights enjoyed by the mass of the rural people. They also suffered from the public humiliation inflicted on them.

As the consequences of being classified as " landlords " and, to a lesser extent, " rich peasants," many thousands of people in North Vietnam were executed, thousands more were imprisoned, and yet thousands more were relegated to the status of outcast " enemies of the people." Although the exact figures may never be agreed upon,[183] even the highest officials in the DRV came to recognize that the brutal way in which land reform had been carried out had been excessive. In late 1956, Ho Chi Minh himself took the initiative in calling for a rectification of the injustices perpetrated under the program. Truong Chinh, the party General Secretary and the architect of the land-reform program, resigned his post, although he still remained a member of the leadership. The campaign carried out in 1957 and 1958 to effect a " rectification of errors" resulted in the release of many men from jail and the reclassification of other putative " landlords " and " rich peasants " as " middle peasants." These efforts at rectification notwithstanding, the basic purpose of the land-reform program was never questioned by the rulers of the DRV. As a method for effecting a radical break with the past, the land-reform program was an unqualified success.

The land-reform program resulted in the expropriation of 810,000 hectares of land from larger land holders and the redistribution of this land among 2,104,100 poorer peasant families.[184] Even more important than the redistribution of land was the radical realignment of authority and prestige within rural society in northern Vietnam:

> Despite all [the] bloody excesses, the mass mobilization campaign for radical land reform and rectification of cadres and organization had produced a revolutionary change in the rural society. It gave rise to a drastic change in rural stratification and revolutionary change in the authority pattern. It cause[d] a phenomenal participation of the usually apathetic poor and landless peasants in local politics.[185]

Following land reform, wealth was eliminated as a basis for attaining prestige and authority in rural society, and sex, age, and lineage membership no longer held their traditional importance. In the place of the traditional ascriptive criteria for social differentiation in Vietnamese society, the leaders of the DRV sought to institute the nonascriptive criterion of work.[186] Such institutionalization was a primary purpose of the next phase in the creation of a socialist society in North Vietnam, the period of cooperativization.

Building Socialism and the Cooperativization Program

The establishment of cooperatives in North Vietnam began in 1959 and was initiated before the " individualistic and capitalistic " tendencies of the peasants could result in the reemergence of the old system, albeit with different personnel.[187] Cooperativization (*hop tac hoa*) entailed a three-stage process of socioeconomic change:

> In the first stage, peasants belong to nothing more than " labor exchange teams " (*to doi cong*) which can be either seasonal or year-round and which are considered to be no more than the " sprouts " (*mam mong*) of socialism. In the second stage, peasants join " low rank " agricultural cooperatives, considered to be partly socialistic. Only some production tools are owned in common, and private land ownership rights are not completely dissolved. In the third stage, peasants enter " high rank " agricultural production cooperatives, deemed fully socialistic, in which all the means of production, including the land, are owned in common.[188]

The work exchange teams were relatively small neighborhood groups, consisting of about ten to twelve families. The low-level cooperative appears to have been very much a transitional entity, consisting of about eighty households. It had practically disappeared by 1968, having given way to the high-level cooperative, which by this time accounted for 79.4 per cent of all cooperatives:

> At the end of 1968 the average northern cooperative embrace 136 families, 276 laborers, and 77 hectares of land. The average delta cooperative was larger; 270 families, 405 laborers, and 128 hectares of land . . . The monster cooperative is probably most commonly found in the suburban areas of large cities . . . But most northern cooperatives do not represent a significant inflation of traditional settlement sizes.[189]

The average size of cooperatives in Vietnam is significantly smaller than the average size of cooperatives in China, which at the end of 1956 was 246.4 households. " In addition, most of the Vietnamese co-operatives were not (and still are not) coextensive with whole administrative villages as were most of the Chinese counterparts in 1956–7."[190]

At the outset, many peasants were reluctant to join the cooperatives, but by 1960–1961 very few continued to hold out against the new program. The evidence seems clear that peasants decided to join not because they were forcibly coerced, but because they concluded that it was to their economic advantage to do so:

> Participation in the activities of the cooperatives was accomplished through an incentive system. It was more profitable to join than to remain outside because of the subsidization of necessities of life through the cooperatives, while they remained considerably more expensive on the outside.[191]

Cooperativization did not result in the appropriation of all privately owned land from the peasantry. By law up to 5 per cent of all the land owned by a cooperative could be allocated to the members of the cooperative for private ownership. This " 5 per cent land " has made it possible for some private production to coexist with socialized production.

The concentration of land the cooperative structure has brought about has permitted a more efficient use of land, implements, animal power, and human labor than was possible on small holdings. If there had been a totally equitable distribution of land in the land-reform period, the amount of arable land available per capita would have been only 0.108 hectares. Moreover, given the poor characteristics of much of the land in the area and the methods of cultivation, the possibility of cultivators producing much surplus beyond consumption needs was very low:

> North Vietnamese leaders argued, at best, under individual farming, a peasant could produce enough for himself and capacity of accumulating funds would be next to nil; at worst, the peasant would suffer famine and permanent hunger.[192]

With cooperativization, many of the decisions concerning agricultural work were no longer made by individuals but by a management committee on behalf of the whole cooperative. This management committee is elected by the representatives of the cooperative assembly, which includes all members of the cooperative. These elections are manipulated so that control lies in the hands of the local party leadership. For example, in one cooperative in Xich Dang Village, Lam Som Commune, Hung Yen Province, the cooperative assembly of 644 people elected sixty-five representatives who in turn chose a management committee of 17 members. Twelve of these seventeen were members of the Party.[193] Party domination of the cooperative management committees appears to be a prevailing pattern throughout North Vietnam.[194] Tran states that " the secretary of the party chapter is also the chairman of the cooperative management board."[195]

The role of the Party in the cooperativization process has been summarized by Elliott as follows:

> The political system that the DRV set out to construct as it embarked on a program of agricultural cooperativization was a combination of three elements: (1) highly centralized state institutions, (2) local communities based on mutual social and economic interests, and (3) the Party which linked the two. While the Party played a key role at all levels, its linkage role most clearly set it apart from the other sectors of the political system.[196]

In this new arena, village political and administrative institutions, even as modified so that councils of notables had been replaced by elected people's councils, were left with no function other than informational and educational ones. Chaliand describes how such a pattern operated in one village in Hung Yen province:

> The prime task of an Administrative Committee is to expound the policies of the central government. These are studied in concert with the People's Council, which is responsible for passing them on to the rest of the community.[197]

The Administrative Committee, the executive body of the People's Council, even though it has very restricted functions, is still dominated by the Party. Thus, while local administration and cooperative management appear on paper to be separated functionally, they are, in fact, integrated because leadership of both is held by those who lead the local Party:

> The real power in rural North Vietnam . . . lies . . . not with the cooperative congresses or control boards themselves but with the party cadres. They belong to the " network of guidance " . . . extended by the district down to the cooperatives . . . In the last analysis, the successful post-colonial reconstruction of northern society obviously depends upon the reliability of the thousands of cadres who serve the regime as revolutionary middlemen.[198]

The role assigned to these revolutionary middlemen in the period of cooperativization necessitated a considerable increase in Party membership over that which had existed in 1958:

> The overall ratio of Party members to population in North Vietnam was about 2 per cent at the outset of cooperativization. Moreover only 40 per cent of Party members were at the village level.[199]

Throughout the period since 1958, there has been considerable emphasis on recruitment ιo the party. This recruitment has had to give emphasis to rather different qualities than those desired in party members recruited during the war with the French. The new party members must be people who are not only ideologically committed, but also skilled in management and administration.

In theory, party membership, as with all significant social statuses within northern Vietnamese society, is attained by merit, demonstrated through one's work, and able to be gained irrespective of one's social background. In fact, this universalistic basis for acquiring social status in north Vietnamese society is subject to certain qualifications. If a person be a member of an " enemy " class that is, if one be classed as a " landlord," a " reactionary," or some other type of " bad element "—then one is not only ineligible for party membership but also barred from enjoying the privileges and rights of all other ordinary citizens.[200] Moreover, kin ties have continued to be important in determining access to social status, including Party membership, despite official policies to the contrary. Although a significant change has been effected in the status of women in northern Vietnamese society, women are still reported to have less opportunity than men for education, to work longer hours than men, and to receive fewer work points for the same amount of work.[201]

These qualifications notwithstanding, there can still be no question but that the socialist revolution effected in northern Vietnam has resulted in a radical devaluation of ascriptive criteria for determining access to social status in favor of the criterion of demonstrated merit through one's own work.

Socialist Programs and the Conditions of War

The escalation and expansion of the war from 1965 on created a set of conditions that made it possible to accelerate socialist transformation in northern Vietnam. Most significantly, with increasing numbers of young men being recruited to fight and with many of these men never returning from the war, women have had to take on many jobs not previously open to them. In 1965, the government of the DRV proclaimed the policy of " the three assumptions of duty," which " required women to assume greater duties in production and in the labor force, in the family, and even in military work, for example by service in anti-aircraft details."[202] The needs in both the labor force and the military brought about by the intensification of the war have also led to the rehabilitation of some who were formerly ostracized as members of " enemy " classes. Yet, although the war served to accelerate socialist efforts to replace ascriptive criteria by universalistic criteria in determining access to social status, it also required that certain other socialist goals be compromised.

In order to adapt to the damaging effects of the American bombing of northern Vietnam and to meet the requirements of supplying and supporting an enlarged army in southern Vietnam, the DRV government found it necessary to alter several of the economic priorities it had set in the Five-Year Plan for 1961–1965. Factories and industrial plants in larger urban centers were recognized to be particularly vulnerable to American bombing. The government determined, therefore, to decentralize industry. At the same time, it also began to encourage the creation of small-scale light industry, which was not only more suitable than heavy industry to be carried out at the local level, but also better adapted to the needs of the war economy.[203]

The decentralization of the economy and the shift to small-scale industry was already evident by 1967, when Chaliand visited various rural areas in northern Vietnam. In Hung Yen province, for example, Chaliand was told that there were 400 miniature repair shops and engineering workshops, a small factory for making jute sacks, a fruit canning factory, and a paper factory.[204] He also reported that agricultural tools and machinery were being produced locally in Thai Binh province and that in Ha Tay province he visited a cooperative whose primary production was cloth woven on hand looms.[205]

When the war was at its height, the DRV softened its previously doctrinaire attitudes about agricultural production. Given the increasing demand for foodstuffs to meet the needs of the armed forces and the limited capacity of the cooperatives to produce enough to meet these needs, the state gave open encouragement to the production of crops on private " 5 per cent land ".

This pragmatic approach toward production was matched by a similarly pragmatic approach toward the distribution and marketing of goods. In the period between 1958 and 1960, the DRV had attempted to eliminate traditional peasant markets and to replace them with " a planned mechanism of distribution by the state."[206] Although state trading firms were given the prior right to purchase village produce, including that raised on private land, this arrangement was not altogether successful in facilitating the flow of goods from producers to consumers. The government was therefore forced to permit the continued existence of rural " free " markets.[207] In 1967, Chaliand found a situation in which local village trading committees, representing the state, made purchases from both the cooperatives and from private individuals. Private individuals were also allowed to sell on the free market if they had already sold 75–80 per cent of their produce to the state. Chaliand states that: " The free market makes up for the deficiencies of the state market, whose aim is (a) to supply the basic necessities at low prices and (b) to provide a guaranteed outlet for production."[208] In addition to the state market and the free market, Chaliand also reported the existence of a black market that dealt " chiefly in oil, petrol, tobacco, sugar, and pork."[209]

Despite the war, the DRV pushed ahead with programs designed to improve the health conditions of the people. According to official statistics, the number of doctors increased from one per 150,000 inhabitants in 1955 to one per 8,700 in 1965, while the number of health officers increased from one per 80,000 to one per 1,850 in the same ten year period.[210] Most of the village doctors would appear to be " assistant physicians " (*y si*), or those who had completed three years of medical training rather than full-fledged doctors (*bac si*) who had completed seven years of training.[211] Both assistant physicians and full-fledged doctors, whose training has been in " modern " medicine, have not entirely supplanted traditional medical practitioners. Chaliand reports that in 1967 there were about 15,000 practitioners (around one per 1,275 people) of traditional medicine. About 10,000 of these practitioners were members of a state-recognized " Society of Traditional Medicine." However, an Institute of Traditional Medicine in Hanoi, which had trained such practitioners, had been disbanded by 1967, thus reflecting the State's desire ultimately to eliminate traditional medical practitioners as part of the health care delivery system of northern Vietnam.[212]

In addition to radical improvement in health-care delivery in northern Vietnam, the DRV has also instituted a number of very successful programs of preventive medicine. As the result of vaccinations, smallpox, diphtheria, and typhoid essentially have been eliminated, and polio has been reduced. VD has also been brought under control. The Ministry of Health also sponsored the building of wells in rural villages with the aim of ensuring potable water for the population. By 1966 nearly every village had a well.[213]

In keeping with programs in preventive medicine, the government of the DRV has also promoted birth control. The rate of population increase in the DRV prior to the intensification of the war was as high or higher than any other Third World country. Between 1960 and 1965 the population grew from 16.1 million to 18.5 million.[214] The significance of the increasing population has been recognized by the leaders of the DRV, and, from 1962 on, birth control was officially advocated. However, it was not until 1966 that a birth control campaign was launched, the delay being a function in part of the nonavailability of contraceptives. By 1967, the program had still not achieved significant popular support. In one district in Hung Yen province, with a total population of 95,000, only three hundred women had been fitted with a coil, whereas in another districts, the program was described as still being " at the experimental stage."[215] The tremendous loss of life suffered by the northern Vietnamese as a result of the war will most likely result in a significant decline in the rate of population growth for some years to come. Although exact statistics are not yet available, the fact that a very high percentage of men between the ages of 15 and 30 were killed in the war certainly means that many women in the same age group will never marry and will never have children.

Technological Revolution and the Socialist Society

Although the war has necessitated a realignment of priorities and tolerance of some nonsocialist practices, the basic commitment of the DRV to creating a socialist Vietnam has not been compromised. As early as 1970, policies were established to bring priorities back into accord with this effort as soon as the war was over.[216] The creation of a socialist Vietnam has been conceived of by the leadership of the DRV as requiring " three revolutions." The essence of what these revolutions entail was related to Chaliand in an interview in 1967 by a man who was both a member of the Provincial Committee of the Party and a member of the Provincial Administrative Committee in Nin Binh Province:

> In spite of the war, we are carrying out three revolutions at once: a revolution in productivity, which we are trying to bring to a peak; a technical revolution, in the agricultural as well as the industrial sphere; and finally an ideological and cultural revolution.[217]

The revolution in productivity involved a radical alteration of the political economy of Vietnam in order to make more efficient use of the available labor force and the factors of production. This revolution was undertaken through programs of land reform and cooperativization and has continued despite the war. The technological revolution in Vietnam, in contrast, has barely begun and is still subject to considerable debate.

The technological revolution in north Vietnamese terms involves a shift from an agricultural base to an industrial base and the introduction of scientific efficiency into both agriculture and industry. The technological revolution thus necessitates a distinction between industrial workers and agricultural workers and between scientific " experts " and the relatively uneducated workers and peasants. The first distinction poses no theoretical problems for orthodox Marxists, since the industrial proletarian is accorded a more exalted place in the ideology than is the peasant. In practice, however, such a distinction has tended to exacerbate rural-urban differences in northern Vietnam. The decentralization of industry and the de-emphasis of heavy industry in favor of light industry during the war has ameliorated this problem, but it is likely to reemerge now that the war is over. Indeed, this problem is likely to become even more acute once major efforts are made to integrate the economies of northern and southern Vietnam, since a much larger proportion of the population of southern Vietnam than of the population of northern Vietnam has worked in urban rather than in rural occupations.

At the outset of the program to build socialism in northern Vietnam, greater reliance was placed upon being ideologically correct (i.e., being " Red ") than on being scientifically trained (i.e., " expert "). However, experience has revealed to the leaders of North Vietnam that social restructuring, engineered by the ideologically aware, cannot in and of itself effect a technological revolution. Although high production quotas were set for agriculture by the government in the first Five-Year Plan (1961–1965), these quotas were not met and it appears that rice yields actually declined somewhat over this period, yields being 2,283 kilogram/hectare in 1959 and 1,894 kilogram/hectare in 1965.[218] However, it should be noted that the average yield of 1,894 kilos per hectare realized in North Vietnam in 1965 was still significantly higher than the average of 1,519 kilos per hectare realized in Thailand for the period of 1965–1967.[219] Moreover, although the rural populace of northern Vietnam was not able to meet the quotas set, " the DRV must be credited with a substantial success in simply holding rural income steady and overcoming potential [sic] calamitous weather conditions during the first years of cooperativization."[220] Still, the fact remains that without a radical change in technology, agricultural production in North Vietnam cannot be pushed to significantly higher levels solely by increasing inputs of labor. Given the population densities in North Vietnam, production of grains by traditional methods has long been insufficient to meet the demand. North Vietnam is dependent on the import of grains from other countries in order to have enough to feed all of its population.[221]

Given the need to achieve significant increases in agricultural production as well as nonagricultural production in order to obtain foreign exchange, the DRV has encouraged the training of specialists, although it insists that these be " Red " as well as " expert." But the emergence of scientific specialists has created yet another problem for the DRV:

> The pressures of the need for agricultural change have led to the appearance of small groups of specialists in the north, and these groups have in turn produced their own scientific parochialisms . . .
>
> [T]he problem is that each group of specialists wishes to ordain the direction of agricultural modernization. And the limited quantity of state resources makes it unlikely that all the specialists can have their way . . . The only priority in agricultural development policy that seems to be universally accepted in the north is that of water control—flood defenses and better irrigation.[222]

Now that the war is over, it is likely that the debate over the priorities to be set in the effort to bring about agricultural modernization will develop in intensity. It may even be that " experts " from southern Vietnam, even though they are patently not " Red," will contribute to this debate.

Although the exact course of the technological revolution in northern Vietnam, and now in southern Vietnam as well, cannot be predicted, the goals are clear. These goals were set out in an important speech given by Le Duan in February 1970. In this speech, Le Duan quoted Lenin to the effect that: " The only possible economic basis of socialism is mechanized heavy industry. Whoever forgets this is not a Communist." In addition to an emphasis on transforming the economic base of Vietnam from agriculture to heavy industry, Le Duan spelled out the goal for those who remained in agriculture. The program for this sector is the " urbanization of villages," meaning, according to Woodside, " the continued development of large cities that will serve as political and economic and cultural centers for the entire country but also the creation of many new ' moderate and small ' cities for the purpose of " direct action " against sluggish rural regions."[223]

Both the revolutions in productivity and in technology depend on the final revolution, the revolution in ideology and culture. In the final section of this chapter we turn to a consideration of the ideological and cultural characteristics of life in communist Vietnam.

IDEOLOGY, EDUCATION AND VALUES IN COMMUNIST VIETNAM

Traditional Culture and Traditional Values in the D.R.V.

The central value which Communist in North Vietnam emphasizes is that through work or labor one realizes one's place in society. The name of the Communist party in Vietnam, *Dang Lao Dong*, gives evidence of this central value; it is the party of workers. How different is this value to that expressed in the early nineteenth-century poem, *The Tale of Kieu*—a poem better known to

Vietnamese than Shakespeare's plays are to Westerners. In this poem, written by Nguyen Du, the heroine Thuy Kieu is unable to realize her great talent because heavenly-decreed fate, or Karma (as interpreted in Vietnamese terms) has destined her for a life of suffering. The poem concludes with the assessment that one cannot create the world in which one lives; one can only adapt to what Heaven ordains:

> All things are fixed by Heaven, first and last.
> Heaven appoints each creature to a place.
> If we are marked for grief, we'll come to grief.
> We'll sit on high when destined for high seats.
> And Heaven with an even hand will give
> Talent to some, to others happiness.
> In talent take no overweening price—
> Great talent and misfortune make a pair.
> A Karma each of us has to live out:
> Let's stop decrying Heaven's quirks and whims.
> Within us each there lies the root of good:
> The heart means more than all talents on earth.[224]

Although Communists have been politically dominant in North Vietnam since 1945 and have been leaders of an independent government there since 1954, the Communist version of the " work ethic " has still not been accepted by all. Many still adhere to traditional values that lead people to accept the world as it is.

The traditional institution in Vietnam that served to reinforce the value of accepting a preordained position within society was the extended family. Within the family, the child was taught that his or her position in the world was determined by his or her ancestry. Through the obligations one was taught one had toward males, toward elders, and toward ancestors, one acquired the value of acceptance of the world as it is. Although ancestor worship has long been officially disapproved of in the DRV, it still continues to be practiced there. In 1967 Chaliand observed an ancestral shrine in one peasant home, and another peasant made specific reference to his performance of the ritual.[225]

German author Peter Weiss, who visited the DRV in May–June 1968, provides further evidence of how the family continues to teach ideas that lead people to feel themselves subject to impersonal forces beyond their control. In addition to the perpetuation of ancestor worship,[226] he reports the continuation of the practice of changing children's names to confuse malevolent spirits:

> Even today in the villages children are not addressed by their own names. Out of respect for the spirits, which may do a child harm or kidnap him, a cover name is used. A girl whose name means " pearl " is addressed as " cow ". The child is aware that he has another given name but responds to the nickname. Thus the spirits are outwitted.[227]

Weiss also reports that villagers continue to use the large array of traditional pronouns that permit them to make fine distinctions regarding the relative social superiority and inferiority of those with whom they interact.[228]

While the family continues to promote traditional values, the village no longer has the same connotations it had traditionally. The radical restructuring of the local community following land reform and the establishment of co-operatives served to undermine the cult of the guardian spirit of the village. Chaliand was told by one informant that

> As for the spirit that is supposed to watch over the village, anyone who wishes to pay homage to it is free to do so; few people bother, except the old. Since 1957 there has been no more talk of the guardian dragon objecting to wells being dug, and villagers are no longer sent into trances at ritualistic ceremonies designed to ward off diseases.[229]

The discrediting of the cult of the guardian spirit has been accompanied by a discrediting of the Buddhist monks and astrologers who traditionally served to interpret to villagers what heaven had decreeed.[230]

In folk drama and popular literature, however, the traditional values remain. The *hat cheo* or popular theater is reported still to be ubiquitous, and its themes still emphasize the acceptance of the world as it is found by confronting its incongruities with laughter rather than action.[231] Perhaps most significantly of all, *The Tale of Kieu* still remains the most well-known piece of literature in North Vietnam. Weiss reports coming across a young woman, acting as guard to a hospital located in a cave, sitting " bent over a dog-eared copy of *Kieu*". He also reports more generally that

> The greatest of the classical poems *Kieu* is known everywhere through oral transmission . . . Everybody can repeat excerpts from the *Kieu* epic in recitative.[232]

EDUCATION AND CULTURAL LEADERSHIP IN COMMUNIST VIETNAM

The promotion of the Communist version of the " work ethic " in contradistinction to the fatalism of traditional values has been carried out primarily through two institutions, the educational system and the Party. Once the Viet Minh came to power in August 1945, a concerted effort was undertaken to eradicate illiteracy.[233] Although the war with the French made this campaign difficult to wage, it achieved a considerable degree of success.

Following the establishment of the DRV in 1954, efforts to develop education were intensified greatly. The regime sought to eliminate illiteracy, to create a body of skilled personnel, and, above all, to raise the ideological consciousness of the general populace. According to official statistics, the total number of students increased from 746,000 in 1955 to 2,666,000 in 1964–5; the increase in higher education was proportionately more dramatic, rising from 1,200 in 1955 to 26,300 in 1964–5.[234]

The curriculum of the elementary schools in North Vietnam lays heavy emphasis on basic language and mathematical skills and on the rudiments of science.[235] Those who continue their education at higher levels gain increasingly specialized training in scientific agriculture or some other modern skill. From the very beginning of schooling, ideological values are also emphasized. In geography, students learn about the unity of Vietnam and about those countries with close ties with Vietnam—for example, China, Laos, Cambodia, and the Soviet Union. In history, students are taught the stories of national heroes and especially themes from modern Vietnamese revolutionary history. The books read for literature classes include such novels as Ngo Tat To's *When the Lamp was Extinguished,* which describes " peasant life in the delta during the days of colonial rule."[236] Anti-American themes were stressed during the period of the second Indochina War. The importance of combining " study and work," " theory and practice," " intellectual work with manual work " is also stressed from these second-phase course (i.e., upper elementary level) on. For the latter purpose, schools are allocated land on which practical work can be carried out.[237]

The DRV has also expended considerable effort to provide continuing education for adults as well as for children:

> [T]he vigorous development in adult education was another great feature of the North Vietnamese education program. According to government reports, more than 3 million persons attended education courses between 1961 and 1964 . . . The majority of persons enrolled were industrial workers and cadres of agricultural cooperatives.[238]

Today, a very large percentage of the adult population of northern Vietnam has been educated according to the syllabuses established by the Ministry of Education in the DRV.

The leaders of the DRV face major problems if they are to see the form of education now established in the north extended to the south as well. The majority of the people of South Vietnam did not receive their education under the Communist system. Rather they studied at schools sponsored by the government of the Republic of Vietnam, by the Catholic Church, by the Buddhist, and by private parties. Thus, the leaders of the DRV face a dual challenge: how to extend basic education throughout the countryside and how to re-educate those trained under totally different systems.

A situation in which the Communist leaders of Vietnam find themselves seeking to educate a population raised with different values from their own is not new to them. A similar situation prevailed when they first began their efforts to create a Communist state in Vietnam. To overcome the problems facing them, Communist leadership from the start has placed great reliance on the cadres (*can bo*) of the party, and the *can bo* remain today as the cultural, as well as the political, vanguard of the revolution.

The *can bo* are not mere party functionaries as they are sometimes portrayed; more accurately, they are the functional equivalent of a priesthood or a cross between priests and mandarins. The aspirant to *can bo* status must first undergo intensive education in Marxist-Leninist doctrine in much the same way that a priest is educated in sacred texts or the mandarin in the writings of Confucius. From his training, the fundamental ideas of conflict between classes and especially between colonial oppressors (first the French, then the Americans) and oppressed, of historical determinism (" history is on our side "), and of creating a new world through work have been deeply ingrained in the cadre's mind.[239]

Having demonstrated his or her grasp of doctrine, the aspirant to *can bo* status is then initiated. Such initiation is said to have taken place, at least in South Vietnam, in the context of a " solemn ceremony " at which the aspirant dedicates himself or herself to the Party.[240] This dedication is periodically reinforced by the " ritual " of *kiem thao* (" self-criticism "), which has striking similarity to the ritual of confession practiced by chapters of Theravada Buddhist monks.

Although some cadres (like some priests) have compromised their original pledge or have placed their own self-interest above that of the party, most have proven to be highly disciplined. No other ideology prevalent in modern Vietnam has been communicated by such a dedicated group of men. Herein lies the success of the revolution in Vietnam.

The struggle against " colonialism " (as it has been construed in Vietnamese Communist terms) has ended; however, efforts to build a Socialist and then a Communist society are still very much in process. Even in the north, vestiges of traditional values are to be found; in the south large segments of the population are strongly committed to values other than those promoted by the Communists. For all the cultural problems Vietnam has yet to face, it still seems likely, however, that its future lies with those who believe that humans can create a new world, a better world, through their own labor.

NOTES

Chapter 4

1. George Coedès, *The Making of South East Asia* (tr. by H. M. Wright; Berkeley and Los Angeles: University of California Press, 1966), pp. 39–43. For general surveys of Vietnamese history, see Joseph Buttinger, *The Smaller Dragon: A Political History of Vietnam* (New York: Praeger, 1958); Jean Chesneaux, *The Vietnamese Nation: Contribution to a History* (tr. by Malcolm Salmon; Sydney: Current Book Distributors Pty., 1966); Le Thanh Khoi, *Le Viet-Nam: Histoire et Civilisation* (Paris: Editions de Minuit, 1955).

2. The mode of ecological adaptation that became dominant in northern Vietnam contrasted in both irrigation and terracing with the mode found elsewhere in mainland Southeast Asia. See Paul Wheatley, " Discursive Scholia on Recent Papers on Agricultural Terracing and on Related Matters Pertaining to Northern Indochina and Neighbouring Areas," *Pacific Viewpoint*, VI, 2 (1965), pp. 123–44.

3. See Tran Van Giap, " Le Bouddhisme en Annam des origines au XIIIe siècle," Bull. de l'École Française d'Extrême-Orient, XXXII (1932), pp. 191–268.

4. See Alexander Woodside, *Vietnam and the Chinese Model* (Cambridge: Harvard University Press, 1971). Woodside's is by far the best study of the Vietnamese tradition as it existed in the period just prior to the expansion of the French into

the area. For a detailed ethnographic reconstruction of the Vietnamese tradition, see Pierre Huard and Maurice Durand, *Connaissance du Viêt-Nam* (Hanoi: École Française d'Extrême-Orient, 1954).

5. Woodside, *op. cit.*, p. 3.

6. *Loc. cit.* For further discussion of peasant uprisings in Vietnam and a Marxist interpretation of the Tay-son rebellion, see Chesneaux, *op. cit.*, pp. 31–46.

7. By far the best study of the ecological adaptation of Vietnamese rice farmers is Pierre Gourou's *Les Paysans du Delta Tonkinois* (Paris: Publications de l'École Français d'Extrême-Orient, XXVII, 1936); English translation by Richard R. Miller, *The Peasants of the Tonkin Delta* (New Haven: Human Relations Area Files Press, 1955).

8. Gerald C. Hickey, in his study, *Village in Vietnam* (New Haven: Yale University Press, 1964), p. 147, reports that villagers in the Mekong Delta village of Khanh Hau in the early 1960s considered double cropping a rather " risky venture."

9. Woodside, *op. cit.*, p. 31.

10. *Ibid.*, pp. 31–32.

11. John Crawfurd, *Journal of an Embassy to the Courts of Siam and Cochin China* (Kuala Lumpur and London: Oxford University Press, 1967; orig. 1828), p. 214.

12. *Ibid.*, p. 470; Woodside, *op. cit.*, p. 31.

13. Crawfurd, *loc. cit.*; Woodside, *op. cit.*, p. 277.

14. Woodside, *op. cit.*, p. 30.

15. *Ibid.*, p. 31.

16. Woodside (*op. cit.*, pp. 37–50) has provided an analysis of Vietnamese kinship as manifested in both law and actuality in the first half of the nineteenth century. In my discussion, I will also draw on studies of Vietnamese kinship made in the colonial and postcolonial periods, where such studies clarify certain practices. See Pierre Lustéguy, *La femme annamite du Tonkin dans l'institution des biens cultuels (huo-hoa)* (Paris: Nizet et Bastard, 1935); English translation as *The Role of Women in Tonkinese Religion and Property* (tr. by Charles A. Messner; New Haven: Human Relations Area Files Press, 1954); Paul K. Benedict, " An Analysis of Annamese Kinship Terms," *Southwestern Journal of Anthropology*, III (1947), pp. 371–92; Pierre Gourou, " Les noms de famille ou ' Ho ' chez les Annamites du delta Tonkinois: Essai d'étude statistique et geographique," *BEFEO*, XXXII (1932), pp. 481–95; Gourou, *Les Paysans du delta Tonkinois, op. cit.*; Robert Lingat, *Les Régimes matrimoniaux du sud-est de l'Asie: Essai de droit comparé indochinois* (Hanoi: Publications de l'École Française d'Extrême-Orient, XXXIV, 1952); Nguyen Huy Lai, *Les régimes matrimoniaux en droit annamite* (Paris: Les Éditions Domat-Montchrestien, 1934); Robert F. Spencer, " The Annamese Kinship System," *Southwestern Journal of Anthropology*, I (1945), pp. 283–309; Tran Van Trai, *La famille patriarcale annamite* (Paris: P. Lapagesse, Thèse, Univ. de Paris, 1942); English translation in Human Relations Area Files (Source AM1, No. 4) by C. A. Messner.

17. See Robert Lingat, *op. cit.*, pp. 40f.

18. Lustéguy, *op. cit.*, pp. 73ff.

19. Woodside, *op. cit.*, p. 41.

20. *Ibid.*, p. 45; Lustéguy, *op. cit.*, pp. 108–109; Gourou, *Paysans* . . . , *op. cit.*, pp. 353, 359; Hickey, *op. cit.*, p. 132.

21. Lingat, *op. cit.*, pp. 40ff; Lustéguy, *op. cit.*, pp. 24–26.

22. Lustéguy, *op. cit.*, pp. 95f; also compare Hickey, *op. cit.*, pp. 91–93.

23. Woodside, *op. cit.*, p. 44; Gourou, *Paysans* . . . , p. 116; Lustéguy, *op. cit.*, pp. 23n, 107; Hickey, *op. cit.*, pp. 82–83, 89, 248–51, 280–81.

24. See Maurice Freedman, *Lineage Organization in Southeastern China* (London: Athlone Press, London School of Economics, Monographs in Social Anthropology, No. 18, 1958); Freedman, *Chinese Lineage and Society* (London: Athlone Press, London School of Economics, Monographs in Social Anthropology, No. 33, 1966).

25. Gourou, *Paysans* . . . , pp. 126–27. Gourou reports that for the whole of the Tonkin Delta region in the 1930s, there was a total of 202 surnames (*ho*), of which 11, and especially Nguyen, were by far the most numerous (Gourou, *op. cit.*, p. 127). Apparently, little importance was attached to possession of a common surname, if there was not also concomitant membership in the same patrilineage. Cf. Lustéguy, *op. cit.*, p. 23n.

26. Woodside, *op. cit.*, p. 44.

27. Lustéguy, *op. cit.*, p. 22.

28. Hickey, *op. cit.*, p. 82.

29. For a discussion of the Vietnamese village as found in the first half of the nineteenth century, see Woodside, *op. cit.*, pp. 152–58. Also see Ralph Smith, *VietNam and the West* (Ithaca, N.Y.: Cornell University Press, 1971 [first published 1968]), pp. 42–46. As in the foregoing discussion of kinship in traditional Vietnamese society, I also draw on studies made during the colonial and postcolonial periods, where such studies help to clarify or elaborate certain aspects.

30. Gourou, *Paysans* . . . , pp. 249–50. Other studies of Tonkinese villages, all made during the colonial period, include P. Ory, *La Commune annamite au Tonkin* (Paris: Challamel, 1894); C. Robequain, *Le Thanh Hoa* (Paris: van Oest, 1929); and Vu Van Hien, *La propriété communale au Tonkin* (Paris: Presses modernes, 1939); also Hanoi: Impr. d'Extrême-Orient, 1939).

31. Woodside, *op. cit.*, p. 153; Gourou, *Paysans* . . . , p. 225n.

32. Gourou, *Paysans* . . . , p. 235.

33. Several studies of Central Vietnamese villages were made in the late colonial and postcolonial periods: Gustave Langrand, *Vie sociale et réligieuse en Annam* (Lille: Editions Univers, 1945; Summary English translation by Patricia Hanson; New Haven: Human Relations Area Files Press, 1950); Guy Moréchand, " Caractères économiques et sociaux d'une région de pêche maritime du Centre-Vietnam," *BEFEO*, XLVII (1955), pp. 291–354; J. D. Donoghue, *Can An: A Fishing Village in Central Vietnam* (Washington, D.C.: Agency for International Development, Michigan State University, Vietnam Advisory Group, 1962).

34. P. Kresser, in his *La commune annamite en Cochinchine* (Paris: Donat-Montchrestien, 1935), provides the best description of traditional southern Vietnamese villages and of the changes that occurred in village life in the south under French administration. For recent studies of Mekhong delta villages see

J. D. Donoghue and Vo Hong Phuc, *My-Thuan: The Study of a Delta Village in South Viet Nam* (Saigon: Michigan State University Vietnam Advisory Group, Provincial-Local Administration Series, 1, 1961); J. B. Hendry, *The Small World of Khanh Hoa* (Chicago: Aldine, 1964); and Hickey, *op. cit.*

35. Hendry, *op. cit.*, p. 7.

36. *Ibid.*, p. 5.

37. *Ibid.*, pp. 3–7.

38. Gourou, *Paysans* . . . , p. 366; Smith, *op. cit.*, p. 42.

39. Gourou, *Paysans* . . . , p. 266.

40. See Woodside, *op. cit.*, pp. 154–55; Gustave Dumotier, *Les cultes Annamites* (Hanoi: Schneider, 1907), pp. 305 *et seq.*; Nguyen Van Khoan, " Essai sur le dinh et le culte du génie tutélaire des villages au Tonkin," *BEFEO*, XXX (1930), p. 132. English translation by Charles R. Temple, Human Relations Area Files (Source AM1, No. 133); Pierre Pasquier, *L'Annam autrefois* (Paris: Société des Éditions Géographiques, Maritimes et Coloniales, 1907), pp. 48–49; Kresser, *op. cit.*, pp. 17, 22–23.

41. Woodside, *op. cit.*, p. 155.

42. See Marcel Rouilly, *La commune annamite* (Paris: Presses Modernes, 1929), p. 51. In south Vietnam, according to Hickey, the village chief in the traditional council " was dean of the notables by virtue of age "—Hickey, *op. cit.*, p. 179. Whether this was also true in South Vietnam traditionally or not is not clear.

43. Smith, *op. cit.*, p. 43.

44. Gourou, *Paysans* . . . , p. 260.

45. Leopold Cadière, *Croyances et pratiques religieuses des Annamites* (Deuxième Ed., Saigon: Publications de la Société des Études Indochinoises, 1958 [orig. published 1944]), Vol. 1, pp. 30–31.

46. Nguyen Van Khoan, *op. cit.*, p. 110; Human Relations Area Files translation.

47. *Ibid.*, pp. 107, 116–17.

48. Hickey, *op. cit.*, p. 6. Nguyen Van Khoan (*op. cit.*, pp. 137–38) cites a supposition to the effect that the practice of an emperor granting patents to guardian spirits began in the sixteenth century.

49. Nguyen Van Khoan, *op. cit.*, pp. 118–119; Gustave Dumoutier, *Les Cultes Annamites* (Hanoi: H. F. Schneider, 1907), pp. 21–22.

50. Nguyen Van Khoan, *op. cit.*, pp. 131–132; Lustéguy, *op. cit.*, p. 110n.

51. Hickey, *op. cit.*, p. 221; also cf. Gourou, *Paysans* . . . , p. 270; Nguyen Van Khoan, *op. cit.*, pp. 124f.

52. Nguyen Van Khoan, *op. cit.*, p. 131.

53. Gourou, *Paysans* . . . , pp. 367–71.

54. Traditionally, the term *thay* applied also to middle level officials. See Woodside, *op. cit.*, p. 181.

55. *Ibid.*, p. 235.

56. Cf. Buttinger, *op. cit.*, p. 368n.

57. Woodside, *op. cit.*, p. 135.

58. For a detailed and incisive analysis of the educational and examination systems under the Nguyen, see Woodside, *op. cit.*, pp. 169–233.

59. See Nghiem Dang, *Viet-Nam: Politics and Administration* (Honolulu: East-West Center Press, 1966, p. 22; Buttinger, *op. cit.*, p. 144; Tran Van Giap, *op. cit.*

60. Talcott Parsons, *Societies: Comparative and Evolutionary Perspectives* (Englewood Cliffs, N.J.: Prentice Hall, 1966), p. 72.

61. Smith, *op. cit.*, pp. 20–21.

62. Woodside, *op. cit.*, p. 80.

63. *Ibid.*, p. 253.

64. *Ibid.*, p. 254.

65. *Ibid.*, p. 220.

66. Smith, *op. cit.*, p. 15. On traditional Vietnamese religion, also see Nguyen Khac Vien, *Tradition and Revolution in Vietnam* (Berkeley: Indochina Resource Center, n.d. [1974?]), esp. pp. 15–40.

67. *Ibid.*, p. 16.

68. *Ibid.*, pp. 22–23.

69. Cf. Max Weber, *The Religion of China* (tr. and ed. by Hans H. Gerth; N.Y.: Free Press, 1951), pp. 227f.

70. For descriptions and discussions of the *nam giao* rites, see Alfred Meynard, "Sacrifice to Heaven and Earth: the Survial at Hué, in Annam, of the Official Worship Once Performed in China," *Asia*, XXVIII (1928), pp. 799–803; Alan Brodrick, *Little China: the Annamese Lands* (London: Oxford, 1942); M. de Bertren, "Le Nam-Giao," *L'Ethnographie*, XLII (1944), pp. 54–61; Nguyen Khoa Toan, "Le Nam Giao: Ses Origines, son rite, sa signification," *J. Siam Society*, XLI (1953), pp. 19–43; and Cadière, *op. cit.*, pp. 85–128.

71. Hickey, *op. cit.*, p. 57. Although the French maintained the monarchy in Annam and maintained the fiction that they ruled northern and central Vietnam as protectorates, there is no question but that French rule had removed the mandate of heaven from the Emperor. The *nam giao* rites continued to be performed during the French period, but were held only once every three years rather than every year. The last performance of the rites took place on the 28th of March 1942 with Emperor Bao Dai officiating. By this time the loss of the mandate was all too painfully obvious. A contemporary observer wrote: " The old-fashioned mandarins who foretold the collapse of the dynasty and the withdrawal of the Mandate of Heaven from a puppet and doubtfully legitimate ruler, have seen their worst fears realized." (Brodrick, *op. cit.*, p. 11).

72. See Nghien Dang, *op. cit.*, pp. 55–56.

73. Woodside, *op. cit.*, pp. 189–90. The first of these two maxims subsumed the five relationships, whereas the other nine were elaborations on the five virtues with specific reference to the Vietnamese context.

74. P. Ory, *op. cit.*, p. 124; Dumoutier, *op. cit.*, p. 1.

75. Dumoutier, *op. cit.*, p. 1; HRAF translation.

76. Cadière, *op. cit.*, pp. 17–18.

77. Hickey (*op. cit.*, p. 57) reports that in the southern Vietnamese village of Khanh

Hau, villagers believed that men and women both have nine inferior vital principles.

78. By far the best studies on Vietnamese popular religion are those of Father Leopold Cadière. These studies have been collected in three volumes, entitled *Croyances et Pratiques Religieuses des Vietnamiens* (originally published in Hanoi: Impr. d'Extrême-Orient, 1944; volume one republished in Saigon: Société des Études Indochinoises, 1958; volume two republished in Saigon: École Française d'Extrême-Orient, 1955; and volume three republished in Saigon: École Française d'Extrême-Orient, 1957).

79. Woodside, *op. cit.*, pp. 284–89.

80. Langrand, *op. cit.*, p. 74; HRAF translation.

81. Smith, *op. cit.*, p. 20.

82. John Crawfurd, *Journal of an Embassy to the Courts of Siam and Cochin China*, *op. cit.*, p. 499.

83. Tran Van Giap, *op. cit.*

84. Cadière, *op. cit.*, 1958, p. 31.

85. *Ibid.*, pp. 27–29.

86. Brodrick, *op. cit.*, p. 42.

87. Hickey, *op. cit.*, pp. 75–79.

88. *Ibid.*, pp. 70–80.

89. Smith, *op. cit.*, p. 23.

90. *Ibid.*, p. 16.

91. *Ibid.*, p. 23.

92. Woodside, *op. cit.*, pp. 31–34, 270–73; Gourou, *Paysans* . . . , p. 350.

93. See Chesneaux, *op. cit.*, pp. 47–52; Smith, *op. cit.*, pp. 23–24.

94. Summaries and overviews of the history of Vietnam during the colonial period can be found in Le Thanh Khoi, *Le Viet-Nam: Histoire et civilisation* (Paris: Éditions de Minuit, 1955); Jean Chesneaux, *The Vietnamese Nation: Contributions to a History* (tr. by Malcolm Salmon, Sydney: Current Book Distributors, 1966); Joseph Buttinger, *op. cit.*; and D. G. E. Hall, *A History of South-East Asia*, 3rd ed. (London: Macmillan, 1968). For a review, and critique, of French writing on Vietnam that was produced during the colonial period, see Jean Chesneaux, " French Historiography and the Evolution of Colonial Vietnam," in *Historians of South East Asia*, ed. by D. G. E. Hall (London: Oxford, 1961), pp. 236–44. For detailed studies of some aspects of the impact of French colonial rule see the following: Chester Bain, " The History of Viet-Nam from the French Penetration to 1939 " (Ph.D. Dissertation, American University, 1956); André Dumarest, *La formation de classes sociales en pays annamite* (Lyon: Impr. Ferréol, 1935); David G. Marr, *Vietnamese Anticolonialism* (Berkeley and Los Angeles: University of California Press, 1971); Milton E. Osborne, *The French Presence in Cochinchina and Cambodia: Rule and Response (1859–1905)* (Ithaca, N.Y.: Cornell University Press, 1969); Charles Robequain, *The Economic Development of French-Indo-china* (London: Oxford University Press, 1944); Ralph Smith, *op. cit.*; and Truong Buu Lam, *Patterns of Vietnamese Response to Foreign Intervention, 1858–1900* (New

Haven: Yale University, Southeast Asia Studies, Monograph Series No. 11, 1967). Ngo Vinh Long's *Before the Revolution: The Vietnamese Peasants under the French* (Cambridge: MIT Press, 1973) provides detailed summaries and analyses of data on the socioeconomic position of the peasantry under colonial rule. It also includes translated passages from a number of Vietnamese works, mainly fictional accounts, which relate stories from the countryside during the period of French rule. Alexander Woodside's study of modern Vietnamese history, *Community and Revolution in Modern Vietnam* (Boston: Houghton Mifflin, 1976) came to hand only after the writing of this chapter had been completed. Woodside's study is to be highly recommended for its interpretation of the impact of colonial rule on Vietnamese society and culture and of the transformations of Vietnam since the end of French rule.

95. David G. Marr, *op. cit.*, p. 35.

96. *Ibid.*, p. 47.

97. Chesneaux, *The Vietnamese Nation, op. cit.*, p. 102.

98. *La Conference Africaine Française, Brazzaville, 30 janvier 1944–8 fevrier 1944* (Algiers, Commissariat aux Colonies, 1944), p. 35. Donald Lancaster (*The Emancipation of French Indo-China* [London: Oxford, 1961], pp. 122–23) from whom this quote is taken points out that this principle, enunciated with reference to French African territories, became dogma with reference to all French colonial territories.

99. Osborne, *op. cit.*, p. 34. On the debate over " assimilation " and " association," see also Chesneaux, *op. cit.*, pp. 97–98.

100. See Osborne, *op. cit.*, pp. 154–55; also cf. Smith, *op. cit.*, pp. 46–54.

101. Quoted in translation in Osborne, *op. cit.*, p. 151.

102. See Kresser, *op. cit.*, pp. 75–76.

103. John T. McAlister, Jr., and Paul Mus, *The Vietnamese and Their Revolution* (N.Y.: Harper Torchbooks, 1970), p. 58.

104. Marcel Rouilly, *La commune annamite* (Paris: Presses Modernes, 1929), p. 89.

105. Robequain, *Economic Development* . . . , pp. 161, 163.

106. Chesneaux, *op. cit.*, p. 110.

107. Cf. Robequain, *Economic Development* . . . , p. 162.

108. See Robequain, *Economic Development* . . . , pp. 89–127; Great Britain, Admiralty, Naval Intelligence Division, *op. cit.*, pp. 369–443.

109. Marr, *op. cit.*, p. 81; Ngo Vinh Long, *op. cit.*, p. 14.

110. Y. Henry, *Economie agricole de l'Indochine* (Hanoi: Gouvernement Général, 1932), p. 109f.; Gourou, *Paysans* . . . , pp. 360ff. Also see Ngo Vinh Long, *op. cit.*, pp. 14–23; Robequain, *Economic Development* . . . , pp. 82–84; Great Britain, Admiralty, Naval Intelligence Division, *op. cit.*, pp. 289–94.

111. This argument is made, for example, by Chesneaux (*op. cit.*, pp. 112–13) and Ngo Vinh Long (*op. cit.*, pp. 48–51).

112. Gourou, *Payans* . . . , p. 405; P. Gourou, *L'Utilisation du sol en Indochine* (Paris: Centre d'Études de Politique Étrangère, 1940), p. 294.

113. Ngo Vinh Long, *op. cit.*, pp. 48–51.

114. James C. Ingram, *Economic Change in Thailand, 1850–1970* (Stanford, Ca.: Stanford University Press, 1971), p. 48.

115. Gourou, *L'Utilisation du sol en Indochine*, pp. 233–34.

116. Ngo Vinh Long, *op. cit.*, p. 46. Long tends to overstate somewhat the situation regarding tenancy and sharecropping.

117. Chesneaux, *op. cit.*, p. 81; also see p. 101.

118. *Ibid.*, p. 98; Marr, *op. cit.*, p. 80.

119. McAlister and Mus, *op. cit.*, p.36; also see pp. 57–59.

120. Robequain, *Economic Development . . .* , p. 156.

121. For further discussion of the taxes levied against the peasantry, see Ngo Vinh Long, *op. cit.*, pp. 61–76.

122. See Ngo Vinh Long, *op. cit.*, pp. 84–97; Robequain, *Economic Development . . .* , p. 40, 168–171; Great Britain. Admiralty, Naval Intelligence Division, *op. cit.*, p. 293; 364–65.

123. Marr, *op. cit.*, p. 265. Also cf. Ngo Vinh Long, *op. cit.*, pp. 102–117.

124. Figures and interpretation drawn from Robequain, *Economic Development . . .* , pp. 21–31.

125. *Ibid.*, pp. 32–44.

126. Great Britain. Admiralty, Naval Intelligence Division, *op. cit.*, p. 294.

127. Ngo Vinh Long, *op. cit.*, pp. 75–76.

128. Chesneaux, *op. cit.*, p. 133. Chesneaux gives as his source for this calculation a work by a M. Henri Lanoue on industrialization in Indochina, which was published in November 1938 by the Société d'études et d'information économiques.

129. McAlister and Mus, *op. cit.*, p. 38.

130. Marr, *op. cit.*, pp. 44–76.

131. McAlister and Mus, *op. cit.*, p. 37.

132. For a detailed assessment of early French educational efforts in Cochin China, see Osborne, *op. cit.*, esp. ch. 4.

133. Great Britain. Admiralty, Naval Intelligence Division, *op. cit.*, p. 156.

134. Ngo Vinh Long, *op. cit.*, p. 74.

135. Great Britain. Admiralty, Naval Intelligence Division, *op. cit.*, p. 157.

136. *Ibid.*, p. 156.

137. Smith, *op. cit.*, pp. 21–22.

138. Piero Gheddo, *The Cross and the Bo-Tree: Catholics and Buddhists in Vietnam* (tr. by Charles Underhill Quinn; New York: Sheed and Ward, 1970), p. 13.

139. *Ibid.*, p. 15.

140. *Ibid.*, p. 17.

141. Gerald C. Hickey, *Village in Vietnam* (New Haven: Yale University Press, 1964), pp. 120–21.

142. Thich Nhat Hanh, *Vietnam: Lotus in a Sea of Fire* (New York: Hill and Wang, 1967), p. 41.

143. *Ibid.*, p. 40.

144. Theravada Buddhism also exists in south Vietnam where its adherents include not only Vietnamese of Khmer descent, but also some ethnic Vietnamese. Sectarian differences between Buddhists are difficult to identify because of efforts by Buddhist leaders in the country to develop the most inclusive organizations possible in order to give Buddhists a significant role in Vietnamese politics. Even the basic distinction between Theravada and Mahayana Buddhism has been muted. At a congress held at the Xa Loi Pagoda in Saigon in December 1963 and January 1964, the two sects agreed to form a joint organization known in English as the United Church of Vietnamese Buddhism or the Association of Unified Buddhism. For discussions of the role of Buddhism in recent (south) Vietnamese history, see Thich Nhat Hanh, *op. cit.*, pp. 40–49; Gheddo, *op. cit.*, pp. 265–92; Jerrold Schecter, *The New Face of Buddha* (London: Victor Gollancz, 1967), pp. 145–252; and Frances Fitzgerald, *Fire in the Lake* (New York: Random House, Vintage Books, 1973 [orig. published by Atlantic-Little Brown, 1972]), pp. 368–88.

145. Gheddo, *op. cit.*, p. 171.

146. Thich Nhat Hanh, *Zen Keys* (Garden City, N.Y.: Doubleday Anchor, 1974), p. 147, italics in original.

147. Bernard Fall, "The Political-Religious Sects of Viet-Nam," *Pacific Affairs*, XXVIII (1955), p. 244.

148. *Ibid.*, p. 243.

149. Translated and quoted in Fall, *ibid.*, p. 244.

150. For discussions of Cao-daism, see Fall, *ibid.*, pp. 235–43. The major source is Gabriel Fobron, *Histoire et Philosophie du Caodaisme* (Paris: Derby, 1949). I have also consulted pamphlets obtained at Tay Ninh, the "Holy See" of Caodaism: *The Outline of Caodaism* (tr. by Ngoc Doan Thanh; Tay Ninh, 1972) and Phan Truong Manh, *La Voie du Salut Caodaique* (Saigon: Impr. Ly Cong Quan, 1950).

151. Fall, *op. cit.*, p. 237. Caodaists trace the founding of their religion to 1926. See *The Outline of Caodaism, op. cit.*, pp. 8–10.

152. Marr, *op. cit.*, p. 96.

153. *Ibid.*, p. 33.

154. *Ibid.*, pp. 83–86.

155. *Ibid.*, p. 255. A number of biographies of Ho now exist, many of which border on hagiography. Among the more balanced accounts, see Jean Lacouture, *Ho Chi Minh: A Political Biography* (tr. by Peter Wiles, ed. by Jane Clark Seitz; New York: Random House, 1968).

156. McAlister and Mus, *op. cit.*, p. 116.

157. *Ibid.*, p. 117.

158. *Ibid.*, p. 119. Paul Mus is almost the only scholar of modern Vietnamese culture who has been seriously concerned with the " language of politics " as used by Vietnamese Communists. The work cited here is a partial translation of Mus' *Viet-Nam: Sociologie d'une Guerre* (Paris: Éditions du Seuil, 1952).

159. Ho Chi Minh, " Message to Women on the Anniversary of the Two Trung Sisters, and Women [sic] International Day," in Ho Chi Minh; *Selected Works* III, (Hanoi: Foreign Languages Publishing House, 1961), pp. 326–28.

160. Smith, *op. cit.*, p. 185. Douglas Pike in *War, Peace and the Viet Cong* (Cambridge: MIT Press, 1969), p. 15n, asserts that however else a Vietnamese Communist's understanding of Communist ideology might vary, he or she would accept the Communist conceptions of class conflict and historical determinism.

161. For discussion of the events of the period between the end of World War II and the Geneva Agreements of 1954 see Lancaster, *op. cit.*, part III; Phillipe Devillers, *Histoire de Viet-Nam de 1940 à 1952* (Paris: Éditions du Seuil, 1952); Phillipe Devillers and Jean Lacouture, *End of the War, Indochina, 1954* (tr. by Alexander Lieven and Adam Roberts; New York: Praeger, 1960); Ellen J. Hammer, *The Struggle for Indochina, 1940–1955* (Stanford: Stanford University Press, 1966); Bernard B. Fall, *The Two Viet-Nams*, rev. ed. (New York: Praeger, 1964); John T. McAlister, Jr., *Vietnam: The Origins of Revolution* (Garden City, N.Y.: Doubleday Anchor, 1971).

162. Quoted in Fall, *The Two Viet-Nams*, p. 212.

163. Lancaster, *op. cit.*, pp. 335–336.

164. The figures regarding the number of Vietnamese who migrated from the north to the south is subject to considerable debate. Fall (*The Two Viet-Nams*, p. 154) places the total at 860,000 of whom 600,000 were Catholics. Fall calculates that whereas 65 per cent of the Catholic population of North Vietnam fled to the south, only 5 per cent of all non-Catholics fled.

165. Fall, *op. cit.*, p. 157.

166. Roy Jumper and Marjorie Weiner Normand, " Vietnam," in *Government and Politics of Southeast Asia*, ed. by George McT. Kahin, 2nd ed. (Ithaca, N.Y.: Cornell University Press, 1964), p. 472.

167. See Douglas Pike, *War, Peace, and the Viet Cong*, *op. cit.*, p. 1n. On the role of the " Viet Cong " in the second War in Indochina, see also Carlyle A. Thayer, " Southern Vietnamese Revolutionary Organizations and the Vietnam Workers' Party: Continuity and Change, 1954–1974," in *Communism in Indochina: New Perspectives*, ed. by Joseph J. Zasloff and MacAlister Brown (Lexington, Mass.: Lexington Books, 1975), pp. 27–56; and Douglas Pike, *Viet Cong* (Cambridge, Mass.: M.I.T. Press, 1966).

168. Elizabeth Pond, " South Vietnamese Politics and the American Withdrawal," in *Indochina in Conflict: A Political Assessment* (Lexington, Mass.: Lexington Books, 1972), pp. 10f. See, also, the articles by Jeffrey Race, James Bullington and James D. Rosenthal, Samuel Popkin, Allan E. Goodman, John Donnell, MacDonald Salter, William Bredo, and Roy L. Prosterman that appear in a special issue of *Asian Survey*, X (1970) devoted to " Vietnam: Politics, Land Reform and Development in the Countryside."

169. Pike, *War, Peace, and the Viet Cong*, *op. cit.*, p. 34.

170. Pond, *op. cit.*, p. 17.

171. *Loc. cit.*

172. Fitzgerald, *op. cit.*, pp. 569–70.

173. *Ibid.*, p. 571.

174. Pond, *op. cit.*, p. 3.

175. Thayer, *op. cit.*, pp. 51–52.

176. These statements have been republished in *Southeast Asia: Documents of Political Development and Change*, ed. by Roger M. Smith (Ithaca, N.Y.: Cornell University Press, 1974), pp. 403–407.

177. For analyses of Communist administration and impact on rural life in South Vietnam before the end of the war, see Douglas Pike, *Viet Cong, op. cit.*; Pike, *War, Peace and the Viet Cong, op. cit.*; Jeffrey Race, *War Comes to Long An: Revolutionary Conflict in a Vietnamese Province* (Berkeley: University of California Press, 1972); Race, " How They Won," *Asian Survey* X, 8 (1970), pp. 628–50; William Bredo, " Agrarian Reform in Vietnam: Vietcong and Government of Vietnam Strategies in Conflict," *Asian Survey* X, 8 (1970), pp. 738–50; R. L. Sansom, *The Economics of Insurgency in the Mekong Delta of Vietnam* (Cambridge, Mss.: M.I.T. Press, 1970).

178. Pike, *War, Peace, and the Viet Cong, op. cit.*, p. 51.

179. Accessible data on rural life in the DRV is relatively limited. The studies that most closely approximate anthropological studies are Nguyen Khac Vien's report on Hung Yen (now Hai Hung) province in the Red River delta in 1963 (contained in Dr. Vien's *Tradition and Revolution*, pp. 75–125) and Gérard Chaliand's report of " a five-week tour of inquiry among the villages of three provinces in the Red River delta . . . carried out during October and November 1967 " (Chaliand, *op. cit.*, p. 13). Dr. Vien was trained as a medical doctor and has become one of the leading scholars in the Democratic Republic of Vietnam. Chaliand is described in the first page of his book as " history teacher and specialist in underdeveloped countries." In addition to these first-hand reports, there have also been a number of studies based on information published in North Vietnamese sources. The most extensive of such studies, Tran Nhu Trang's "The Transformation of the Peasantry in North Viet Nam " (Ph.D. Dissertation, University of Pittsburgh, 1972), written by a former professor of Law at the University of Saigon, also incorporates some data derived from interviews with North Vietnamese who had defected or been captured in South Vietnam. Also see Alexander Woodside, " Decolonization and Agricultural Reform in Northern Vietnam," *Asian Survey*, X, 8 (1970), pp. 705–23 and David W. P. Elliott, " Political Integration in North Vietnam: The Cooperativization Period," in Zasloff and Brown, *Communism in Indochina*, pp. 165–93.

180. Woodside, " Decolonization . . . ," *op. cit.*, p. 706.

181. *Loc. cit.*

182. Tran Nhu Trang, *op. cit.*, pp. 242–43. Tran here paraphrases the Viet Minh decree of March 5, 1953, " The Differentiation of Class Status in the Country-side."

183. See the discussion of various estimates in Tran Nhu Trang, *op. cit.*, pp. 276–77.

184. Woodside, " Decolonization . . . ," *op. cit.*, p. 707.

185. Tran Nhu Trang, *op. cit.*, p. 287.

186. Cf. *Ibid.*, p. 314.

187. *Ibid.*, p. 317.

188. Woodside, " Decolonization . . . ," *op. cit.*, p. 707.

189. *Ibid.*, p. 708. Also see Tran Nhu Trang, *op. cit.*, pp. 442–45.

190. Tran Nhu Trang, *op. cit.*, p. 445; also see Woodside, " Decolonization . . .", *op. cit.*, p. 718.

191. Elliott, *op. cit.*, p. 184. Peasants interviewed by Chaliand on this subject also gave as their reasons for joining the cooperatives the fact that it was to their economic advantage to do so. See Chaliand, *op. cit.*, pp. 147, 161.

192. Tran Nhu Trang, *op. cit.*, p. 319.

193. Chaliand, *op. cit.*, p. 126.

194. Tran Nhu Trang, *op. cit.*, pp. 327–28, 335, 395–96.

195. *Ibid.*, p. 397.

196. Elliott, *op. cit.*, p. 171.

197. Chaliand, *op. cit.*, p. 118.

198. Woodside, " Decolonization . . . ," pp. 713, 715–16.

199. Elliott, *op. cit.*, p. 173.

200. Tran Nhu Trang, *op. cit.*, pp. 333.

201. Woodside, " Decolonization . . . ," p. 712.

202. *Ibid.*, p. 711.

203. Tran Nhu Trang, *op. cit.*, pp. 404–405.

204. Chaliand, *op. cit.*, p. 80.

205. *Ibid.*, pp. 165, 200f.

206. Tran Nhu Trang, *op. cit.*, p. 314.

207. *Ibid.*, pp. 439–40.

208. Chaliand, *op. cit.*, p. 136; also see pp. 132–33.

209. *Ibid.*, p. 135.

210. Quoted in Chaliand, *op. cit.*, p. 50. Tran Nhu Trang (*op. cit.*, p. 388) calculated that the number of doctors in 1966 was one per 3,200 persons. He also gives a figure of 21,000 midwives for the same year, or about one per 900 people.

211. Tran Nhu Trang, *op. cit.*, pp. 387–88.

212. Chaliand, *op. cit.*, p. 129.

213. Tran Nhu Trang, *op. cit.*, p. 387; Chaliand, *op. cit.*, pp. 128–29.

214. Tran Nhu Trang, *op. cit.*, p. 380.

215. Chaliand, *op. cit.*, pp. 120, 130; Tran Nhu Trang, *op. cit.*, p. 388.

216. William S. Turley, " The DRV since the Death of Ho Chi Minh: The Politics of a Revolution in Transition," in Zasloff and Goodman, *Indochina in Conflict*, pp. 28–30.

217. Chaliand, *op. cit.*, p. 231.

218. Tran Nhu Trang, *op. cit.*, pp. 378–79.

219. Figures for North Vietnam taken from Tran Nhu Trang, *loc. cit.* Those for Thailand are based on data given by James C. Ingram in *Economic Change in Thailand*, *op. cit.*, p. 239.

220. Elliott, *op. cit.*, p. 183.

221. Tran Nhu Trang, *op. cit.*, pp. 454–55.

222. Woodside, " Decolonization . . .", pp. 721–22.

223. *Ibid.*, p. 722. Le Duan's quote from Lenin appears in Turley, " The D.R.V. since the Death of Ho Chi Minh . . . ," Turley, *op. cit.*, pp. 29–30. Both Turley and Woodside draw attention to this important speech as being the " Party line ".

224. Nguyen Du, *The Tale of Kieu.* Translated and annotated by Huynh Sanh Thong (New York: Random House, 1973), p. 142.

225. Chaliand, *op. cit.*, pp. 145, 159.

226. Peter Weiss, *Notes on the Cultural Life of the Democratic Republic of Vietnam* (N. Y.: Dell Publishing Co., 1970), p. 75.

227. *Ibid.*, p. 79.

228. *Ibid.*, pp. 78–79.

229. Chaliand, *op. cit.*, p. 120.

230. *Loc. cit.*

231. Weiss, *op. cit.*, pp. 142–52. The DRV does not appear to have converted the folk theater into an instrument for communicating Communist values to quite the extent that was done in China.

232. *Ibid.*, pp. 120, 81, 83.

233. *Lutte contre l'analphabétisme au Viet Nam* (Hanoi: Éditions en Langues Étrangères, 1959).

234. The same statistics, with only minor variations, are reported in Tran Nhu Trang, *op. cit.*, p. 385 and in Chaliand, *op. cit.*, p. 47.

235. This description of the curriculum of schools in North Vietnam is based on Chaliand's report of 1967. See Chaliand, *op. cit.*, p. 105–106.

236. *Ibid.*, p. 108n.

237. *Ibid.*, p. 106; Tran Nhu Trang, *op. cit.*, p. 386.

238. Tran Nhu Trang, *op. cit.*, p. 386.

239. See Pike, *War, Peace, and the Viet Cong*, *op. cit.*, p. 15.

240. *Ibid.*, pp. 16–17.

CHAPTER 5
CITIES IN CHANGING SOCIETIES
IN MAINLAND SOUTHEAST ASIA

Thus far in this work, we have examined patterns of cultural adaptation and the transformations of these patterns with reference to peoples who live in the rural communities, both peasant and tribal, of mainland Southeast Asia. In this chapter, the focus is shifted from rural peoples to those peoples who live and have lived in the cities and towns of mainland Southeast Asia. It has been in the urban centers that conflicts between different patterns of adaptation found in mainland Southeast Asian societies have been most sharply drawn, and it is with reference to contemporary cities in mainland Southeast Asia that the processes of socioeconomic and ideological change can best be explored.

PRE-MODERN CITIES AND RELIGIOUSLY-ORIENTED SOCIETIES

Ancient and Classical Cities

Until quite recently it was generally accepted that the emergence of cities in mainland Southeast Asia was not an indigenous development but resulted from influences from China and India. Recent archaeological finds, particularly from northeastern Thailand, strongly suggest that rice cultivation, animal husbandry, differentiated pottery forms, specialized bronze and iron tool industries, and perhaps other conditions necessary for urban life were developed independently of influences from outside the region. Yet these developments notwithstanding, it still appears certain that other essential ingredients for the emergence of urban life, namely writing and the religious ideas that could provide the legitimacy for a state, came to mainland Southeast Asia from China and particularly from India. The earliest cities of the region that have been excavated archaeologically —Chansen in Thailand and Beikthano in Burma—clearly show evidence of Indian influence.[1]

Several different types of ancient cities in mainland Southeast Asia can be distinguished.[2] Among the most important of the early cities were those that have called " sacred " or " temple " cities,[3] that is, cities that were believed

259

by the agrarian population of a territory to radiate or generate the religious virtue necessary to ensure their prosperity. Among the more well-known ancient cities are Vyadhapura, the capital of Funan, located in the present-day Cambodian province of Prei Veng; Panduranga and Indrapura, capitals of Champa, located on the coast of central Vietnam; Srikshetra (Old Prome), capital of the Pyu kingdom located in lower Burma; and the capitals of ancient Dvaravati located at what are today the towns of Nakhon Pathom and U Thong in the lower Cao Phraya valley of Thailand. Each of these cities contained religious buildings that were geomantically oriented and that also served as concrete expressions of the power of Buddhism and/or Brahmanism with which the rulers of the state were intimately linked. Although these religious monuments were striking by the standards of the time, and although they certainly would have been impressive to the rural people who were brought to help build them or to support the ruling politico-religious elite living in the cities, they were only foreshadowing of the huge monuments that were later to be found in the classic temple cities at Pagan and Angkor.

The classic temple cities began to emerge about A.D. 1000 and reached their climactic development in the twelfth and thirteenth centuries. Pagan and Angkor, whose characteristics have already been discussed in Chapter 3, were not the only examples of the classic temple cities. Although constructed on a lesser scale and in control of smaller territories, Vijaya, the medieval Champa capital located on the coast of central Vietnam, Lavo (modern Lopburi) and Haripunjaya (modern Lamphun), capitals of kingdoms of the same names in central and northern Thailand, Phimai, the " second " city of the Angkorean empire, located in northeastern Thailand, Hamsavati (old Pegu) and Suddhammavati (old Thaton), capitals of Mon kingdoms in lower Burma, all had the defining characteristics of the temple city. During the same period, smaller " cities " were also built, constructed on the model provided by the dominant neighboring capital.

The primary characteristic of the " temple cities " was that they were constructed to symbolize a sacred cosmography,[4] with a sacred center representing Mount Meru, the center of the cosmos:

> As every human creation repeats the primal cosmogonic act that itself took place at the centre of the world, so the sacred city, the capital inevitably becomes an *axis mundi*, a meeting point of heaven, earth and hell, with a secondary role as centre of its early kingdom. . . . The necessity of selecting auspicious locations for such cities explains the importance of the geomantic art . . . which was . . . formerly widespread throughout Asia from the Mediterranean to the China sea.[5]

Given the overriding importance of geomantic concerns in the temple cities of Southeast Asia, some scholars have been led to query whether they were true cities. Coe, for one, has concluded that they were cult centers that lacked such distinguishing features of true cities as large populations, marketing functions, and the like.[6] McGee takes issue with Coe and argues that " temple cities " were truly urban centers:

What Coe seems to ignore is that even in a Southeast Asian center such as Angkor, there is considerable evidence of trade and diversification of economic activity which supports the argument that such centers deserve the title of city. [7]

Given the demands for labor and wealth involved in the construction and maintenance of the archtectural representations of the cosmos, the temple cities were the chief consumers of the agricultural surpluses produced by the peasants living in the archaic civilizations of Southeast Asia. The temple cities also required the services of large numbers of architects, stone-cutters, sculptors, wood-carvers and other artisans for the work of constructing and decorating the important temples. In addition to the artisans and the service people found in these ancient cities, there were also the rulers, the administrators, and the priests who belonged to a class apart from the rest of the populace. Thus, the classic temple cities were characterized by a significant diversity in their occupational structure.

A second type of ancient city found in mainland Southeast Asia was the " entrepôt " or " trading " city. Although some representatives of this type of city also had sacred functions that were exercised with reference to rural peoples, their characteristic feature was the role which they played in the trade of the region. When the earliest entrepôt cities were founded in mainland Southeast Asia is not certain, but by the first centuries of the Christian era, they existed in some number, not only along the Malay peninsula, but also elsewhere in the region. Among the more important of the early entrepôt cities was Oc-Eo, the so-called port city of the ancient kingdom of Funan and located in what is today South Vietnam. Entrepôt cities in mainland Southeast Asia never assumed the importance that they did in insular Southeast Asia, and the majority of those to be found on the mainland lay along the peninsula. During the period of the classic civilizations in mainland Southeast Asia, the most important entrepôt cities included Takkola and Nagara Sri Dhammaraja, located on opposite sides of the peninsula in what is today southern Thailand. The location of Takkola has long been the subject of considerable debate, although most of the sites suggested are to be found between present-day Trang (capital of a province of the same name) and Takuapa in present-day Phangnga province, both in Thailand. [8] Nagara Sri Dhammarja, often known as Ligor in earlier Western sources, still exists under its traditional name and is the capital of a province on the east coast of southern Thailand. Nagara Sri Dhammaraja was an important city in the medieval " empire " of Srivijaya, which encompassed territories in both peninsular and insular Southeast Asia.

The distinguishing feature of the entrepôt cities was that they " drew their economic wealth from maritime trade and their role as trading emporiums." [9] Although entrepôt cities obtained their food from nearby rural peoples, they did not depend on the control of large peasant populations for their wealth and they rarely exercised control over populations as large as those controlled by temple cities. The entrepôt cities were more cosmopolitan than temple cities; their populations included peoples of such diverse ethnic backgrounds as Indians,

Chinese, and Malays as well as local peoples. This ethnic diversity was associated with an ethnic division of labor: the international merchants were either Indians or, more rarely, Chinese; ship crews were apparently often Malays; rulers, peasants, and servants were drawn from local populations. For most of the ancient entrepôt cities in mainland Southeast Asia—i.e., Oc-Eo, Takkola, Nagara Sri Dhammaraja—the local population spoke Mon-Khmer languages.

A third type of ancient city in mainland Southeast Asia, the Chinese garrison city, was found in the northern part of the region where the Chinese had established their control. In areas, today part of southern China, that were absorbed into the Chinese state, these garrison towns evolved into Chinese provincial cities and towns. In what is today northern Vietnam, however, a different process took place following upon the success that the Vietnamese had in achieving their independence from China. The first capitals to be established by the Vietnamese after they gained their independence from China in A.D. 939 were not particularly noteworthy. Hoa-lu, in the lower Tonkin Delta, which became the capital in A.D. 968, was described as follows:

> The Vietnamese Annals describe the capital, Hoa-lu, as being of great magnificence, but a Chinese envoy who visited it in 990 does not seem to have been particularly impressed, and only mentions several thousand huts built of bamboo or straw which served as barracks. " The palace," he says, " is quite small. The wooden towers raised for the defence of the city are as simple in construction as they are ugly in form."[10]

In 1012, Hoa-lu was in turn abandoned, and a new capital was established at Thang-long, that is, old Hanoi, which had previously been the seat of the Chinese governor when Vietnam was under Chinese rule. Thang-long became, like the Chinese model on which it was based, the cultural and religious center as well as the political center of the state. In 1070, a "temple of literature" was constructed in the capital and dedicated to the cult of Confucius. "A national university was created in 1076, a year after the first literary examinations werel held."[11] From at least this point in time on, Vietnamese capitals were modeled on those of China.

Traditional Cities in Theravada Buddhist Southeast Asia

The great social and cultural upheaval that took place in mainland Southeast Asia between the late thirteenth century and the end of the fifteenth century brought about significant changes in the structure of the city as found in the Indianized parts of the region. Although the capitals of the agrarian-based states continued to be temple cities, and many of the motifs of the classical cities were perpetuated—perhaps most strongly in Burma—religious authority was no longer conterminous with political authority. In the wake of the Theravada Buddhist revolution in Southeast Asia, kings ceased to be deva-rajas encased in an architectural microcosm of the cosmos; rather, they became defenders of the faith who established their right to rule by acts of conspicuous merit making. As a seeker after merit, the king, as all lay persons, was (in theory at least) subordinate to and dependent upon the Sangha.[12]

The separation of political and religious authorities in the capital cities of Theravada Buddhist states is evidenced in the city of Sukhothai, one of the first new Theravadin capitals to be founded. Sukhothai, located on the Yom River in what is today north central Thailand, had originally been founded in the twelfth century as a provincial outpost of the Khmer empire, but with a population that was mainly Tai, organized under their own " chiefs " (*cao*). In the 1220s two of these Tai chiefs rebelled against the Khmer and established an independent Tai kingdom, the first Tai state in what is today central Thailand. Little is known about the early days of Sukhothai as a capital, for there are no inscriptions prior to the end of the thirteenth century. However, with the inscription of King Ram Khamhaeng of 1292, we have a document that gives considerable detail about the city of Sukhothai and about the state of which it was the capital.

The inscription of King Ram Khamhaeng of Sukhothai is the earliest document still extant written in a Tai language (as distinct from Sanskrit or Khmer or Mon).[13] Indeed, King Ram Khamhaeng (1279?–1299?) is credited with having originated the script, which, with some changes, is still used in Thailand today.

By the time of King Ram Khamaeng, Theravada Buddhism was the established religion of the kingdom.[14] The inscription describes what must have been considered one of, if not the major acts of royal merit making, the presentation of *kathina* robes to monks, that is, the presentation of robes (and other offerings) at the end of the rainy season. What is significant in this act is that the king travelled in a procession to a monastery some two kilometers away from the walled city itself. It was at this monastery, where the monks were what is known as " forest dwellers " (Araññavāsi), the senior monk of the kingdom, the " Mahathera Sangharaja, the sage who has studied the scriptures from beginning to end, who is wiser that any other monk in the kingdom."[15] The fact that the senior monk of the kingdom dwelt outside the walls of the city reflects a separation of religion and power that had not existed in the classic cities of mainland Southeast Asia.

Still, while the fundamental relationship between religion and power was expressed in the king's making meritorious offerings to the Sangha, it was also important in Sukhothai, as in every other Theravada Buddhist capital up to modern times, that the king reside in a capital that was cosmologically oriented. In the " Great Relic " (Mahadhatu) shrine was to be found the " magical and spiritual center of the kingdom " of Sukhothai.[16] According to Ram Khamaeng's inscription, the temple of the Great Relic Shrine held statues of the Buddha, including " statues eighteen cubits in height " and was the residence for members of the " city dwelling " (Nāgaravāsi) order of the Sangha.[17] The city itself was surrounded by a triple wall, each of which was separated by a moat. The walled city was probably occupied mainly by royalty and by the monks who resided in the various temple monasteries; the common people may be assumed to have lived beyond the walls. The main market, referred to in the inscription by a Thai rendering of the Persian term, bazaar, was located north of the city.[18] Southwest of the city was a dam that held back a reservoir. From this reservoir, water was canalized through canals and streams and moats to provide for the needs of the city's population.

One final feature of Sukhothai might also be noted as it also was a characteristic feature of most traditional Southeast Asian cities in Theravada Buddhist Southeast Asia. In addition to the association of the city with the cosmos, and with Buddhist merit, the city was also associated with the most powerful spirit of the kingdom.[19] The shrine to the national god of Sukhothai, a god known as Phra Kapung (" holy and exalted "), was not located in the city itself but on a hill south of the city.

Although it is the politicoreligious capitals of the traditional agrarian states such as Sukhothai and Ayutthaya in Thailand, Pegu and Ava in Burma, Oudong and Phnom Penh in Cambodia, and Luang Prabang and Vientiane in Laos that dominate the histories of Theravada Buddhist Southeast Asia from the end of the thirteenth century until the middle of the nineteenth century, these were not the only types of cities that existed in the region during this period. There were also dotted about the region a number of centers whose importance was primarily a consequence of their being the sites of an important shrine. Shrine towns were by no means always seats of political authority, as can be seen in the case of Dagon (Rangoon), which prior to British rule was merely a small village important only because it was the site of the Shwe Dagon pagoda. Such other shrine centers as Côm Thông in northern Thailand, That Phanom in northeastern Thailand, and Phra Phutthabat in central Thailand have remained important to this day solely because of the famous " reminder " of the Buddha with which they are associated. Save for during the time of the year when pilgrims flocked to pay the annual ritual homage to the " remainder," these towns had very small populations.[26]

Far more important than shrine centers were trading centers. The greatest concentration of trading centers was to be found in what is today Burma. Important among these were Moulmein, Martaban, Syriam (this latter being located across the river from what is today Rangoon), and Tavoy and Mergui, which were sometimes subject to the traditional kingdom of Siam rather than to Burma. Nakhon Sithammarat on the isthmus in what is today southern Thailand also continued to be a major entrepôt in traditional times as it had been in earlier centuries.

Certain capitals of the agrarian states also had significant trading functions. Pegu, in lower Burma, which had been the capital of a Mon-dominated state in lower Burma from 1369 until 1539 and then the capital of a Burman-dominated state that included both lower and upper Burma from 1599 until 1613, was also the residence for much of the same period of those foreigners (Indians, Chinese, and later Europeans) who organized the international trade in which Burma was involved. It is significant for the later history of Burma that when the capital of Burma was moved to upper Burma in the early part of the seventeenth century, the political and economic functions of Pegu were separated. Port towns in lower Burma became the new trading centers of the country, while the political capital was removed far inland and divested of its economic capacities.

The traditional Theravadin capital city which, by reputation at least, was important both as a political and trading center, was Ayutthaya, the capital of traditional Siam from 1350 until 1767:

Ayutthaya's reputation as an " emporium of the East " (however ill-deserved) rests largely upon her role as a focus for the transshipment of goods between Europe/India and China/Japan during the fairly frequent and relatively prolonged peaceful interludes of the 16th and 17th centuries; further, this function appears to have been fulfilled, albeit in a minor way and intermittently, from the very inception of this capital which . . . was coincident with the abandonment of overland routes following the deterioration of Mongol power. The nature of the Chinese junk traffic appears a major factor in the development of the Ayutthaya entrepôt. . . . [21]

In 1767, Ayutthaya was destroyed by Burmese armies, after which it was abandoned as the capital of Siam. A new capital was built at Thonburi-Bangkok, on the Cao Phraya River as Ayutthaya had been, but located nearer the coast. Given its location, it was not long before the new capital became a major port. Thus, in marked contrast to the capital of Burma, which at the time was located far away from its chief port, Siam's capital became one with the country's major port. As a result, the Siamese capital remained an important city during the colonial period, while the Burmese capital did not.

Whereas participation in international trade proved to be a major factor in determining why certain cities emerged and achieved importance in traditional Theravada Buddhist Southeast Asia, involvement in domestic trade never achieved so significant a role. Almost all internal trade was localized, each city drawing its immediate hinterland for its needs. No hierarchy of market towns emerged, nor did periodic markets develop in mainland Southeast Asia as they did, for example, in China.

What hierarchies of cities and towns existed in traditional mainland Southeast Asia depended almost exclusively on the politicoreligious functions filled by those centers. Throughout the traditional period—that is, from the beginning of the fourteenth century until the middle of the nineteenth century when Western colonial powers attained dominance in the region—these hierarchies were often rearranged to reflect the fortunes of war. The almost incessant conflict between the Theravada Buddhist polities led to the destruction of existing capitals, the establishment or reconstruction of new capital cities, and the rise and decline of numerous secondary centers. This process continued right into the nineteenth century. [22] In Thailand, for example, the emergence of the new Cakkri dynasty at the end of the eighteenth century was associated with the founding of a new capital, Bangkok (which was made the capital of the country in 1782). The early Cakkri kings pursued a policy of expansion toward Siam's neighbors to the north and east. Following the Lao-Siamese War of 1827–1828, Siamese forces completely destroyed the Lao capital of Vientiane; Vientiane was not resurrected until after the French established their hegemony over Laos at the end of the nineteenth century. Pressured by both the Siamese and the Vietnamese, the Cambodian rulers changed the site of their capital three times in the nineteenth century. From 1618 up to the 1830s the capital was at Oudong, a city located on the Tonlé Sap river upstream from the present-day capital of Phnom Penh. In the 1830s the Khmer moved their capital to Phnom Penh, a city that had been the capital in the sixteenth century. However, when Phnom

Penh was destroyed by the Thai, it was abandoned again in favor of Oudong. In 1866, after the French established their protectorate over Cambodia, the capital was moved yet again to Phnom Penh, where it was to remain until the present day.

The most complex political history of cities in traditional Theravada Buddhist Southeast Asia is to be found in Burma. During the reign of the Konbaung kings, the last kings to rule an independent Burma, the capital was moved no less than six times in a little more than one hundred years.[23] All the capital cities involved lay in upper Burma on or near the Irrawaddy River in what is considered the heartland of Burman civilization. The shift of the capital from Shwebo, then to Ava, then to Amarapura, back to Ava, to Amarapura again, and finally to Mandalay reflected the troubled times that Burma experienced during the reigns of the last kings. Problems surrounding the emergence of a new dynasty, wars with Siam and Arakan and, finally, the two Anglo-Burman wars of 1824–1826 and 1852, whereby the Burmese kings were forced to cede part of their kingdom to the British Empire—all were reflected in the rise and collapse of the chief cities of Burma during this period.

In the history of Mandalay, the last capital of the Burmese kingdom, built by the great king Mindon in 1857,[24] we can trace many of the patterns that characterize the traditional capital city of Theravada Buddhist Southeast Asia. Following the annexation of lower Burma by the British, the site of the capital city of Amarapura was deemed to be inauspicious, and efforts were made to settle on a new site that would prove more fortunate for the country. Mandalay hill, like Mt. Popa near Pagan, although to a lesser degree, was believed to embody many of the characteristics of a sacred mountain. At the time of the founding of Mandalay, a myth was current that the Buddha had visited Mandalay hill during his lifetime, and had prophesied that a great capital would be built at the foot of the hill. After Mandalay was founded, the myth was given concrete representation in the form of a large standing image of the Buddha halfway up Mandalay hill. The iconography of this image was unusual, since with the right hand it pointed " with steadfact finger full at the glittering central spire of the palace rising gracefully over the throne of the Ruler of Existence."[25] Similar phrophesies claimed to have been made by the Buddha about the future founding of a capital city were commonly associated with capital cities in Theravada Buddhist Southeast Asia.

The site of Mandalay was associated with the Buddha in yet another way. Also located near the site was the Arakan Pagoda enshrining the famed Maha Muni image, an image of the Buddha that had formerly been the palladium of the kingdom of Arakan and greatly revered by Burmese Buddhists then as today.[26] The astrologers and monks who helped King Mindon decide on a site for a new capital took into account the sacredness of both the Arakan Pagoda and Mandalay hill. The site chosen was approximately halfway between these two places.

The capital city proper, the *myo* within which the King, the royal family, and the chief nobles lived and the major monasteries and main government offices were situated, was surrounded by walls:

The last royal capital of Burma, Mandalay . . . was designed as a square corresponding to the four cardinal directions and centered around the palace. The gates of the capital were marked with the signs of the zodiac. . . . Thereby the capital—and within it the palace—symbolized the centre of the universe in a microcosmic sense, surrounded (just like Mount Meru) by constellations. Particularly the spire (Pyathat) of the palace above the king— as the throne of Mandalay under him—was . . . conceived as the center of the universe. The royal throne was a microcosm in relation to the empire, and the empire in relation to the universe.[27]

The walls were a mile and one-eighth long and were, in turn, surrounded by a moat. The homes of the common people and of " aliens," the markets, the workshops of the craftsmen and the shops, were located beyond the walls of the capital city. In contrast to Chinese and medieval European cities, the walls of a traditional Theravadin city were built not so much to serve as barriers against potential invaders as to demarcate a sacred space, although, it must be noted, the sacredness of the Therevadin city was not believed to derive solely from the geomancy of the palace and other buildings within the walled capital.

Like the rulers of other Theravadin cities, King Mindon believed it necessary to mobilize the support of local spirits to protect the city. Among the more important spirits, or *nats*, regarded as affecting the prosperity of Mandalay were the Mahagiri *nats* at Mount Popa near Pagan, the *nats* of Mandalay hill, and the *nats* that guarded the capital city itself. For Burmese cities, as for some other cities in traditional Theravadin Southeast Asia, the spirits that were believed to guard a city were those of certain unfortunate people who were buried alive under the gates of the city, the corners of its walls, the palace gates, or the throne itself.[28] There is some debate as to whether or not this custom of human sacrifice was followed when Mandalay was founded, but it had been observed at the founding of previous Burmese capitals.[29]

Although King Mindon, like other Theravadin rulers, ensured that the city was protected by spirits and that it was oriented cosmologically, his primary efforts to draw upon sacred power in ensuring the prosperity of his kingdom followed orthodox Buddhist patterns. King Mindon is still remembered for his great acts of merit, the greatest of which was unquestionably the convening of what the Burmese hold to have been the Fifth Buddhist Council. Convened in 1871, this council had as its purpose the purification and confirmation of the Buddhist canon. Although the council succeeded neither in gaining the support of Sanghas in other Theravada Buddhist countries nor even in effecting unity among the Burmese Sangha,[30] it did result in the construction of what has been described as " the biggest Bible in the world."[31] The text of the *tripiṭaka*, after having been agreed on by the most learned of Burmese monks in sessions that lasted over a five-year period, was engraved upon stones. The 729 engraved " pages " of the scriptures, each of which had their own shrine located at the Kutho-daw (" royal merit ") temple monastery remain to this day as graphic reminders of the great merit that King Mindon acquired.[32]

King Mindon also undertook many other acts of merit, including the construction of temple monasteries in Mandalay and its vicinity. His greatest effort, however, came to naught. Four years before his death, he began the construction of a huge pagoda east of Mandalay. The size of this projected shrine was so immense that a French architect estimated that it would take 84 years to complete with 5,000 men working every day full time.[33] At the time of Mindon's death, only the basement of the shrine has been constructed, and no one after Mindon attempted to complete the project. Mindon's dream of constructing the largest pagoda in the Theravada Buddhist world proved as ephemeral as his dream of reuniting all of Burma under his rule. What is worth noting about Mindon's sponsorship of the building of Buddhist monuments is that they were often built outside the walls of the city. Like Sukhothai and all capitals of Theravada Buddhist states, but unlike the classic cities, religious power was not concentrated solely within the walls of the city.

Although Mindon failed to build the largest pagoda in the Theravada Buddhist world, he did succeed, however, in constructing a new city. The move from Amarapura to Mandalay is said to have involved the resettlement of 150,000 people.[34] The population of the city included not only native Burmans, but also a number of " alien " communities. Among the most important of these was that of the Chinese, most of whom were engaged in trade.[35] In addition to the Chinese, other non-Burmans living in Mandalay included tribal people, Shans, and Westerners, of whom many were not British.[36] Most of these non-Burman groups specialized in some form of trade, and all lived in their own separate and distinctive quarters. Although the number of " aliens " in Mandalay, as in all traditional cities in Theravada Buddhist Southeast Asia, was few, the presence of these distinctive communities foreshadowed the pluralism that was later to characterize the colonial city.

Other distinctive quarters in Mandalay were inhabited by artisans employed in a common craft:

> As in all Eastern towns, those who occupy themselves with a regular handi-craft all flock together. Thus the umbrella-makers and the sellers of saddlery live to the south of the palace, vendors of bamboo-work and lacquered boxes to the west, while the potters and miscellaneous goods shops are mostly along the street that leads to Paya Gyi, the Arakan pagoda.[37]

Such occupationally distinctive quarters can still be found in Southeast Asian cities. The area around the Arakan pagoda in Mandalay, for example, is the only place to find the craftsmen who make the " crowns " (*hti*) placed on tops of pagodas. One street in Bangkok is known as the place where one goes to buy the various artifacts used in Buddhist rituals. A particular street in Chiangmai in northern Thailand is known locally as the " silver village," because that is where the silver craftsmen in the area are concentrated.

Among the most conspicuous inhabitants of Mandalay in the reign of King Mindon were the monks. At the time of his successor, King Thibaw, a king not noted for his piety, they are estimated to have numbered 10,000 and in the reign of Mindon they must undoubtedly have numbered many more. We are told that " King Mindon used to give alms to five thousand of them daily."[38]

Finally there were the members of the ruling class of traditional Burma, consisting of members of the royal family together with the nobles, visually distinguishable by their dress. It was this small ruling elite that was stripped of its power and deprived of its distinctive position in the city of Mandalay when the British conquered upper Burma in 1882.

Under British rule, Mandalay was transformed from the center of the universe into a small provincial town.[39] For many years the palace remained as a monument to Burma's royal past, but during World War II it was destroyed by allied bombing. The focus of Burma during the colonial period ceased to be the palace and became instead the port located in Rangoon.

Traditional Cities in Vietnam

In urban patterns, as in other patterns that were expressions of power in traditional Vietnam, the Vietnamese attempted to emulate Chinese models. The efforts at emulation were most successful in the Tonkin Delta, where a long history of settlement and of Chinese influence combined to render the transplanting of Chinese urban models relatively successful. In southern Vietnam where the Vietnamese city had a shorter history and had usually began as a military outpost in an area originally populated by Indianized Southeast Asians, the Chinese model ran more against the grain.

The greatest development of traditional cities in Vietnam occurred during the Nguyen dynasty, whose founder, Gia Long, unified Vietnam in 1802. Under the Nguyen there was a proliferation of administrative centers—31 provincial capitals and 250 or more district capitals.[40] Although the Chinese model specified that the primary function of the city or town was administrative in that it served as the residence of mandarins whose authority derived from the power of the capital, which in turn derived its power from the cosmos itself, not all traditional Vietnamese cities owed their importance to political and administrative functions. A number of cities in southern Vietnam under the Nguyen were, for example, important as port cities. Sir John Crawfurd, who in his description of his visit to Vietnam in 1822, listed Hatien, Saigon, Nha-Trang, Phu-Yen, Qui Nhon, Fai-fo, Tourane (Danang), Hué, and Hanoi as important port cities—all but the last of these being in southern Vietnam.[41] Given its role as a port city in traditional Vietnam and given its later importance as the major city of French Indochina, it is of some interest to learn what Saigon was like in premodern times.

Saigon had originally been a small provincial outpost of Cambodia known as Prei Kor. In 1623, the Khmer gave the Vietnamese the right to establish a custom house in Prei Kor, " and this was one of the things leading to Vietnamese settlement in the Mekong delta."[42] By the end of the seventeenth century, the Vietnamese had annexed much of what is today southern Vietnam, including the town of Saigon and Saigon became a southern outpost of Vietnamese civilization. Nevertheless something of its previous Southeast Asia character remained even into the nineteenth century. The following is a description of Saigon as seen by Crawfurd in 1822:

The town properly called Saigun, is about three miles distant from the residence of the Governor of the province . . . Straggling houses nearly join the fort and residence of the Governor with Saigun . . . The principal bazaar is a wide and spacious street. The numerous shops were not rich, but sufficiently neat. The principal articles exposed for sale were Chinese earthenware, manufactured silks, chiefly of Tonquin, and of the place itself, and commonly made up into dresses, paper, and great quantities of amazingly coarse tea from the northern provinces . . . There was abundance of poultry . . . Here were also plenty of hogs, of an excellent breed. The want of intercourse, direct or indirect, with European nations, was sufficiently evinced by the general absence of European manufacturers. . . .

Women alone attended in the shops . . . A large proportion of the houses are covered with tiles instead of thatch . . . The Chinese of Saigun amount in all to between three and four thousand in number. They have several temples, and that which belongs to the Chinese of Canton is the handsomest building of the sort I have anywhere seen.[43]

From this description it can be seen that Saigon was in 1822 probably more important as a commercial center than it was as an administrative center. It is worth noting that by Crawfurd's estimate, the Chinese living in Saigon would have accounted for upward of ten per cent of all the Chinese living anywhere in Vietnam at the time.[44] Again, as in the case of certain cities in traditional Theravada Buddhist Southeast Asia, we may see in traditional Saigon the embryo of the subsequent " great " or " primate " city of modern Saigon.

But in 1822, Saigon was not the preeminent city of Vietnam. That honor belonged unequivocally to Hué. In Hué, the Vietnamese elite made its most supreme effort, albeit a belated one, to create a facsimile of Peking. Just as the Nguyen emperors and their attendants attempted to model themselves on Chinese prototypes, so the stage on which they performed had to mirror as closely as possible the architecture, the location of buildings, and the relationships in space found in the Chinese capital.[45] Like the Theravadin city, the Sino-Vietnamese capital was also oriented with reference to the cosmos. At the core of the city, and at the center of the world, was the " forbidden city " with the palace in its center. Crawfurd, who was not permitted to enter the " forbidden city," described it and the palace in these terms:

The palace is situated within a strong citadel, consisting of two distinct walls, or ramparts. Within this we were not invited; but the roof of the palace itself was distinguishable by its yellow colour; and one handsome temple, consecrated to the royal ancestors of the King, was also noticed. This last, which has no priests attached to it, was the only place of worship within the new city.[46]

All the buildings in the " forbidden city " were oriented along a geomantically correct south-north axis.[47] Surrounding the " forbidden city " was a second walled city, called the " Imperial city," and surrounding this was yet another city, the " capital city." Again, geomantic principles determined the orientation and location of buildings, gates, and spaces within each of these outer cities.

What is notable in comparing traditional Hué with any traditional city in

Theravadin Southeast Asia is the absence, as Crawfurd observed, of religious edifices comparable to the temple monasteries. Cosmic harmony alone determined the religious basis of power in Vietnam, whereas cosmic harmony and acts of religious piety that led the king to demonstrate his subservience to a faith were essential in the legitimation of rulers in Theravada Buddhist Southeast Asia. Both Theravadin and Vietnamese capital cities were sacred cities, but the " sacred " had very different implications for the two civilizations.

Hué was not exclusively a politicoreligious center. Its total population of between fifty and sixty thousand in 1822 included only a small number of royalty and mandarins. By far the biggest segment of the population—numbering between twelve and thirteen thousand—was made up of soldiers.[48] Again this fact contrasts to what is known about Theravada Southeast Asian capital cities. It suggests that power was more tenuously held in Vietnam, at least relative to the general populace, than it was in Theravada Buddhist Southeast Asia.

Although Hué did serve certain commercial functions, trade was less important there than in Saigon in 1822. The Chinese community, in whose hands most of the foreign trade of traditional Vietnam lay, numbered only about 600 in 1822.[49] In general, Crawfurd found the general populace of Hué less well off than their counterparts in Saigon: " the greater number of the habitations are poor structures of thatch and bamboo."[50]

The general populace does not appear to have been overawed by the presence of the court; indeed, they did not fully comprehend the meanings of the complicated rituals that took place in the city:

> Nguyen court records document episodes in which the people of Hué interfered with imperial processions through the streets, offered little respect of officials in sedan chairs, and indulged in hooliganism. Hué in the early 1880's was renowned for its discordantly noisy food peddlars, whom a desperate Minh-mang tried to license. The Sino-Vietnamese imperial dream coexisted uneasily with the Southeast Asian market town.[51]

With the establishment of colonial rule in Vietnam, Hué suffered much the same fate as Mandalay. It declined in importance relative to Saigon and also Hanoi, the commercial and administrative centers, respectively, of French Indochina. However, unlike the British in Burma, the French in Vietnam maintained the imperial court. Thus, the rituals of a Sinified Vietnamese court continued to be performed as empty survivals from the past right up to World War II. With the abdication of Bao Dai, the residual importance of Hué as a center of power was totally eliminated. Although the old city was scarred by the war, enough of it still remains today to serve as a museum for future generations of Vietnamese.

While Mandalay and Hué and cities like them continue to attract the attention of those interested in premodern culture in Southeast Asia, they provide only a limited insight into urban life in the region as it developed during the colonial period. To understand fully modern urbanization in mainland Southeast Asia, we must explore the characteristics of the " great cities " of the region, which emerged during the colonial period.

COLONIAL CITIES IN PLURAL SOCIETIES

Types of Cities During the Colonial Period

The establishment of European domination in mainland Southeast Asia radically transformed both the cities of the region and the societies in which these cities were located. Europeans had played a significant role in the urban life of Southeast Asia since the sixteenth century, but prior to the nineteenth century there were no European " garrison fort settlements " or " permanent stabilized centers " of colonial power in mainland Southeast Asia such as were to be found in peninsular and insular Southeast Asia.[52] Initially, the Europeans in the cities of mainland Southeast Asia engaged in a limited international trade and were restricted to segregated quarters in capital cities or port towns.

European colonial rule was first established in mainland Southeast Asia following the Anglo-Burman war of 1824–1826. However, the full impact of European influence on mainland Southeast Asian societies was not really felt until after 1869, the year the Suez canal was opened. The industrial revolution spurred Europeans' searches for overseas markets for their manufactured goods and for sources of raw materials. Once the Suez canal was opened, Europeans found that their trade with Asia could be carried out far more efficiently and less expensively than had previously been the case. From the 1870s on, trade became as much a characteristic feature of European influence in mainland Southeast Asia as was political domination. Economic colonialism and political colonialism frequently went hand in hand, although such was not always the case, as developments in Thailand and Laos reveal for differing reasons. Although Thailand, for example, never became a European dependency, it became solidly incorporated into the European sphere of economic influence. Laos, on the other hand, became a European dependency, yet its economy changed little throughout the colonial period. Whether the impact of European influence was felt at the political, the economic, or at both levels, however, it led to radical changes in mainland Southeast Asian societies and in particular in the cities and towns of these societies.

By far the greatest changes in urban life in mainland Southeast Asia during the colonial period took place in those cities that were also ports. The major port cities—Rangoon, Bangkok, and Saigon-Cholon—grew so rapidly that they developed into the " primate cities " or cities qualitatively different in size and importance than the other urban settlements of the countries in which they were located.[53] In Thailand, Bangkok's primacy went unchallenged; Bangkok was its only international port. In Burma and Indochina, however, other cities besides Rangoon and Saigon-Cholon also played major roles in international trade. The ports of Haiphong in Tonkin and Moulmein in Burma, for example, both showed characteristics similar to those of the primate cities. Phnom Penh, although located inland and economically dependent on Saigon, also played an important role in the regulation of trade into and out of Cambodia.

Both the "primate city" and those other cities that played important roles in international trade during the colonial period developed certain distinctive characteristics. Around the ports with their associated godowns or warehouses, where goods awaited shipment in and out of the country were stored were to be found the major trading and processing firms that regulated the import of manufactured goods and the export of raw materials such as rice, teak, rubber, and other products. In the major colonial cities Western banks were set up to provide credit, regulate capital investment, and transmit profits to the home country. The areas around the ports and in the central business districts where the international trading functions of the great cities were organized took on a distinctly Western character.

The character of cities in mainland Southeast Asia during the colonial period reflected not only their role in international trade but also their political role. Although the traditional capital cities of mainland Southeast Asia such as Mandalay, Bangkok, Phnom Penh, or Hué had, in theory, been the centers of their respective kingdoms, their importance had been more symbolic than real. Communication between capital city and outlying areas was difficult and time consuming,[54] with the result that provincial centers in traditional Southeast Asia enjoyed considerable local autonomy. In the very difficult geographical terrain of the Shan States and other parts of upper Burma, northern Thailand, upper Laos, and northwestern Tonkin, local lords were often, in effect, politically independent of the major centres of the region.

During the colonial period the semi-independence on the part of outlying chiefs was radically curtailed and often eliminated. This was as true in Thailand, which had never become a colonial dependency, as it was in the colonies of Burma and Indochina. Political centralization was made possible by the improvements effected in communications during the colonial period. By the end of the nineteenth century, the great cities of Southeast Asia were all connected by telegraph lines to the outside world, and provincial centers were starting to be linked by telegraphy to the major cities of Rangoon, Bangkok, Saigon-Cholon, and Hanoi. Of particular importance to the centralization of authority in mainland Southeast Asia during the colonial period was the development of railways. The first railways in the region were built by the British in Burma shortly after the opening of the Suez canal, and by the end of the nineteenth century the beginnings of rail systems also existed in Indochina and Thailand as well. These systems were expanded throughout the colonial period, until by 1940 there were over 2,000 miles of rail lines in both Burma and Thailand and only a little less than that length in Indochina.[55]

Political centralization was not, however, a function of improved communications alone. Rather, in each country of mainland Southeast Asia during the colonial period, political centralization was undertaken as a deliberate policy. Local chiefs were replaced by or transformed into bureaucrats responsible to functionally defined centralized offices.[56] In Burma and Thailand, political centralization was focused on the same cities as were also centers of international trade, that is, on Rangoon and Bangkok. Political centralization in French Indochina, however, was more complicated. Although Saigon-Cholon became the economic center of Indochina, Hanoi became its main political center. The fact that Indochina was composed of five constituent polities was reflected, however, in the fact that Hué in Annam, Phnom Penh in Cambodia, and

Vientiane and Luang Prabang in Laos all continued to have greater political significance than did secondary cities in Thailand or Burma.

In addition to the major cities that developed in mainland Southeast Asia during the period of colonial rule, Western domination of this part of the world resulted in the emergence of a number of new towns, which grew up primarily to serve specialized Western needs. Towns such as Dalat in Vietnam and Taunggyi in Burma, for example, were built as " hill stations," which served as retreats for Westerners who wished to escape the heat of the lowland cities during the height of the hot season.

The typical provincial town in mainland Southeast Asia during the colonial period was neither a " hill station " nor a secondary port city such as Haiphong or Moulmein. Rather, it was a node in the administrative and economic networks of the countries in which it was located. Generally speaking, provincial towns remained quite small during the colonial period, their growth rate being far less marked than that of the major port/capital cities. Indeed, one of the more outstanding features of urban change in mainland Southeast Asia during the colonial period was the increasing disparity in size between the great metropolises of the area and all other towns of the region. During the colonial period, Rangoon and Saigon-Cholon became two to three times larger than the next largest cities in British Burma and French Indochina respectively, while Bangkok became perhaps ten times larger than the next largest city in Thailand. Their dominance, politically and economically, as well as their size, led observers to term cities such as Bangkok, Rangoon, and Saigon-Cholon " primate cities."[57]

Economic Role of the Colonial City

Economic life in the primate cities of mainland Southeast Asia during the colonial period reflected the fact that these cities were major *loci* for European capitalist expansion. It was in these cities that the capitalist firms such as shipping companies, warehousing enterprises, processing factories, and international financial institutions were located. Economic life in these cities was not, however, organized exclusively to meet capitalist demands. Coexisting with the " firm-centered " economy was what has been termed the " bazaar-centered " economy.[58]

The bazaar-centered economy has been described as " one in which the total flow of commerce is fragmented into a very great number of unrelated person-to-person transactions."[59] In a recent article, McGee has further elaborated on the model of the bazaar-centered economy.[60] In addition to the fragmentation of trade, he notes that the bazaar-centered economy is one in which labor is recruited primarily through family ties rather than through contract. For the " enterprise" in the bazaar-centered economy, capital is scarce, hours of work irregular, regular wages are not paid, inventories are small, relations between seller and customers personal, prices negotiable and fixed costs negligible. Many features of the "enterprise" in the bazaar-centered economy are the same as those of the peasant system of production found in the rural areas.[61] For this reason, McGee has argued that those engaged in bazaar-centered enterprises in the cities can be considered " peasants in the cities." Both the bazaar-centered enterprise in the city and the peasant system of production in the countryside contrast with the capitalist firms that regulate trade and processing in the city and may also exist in the countryside in the form of plantations, mines, and so on. In other words, the economic " dualism," that is, the coexistence of capital-intensive and labor-intensive economic systems, which has been recognized as characterizing colonial societies as a whole, is also to be found within the colonial great cities.[62] Moreover, as we shall see, economic dualism did not disappear with the ending of the colonial period, but still exists in Southeast Asia, including in its major cities, today.

Although the division of the economy between firm-centered and bazaar-centered sectors was an overriding feature of the colonial city, it was not the only significant economic characteristic. Aside from factories built to process raw materials for export, industrial manufacturing was almost totally absent from the colonial economy. A few factories, such as cement plants in Haiphong and Bangkok, match and paper factories at Hanoi, Ben Thuy, and Ham Rong in Tonkin and in Bangkok and Rangoon, and a number of distilleries located throughout the region were established during the colonial period, but they employed only a small proportion of the total labor force in mainland Southeast Asian societies during that period. In Burma in 1940 there were 1,027 factories employing just under 90,000 people out of a total population of about 16 million.[63] Well over half of those employed in manufacturing worked for firms that processed raw materials and foodstuffs for export. In Indochina in 1937 the total number employed in both mining and manufacturing was 140,000 out of a total population of about 23 million.[64] All but a small number of this total were employed in mining and in processing goods for export. In Thailand in 1937, " manufacturing industries," again most of which involved the processing of rice and other products for export, employed 111,000 people out of a total population of $14\frac{1}{2}$ million.[65]

Whereas " modern " industry was hardly developed at all during the colonial period, small-scale traditional craft production, such as weaving, pottery making, metal working, lacquerwork, basketry, matmaking, wood carving and furniture making continued to exist during the colonial period, mainly to meet local demand. Although these handicrafts were produced primarily in rural areas, every city and town in mainland Southeast Asia during the colonial period included in its population at least a small number of craft specialists.[66] Although the production of handicrafts continued during the colonial period, its importance declined, however, as cheap manufactured goods from the industrial countries were imported into mainland Southeast Asia.

By far the largest percentage of the labor force in the colonial cities of Southeast Asia were employed in the tertiary sector. The colonial Southeast Asian city " was a city of clerks, retailers, administrators, hawkers, retail merchants and transport workers."[67] For example, in 1931, 62 per cent of the labor force of Rangoon was engaged in tertiary occupations, while only 24 per cent was engaged in industry.[68]

Not only were large percentages of the working populations of colonial cities employed in tertiary rather than industrial occupations, but most of those employed in the tertiary sector were in occupations connected with the bazaar-centered economy:

> The proliferation of petty traders, pedicab drivers, footpath astrologers, trinket vendors and food sellers in the colonial city was not a reflection of growing demand, but simply the result of employment opportunities not growing at a fast enough rate to absorb city population.[69]

More precisely, the employment opportunities created by economic development focused on international trade were not sufficient to provide opportunities for all those employed in cities to find work in the firm-centered or capitalist economy. By the same token, industrial development, being minimal, failed to provide employment opportunities for very many of the people living in cities. Thus, many urban dwellers, some migrants from rural areas, but also including many born in the city, could find employment only in the bazaar-centered economy.

Despite the limited economic opportunities available in the primate cities of Southeast Asia during the colonial period, such cities grew rapidly. Rangoon grew from an estimated 46,000 in 1855 to 400,000 by 1931.[70] Bangkok had already experienced considerable growth prior to the colonial period, its population having risen from approximately 50,000 in 1822 to 300,000–400,000 in 1854–1855.[71] The city continued to grow during the colonial period. In the 1937 census, the total population of the two provinces of Bangkok and adjacent Thonburi was nearly 900,000, of which the greater percentage were urban dwellers.[72] Saigon, as we have already noted from Crawfurd's account, was a city of only several thousand people in 1822,[73] but after the French conquest its numbers began to increase rapidly, and by 1936 Saigon and its twin city Cholon had a total population of 256,000. That Saigon-Cholon was not as large as either Rangoon or Bangkok reflects the fact that in French Indochina there were other cities whose political significance was far greater than that of any of the secondary cities of Thailand and Burma. In 1936, Hanoi had a population of 149,000 and Phnom Penh a population of 103,000.[74]

During the colonial period, migration greatly swelled the populations of the primate cities of Rangoon, Bangkok, Saigon, and, to a lesser extent, certain other colonial cities in mainland Southeast Asia such as Hanoi and Phnom Penh. Migrants to these cities were drawn primarily by the demand for labor created by the expansion of trade in which the Southeast Asian colonial city played a key role. The majority of migrants were not natives of the countries to whose cities they migrated but " alien Asians."

The alien Asians who settled in the cities of Burma, Thailand, and Indochina tended to specialize in those occupations that were not engaged in by either the natives of the country or the European colonialists. Thus, the economy of the colonial city in mainland Southeast Asia came to be characterized by ethnic specialization by occupation. Such specialization can clearly be seen, for example, in Rangoon's occupation structure in 1931. There Europeans were concentrated in the upper echelons of the colonial administration, in the management of the trading firms and banks, and in the professions. The Chinese were heavily concentrated in middle-level trading occupations, whereas the Indians provided most of the unskilled labor. Middle-level administrative positions were filled mainly by Eurasians. Natives of Burma living in Rangoon at that time were employed mainly as unskilled laborers, as craftsmen, and, to a minor extent, in the professions.[75]

Allowing for the fact that in Saigon-Cholon Indians constituted only a very small percentage of the population and that the overwhelming majority of Asians aliens were Chinese, that city showed much the same pattern of ethnic division of labor as did Rangoon. In Phnom Penh the pattern also obtained, but with Vietnamese as well as Chinese being the most important alien Asians.[76] In Bangkok, Chinese, as well as a small number of Indians and Vietnamese, were specialized by occupation, although Thais rather than Europeans or Eurasians held most government positions.[77]

This ethnic division of labor in the major cities of Southeast Asia during the colonial period extended beyond the city to the entire local economy. For example, until quite recently, commercial rice mills upcountry as well as in the capital cities of Thailand and Indochina have almost always been owned and operated by those of Chinese descent. The question of why there should have been such a " persistent tendency toward specialization along ethnic lines"[78] in colonial societies has received considerable attention by social scientists concerned with understanding the process of change in Southeast Asia.

The Colonial City in a Plural Society

J. S. Furnivall, an Englishman who served for many years as a colonial official in Burma and who made intensive studies of the political economies of Burma and the Dutch East Indies, characterized the colonial society in which there was an ethnic division of labor as a " plural society." Furnivall's ideas were first articulated just prior to World War I, but his fullest analysis of them occurs in the context of his studies of Burmese and Indonesian colonial societies made just prior to and during World War II.[79] Furnivall defines a plural society as one " comprising two or more elements or social orders which live side by side, yet without mingling, in one political unit."[80] These elements —which we may recognize as distinctive ethnic groups, do not " mingle" because they do not have a common " social will." By this Furnivall means that the different groups that comprise a plural society do not share a common religion or culture that would lead them to agree on the priorities to be set for effecting improvements in life.[81] In contemporary terms, the groups that " mingle " in a plural society can be said not to share any fundamental cultural values.

What the constituent groups in a plural society do share in common is an interest in the market place:

> [T]here is one place in which the various sections of a plural society meet on common ground—the market place; and the highest common factor of their wants is the economic factor.[82]

The interaction of the groups in the market place is not, however, on the same terms. Each group acts in terms if its own values, the social demand these values generate being different in each case:

> Every social want, then, has its economic aspect, and in any community the resultant of such social wants is the economic aspect of its cilvilization or, in other words, the social demand of the community taken as a whole. But, in a plural society, social demand is disorganized; social wants are sectional, and there is no social demand common to all the several elements. [83]

Moreover, the different groups have specialized niches within the economy: " each section comes to have its own functions in production, and there is a tendency towards the grouping of the several elements into distinct economic castes." [84] Caste-like, but not true castes since the plural society, unlike Indian society, lacks the religious sanction that would cement the specialized elements. [85]

According to Furnivall, the ethnic groups or elements that constitute the plural society in Southeast Asia are basically of three types: (a) Europeans, (b) " alien Asians," and (c) natives. The first includes the Europeans who work in colonial dependencies and client states but do not have their permanent residence in the dependencies. Europeans who were colonial administrators or managers of capital-intensive firms (estates, trading companies, and so on) only resided in the colony to carry out their functions; eventually they returned " home " to England, France, or wherever they might come from. For the European businessman, his " life in the tropics centers round his business, and he looks at social problems, political or economic, not as a citizen but as a capitalist or an employer of labor." [86] Although Europeans (and Americans) who lived as temporary residents in Southeast Asia during the colonial period were the subject of attention by novelists (e.g., George Orwell in *Burmese Days*), they have received almost no attention from social scientists. [87]

On the periphery of the European world and holding a rather ambiguous position in it were the Eurasians. As Koop, who has made one of the few studies of Eurasians in Southeast Asia, shows, Eurasians are often descended from Europeans other than those who were the colonial rulers of the country in which they are found. [88] Some Eurasians held European citizenship; others did not. Where they comprised a distinctive group, as they did in Burma, they held a special place in the occupational structure. In Burma, Eurasians were likely to be found working in government service and in the clerical positions of the large trading firms, banks, and other foreign businesses. Eurasians never constituted a very large sector of the population of any society in mainland Southeast Asia. In Burma, where there was a distinctive Eurasian community, the total number of Eurasians there reached perhaps as many as 22,000 just before World War II, over half of whom lived in Rangoon. Their numbers declined following World War II and the creation of an independent Burma. [89] In Indochina, Eurasians tended to be invisible, having been assimilated either to the European or to the native (only rarely to the Asian alien) communities. In Thailand those few Eurasians who did exist also tended to be invisible, having been assimilated into the native Thai community.

Although Europeans living in colonial Southeast Asia have been relatively neglected as objects of study, the same has not been true of the " alien Asians." At first glance it may seem rather strange to group together under a single rubric overseas Chinese and overseas Indians, the two groups that account for the overwhelming majority of " alien Asians " in Southeast Asia. Quite obviously Chinese and Indians come from different cultural backgrounds. These differences notwithstanding, both overseas Chinese and overseas Indians in Southeast Asia (as well as elsewhere in the colonial world) share certain features that make it possible to treat them for some purposes as being of the same type.[90] Both overseas Chinese and overseas Indians living in colonial Southeast Asia had their origins in immigration.[91] Although some Indians and more Chinese had settled in Southeast Asia, and particularly in Southeast Asian cities, prior to the colonial period, large-scale migration was a concomitant of colonialism. It is important to note, however, that the Chinese migrants who arrived during the colonial period found well-established Chinese communities that had long held specialized roles in trade in Southeast Asia. The same was not true for the Indian migrants, who rarely found any niche that antedated the colonial period. Until the end of the nineteenth century most Chinese migrants were " merchantentrepreneurs " who established themselves in existing Chinese-dominated commercial networks.[92] However, by the end of the nineteenth century when large-scale migration of Chinese began, the typical Chinese migrant was very much like the typical Indian migrant. Both were likely to have come from poor backgrounds, usually poor rural backgrounds, to be uneducated and to be without skills or capital. In other words, about all that the migrant brought with him was his labor. Without the necessary capital to finance his own trip to Southeast Asia, the migrant had either to indenture himself or to take out a loan, which, since it was repaid by labor, often amounted to the same thing.[93]

It is important to stress that the overseas Chinese and overseas Indian communities in Southeast Asia did not represent cross sections of their home societies. Those who came were usually strongly motivated by economic values, pushed by the poverty of their home environments and pulled by the opportunities they believed awaited them in Southeast Asia. The migrants were not carriers of the values associated with the elite strata of the societies from which they came.[94]

Initially, most Chinese and Indian migrants were males. This fact was a function of another characteristic of migrants, both Indian and Chinese. Migrants set out from home with the idea that they would work until they had acquired significant savings and then they would return to their homes in India or China. In fact, most overseas Indians did return to India after a sojourn of from five to seven years.[95] Most Chinese returned home as well, the relative proportion who stayed rather than returned being a function of the degree of economic opportunity and security available at different periods of time in China vis-à-vis the host country.[96] The fact that the normal pattern was for the migrant to return provided both the overseas Indians and Chinese themselves and the natives of the countries into which they moved with strong evidence that

Indians and Chinese were inherently " aliens " in Southeast Asia. Further, the growth of nationalism in India and China provided an added incentive for overseas Indians and overseas Chinese to maintain their alien status.[97] The governments of the Southeast Asian societies gave legal recognition to the alien status of overseas Chinese and Indians and circumscribed the rights and responsibilities such aliens might have.

Members of overseas Chinese or overseas Indian communities were usually set apart from the native inhabitants of the countries to which they had migrated not only by virtue of being aliens, but by virtue of being concentrated into the same occupations, occupations that were rarely filled by natives or Europeans. Although the conventional picture of the occupational specialization of overseas Indians and Chinese is as moneylenders (in Burma) and middlemen (in all parts of Southeast Asia), respectively, in fact a variety of occupations were filled by both Indians and Chinese. Although some Indians in Burma were moneylenders, many more were unskilled laborers or stevedores who worked at the port in Rangoon for very minimal wages. Although Chinese were more likely than Indians to be middle-level traders, even in Burma, cloth and jewel merchants throughout Southeast Asia are commonly Indians. In Bangkok during the colonial period, Chinese were large-scale merchants, small shopkeepers. hawkers, and unskilled laborers among other occupations.[98] In more general terms, during the colonial period overseas Indians and Chinese were more often members of the urban proletariat than they were merchants.

Being recognized as aliens, the overseas Chinese and Indians were administered in a manner different from that of the rest of the population. In Rangoon, the Indians had communal representatives who met with the officials of the colonial regime. In Saigon-Cholon, Phnom Penh, and elsewhere in Indochina where Chinese were found, Chinese communities—usually grouped together on the basis of dialect differences—were organized as distinctive *congrégations* under their own *chef* and *sous-chef*. Skinner has identified the pattern of leadership in overseas Chinese communities during the colonial period as being fundamentally the same regardless of the country in Southeast Asia in which it might be found. The leader was likely to be a man who was recognized, by virtue of his economic success, as a natural leader of the Chinese community and thus, an excellent choice for the person through whom the government would administer the Chinese community.[99]

Along with being set apart socially and economically, the Indian and Chinese communities were often set apart spatially from the indigenous population. The Indians in Rangoon (and elsewhere) and the Chinese in Bangkok, Rangoon, Saigon-Cholon, and Phnom Penh tended to be concentrated in distinctive quarters of the city.

Although the colonial cities of Southeast Asia included within their populations distinctive groups classified as " Indians " or " Chinese," many overseas Chinese and Indians did not retain all the distinctive cultural characteristics that would mark them as Chinese or Indian. Within the communities of overseas Chinese and Indians were those whose patterns of dress, cuisine, kinship, language usage, and so on were much more similar to patterns found among native Southeast Asians or among Europeans than they were to those of Chinese and Indians in their home countries. What Freedman has said of the overseas Chinese is equally applicable to the overseas Indians: " ' Chinese ' . . . begins to emerge as a label for some kind of political and social status (varying as between countries) and to recede as a name for a way of life or culture."[100] In Thailand, the process of cultural change led eventually to assimilation into Thai culture. Second- and third-generation Chinese in Thailand generally held " double identities," being able to move in both Chinese and Thai communities.[101] In contrast to the overseas Chinese in Thailand, overseas Indians in Burma and overseas Chinese in Indochina, despite cultural change, rarely assimilated to local cultures.

The reason for differences in assimilation patterns can be found in the political, as distinct from the economic, characteristics of colonialism. However similar Thailand may have been to Burma and Indochina in the degree to which it was subjected to Western capitalist expansion, Thais still remained rulers in their own society. This made possible the maintenance of a dominant " social will " (to use Furnivall's term) derived from indigenous culture, that was not true of the colonial society. The European rulers of Burma and Indochina saw little reason for encouraging the assimilation of Chinese or Indians to indigenous cultures, since the values derived from such cultures were not held by Europeans. On the contrary, if any assimilation was to be encouraged, it was the assimilation of natives and Asian aliens alike to Western culture. As we have already seen, assimilation to French culture was a stated end of French rule in Indochina, although the means to effect this end were implemented in only a very limited way. Although the British never advocated assimilation in the same way as did the French, adoption of British cultural patterns by natives and by alien Asians did occur in all British colonies, Burma included. In Thailand, by contrast, the fact that the Thai were the rulers of the country as well as the natives provided a strong impetus to those who saw Thailand as their permanent residence to assimilate to Thai culture.[102]

The " natives " who formed the third division of society in Furnivall's model of plural society were left largely with only residual positions in the political economy of colonial Burma and Indochina. In Thailand, as elsewhere in the region, few natives held management positions in capitalist firms. However, unlike natives elsewhere in the region, native Thai held power in their own society. Not all the " natives " of Thailand were culturally the same as the Siamese who ruled the country, however. Toward certain culturally different groups—notably the Malays, the tribal peoples, and even to some extent the Tai-speaking " Lao " of northern and northeastern Thailand—the Siamese elite engaged in what can only be termed " internal colonialism." Those who were identified as members of these various groups were not allowed access to the same rights and privileges accorded the dominant Siamese. Although other groups, for example, the Mons, were not subjected to disadvantages because of their ethnicity, they tended to occupy rather limited niches in the Thai economy.[103] These qualifications notwithstanding, there was a fundamental difference between a society such as Thailand in which there was a dominant " social will " grounded in indigenous cultural values and the society in which " social will " was fragmented because the dominant political group acted in terms of cultural values that were meaningful in Europe rather than in Southeast Asia. This difference had marked implications for the cultural roles the cities played in mainland Southeast Asian societies both during the colonial period and in the post colonial period as well.

POLITICAL CULTURE AND CONTEMPORARY CITIES IN MAINLAND SOUTHEAST ASIA

The Emergence of Nationalism and the Cultural Role of Cities

During the colonial period the cultural role played by the major cities of Southeast Asia was an ambiguous one.[104] Because of the dominance of Europeans during the period, cultural institutions that purveyed Western culture were very conspicuous in the larger cities. Even in Bangkok, many of the elite sent their children to Catholic or Protestant schools. In addition to schools whose media was English or French and whose curricula were structured along lines similar to those found in schools in England or France, there were also Catholic and Protestant churches and missions and French- and English-language periodicals. In Rangoon, Saigon, Hanoi, and, to some extent, in Bagkok, groups would meet to study the writings of various Western literary figures such as Shakespeare or Molière, or the works of Western political theorists, most notably Marx. Even the architecture of some of the buildings in the major cities of Southeast Asia during the colonial period, not excluding Bangkok, gave expression to Western cultural concepts of the social use of space.

In addition to the forms of Western culture to be found in the cities of colonial Southeast Asia, there were also a variety of cultural forms that served to preserve and promote the traditions of Asian aliens. Every major city had its Chinese temples, lineage halls, and meeting halls for various Chinese associations. Often there were also Chinese-media schools and Chinese-language periodicals as well. In Rangoon, as well as in other cities where there was a significant Indian population, one found Hindu shrines, mosques, and Sikh temples. Indians also established their cultural associations and sometimes published periodicals in one or another Indian language. In Rangoon, schools existed in which the media of instruction was an Indian language. In Bangkok and Phnom Penh, various cultural institutions such as Mahayana Buddhist temples and Catholic churches served the Vietnamese communities. Although Western and alien Asian cultural institutions coexisted in all the major colonial cities of mainland Southeast Asia, the scope of their influence, however, differed considerably. Western cultural patterns and institutions had marked influences on the indigenous populations throughout the larger societies of mainland Southeast Asia, whereas those of the alien Asians were restricted primarily to the

Chinese, Indian, and Vietnamese communities they served. A major exception to this generalization are the nationalist organizations that emerged among the overseas Indians and Chinese and among the migrant Vietnamese. The Indian Congress Party, the KMT, and later the Viet Minh were all to serve to some extent as sources of nationalist ideas for the indigenous peoples of mainland Southeast Asia.

Institutions and forms that gave expression to indigenous cultures in the Southeast Asian societies persisted in the cities and towns during the colonial period. Buddhist shrines and temple monasteries throughout Burma, Thailand, Cambodia, and Laos remained foci of local cultural life, and especially well-known temples such as the Shwe Dagon in Rangoon continued to attract pilgrims from distant as well as local communities. In Vietnam, where the elite culture was strongly discredited by the French conquest, traditional cultural institutions were less influential than were the Buddhist institutions of Vietnam's neighbors. Nonetheless, traditional rituals centering on the emperor were performed in Hué, and traditional Confucian shrines and schools were frequented by Vietnamese in a number of cities in Tonkin, Annam, and to a lesser extent in Cochin China.

Although the indigenous culture continued to be conveyed through traditional institutions in the cities of colonial Southeast Asia, during the colonial period new organizations began to appear that sought to revitalize or reinterpret traditional culture. Woodside's description of the emergence of modern Buddhist organizations in the colonial cities in Vietnam provides an example of the significant role played by new cultural organizations in Southeast Asian cities:

> More modern religious organizations appeared in the cities in the early 1930s, with the rise of urban Buddhist associations like the Cochinchina Association of Buddhist Studies Research ... in Saigon in 1931, the Association of Buddhist Studies of Annam ... in Hué in 1932, and the Association of Vietnamese Buddhism ... in Hanoi in 1934. At first, of course, such Buddhist associations were purely urban phenomena, resting upon a very narrow social base ... The climax to their organizational efforts came in 1935, when the first modern public celebration of the Buddha's birthday in Vietnam was held in the city of Hué. Thousands of Hué residents hung out flags and lined the streets, or attended the ceremonies at the Dieu-de temple. This was a new kind of urban festival, one which superimposed upon the old concept of the city as an administrative center and market the new concept of the city as a consciously planned theater of social (and sectarian) commitments.[105]

Similar to the new Buddhist organizations of the Vietnamese cities were the Young Men's Buddhist Association and the General Council of Burmese Associations in Burmese cities, and the Young Buddhists and the Dharma Society in Thai cities. The new associations often proved to be seedbeds of nationalism and as such were barely tolerated, if they were not actually repressed, by colonial officials. Even in Thailand they were viewed with some suspicion, since certain members of these organizations were known to hold radical views.[106]

The Southeast Asian city during the colonial period did not, then, present a single dominant cultural image. Facets of Western culture, some of which were in conflict with one another, coexisted uneasily with elements of traditional and revitalized indigenous cultures, and cultural traditions imported by migrants from other Asian countries added yet a further dimension to the urban cultural scene. Out of the cultural dialectic between indigenous and Western traditions, which was played out in a context in which the growing nationalism of the Asian aliens was an important catalyst, emerged the different varieties of Southeast Asian nationalism.

The various nationalist movements that developed during the colonial period in mainland Southeast Asian societies looked beyond the elimination of European rule to a time when Southeast Asian political leaders could once again provide a sense of common purpose to the peoples of the countries they led. At such a time, the cities of the region, and particularly the capital cities, would once again have an " orthogenetic " role, that is, a role in defining and disseminating the essence of national culture.[107] The achieving of political independence was regarded as a prerequisite to the cities in Southeast Asia being able to play such a role.

The end of the colonial period did not affect the status of Bangkok as a national capital, as Thailand had been independent throughout the colonial period. In Burma, the colonial capital was retained as the national capital of an independent Burma, while the last traditional capital, Mandalay, retained its subordinate status. In Indochina, however, the end of colonial domination brought about a radical change in the political position of a number of its cities. Under the French, Hanoi, as the seat of the Governor General and the locus for such cultural institutions as the University of Hanoi, the only university in the colony, the Bibliothèque Centrale de l'Indochine, and the École Française d'Extrême-Orient, had been the preeminent center of political culture in Indochina. Although Saigon, Hué, Phnom Penh, and Vientiane had each been the political center of one of the units that made up French Indochina, all had been subordinate to Hanoi culturally as well as politicoadministratively. After the Geneva Agreements of 1954, however, Hanoi, Saigon, Phnom Penh, and Vientiane all became capitals of idependent states, while Hué was relegated to a secondary position within the new State of Vietnam. Hué's position declined yet further in importance when the State of Vietnam was transformed into the Republic of Vietnam and the institution of the monarchy was abolished. It should also be noted that although Vientiane became the center for all political and administrative action in independent Laos, the king of Laos, who served as ceremonial head of state, resided not in Vientiane but in Luang Prabang. The importance of Luang Prabang as the royal capital of Laos ended only in 1975 when the King of Laos abdicated and a People's Republic was established with Vientiane as its capital. Thus, although from 1954 onward Rangoon, Bangkok, Phnom Penh, Vientiane, Saigon, and Hanoi all became capitals of independent states in mainland Southeast Asia, they differed greatly in the roles they came to play as fountainheads of national culture in the region.

Cities and the Displays of National Symbols

The claims of many nationalist groups notwithstanding, there is nothing inherent in the definition of a national identity; rather, such an identity always, in the end, depends on political decisions. Such decisions are evident in the symbols displayed at public celebrations on national holidays, in the school curricula, in the radio and TV programming of the particular country, and in the degree of control of newspapers and periodicals, and so on. This said, it must also be observed that such political decisions are strongly influenced by the knowledge that certain cultural traditions are deeply meaningful to large sectors of the populace of a country, often including those in positions of power.

In recognition of the deep-seated meaning of certain traditions for the peoples of the societies of mainland Southeast Asia, the rulers of these societies have incorporated some indigenous symbols into the national cultures that they have worked to construct in the postcolonial period. For example, in all countries of mainland Southeast Asia, except the Democratic Republic of Vietnam, certain religious holidays have been designated official holidays. Even in the DRV, notice is taken in patriotic speeches made by the leaders of the country of such traditional feast days as Tet, the Vietnamese New Year. In South Vietnam, prior to the end of the war in 1975, many traditional religious holidays were officially observed. A publication under the auspices of the Saigon government in 1969 lists no less than ten such holidays, but gives no attention whatsoever to other official holidays recognized in South Vietnam.[108] Although traditional holidays have been incorporated into the calendars of official national holidays, the observance of Tet in Vietnam, of Songkran, the traditional New Year, in Thailand, of the Bun Bong Fai or fire rocket festival in Laos, of Thadingyut, the festival of lights, in Burma, or of Prachum, the festival for the dead, in Cambodia, remains, however, far more elaborate in the villages than in the cities of mainland Southeast Asia.

Nonetheless, towns and cities in mainland Southeast Asia are used as display sites for certain traditional symbols that have been incorporated into national cultures. In up-country towns in Thailand, for example, a number of Buddhist shrines of long-standing local importance—for example, That Phanom in northeastern Thailand, Phra That Doi Suthep in northern Thailand, Phra That Nakhon Sithammarat in southern Thailand, and Phra Pathom in central Thailand—have been brought under royal patronage and thus linked with the nation. In both Thailand and Laos, images of the Buddha serve as palladiums of their respective nations. The Emerald Buddha, located at a chapel in the Grand Palace complex in Bangkok, and the Phra Bang image, located in a temple in Luang Prabang, the royal capital of Laos, are objects of periodic ritual attention by royalty and other high-ranking officials. In Cambodia, a sacred sword, believed to have been obtained from tribal peoples by rulers of

Angkor, has been ritually displayed in Phnom Penh in ways that serve to link the contemporary Khmer nation with its traditional past.

Traditionally, as we have seen, the capital city of mainland Southeast Asia served through its architecture and the ritual actions of the monarch conducted in it and its environs to link the destiny of the country with sacred powers. Some efforts have been made to use meanings associated with the traditional role of capital cities in the fostering of nationalism in postcolonial mainland Southeast Asia. These efforts have been limited, at the very least, by the fact that the world in which these capital cities exist today is not the precolonial world. Moreover, even when monarchies have persisted into the postcolonial period, they have been invested with meanings quite different from those associated with kingship in traditional societies.

Laos emerged from the colonial period nominally a kingdom with the king of what had formerly been the principality of Luang Prabang as its monarch. Up till quite recently, the last two kings of Luang Prabang continued to perform several completely traditional rituals at the royal capital city. However, these rituals continued to hold symbolic significance for those living in the territories that had formerly comprised the principality of Luang Prabang. In the southern part of Laos, the most symbolically important figure was not the King residing in Luang Prabang but a descendant of the Prince of Campasak.[109] Moreover the day-to-day concerns of national politics were conducted not at Luang Prabang but in the city of Vientiane in central Laos, and rarely involved the King at all. In short, neither King Sisavang Vong (1909–1959) who had been proclaimed by the French in 1941 as King of all Laos nor King Savang Vatthana who came to the throne in 1959 ever succeeded in making the Luang Prabang monarch a modern national symbol for all Laos. Whatever potential the Lao kingship had for becoming such a symbol was aborted in late 1975 when King Savang Vatthana abdicated and Laos became a People's Republic.

In Burma, U Nu, while not a king, attempted to conform as closely as possible to the model of the ideal Buddhist ruler. Like the former kings of Burma, he saw the role of Rangoon as being, at least in part, that of a sacred city wherein actions such as the building of shrines, the offering of charity, and even the propitiation of *nats* (spirits) would ensure the prosperity of the nation. U Nu consciously emulated King Mindon by organizing a Great Buddhist Council; the Sixth (according to Burmese reckoning) Buddhist Council was convened in 1954 and lasted for two years. " The Council's greatest significance was symbolic; it dramatized in unforgettable fashion the government's commitment to the promotion of Buddhism, which was regarded as an essential component of the Burmese national identity."[110] Prior to this, U Nu had obtained government support for the construction of the Kaba Aye or World Peace Pagoda on the edge of Rangoon. Through the construction of this pagoda, it was believed that peace would come not only to Burma but to the whole world. " The Kaba Aye Pagoda was undoubtedly related to a ' vibrational ' ideology according to which numbers, letters, cardinal directions, and such are placed in relation, by magic ritual, with the attainment of certain worldly aims."[111] Theater politics played out on the stage of Rangoon were brought to an abrupt end in Burma in 1962 when Ne Win replaced U Nu as Prime Minister.

In Vietnam, the leaders of both the Democratic Republic of Vietnam and the Republic of Vietnam rejected the symbolism of the traditional monarchy in their efforts to construct postcolonial national cultures. As a result, Hué was relegated to the position of a museum rather than representing the center of the state. Although the actions of a past emperor such as Le Loi (fifteenth century) were deemed sufficiently important to South Vietnamese nationalism to be commemorated by a holiday, they were regarded as important not because they were the actions of an emperor but because, like the actions of other cultural heroes commemorated by national holidays, they symbolized Vietnamese efforts to resist foreign conquerors.

The monarchy in Cambodia survived the colonial period and became an important source for Khmer nationalist themes up till 1970. The architecture of the grand palace in Phnom Penh and the performance, also in Phnom Penh, of such royal rituals as plowing the holy furrow and paying homage to the ancestral spirits of former kings gave the monarchy, and Phnom Penh as the capital, something of a traditional aura. This aura notwithstanding, immediately after independence in 1954, Sihanouk began to redefine the monarchy and, in the process, to redefine Khmer nationalism. After independence, Sihanouk abdicated in favor of his father, and when his father died in 1960 Sihanouk assumed the role of head of state, although he did not take on the legal position of monarch. Unlike his traditional forebears and the rulers of Angkor, Sihanouk did not confine his activities to the capital; rather, he made a concerted effort to make constant contact with the people in all parts of the country and to construct the image of himself as a king of the people. In response, people often addressed him as *Samdech Euv*, " Papa Prince."[112] In 1970, Sihanouk was overthrown by Lon Nol and the Kingdom of Cambodia was transformed into the Khmer Republic. It would appear, in the light of the events of 1975, however, that the link with the traditional monarchy that Sihanouk represented still held meaning for the populace even after the 1970 *coup*. After the establishment of a new government under the National United Front of Cambodia, Sihanouk resumed his role as head of state, although he held no real power. Even this symbolic role ended in 1976, however, when Sihanouk resigned as head of state and was pensioned off.

As in Cambodia, the nature of the monarchy in Thailand has been markedly reinterpreted in modern times. Nevertheless, Bangkok still retains certain characteristics of the traditional sacred city in which resides the king whose actions determine the prosperity of the nation. Although the present royal family of Thailand maintains palaces in Hua Hin in the south and in Chiang Mai in the north, Chitralada Palace in Bangkok remains the chief residence of the family. It is also along the Cao Phraya river in Bangkok that King Phumiphon procedes by royal barge to present robes to members of the Sangha at the end of Buddhist lent each year. The merit accrued by this act of royal charity is still believed by many to redound to the nation as a whole. Bangkok is also the locus for other traditional rituals in which the king fulfills an important role, the most important of such rituals being connected with the coronation ceremony and with funerary rites conducted for high-ranking members of the royal family, the Sangha, and certain other people of major stature. However, many of the state ceremonies carried out traditionally are no longer performed, and even such a recently resurrected ceremony as the ritual first plowing traditionally performed by the monarch is today performed by the Minister of Agriculture rather than the king.[113]

Since 1932, when a group of civilian " promoters " succeeded in transforming Thailand from an absolute to a constitutional monarchy, the meaning of the monarchy for Thai national culture has undergone considerable change. The several national holidays in which the Thai monarchy forms the central image are all of recent vintage: Cakkri Day, which commemorates the founding of the present dynasty; Coronation Day, which commemorates the crowning of King Phumiphon, the present king; the birthday of the present queen, Queen Sirikit; Chulalongkorn Day, during which homage is paid to the ruler during whose reign (1868–1910) modern Thailand was created; and King Phumiphon's birthday, which is also celebrated (on the model of Great Britain) as Thailand's national day. Although the celebration of each holiday involves some linking of the monarchy with Buddhism, what is striking in the way in which the monarchy is portrayed as the institution that unifies all the constituent groups in the nation, Buddhist and non-Buddhist alike. Photographs appear in local newspapers on the King's birthday, for example, showing representatives of the Indian, Chinese, Muslim, or Catholic communities conveying their best wishes to the King. King Phumiphon himself has attempted consciously in recent years to redefine the monarchy so that it is meaningful to minority groups as well as to the dominant Thai. This effort has led the King to travel to remote parts of the Kingdom, far distant from the palace in Bangkok. Although these efforts have been successful to some degree, particularly among tribal peoples in northern Thailand, the modern national meaning of the Thai monarchy is still best understood in the cities and towns rather than in the countryside. The national holidays that focus on the monarchy are observed almost exclusively in towns and cities.

The towns and cities of Thailand also serve as contexts for the display of Buddhist symbols reinterpreted for postcolonial national purposes. Three new national Buddhist holidays have been established in Thailand in modern times—Magha-puja, Visakha-puja, and Asalaha-puja—each of which emphasizes " fundamental " Buddhist doctrines stripped of the particularistic embellishments associated with traditional Buddhist holidays. The first two holidays are also observed in Burma, Cambodia, and Laos; in all four countries observance is limited mainly to urban temple monasteries. In South Vietnam prior to the end of the War, Vesak (Thai, Visakha-puja), on which day the birth, enlightenment, and death of the Buddha is celebrated, Confucius' birthday, and Christmas were all recognized as national holidays. Of these, only Confucius' birthday has a premodern origin in Vietnam, and it had traditionally been observed only by the elite. The presence of all three holidays in the list of national holidays of post-colonial South Vietnam reflects the religious and cultural pluralism of modern South Vietnam rather than the continuity of traditional religion.

Although the national cultures of all modern Southeast Asian societies have incorporated certain symbols from the traditional past and others that represent revitalized or reinterpreted traditional cultures, all these cultures also include symbols whose meanings are grounded in the experience of the colonial confrontation with Western societies and cultures. Hanoi, Saigon, Rangoon, Phnom Penh, and even Vientiane have monuments dedicated to independence. In Bangkok, a comparable monument is the Victory Monument that commemorates Thai success in a 1941 war with the French.

The modern events chosen by the countries of Southeast Asia to be commemorated by holidays reveal considerable variations in the national cultures of the various countries. Thailand has only one such holiday, Constitution Day, which serves to remind the populace that power resides with the people, not with the king. This holiday commemorates the occasion in 1932 when King Prajadhipok was forced by a revolutionary group of civil servants and military officers to grant a constitution to the country. Constitution Day still carries little meaning for Thai villagers, but holds considerable significance for those urban groups committed to the ideal of democracy in Thailand, particularly during those periods in recent Thai history when military rulers ruled the country without a constitution.

In addition to a Constitution Day, Laos also had its Independence Day. An Independence Day and a Constitution Day were also the only modern national holidays created in Cambodia after 1954. After Lon Nol overthrew Sihanouk in 1970, Constitution Day was replaced by a National Day held on another date. After Diem came to power in South Vietnam, two national holidays were established—one to commemorate the founding of the republic and the promulgation of the first constitution and the second, called " Shameful Day," to recall the tragic effects claimed by the government to be consequent upon the signing of the Geneva Agreements. Following the overthrow of Diem in 1963, the first of these holidays was abolished in favor of National Day or Revolution Day, which commemorated not only the founding of the republic but also the end of Diem's regime. In 1965, " Shameful Day " was changed by then Air Marshal Ky to become " National Unity Day for the Liberation of North Vietnam." The government that came to power after Burma gained independence established a considerable number of holidays that commemorated events and people connected with the gaining of independence: Independence Day, Union Day (commemorating the signing of an agreement in 1947, which was the basis for uniting minority groups into an independent Burma), Resistance Day (commemorating Burmese resistance to the Japanese during World War II), Martyrs' Day (honoring General Aung San, the architect of Burmese independence, who together with eight of his associates was assassinated in 1947), and National Day. In all these countries, the observance of national holidays commemorating events in recent history has been restricted primarily to cities and towns where officials could draw on the resources required to make the necessary decorations and mobilize people to attend the various events.

In marked contrast with the other countries of mainland Southeast Asia, many of the modern national holidays observed in the Democratic Republic of Vietnam are observed in the villages as well as in the cities and towns. Although some of the modern holidays in the DRV, such as the birthday of Ho Chi Minh and the founding of the DRV in 1945, have national implications, literally hundreds of days are set apart to be commemorated by the villagers or occupational groups to whom they are most meaningful:

> The creation of a new political calendar crowded with the dates of hundreds of memorial days whose interest is confined entirely to the people in a given occupational ambit or a given village demonstrates Hanoi's belief in the importance of revitalizing nationalism and other political loyalties by keeping them firmly aligned with group attachments and parochialisms, rather than by allowing such alignments to wither.[114]

In the Democratic Republic of Vietnam, Ho Chi Minh, both during his lifetime and since his death, has been symbolized as the embodiment of the revolution. Although his personal appearances in later life were confined mainly to events in Hanoi, his portrait was and still remains ubiquitous. It is not uncommon to see Ho's picture hung in village homes in the place where the family altar once (and sometimes still is) located.

Of particular importance in the postcolonial national cultures that leaders of each society in mainland Southeast Asia have attempted to construct are those symbols drawn from ideologies established for the guidance of national policy. In Thailand this ideology has been a modernized Buddhist-based constitutional monarchy, the main symbols of which have already been noted. In Burma, U Nu attempted to promote the " Burmese Way to Socialism " grounded in traditional Buddhism. Ne Win, who replaced U Nu in 1963, has discarded all the religious bases for national ideology and has given greater stress to Socialism. In Burma today, the most important holidays are Labor Day (May 1) and Peasants' Day (May 2) on which occasions seminars are held in Rangoon for labor and peasant groups drawn from throughout the country. In 1974 the Ne Win government gave the country a new name, a new flag, a new national seal and a new national anthem, all of which incorporate symbols of secular socialism. In Cambodia. Sihanouk attempted to combine Socialist ideas together with aspects of constitutional monarchy and of modern Buddhism into a viable national ideology for his country. These efforts were brought to a halt when Lon Nol overthrew Sihanouk in 1970. Under Lon Nol no new national ideology took root as the country became enveloped in an ever-widening civil war. It seems highly likely that the new government of Cambodia, established in 1975 by the National United Front of Cambodia, will emphasize Socialist/Communist themes almost to the total exclusion of other possible ideologies. The same is probably also true of the new Pathet Lao government in Laos—a government that has already eliminated the monarchy. As noted in the last chapter, the South Vietnamese government never succeeded in establishing a legitimating national ideology to compete with the Vietnamese Communist ideology developed in the North. The DRVs commitment to Communism, already discussed at length, is further evidenced in its holding of national holidays that celebrate Lenin's birthday and international Labor Day (May 1).

The efforts of all the postcolonial countries of mainland Southeast Asia to establish new national ideologies have not been restricted merely to the display of national symbols. As the meanings of these new ideologies are often ill understood, if understood at all, by the rural populace of the countries concerned, it has also been found necessary to establish means for the dissemination of national cultures. In such dissemination, the cities have been made to play central roles.

Cities and the Dissemination of National Culture

Throughout mainland Southeast Asia, the means for the dissemination of national culture have been centralized in the national capitals of the region. It is in the capital cities that national newspapers and many of the periodicals and books produced are published. It is in the national capitals that most of the programming for radio and TV is determined. The national capitals also serve as sites for the headquarters of most national cultural organizations such as religious and professional organizations and charities. National museums and other national cultural institutions are also located in the national capitals. Above all, it is in the capital cities of mainland Southeast Asia that policies relating to national educational curricula and institutions are established.

In Thailand, Bangkok has been the locus of all major policy-making regarding education for the whole country ever since the last decades of the nineteenth century when King Chulalongkorn and his advisors first devised a plan for a national system of education.[115] It has been a fundamental tenet of Thai educational policy ever since Chulalongkorn's time that all children in the country be given a basic education and that all students, no matter what their background, be educated according to the same curriculum, particularly with regard to the basic elements of national culture. By the 1930s the task of extending compulsory primary education throughout the country had essentially been completed. In 1919, a Private School Act was promulgated designed to make schools for the Chinese community and those run by missionaries and other Europeans teach the same basic curriculum as that taught by the public schools and employ Thai as the primary medium of instruction.[116] Although this law was not always enforced in the prewar period, by the 1950s all private schools had been required to conform with it.

The fact that the medium of instruction for almost all formal education in Thailand is standard Thai has meant that most of the people of the country have some competence in the national language, both written and spoken, whatever their home language might be. Through the texts used in the compulsory primary schooling, as well as in more advanced education, students throughout

Bangkok. View of the Grand Palace from across the Cao Phraya river. (*C. F. Keyes, photograph*).

Thailand learn to identify with and use national symbols such as the flag, the national anthem, and pictures of the King and Queen. They are taught that they share a common history with others in the country, and that they have common rights and responsibilities with the other citizens thereof. They are taught that Thailand is a monarchy, that Buddhism is the national religion, and that the King and religion are closely related.[117]

Not only is Bangkok the center of the educational system for the whole country, but it is also the site of most of the major institutions of higher education found in the kingdom. Although provincial universities now exist in Chiang Mai in the north, Khọn Kaen in the northeast, and Songkhla in the south and teachers' colleges exist in a number of other provincial centers, the longest established and most highly regarded universities are in Bangkok. There, too, are to be found two of the country's three medical schools, its major agricultural university, the main branch of the Fine Arts university, its National Institute of Development Administration, its military academies, its District Officer Academy, and its two Buddhist Universities. Almost anyone who wishes to attain the most advanced training in any subject must eventually go to Bangkok.

In Laos during the colonial period, very few Lao received any education other than the traditional religious-centered education offered at local temple monasteries. Many received no education at all. In 1951, a law established a system of compulsory primary education, but the law could not be fully implemented owing to the lack of trained teachers, the difficulties of communication and transportation in Laos, and the *de facto* political division of the country. Secondary education in Laos even after independence continued to be in French and was structured according to a French curriculum. Only in the 1960s were secondary schools finally established in which Lao was the language of instruction. During the 1960s and the 1970s, prior to the change of government in late 1975, both primary and secondary education sponsored by the Royal Lao government was restricted primarily to urban contexts.[118] What limited higher education existed in Laos—i.e., at teachers' colleges, at a Buddhist Institute, a School of Medicine, and a School of Public Administration—was found mainly in Vientiane. Throughout the entire period of modern Lao history, from independence in 1954 until the change of government in 1975, the Pathet Lao maintained a separate educational system, one modeled on that in North Vietnam. It now seems likely that it will be this system that will be extended throughout the country.[119]

Education in Cambodia under the French was only a slight improvement over education in Laos. The same basic dichotomy existed there as in Laos between popular education based on the temple monastery and elite education structured along the same lines as education in France. Moreover, private schools for the Vietnamese and Chinese communities also existed. After independence, the Khmer government under Prince Sihanouk began to develop a national educational policy to be implemented throughout the country.

Temple-monastery schools were first incorporated into the national system and then, as resources and personnel allowed, phased out in favor of secular government schools. By 1967, only ten per cent of the primary schools were of the temple-monastery variety. Enrollments increased rapidly from the 1950s on, and by 1966 primary education was available to most of the school age population. However, almost one fourth of the students in primary schools in 1966 dropped out after only one year of education.[120]

Although the Khmer government under Sihanouk made major strides toward extending primary education throughout the country, it was not very successful in eliminating the marked cultural differences that existed at the secondary and higher levels. Most of the elite secondary schools continued to be oriented toward the French system and all higher education was structured according to French curricula as well as taught in French. The Vietnamese and Chinese communities also continued to have their own schools. This situation notwithstanding, pressures were mounting under Sihanouk for the nationalization of education in the country and for the restructuring of all education to reflect national priorities established by the Khmer government in Phnom Penh.

The strides toward educational development made during the period between 1954 and 1970 were greatly undercut by the civil war that followed Lon Nol's overthrow of Sihanouk. In the first year of the war alone, the number of elementary schools in areas under the control of the Lon Nol government were reduced to 20 per cent of the number of schools in existence in 1969–1970.[121] The situation continued to deteriorate until by early 1975, prior to the end of the war, education had all but ceased to exist in the Lon Nol controlled areas. That is to say, education has ceased to exist in Phnom Penh, since most of the countryside by this time was in the hands of forces associated with the National United Front of Cambodia.

The National Front of Cambodia had its own system of education, again modeled on that of the North Vietnamese:

> A spokesman of the National United Front of Cambodia . . . in early 1972 asserted that education in areas under its control was entirely free and was in the Khmer language, that literacy classes were functioning, and that the curriculum of schools included political economy and military and medical science. It was claimed that instruction in the arts and cultural subjects was also being carried out.[122]

Now that the Khmer Rouge controls the entire country, including Phnom Penh, it is probable that a completely unified system of education will be established in Cambodia.

Although the British in Burma did more to develop education than the French in Cambodia, the Burmese government that took power in 1948 was faced with problems not dissimilar to those faced by postindependence Khmer leaders. Secular primary education had not been extended to the entire populace, and many of those receiving basic education were still gaining only the traditional education offered by the local Buddhist temple monasteries. In addition, a number of schools strictly served certain ethnic minorities such as Indians, Chinese, Karens, Shans, and others. Elite education at the secondary and higher levels showed a markedly English orientation.

U Nu's government determined to place all educational planning under the Ministry of Education in Rangoon. The Ministry devised an educational policy designed to produce a uniform system throughout the country. Although some progress was made under U Nu in extending primary education into the countryside, the fundamental educational problems Burma had inherited from the colonial period remained when Ne Win assumed power in 1963. Education received by those living in cities and towns was, in most instances, radically different from that received by rural people.[123]

Ne Win's government has had considerably more success than did U Nu's government in extending primary education throughout Burma and in making all schools conform to uniform policies devised by the Ministry of Education in Rangoon. In 1965, primary education was made compulsory, and it has been estimated by the United Nations that the implementation of the policy of compulsory primary education will be completed by 1980.[124] During 1963 and 1964 most of the private schools in the country were nationalized, and by 1965 the only private schools remaining were local temple-monastery schools in areas where government primary schools had not yet been established.[125] In all schools today, Burmese is the only permitted medium of instruction. The goals of education are the inculcation in the populace of a commitment to socialist development in Burma and of the skills necessary to make such development possible.

The educational changes implemented by Ne Win's government have been unwelcome to a number of groups of people. Many Burmese monks have been concerned about the downgrading of the temple-monastery schools and about the elimination of Buddhist instruction in the government schools. Ethnic minority groups have resented the requirement that education be in Burmese and that it stress Burman history and national identity. In those areas of Burma controlled by insurgent groups opposed to the central government, the government has been unable to implement its educational programs, and alternative forms of education continue to exist. Some of the old elite have argued that the downgrading of English has reduced the access of Burmese to Western knowledge. Yet despite the resistance by certain groups to the implementation of a uniform system of education, the Ne Win government has pressed ahead with its plans.

Prior to the end of the colonial period, the only institutions of higher education in Burma, in Rangoon and Mandalay, respectively, were structured primarily to produce personnel for the British-dominated colonial service. Under U Nu, and particularly under Ne Win, efforts have been made to restructure higher education in order to train people in skills needed for economic development. Although a number of new institutions of higher and vocational learning have been established, including colleges in Moulmein, Bassein, Taunggyi, Myitkyina, and Magwe, Rangoon University has remained the most prestigious institution of higher education in the country. Despite the fact that most students who go to Rangoon University are destined for important jobs in the leadership in the country, it has been the source also of some of the most outspoken dissent to the national policies of Ne Win's government. This dissent has led on several occasions to bitter and violent confrontations between students and certain professors on the one side and the government on the other.[126]

The educational system inherited from the French by the Democratic Republic of Vietnam and the Republic of Vietnam again showed the characteristic features of a poorly developed system of vernacular primary education for the masses and a Western-structured system of education for the elite. To overcome this legacy, the two Vietnams took very different approaches. In the South, what could only be described as educational " free enterprise " was encouraged. In the North, the central government determined the fundamental parameters of educational policy, but great emphasis was placed upon local efforts.[127]

In South Vietnam, the various governments from Diem's on placed heavy emphasis on extending primary education into the villages and on combatting illiteracy. The latter campaign had been influenced, unquestionably, by the great efforts made by members of the Viet Minh to promote literacy even before they came to power in the North. Although the governments of South Vietnam did succeed in extending basic education to a considerable proportion of the population, they left the development of post-primary education mainly to private entrepreneurs:

> Of the some 600,000 middle-school students in southern Vietnam in the early 1970s, about 400,000 attend private schools. The Saigon government has customarily ignored the private schools, allowing their owners, like petty sovereigns, to do almost anything they wished.[128]

The numbers of private schools established in South Vietnamese towns and cities increased to meet the growing demand for higher education, a demand that was stimulated in no small part by the fact that a school certificate could mean military deferment. The most prestigious private secondary schools continued to provide the elite with a French-oriented education—an education which by the 1960s had almost no relevance to the local scene. The most prestigious institutions of higher education—including most notably Saigon University— also continued to be organized according to French patterns with most of the professors being French-educated. Some of the less-prestigious institutions as well as some of the lesser faculties in Saigon University and at other centers had begun, by the end of the war, to show the effects of American influence. Whether the influence in higher education was French or American, the universities of South Vietnam failed to generate " a national consciousness or a spirit of national service . . . because leadership in the universities was still chained to foreign, colonial standards."[129] Moreover, those universities that were supposed to provide education tied to indigenous traditions—e.g., Van Hanh University, the Buddhist University in Saigon, the Hoa Hao University in Long Xuyen, and the Cao Dai University in Tay Ninh—never had the opportunity to realize their potential.[130] In sum, education in South Vietnam was never fully decolonized nor made to serve in any truly effective way the cause of South Vietnamese nationalism. The South was " a society where the best organized sources of nationalism lie completely outside the governmental sphere, in such places as the student movement (anti-American) and Hoa Hao Buddhism (anti-Communist)."[131]

A very different story exists in North Vietnam. From the time of the August Revolution of 1945 on, great stress was laid upon education as the primary means for effecting the creation of a new nation. Initially, the leadership in the North placed primary emphasis on combatting illiteracy. Almost anyone who was literate and who was not fighting in the resistance during the period between 1945 and 1954 was pressed into service to teach others.[132] After independence the war against illiteracy was continued, and by 1958 it was said to have been won.

Since 1954, a comprehensive system of education has been created in North Vietnam which includes basic compulsory primary education, secondary education—much of it vocational, higher education that has been geared to producing the " experts " needed for the economic development of the country, and the most extensive program of adult education found anywhere in Southeast

Asia. Although the whole educational system is managed by central authorities, the curricula of primary and secondary schools have been made to " match the particular economic, technical and social needs of the villages immediately around them."[133] Local teachers have been told to make use of local history and experience that reflects the general premises of North Vietnamese nationalism. Through the " carefully calculated cultivation of parochial loyalties,"[134] the essential elements of North Vietnamese nationalism are made meaningful to the North Vietnamese. Parochial loyalties may be those of kinship and community in Vietnamese villages, or they may be tribal in villages in minority areas. In minority areas, the medium of instruction in the lower grades is not rarely in a minority language.

A concomitant of the " localization " of education in North Vietnam has been the downgrading of the urban center as the major locus of national culture. " This kind of decentralized patriotic education presupposes a society where the physical mobility of most of its people will be very limited."[135] Very few in North Vietnam have access to the thirty-seven universities and technical colleges of North Vietnam that are still urban based. " Upward mobility is conservatively managed in the north, by means of a marathon of sieve-straining through student-selection boards and ' cultural control examination periods'. . . "[136]

Now that South Vietnam has been brought under a government with the same national goals as that of the North, it will be interesting to see what type of educational system is created in the South. Rather unexpectedly, there are probably more similarities between nationalism in the North and the South than might have been thought. Much the same pantheon of historical heroes is recognized in the South as in the North. Moreover, politicians and other leaders in South Vietnam before the collapse of the Saigon regime often borrowed symbols and ideology from the Communists in order to combat Communism.[137] Nonetheless, the fragmented, entrepreneurial education system of the South, with the strong Western orientation at secondary and higher levels will require considerable overhauling before it can be articulated with the system in the North.

Cities and Revolution in Mainland Southeast Asia

The efforts of the postcolonial governments of mainland Southeast Asia to define, portray, and desseminate new national cultures have involved revolutionary breaks with both the colonial and traditional pasts. In this revolutionary context, the major cities of the region are seen to have played two very different roles. On the one hand, they have appeared to be the last bastions of the traditional and/or colonial past, resisting revolutionary forces whose support is the peasantry. The triumph of the revolution, according to this model, comes when " a rural-based revolution ' captured ' the city-based power structure of the country."[138] Contrariwise, the cities have been seen as the seedbeds of revolutions, the places within which revolutionary ideologies are forged and subsequently the places from which these ideologies are disseminated. Both models involve some distortion of reality, but their opposition in theory does provide a useful springboard for raising the question of what role cities have played in revolutionary change in mainland Southeast Asia.

During the colonial period there were a number of uprisings in mainland Southeast Asia almost all of which were entirely peasant based. However, such uprising as the Saya San rebellion in Burma and the " men with merit " uprisings in northeastern Thailand and Laos did not lead to revolutionary change in mainland Southeast Asian societies. Not only did the peasant rebels lack the force required to gain power, but they also lacked access to cultural ideas that would make possible the construction of a viable ideology. Instead, they were carried along by visions of utopias that never eventuated.

It was in the cities that the contraditions between the colonial world as it was experienced and the world as tradition had led people to expect it to be were even more apparent than they were in the countryside and where viable revolutionary ideologies were forged. The revolutionary leaders of the mainland Southeast Asia societies have all been people who have studied various aspects of Western thought—Christianity, liberalism, democracy, socialism, communism. And they have been able to study such because of the schools, the study groups, and the Western books and periodicals available to them in the cities of Southeast Asia. Vietnamese Communism and Burmese Socialism as well as modern Thai Buddhism all have their origins in urban contexts. Even in the postcolonial period, the debates over the ideological alternatives for the peoples of mainland Southeast Asia are still carried out either in urban contexts or by those who have had urban educations. In Rangoon, in Saigon, and especially in Bangkok these debates have been, and in Rangoon and Bangkok still are, spurred by the student movements. And most of the leaders of the National Liberation Front for South Vietnam, of the National Front of Cambodia, and of the Lao National Front (the Pathet Lao) are people who have received much of their training in urban contexts.

A revolution is not made, of course, by an ideology alone. Revolutionaries must also gain power, before they can implement their ideas. Revolutionaries do not, however, always come to power in the wake of a violent upheaval. King Chulalongkorn of Thailand, Prince Sihanouk of Cambodia, and U Nu of Burma, all of whom instituted varying degrees of revolutionary changes in their societies, each came to power following an orderly transfer from the previous power holders. Even when revolutionaries come to power through violent means, such violence may be restricted entirely to the urban context. For example, the 1932 Revolution led by civil servants and military officers and the 1973 student-led Revolutions in Thailand both took place almost entirely in Bangkok. Similarly, the actions that led to the overthrow of Diem in South Vietnam in 1963 were confined mainly to Saigon. Ne Win's *coup* against U Nu was played out in Rangoon. Even the Pathet Lao, who had for so long fought a war from rural bases, ultimately gained power through maneuvers in Vientiane. Pressures for further revolutionary change are still being exerted by urban groups such as student bodies, labor movements, and religious organizations in both Bangkok and Rangoon, and to a lesser extent in other cities in Thailand and Burma.

In Vietnam and Cambodia revolutionary change has been preceded by a violent struggle ending with a peasant-based movement capturing power in the capital cities. Even in these cases, it must be noted that most of the leaders of the Viet Minh, of the National Liberation Front for South Vietnam, and of the National United Front of Cambodia were urban educated. However, given the force commanded by those who exercised power in Hanoi prior to 1954, in Saigon from 1954 to 1975, and in Phnom Penh from 1970 to 1975, it was not possible for the revolutionaries to attain power through the mobilization of the strength found in the cities alone. By turning to the peasants for support, the revolutionary movements in these countries changed not only tactically but also fundamentally. The interest situations of the peasants in Vietnam and Cambodia have been taken into account by revolutionary leaders in those countries to a much greater degreee than they have by revolutionary leaders in Thailand or Burma.

Once the revolutionary leaders gained power in Vietnam and even in Cambodia, the city was once again recognized as the center for the dissemination of ideas and orders. Hanoi and Saigon are today both seats of revolutionary governments and even Phnom Penh, which the Khmer Rouge at first appeared intent on turning into a ghost town, has reemerged as the capital of Cambodia.

In the final analysis, the role a city in Southeast Asia or elsewhere plays in the process of revolutionary change is not to be determined by whether revolutionary leaders have come to power through actions within the city itself or through the " capture " of a city by a peasant-based revolutionary movement. The seeds of revolution are almost invariably found first in the city. Although it may later prove necessary to base the struggle for power in the countryside, the city in the end becomes the center for the dissemination of changes that will affect the whole society, rural and urban alike.

THE ECONOMIC ROLE OF CITIES IN CONTEMPORARY MAINLAND SOUTHEAST ASIA

Urbanization and the Growth of Cities

Since the end of the colonial period, all the countries of mainland Southeast Asia have experienced considerable population growth, ranging from about 2.0 to 3.0 per cent per annum in all countries except Thailand, where the growth rate has been even higher. Population growth in the cities of these countries has been even greater than that of the countries as wholes, indicating that all of them have undergone continuing urbanization. Although urbanization has occurred in all of the countries concerned, it has not occurred to the same extent in each, nor always for the same reasons.

In all the countries of mainland Southeast Asia, one city, the capital city in each case, has grown much more rapidly than other cities in the country. In 1941, Rangoon, which then had a population of a little over 500,000, was three times larger than the next largest Burmese city, Mandalay, with a population of about 163,000. By 1953, the population of Rangoon has grown to 737,000 and was 3.9 times larger than that of Mandalay and twice as large as the next three largest cities combined; by 1970, Rangoon was estimated to have 1,800,000 people and to be 2.1 times larger than the next three largest cities combined.[139]

Bangkok presents a more dramatic illustration of the top-heavy growth of the primate city in mainland Southeast Asia.[140] In 1947, the Bangkok-Thonburi metropolitan area had a population of 782,000 and was 14.5 times larger than the next largest city, Chiang Mai; in 1960, its population was 1,633,000 and it was 25.9 times larger than Chiang Mai.

> Bangkok's 1970 population of 3 million persons . . . makes it 32 times larger
> than the next largest urban place in Thailand. The city contains over half
> of Thailand's total urban population and accounts for almost two-thirds of
> the country's urban population growth.[141]

Bangkok has obviously grown more rapidly than Rangoon, for although in about 1950 the cities were roughly the same size, by 1970, Bangkok had become about one and two-thirds times larger than Rangoon.

Although Vientiane, Laos, hardly counts as one of the major cities of Southeast Asia, it has shown much the same pattern of growth as other capital cities in the area. In 1943, the population of Vientiane was about 23,000, making it 4.7 times larger than Luang Prabang; by 1958, Vientiane had a population of 68,000 and had become 6 times larger than Luang Prabang. During the 1960s the cities of Laos were swelled by refugees from the war. Most of the refugees flowed into Vientiane, Savannakhet, and Pakse. By 1970, the population of Vientiane had grown to about 200,000, that of Savannakhet to about 50,000, and that of Pakse to about 45,000. Luang Prabang had not grown so rapidly as these other cities and in 1970 had a population that was probably about 30,000.[142]

Phnom Penh, in 1936, had a population of 103,000 and was 5.2 times larger than Battambang, the next largest city. In 1960, Phnom Penh's population had grown to 450,000 and it was 12.7 times larger than Battambang. By 1970, Phnom Penh's population has more than doubled, reaching over 1,000,000; in the next four years it doubled again, reaching, according to news accounts, about 2 million just before the collapse of the Lon Nol regime. Since the National United Front for Cambodia took power, large numbers of people were forced to leave or chose to leave the capital city to return to the countryside, so that today it is likely that the population of Phnom Penh has shrunk to below one million.[143]

In 1936, the combined cities of Saigon-Cholon had a population of 256,000, a population that was about 6 times larger than that of the next largest city—Hué—in what was to become South Vietnam. In 1960, the population of Saigon-Cholon had swelled to over two million, and it was then 22 times larger than the next largest city, Danang. By 1970, the Saigon metropolitan area had a population of 3,320,000, but since Danang had grown rapidly in the intervening decade, Saigon was then only about 9 times larger than Danang, the next largest city in South Vietnam.[144] South Vietnam has also experienced the greatest overall urbanization of any country in mainland Southeast Asia. By 1970, 35 per cent of the people of South Vietnam were living in urban centers compared with 24 per cent in North Vietnam, 13–15 per cent in Thailand, 16 per cent in Burma, 13 per cent in Cambodia. and 13 per cent in Laos.[145] As in Cambodia, some of the urban population of South Vietnam was forced to return to the countryside after the Communist takeover. How extensive this exodus has been in still not fully known.[146]

In 1936, Hanoi had a population of 149,000, which was 2.1 times larger than the population of Haiphong, the second largest city in what was to become North Vietnam. In 1962, the population of Hanoi was 643,000 and Hanoi was then only 1.7 times larger than Haiphong. During the early 1960s the boundaries of Hanoi were extended considerably, accounting for the very rapid jump in population over the subsequent decade. By 1970, the population of Hanoi proper is estimated to have been about 700,000 while the greater Hanoi population was between one and 1.4 million. Depending on the figure used, the population of Hanoi in 1970 would have been between 1.2 and 1.7 times larger than the next three largest cities combined.[147] In other words, despite the bombing and the policy emphasis on decentralization that were also features of the same decade, North Vietnam has continued to experience urban growth.

How is one to account for the growth of cities in postcolonial mainland Southeast Asia? As noted at the outset of the chapter, growth rates in the cities of the region has all been higher than the growth rates of the overall populations of the countries in which these cities are located. Thus, while natural increase has accounted for some of the growth of cities, it has not accounted for all the growth. We have also seen that the extension of the boundaries of Hanoi brought about a marked increase in the population of that city in the 1960s. Similarly, Bangkok took in additional population when it expanded in area from 49.5 square kilometers in 1947 to 124.7 square kilometers in 1960, and it has continued to add population through extension of boundaries in the past decade and a half as well. Yet although cities do extend their boundaries, they rarely extend them as rapidly as the population increases and the transformation of land use from agricultural to nonagricultural takes place on their peripheries.[148] By far the most important factor in the growth of cities in mainland Southeast Asia as elsewhere in the Third World, has been the in-migration of peoples into the cities. Studies on urbanization in the Third World have been primarily concerned with the questions of who comes to settle in cities, where do they come from, and why do they come.

During the colonial period, as we have seen, most of those who migrated to the major cities of mainland Southeast Asia came not from the rural areas of the countries in which these cities were located but from other Asian countries. In the first decade of the twentieth century, Bangkok had so large a Chinese population, accounting for well over one quarter of those living within its orbit, that it " had the stamp of a Chinese city."[149] In the 1920s the Chinese population of Phnom Penh may have accounted for half the total population of the city,[150] and if the Vietnamese population was also taken into consideration, then it would seem that the Khmer formed only a minority of the population of Phnom Penh at that period. By 1911, over 50 per cent of the population of Rangoon was Indian, whereas the Burmese accounted for only 31 per cent of the population of the city.[151] Cholon, which for most of the colonial period was larger than its twin city, Saigon, was founded and mainly populated by Chinese.

All of the governments of postcolonial mainland Southeast Asian societies have placed severe restrictions on the immigration of Asian aliens into their countries, including their cities. Moreover, new laws have been passed in each of these countries excluding aliens from certain of the privileges and rights held by citizens, thus providing a strong incentive for aliens to either become citizens or leave the country. The restrictions on immigration from other countries together with the legal constraints on aliens imposed by Southeast Asian governments have essentially ended the inflow of Indians and Chinese into the cities of mainland Southeast Asia. Given the end of immigration, the fact that many aliens have assimilated to the culture of their adopted countries, and the emigration of many who have felt they could not live under the restrictions placed on aliens, the proportion of alien Asians in the populations of mainland Southeast Asian cities has declined in the postcolonial period.

After 1954 both Vietnams severely restricted the legal migration of Chinese into their countries. In South Vietnam citizenship was conferred on all those born in the country, thus making citizens out of many Chinese who did not necessarily wish to be citizens. But while a number of Chinese resisted becoming citizens, the economic disadvantages incurred by those who remained aliens were sufficient to persuade most of those who continued to reside in the country to take out local South Vietnamese citizenship, even though the majority of the Chinese in South Vietnam still remained ethnically Chinese. The total Chinese population of Saigon-Cholon is estimated to have been 570,000 in 1957, a figure which would have accounted for about one third of the total population of the city at that time.[152]

The Chinese community in North Vietnam was never very large, particularly when compared with that of the South. In 1936–1937, the total number of Chinese in Tonkin was said to have been 35,000,[153] and although this figure is probably an underestimate, it suggests that the Chinese did not form a significant proportion of the population of northern Vietnam. It is probable that the majority of Chinese living in northern Vietnam in the colonial period were to be found in Haiphong, the chief port of the area. In 1954, the Chinese population in North Vietnam may have numbered about 100,000, of whom about 45,000 are said to have migrated to South Vietnam after partition.[154] Although the remaining Chinese were relatively well integrated into the new society being created in North Vietnam, distinctive Chinese communities still exist in Haiphong and elsewhere in the country.[155]

In Cambodia " it appears that immigration effectively ceased in 1952 or

1953, after which time very few Chinese have been admitted to residence in Cambodia."[156] Citizenship laws made it more difficult in Cambodia than in South Vietnam for Chinese and others classified as aliens to gain citizenship. Nevertheless, many Chinese succeeded, often through bribes and other extra-legal means, in obtaining Cambodian citizenship.[157] As the result of restricted immigration and change of citizenship, the proportion of Chinese to the Khmer population declined both in Cambodia as a whole and in Phnom Penh, the Khmer capital. Nonetheless, Chinese still constituted one third of the population of Phnom Penh in 1962–1963 and comprised significant proportions of the populations of Battambang, Kampot and Kampong Cham.[158]

Skinner estimated in 1957 that " at least half of the China-born Chinese living in Thailand today first immigrated during the 1918–1931 period."[159] As a result of the Depression and then of World War II, and followed by the legal restrictions imposed on Chinese migration once World War II ended, Chinese migration to Thailand was first slowed and then essentially ended by about 1950. Beginning in 1913/1914 when a Nationality Act was promulgated, successive Thai governments have attempted, through legal incentives, to encourage Chinese to become citizens. Although many Chinese migrants to Thailand eventually returned to China, and many more remained intent on doing so, the number who decided that they would remain in Thailand and who took out citizenship continued to grow. During World War II and again in the late 1940s and early 1950s, strong pressures were put on the Chinese not only to become citizens, but also to assimilate to Thai culture. These pressures have been resisted, at times violently, by the Chinese, but Chinese assimilation has, in fact, been very high in Thailand.[160]. Skinner provides figures that show that the percentage of Chinese nationals in the total population of Bangkok (not including Thonburi) declined from 28.3 per cent in 1950 to 23 per cent in 1955. However, many Chinese who took out Thai citizenship still remained ethnically Chinese. Skinner estimates that the proportion of ethnic Chinese in the Bangkok-Thonburi population, which in 1955 totaled 1,057,280, was 45 per cent.[161] By the time of the 1960 census, less than 10 per cent of the total population of Bangkok-Thonburi were Chinese nationals.[162] Figures on what percentage of the population remained distinctive as ethnic Chinese, even though Thai by nationality, are not available, but assimilation has certainly eroded the size of the ethnic Chinese community relative to the Thai community in Bangkok-Thonburi as elsewhere in the kingdom.[163]

By far the most dramatic decline in the proportion of Asian aliens in a mainland Southeast Asian society and in its capital city has taken place in Burma. In 1931, at the time of the most complete census taken in Burma, there were a total of 1,017,825 Indians in the country, comprising 6.7 per cent of the overall population. 211,692 lived in Rangoon, where they constituted 52.9 per cent of the population of that city. The Depression, the severance of Burma from India in 1937, World War II, and finally independence all resulted in greater out-migration of Indians from Burma than in-migration. By 1953, it is estimated that the number of Indians in the whole population was about 600,000, representing about 4 per cent of the total. In that year, the total urban population of the country was 2,940,704 of whom 287,003 (9.7 per cent) were Indians. Rangoon had an Indian population of 140,396 out of a total of 737,079, that is, 19.2 per cent of the total. At the time of independence, liberal citizenship laws made it relatively easy for Indians to obtain Burmese citizenship. Yet it would appear that perhaps only 10 per cent of the Indian community opted for Burmese citizenship. Thus, most of the Indians in Burma remained aliens. Under the U Nu regime, and particularly under Ne Win, aliens have seen their privileges heavily curtailed, and have been severely restricted in their access to occupations. As a result of these restrictions, between 1962 and 1970, somewhere between 200,000 and 500,000 Indians (precise figures are not available) left Burma. The large-scale exodus of Indians from Burma, and particularly from Rangoon, unquestionably slowed the rate of urbanization in Burma.[164]

Although the migration of Asian aliens into the cities of mainland Southeast Asia has been halted and in some cases reversed in the postcolonial period, these cities have still continued to grow as the result of migration. It is clear, then, that postcolonial migrants to cities in mainland Southeast Asian societies have come not from other Asian countries but from rural communities within the countries themselves.

One major reason rural peoples leave their homes to go and live in the city is that they find life in the countryside insecure. This was undoubtedly the overriding factor behind the migration of people to Saigon-Cholon between 1964 and 1972. Goodman and Franks, who interviewed a number of migrants who moved to Saigon-Cholon during this period, found that two-thirds of their sample stated that factors relating to the war were among the major reasons they had left their homes to settle in the Greater Saigon Metropolitan Area.[165] By 1975, just before the end of the war, Phnom Penh had become a city in which at least half the population consisted of war refugees. In North Vietnam, the war produced an opposite effect. Since American bombing was focused mainly on urban targets, the government attempted to evacuate part of the population of the cities to sanctuaries in the countryside. It is apparent, however, that this depopulation of North Vietnamese cities was temporary and limited. The insurrections in Burma, at least in the early years after independence, also created a body of refugees who sought safety in Rangoon.[166] The subsequent restriction of the fighting in Burma to the peripheries of the country has all but eliminated insecurity in the countryside as a reason for the migration of people into Rangoon, although it is still a factor behind migration to some up-country cities in Burma. Bankok appears to be the only major city in Southeast Asia that has not at one point or another in recent years received a sizable influx of rural migrants who have left their homes because of a sense of insecurity.

Bangkok is also the only city in mainland Southeast Asia for which there exists a substantial number of studies that deal in part or whole with migration.[167] According to data from the 1960 census, 28 per cent of the population of the Greater Bangkok Metropolitan Area was born outside of the city, 19 per cent having been born in other provinces of the country, and the remaining 9 per cent abroad (mainly in China).[168] Of migrants from other provinces recorded as living in Bangkok in 1960, 25 per cent had come into the city during the period between 1955 and 1960. It was during this period that Bangkok also began to undergo marked economic expansion. The rate of migration has continued to accelerate since 1960:

> The rapid growth of Greater Bangkok between 1960 and 1967, which far exceeded natural increase, suggests that the rate of migration to the capital had accelerated and that recent migrants represent an increasing proportion of the total migrants and of the total population.[169]

Two-thirds of the migrants to Bangkok recorded in the 1960 census came from areas within 150 kilometers of the Greater Bangkok Metropolitan area. " The capital . . . gained only one fifth of its net in-migrants from the 45 [provinces] and two-thirds of the kingdom's population which are found outside the Central Region."[170]

A somewhat different pattern emerges, however, if recent migrants are singled out for examination. " Significantly, more of the recent migrants (those of the period 1955–1960) came from distant provinces and particularly from the northeastern and peninsular portions of the country. . . ."[171] Studies made in the early 1970s in six slums in Bangkok strongly suggest that northeastern Thailand was the second most important source of migrants into Bangkok, exceeded only by the provinces immediately surrounding the capital city.[172] It is important to note that although provinces in central Thailand near Bangkok and provinces in northeastern Thailand have experienced population pressures in recent years, the two regions differ markedly in their economic characteristics. Agriculture in the provinces in central Thailand nearest Bangkok has been commercialized for nearly 75 years, while agriculture in northeastern Thailand remained tied primarily to the subsistence needs of villagers in the area. In other words, whereas migrants to Bangkok from provinces in Central Thailand appear to be drawn by the economic advantages offered in the city, those from provinces in northeastern Thailand appear to be driven more by the conditions of poverty in their own home villages.

Migrants to Bangkok tend to be young. Male migrants predominate over females; according to the 1960 census, 120 males came to Bangkok for every 100 females. Many migrants do not stay permanently, but return to their homes after a short period. This pattern of temporary migration is quite common in Third World cities. Even in Saigon, about half the migrants interviewed in a survey made in 1972 said that they intended to return to the countryside when conditions permitted.[173] Yet although migrants from rural areas in mainland Southeast Asia often see their move to the city as being temporary, they often end up settling in the city permanently.

Whether or not rural migrants stay in a city depends in part on whether they perceive the economic opportunities available in the city as greater than those at home in the village. In a sample survey carried out in the large squatter slum near the port of Bangkok at Klong Toey, 80 per cent of those interviewed gave what they perceived as being the economic opportunities available to them in Bangkok as one of their reasons for migrating to the city. In a sample survey carried out in four other slums in Bangkok, 61 per cent of the respondents gave similar reasons.[174] Even in the greater Saigon Metropolitan area where many migrants had settled because of war-created insecurity in their home areas, 35 per cent of respondents in a sample survey of migrants still gave as a major reason for migrating their perception that economic opportunities were greater in Saigon than in their home areas.[175]

What jobs migrants actually find in the cities of mainland Southeast Asia depends in part on the type and degree of economic growth that the city is experiencing. It is also a function of the social patterns that restrict or facilitate access to certain types of occupations. In order to understand fully the reason why Southeast Asian cities have grown as the result of migration of people from rural areas, we must consider the economic development and occupational structure of the cities of the region.

Economic Development and Occupational Structure in Contemporary Mainland Southeast Asian Cities

McGee has argued that migrants to many Southeast Asian cities are able to find employment only in the tertiary sector, if at all. According to this argument, the limited economic development of Southeast Asian societies has generated very few new jobs to date, with the result that migrants are forced to take on work as unskilled laborers in whatever jobs they can find or create work for themselves by becoming hawkers and vendors of any commodity that can be sold in small quantities. Many can find no employment at all.[176] McGee also argues that the occupational structure of Southeast Asian cities in the post-colonial period, as in the colonial period, continues to be characterized by an ethnic division of labor. Finally, occupation is affected by the existence of fairly rigid stratification along class lines, albeit with a native elite now ruling the countries concerned in place of the European colonialist.[177] The model constructed by McGee appears to be more applicable to Southeast Asian cities as they emerged from the colonial period than to these cities as they have been transformed in more recent years.

Prior to Ne Win's coup in 1962, the economy of Burma was growing at a slower rate than was urbanization, an ethnic division of labor continued to obtain, and entrance into the small Burmese middle and upper classes was very hard to achieve. In this context, Rangoon showed all the salient characteristics of a postcolonial primate city in a society experiencing urbanization without development.[178] After Ne Win took power, all economic activity was nationalized, one of the most far-reaching consequencies of this policy being that most of the Indians living in Burma left the country. Given the Ne Win government's commitment to socialism, the privileges of the former elite were also sharply curtailed. There is, however, evidence to suggest that the officer corps has become the new elite of Burma, and that entrance into this corps is almost as difficult to achieve as entrance into the old civilian elite once used to be.

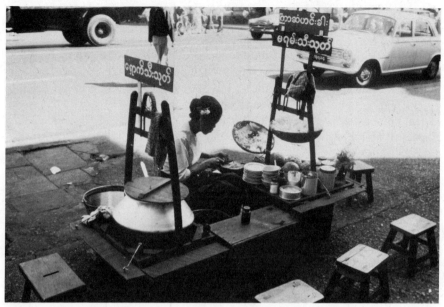

Rangoon. A portable restaurant on a main street, an example of a bazaar-economy enterprise. *(C. F. Keyes, photograph).*

Under the Ne Win regime, Burma has actually undergone economic decline, although it may be that the first ten years of Ne Win's rule represented, as the government has claimed, a transitional period during which the basis for a socialist economy was laid. However this may be, economic stagnation and the emigration of much of the Indian population of the country had led to a considerable slowing down of the process of urbanization in Burma. Statistics on the subject are not available, but it may well be that during the past few years, Rangoon and other cities in Burma have increased in size mainly as a consequence of natural increase rather than as a result of migration.

Prior to 1970, urbanization in Cambodia appears to have proceeded in step with economic development. Under Prince Sihanouk, the Cambodian economy expanded as the result of the increased export of such commodities as rice, rubber, pepper, kapok, and oil seeds, of the import of manufactured goods, and of a small degree of industrial development. Expanded trade not only spurred urbanization in Phnom Penh but also led to the founding of a new port city, Sihanoukville (Kampong Som), which was created in order to eliminate Cambodia's dependence on the port of Saigon. Although some new jobs, created by the expanding economy of Cambodia during the late 1950s and early 1960s, were filled by migrants from the countryside, most occupations associated with commerce and administration remained closed except to those of particular ethnic or class backgrounds.

After Sihanouk's fall from power and with the spread of civil war throughout the country, most of the economic gains made during the previous decade were wiped out. Country people began to flock to Phnom Penh not because the city offered employment opportunities but because it was seen as a refuge from the war. Under these circumstances, many Khmer who saw their own economic position weakening, came to look on the protected economic position held by the Vietnamese and Chinese as unacceptable. Between 1970 and 1975 several violent demonstrations against the Vietnamese and Chinese in Cambodia took place. In 1970, thousands of Vietnamese were killed by Khmers, and in March 1975 just prior to the fall of Phnom Penh anti-Chinese riots broke out in that city as the result of economic grievances.[179]

When the Khmer Rouge came to power, they are reported to have forced the greater part of the population to leave the city. Although some observers of Cambodian events have suggested that the new government is intent upon returning the nation to an agrarian economy in which cities would have no significant place, the government itself has stated that its intention is to promote industrialization. In a broadcast from Radio Phnom Penh in August 1975, it was reported that efforts were underway to reconstruct at least some prewar industries, including primarily those in Phnom Penh:

> Only three months after the liberation, more than 80 large, medium and small industrial plants have been repaired and are now functioning. In Phnom Penh, textile mills, tyre factories, electric plants, water plants and food and dry-battery shops are now functioning and producing appreciable quality and quantity for local consumption.[180]

Yet, although some people may be employed in the reconstructed industries in Cambodian cities, it will be some years before a new pattern of industrialization will emerge in the country. Economic development in Cambodia must begin again almost from scratch.

What economic development occurred in Laos during the period between 1954 and 1975 was almost totally subsidized by American aid. There was no industrialization, few goods were exported, and imports were obtained under a program funded by the United States government. What little urbanization has taken place in Laos has come about not as the result of economic growth, but rather through the swelling of Vientiane and other Lao towns by migrants fleeing from the war. The Pathet Lao takeover of the Lao government at the end of 1975 will unquestionably lead to some radical changes in the urban economy, as well as in the economy of the country as a whole. It would seem unlikely, for example, that the Pathet Lao government will tolerate the perpetuation of class and ethnic criteria for determining access to certain occupations. On the other hand, the new government will face grave difficulties in attempting to promote economic development in Laos for at least several years to come, and it is quite probable that the rate of urbanization in Laos will remain low for the foreseeable future. Indeed, the government of Laos, like the governments of Cambodia and Vietnam, has encouraged refugees living in the cities to return to the countryside.

Urbanization in South Vietnam has been much more a function of the war than of economic development. Buu Hoan, a South Vietnamese official who had also worked for the Asian Development Bank, estimated that in 1970 " aid-supported Government expenditures and expenditures by the allied armies . . . overwhelmingly determine the level of income."[181] In essence the war, produced an economic boom as a rapid increase in the demand for labor occurred at the military bases and ports and in the various facilities providing services to South Vietnamese, American, and other servicemen fighting in the war. Although some war-created jobs, such as those of mechanics, carpenters, stenographers, and so on, were skilled or semiskilled, many more were unskilled. Women became prostitutes or servants or street hawkers whereas men became cyclo drivers, road construction laborers, and petty traders. Even with the boom, the number of rural migrants who flowed into the cities as a result of the war greatly exceeded the number of new jobs available. Goodman and Franks found that a significant proportion of the migrants they interviewed in Saigon were unemployed.[182]

The war never seriously threatened the class structure that had been inherited from the colonial period. The Chinese, a small number of French people who remained in South Vietnam, and a French-educated elite continued to control trade, the bureaucracy, and the educational system until the fall of Saigon in April 1975. Some in the middle and upper classes, particularly those who held positions in the bureaucracy that permitted them to manipulate regulations and those involved in managing the services and trade on which the military bases depended, made enormous profits during the war. It was also this same group who were most upset to see the Americans withdraw.

The American withdrawal seriously dislocated the South Vietnamese economy. When the job market contracted rapidly owing the the closing of American installations, the number of migrants to the cities of South Vietnam increased greatly because of the heightened insecurity in the countryside. The image of the last days of the Republic of Vietnam is that of great streams of refugees flowing from war zones to the cities and from one city to another as the Communist troops moved south.

The end of the war left the cities of South Vietnam with greatly inflated populations. At the same time, a significant portion of the middle and upper classes were successful in fleeing from Vietnam to sanctuaries abroad. After the Communists took over, they strongly encouraged the refugees to return to the countryside, but this policy was not pushed with the insensitivity that it was in Cambodia. The new Vietnamese rulers organized work that made possible the reopening of many of the roadways and railways of the country and also pro-vided gasoline cheaper than the going rate to bus operators so that people could travel back to their homes more easily. The new government is also reported to have made land available to those who are willing to return to agricultural pursuits. According to a report in the *Far Eastern Economic Review*, the new government's " objective was not only to resettle the latest wave of refugees but also to thin out the concentration of population in urban centers where unemployment was high. The administration was believed to be planning to reduce the 3 million population in Saigon to 1 million."[183] However, in May 1976, the population of Saigon was said in a Saigon Radio broadcast to still number three million, of whom one million were unemployed.

In this same broadcast, it was said that Saigon would be transformed into " ' a productive city ' with a smaller inner core and an outer industrial and agricultural belt."[184] It would appear that while South Vietnamese cities will play some part in the planned industrialization of a united Vietnam, they will not have as important role in this regard as will cities in the north.

During the colonial period there had been somewhat more industrialization in northern Vietnam than in the south, but still the French left the new government of the DRV with only twelve large-scale manufacturing enterprises in 1954. The DRV undertook a program of industrialization and in the period of the first Five Year Plan (1961–1965) emphasis was given to the creation of heavy industry. Not only were new industries created in Hanoi, which in 1964 had 88 major industrial enterprises, and in Haiphong but also in new centers, the most important being the complex at Thai Nguyen with its iron and steel factories, steel-rolling mills and factories producing pipes and cables. Hanoi, however, was and is the most important industrial centres in the DRV.

In addition to its primary role in industry, Hanoi also retained its pre-eminence as the administrative capital and cultural center of the country and as the major node in the transportation system. The post-1954 expansion of industry, of government services, and of transportation created new jobs in the cities of North Vietnam. Although migrants were drawn to the cities because of these jobs, there is some evidence to suggest that prior to 1965 (when the American bombing began) the rate of urbanization was greater than the rate of economic growth.[185]

The American bombing of North Vietnam, which was concentrated in 1965–1968 and again in 1972, led to radical changes in urban life in the country. Industries that were destroyed by bombing or that were primary targets were often relocated elsewhere in the country. Within the cities themselves, some industries literally went underground. Part of the labor forces in the cities was mobilized to construct bomb shelters and to work in reconstructing public facilities and factories destroyed by the bombs. Migration into the cities was slowed in part because of the insecurity of the cities compared to the countryside and even more importantly because many who might have joined the urban labor force were recruited into military service or else filled jobs in the countryside left open by those who became soldiers. Some people also left the cities in order to escape the threat of bombing or to follow the factories to their new locations.

Between 1965 and 1972 the DRV was forced to subordinate economic development plans to the war effort. Although Hanoi and other cities in North Vietnam remained among the most industrialized of all cities in Southeast Asia, the growth that took place was mainly in light industries and in manufacturing tied specifically to the needs created by the war. After 1972, however, the DRV once again embarked upon a program of industrialization, with emphasis being given to heavy industry. It appears that in the new united Vietnam heavy industry will be concentrated in the north, while some light industry and agricultural processing enterprises will be located in the south.

Despite the efforts to revolutionize and socialize life in the DRV, the city in North Vietnam still shows some vestiges of its past. A bazaar economy still exists, albeit on a small scale, and there still remains some ethnic specialization by occupation, although the few remaining ethnic Chinese have been strongly encouraged to identify with those who share their same economic situation and to think of Vietnam as their " second ancestral land."[186] Vestiges aside, the economic role of cities in North Vietnam has clearly been transformed from a colonial to a socialist role.

Throughout the 1960s, Thailand experienced a rate of economic growth that was probably higher than that of any other country in mainland Southeast Asia. Prachoom Chomchai has calculated that the average rate of growth of the Gross National Product and the Gross Domestic Product was 8.1 per cent per year for the period between 1961 and 1969.[187] The greatest growth has been in mining and quarrying, manufacturing, construction, electricity, and water, and in banking, insurance, and real estate, all but the first being centered in the urban context, and particularly in Bangkok. Industrialization has been concentrated overwhelmingly in the creation of enterprises that produce consumer goods. Of the over 260,000 people employed in manufacturing in Bangkok in 1972, 85.5 per cent were employed by firms producing consumer goods. Moreover, most of the manufacturing firms were small, 87 per cent of the total of 18,340 firms employing nine or fewer employees. However, these firms employed only 31.2 per cent of the total industrial labor force. The 296 large-scale enterprises (employing one hundred people or more) employed 43 per cent of the industrial workers.[188]

Jobs created both in manufacturing and in other sectors of the Thai economy that have experienced development over the past two decades have provided opportunities for rural migrants to the cities. However, development still has not been sufficient to meet the demand for work created by rural migrants and urban dwellers who have entered the work force during this period. The third Five Year Plan of Thailand (1971–1976) only projected the addition of 70,000 to the industrial labor force during a period when 2.6 million people would be entering the labor force.[189] And it is likely that this goal has not been reached. Many of the rural migrants to Bangkok and to other Thai cities still can find work only in the tertiary sector.

Economic development has served to break down the ethnic division of labor in Bangkok. Prior to World War II, the proletarian labor that existed in Bangkok was supplied mainly by the Chinese. The majority of those employed in the construction business or in the few factories then existing were of Chinese descent. As the result of both the ending of Chinese immigration and the upward mobility of Chinese laborers, who seized on the opportunities created by economic growth, laboring jobs ceased to be filled by the Chinese and instead became filled by Thai. Today even firms engaged in such ethnically linked occupations as the production of " Chinese " noodles and " Chinese " pottery often employ predominantly Thai workers.[190] Meanwhile, many of those who are of Chinese descent have taken on occupations—notably in the professions, in the management of new businesses, and in government service—distinguished by class rather than by ethnic status.[191] Even those occupations, particularly in the business sector, traditionally held by the Chinese are becoming defined more by class than by ethnic terms now that the relatives and associates of those who fill these occupations are increasingly likely to be Thai rather than Chinese.

As Chinese residents in Thailand have become citizens, their investments have changed from being " alien " to being " national." However, foreign control of part of the Thai economy still continues to persist in modern Thailand and is perhaps most evident in the industrial sector. Although foreign firms account for less than one per cent of all firms existing in Bangkok in 1972 (n = 18,340), they account for nineteen per cent of those firms that employ 100 or more people.[192] Although there has been increasing criticism of foreign firms mounted not only by students but also even by conservative politicians and although there have been in the 1970s stringent laws created that regulate foreign investment, the Thai government still continues to encourage some foreign investment. Such investment, it is felt, brings with it more rationalized management and more advanced technology, both of which are desired. Foreign firms also pay higher wages than do domestic firms, skilled and unskilled workers in foreign firms receiving about one and a half times and executives two and a half times the rate received by comparable employees in domestic firms.[193]

The economic role of cities in Thailand was shaped, in part, during the 1960s and early 1970s by American influence generated by the war in Indochina. Not only were several towns in Thailand (Udorn, for example) economically structured with reference to nearby American bases, but a significant part of the labor force in Bangkok was also employed in service occupations for American military and aid missions or in jobs, such as those of bar hostess, masseuse, chauffer, and so on, which catered to American soldiers on leave from the war or from bases within Thailand. The withdrawal of American forces from Indochina and from Thailand itself resulted in some economic dislocation, most severely in the towns near bases. Tourist traffic (which in recent years has come more from Europe than the United States) has kept the demand high for some services previously offered to American soldiers, but it has not been sufficient to offset the economic dislocations caused by the American military withdrawal.

During the period of economic growth, the absolute number of those in upper and middle classes increased markedly, but urban society in Thailand still remains a fairly rigidly stratified system.[194] The benefits derived from economic growth have been enjoyed largely by the political elite of the country and by influential members of the Sino-Thai community. In a real sense, the Revolution of October 1973 was a middle-class revolution aimed at providing the by now rather large middle-class urban population of Thailand with greater access to the wealth and power of the society than had previously obtained.

Serious doubts have been raised as to whether Thailand can continue to sustain in the 1970s the rate of economic growth it enjoyed during the 1960s. Increasing pressures exist to bring about a more equitable distribution of the benefits of development. The overcentralization of the economy and polity in Bangkok has come under growing criticism. Serious suggestions have been put forward in high political circles for the constructing of new ports so that the country will not have to depend so heavily on that of Bangkok, for the decentralizing of industry to make it more responsive to Thailand's needs, and to give higher priority to agricultural development than has been the case in the past. Although Bangkok's position as a great primate city in unlikely to change rapidly, it does appear that the city is beginning to assume a rather different role from that which it played during the colonial and first decades of the postcolonial eras.

Considerable debate has taken place among students of urbanization in Third World cities about whether primate cities play " catalytic " roles in the promotion of economic development or whether they are " parasites " that drain the natural resources of a country and exploit the labor of the peasantry in order to meet the demands of industrialized countries for raw materials and foodstuffs. The wealth generated by such exploitation is used, so the argument goes, to purchase imported goods consumed primarily by the small percentage of a country's population comprising its urban middle and upper classes. Another view, and that shared by Bert F. Hoselitz, who first proposed the concept of the " parasitic city," is that although initially a city may act as a parasite on the countryside, the wealth generated through trade passing through that city can be invested in such a way as to generate the overall economic development of a country.[195]

In mainland Southeast Asia, Rangoon, Bangkok, Phnom Penh, Saigon, and even Vientiane all showed " parasitic " characteristics at the outset of the postcolonial period. Hanoi, on the other hand, assumed a " catalytic " role after the founding of the DRV in 1954. By the late 1960s and early 1970s, Rangoon had ceased to play either type of role and had simply stagnated; Phnom Penh, Saigon, and Vientiane were all caught in the vortex of war, and Hanoi's potential as a catalyst for economic development could not be realized, also as a result of the war. Bangkok, on the other hand, posed the picture of a parasitic city that yet was also generating economic development. Although the future economic roles of the major cities of mainland Southeast Asia are unclear, the radical political changes that have occurred in the region in the past few years make it unlikely that any of these cities will ever become permanent parasites on their rural hinterlands.

LIFE IN CONTEMPORARY CITIES IN MAINLAND SOUTHEAST ASIA

The Patterning of Social Life in Contemporary Cities in Mainland Southeast Asia

Those who live in the cities of mainland Southeast Asia rarely conceive of their cities in terms of grids, the lines of which represent boulevards, streets, and lanes organized into a unified system. Larry Sternstein, an urban geographer who has made a preliminary and almost unique study of the image of the city held by urban dwellers in Southeast Asia reports that in Bangkok:

> For the 193 residents interviewed the image [of the city] is vague and distorted; the " Bangkok eveyone knows " nonexistent . . . Compared with the actual configuration of the elements noted, the interviewees' image condenses overall area, loses angularity and distorts size; compared with my [Sternstein's] image, that of the interviewees suggests a profound lack of appreciation of the component parts of the city and their coherence.[196]

Sternstein concludes that the " virtually formless ' public image ' of Bangkok " suggests that public opinion in Bangkok must be " uniformed or disinterested."[197] There is an alternative interpretation that may, perhaps, be closer to the truth. It is doubtful whether most of the people who live in large cities such as Bangkok, Saigon, Hanoi, and Rangoon conceive of these cities as being total systems that include, among other places, the areas where they live and work. For those in Saigon, for example, who live and work on sampans along the rivers, the area of the city that urban geographers refer to as the Central Business District is probably as remote from their thoughts as it would for villagers living in upcountry Vietnam.[198] No single image of Saigon, or Rangoon, or Bangkok can be drawn; rather, a composite of images exists reflecting the particular patterns of adaptation of the peoples who live and work in these cities.

Of patterns of social adaptation in the cities of mainland Southeast Asia, the best known concern patterns of residence. And of these last, those patterns that characterize slums and squatter settlements have been studied in greater depth than those of other city dwellers, largely because slum residents and squatters are considered to pose " social problems." Perhaps the most characterisitic mainland Southeast Asian slum, where, unlike squatter settlements, legal ownership of dwellings is not in question,[199] is to be found in the tenement blocks clustered in the " China towns " of these cities. Such slums have often been in existence for a considerable length of time. Buildings that may once have been well built have since been allowed to deteriorate. The following description of a slum in Bangkok, while now inhabited by Thai as well as Chinese, is not atypical of tenements in " China towns " throughout the region:

> [The slum behind the Manangasila Guest House] is an old, established residential area . . . almost 3,000 people live here, and most of them do not regard the area as a slum . . .
>
> Forty-six per cent of the dwellings here are between 16 and 30 years old, and another 19 per cent are 31 years old or older . . . There are 224 houses,

485 households in the area; most consist of one or two rooms, but they vary greatly in size and composition . . .

Manangasila is a maze of narrow, twisiting passages between crooked rows of houses. Although 82 per cent of the dwelling unts are detached houses, there is almost no space between them. . . .[200]

Slums such as Manangasila in Bangkok are usually populated mainly by people who were born in the city, although with increasing urbanization migrants may come in to take the places of those who have moved out of the slum as a consequence of upward mobility.

Squatter settlements are often made up of recent migrants. A survey of migrants to Saigon made in 1972 found that

Few migrants have legal tenure where they live. Most of the land they occupy is either owned by the government, by Chinese merchants, or by absentee Frenchmen. Houses built on these lands—either by the migrant or as rental property—have no title.[201]

In the squatter settlement at Klong Toey, the port of Bangkok, and probably the largest squatter settlement in the city, 80 per cent of family heads were migrants to the city.[202] In Rangoon, Phnom Penh, and Saigon just before the end of the war, some squatters were to be found who had no physical residence and who found a bed on the pavement or in a doorway. The latter pattern is much rarer in Southeast Asia than in India, however, and the existence of a body of totally homeless refugees in Phnom Penh and Saigon was predominantly a function of the war.

Although ethnic differences have become somewhat blurred in the postcolonial era, areas of Southeast Asian cities still remain distinctive in ethnic flavor. In Bangkok, "China town" is located in the Sampaeng area, a district composed chiefly of retail and wholesale stores where the homes of the people who work in the area are located above the commercial establishments. In Saigon, the center of the Chinese community is to be found in Cholon; in Haiphong, "China Street in the Hong Bang street zone" still exists.[203] In these districts population densities are probably greater than in any other part of the city. As cities have expanded in size, the Chinese have also established secondary centers within the city where they have recreated the typical pattern of a shop with a residence located above it. In Rangoon, the tightly packed commercial/residential area was associated mainly with Indians. However, with the departure of much of the Indian population that had resided there and with the nationalization of commerce, this area has changed very much in character. Many buildings formerly used as shops have now been converted into government houses, and as the latter are occupied by Burmese, not Indians, the ethnic distinctiveness of many parts of Rangoon has disappeared.

Parts of every Southeast Asian city display characteristics that reveal that they have only recently been converted from villages into urban areas. Although village-type housing is most conspicuous on the fringes of the city, it can sometimes be found within the city itself. For years there was a totally encapsulated village in the Sukhumvit area of Bangkok, an area otherwise devoted to expensive upper class and European housing. Only after land prices in the district rose to extremely high levels did it become impossible for the village to maintain its existence.

The political elites of the postcolonial states of mainland Southeast Asia have often displaced Europeans not only in terms of occupation, but also by living in the houses the Europeans formerly occupied. When the British left Rangoon, the houses in which they had lived, located mainly to the southwest of the Shwe Dagon Pagoda, were taken over by Burmese and Indians of power and wealth. Today, with the political and economic austerity that has been imposed on Burma, many homes have deteriorated greatly, and not a few are being used as warehouses and shops as well as for residential purposes. In Bangkok, the " good " residential areas have greatly expanded, and thousands of new " compounds " have been created in the suburbs of the city.

A number of the governments of mainland Southeast Asian societies have sponsored the construction of subsidized housing in their cities. Such housing may be for the poorer residents of the city, to enable the relocation of those living in slums and squatter settlements, but more often it is built to provide housing for government employees. Privately financed middle-class housing has become especially conspicuous in Bangkok, where private interests have constructed entire communities of tract housing, often located miles from the main centers of the city.

Just as residential patterns reveal the class and ethnic divisions of cities in mainland Southeast Asia, so, too, do social patterns. Considerable attention has been given by researchers to whether family ties are strengthened or weakened when rural people move into cities. Research among migrants in Saigon in 1972 found that the " family " (which is not broken down further in the study) remained the basis of social life for migrants. Once a person had become established in Saigon, he would begin to attract other family members, and they in turn would attract still further family members to their fold. Compared to all other patterns for the organization of social life, family ties remained by far the most important for migrants to Saigon.[204] The more detailed findings on social patterns among residents in slums in Bangkok also reveal the importance of kin ties for migrants, as well as for those longer resident in the city. One third of slum households consisted on " extended families," which included nuclear families together with grandparents and sometimes aunts, uncles, and cousins.[205] As in the rural areas, the head of the household in Bangkok slums is usually male, although there were a small number of households headed by women even though their husbands were present. As Morell and Morell have pointed out, " this reflects the husband's inability to find work incapacity because of illness or injury, or irresponsibility."[206] As in villages, it is common in the slums of Bangkok for young couples to reside with the parents of the wife after marriage. Although the urban slum family has many characteristics similar to those of the rural family in Thailand, important differences exist between them.

> The most obvious differences in family life between rural village and urban slum lies in the work habits of parents. In the village, children and parents work together at home and in the field . . . In the slum, father may rise to go to work before children are awake. He may work 12 or 14 hours, returning when children are again asleep. Mother is often forced to work as well. [207]

Parents who both work rarely work at the same job, and their children rarely see them at work. This pattern is less true if the employment of one or the other parent is that of hawking. In such cases, a wife and children may help make the product the father then hawks about the streets. " The sight of an itinerant vendor with a small child astride her hip is not an uncommon sight on the streets of Bangkok."[208] When both parents work, the children are often cared for by grandparents, other relatives, or neighbors. However, in the slums of Bangkok, it is still uncommon for mothers to work, at least away from home.

Whereas the kinship ties that bind people together in the countryside of Southeast Asian societies still appear to be important for rural migrants to the cities of the region, Chinese migrants did not maintain the kinship patterns of their home society. What Skinner has said of the Chinese in Thailand is equally true of the Chinese throughout the region: " Unlike organized lineages in China, actual kinship was unimportant, and considerations of generation and age in the selection of leaders were entirely subordinate to those of wealth."[209] Willmott has traced this change in kinship patterns to the process of immigration:

> The argument can be summarized briefly as follows: since most Chinese immigrants are unaccompanied adult males, and since many of them owe allegiance—at least at first—to a lineage in China, a system of lineages cannot be elaborated in the urban Chinese community abroad. [210]

Willmott reports, however, that there were rare exceptions to this generalization that lineages of considerable depth did not exist among overseas Chinese. In particular, he cites the instance of the Hainanese community of Kampot province, Cambodia. [211]

Essentially no research has been done on family patterns among the middle and upper classes of cities in mainland Southeast Asia. The impressions of those who have known families in Saigon, or Bangkok, or Phnom Penh, is that the extended family is common. In Thailand, novels of manners, popular among the upper classes, show the lives of the protagonists as influenced by a large number of kinsmen. The plots of such novels and also of films often turn on love affairs in which class is an important factor.

Just as little research has been carried out on urban and middle-class family patterns in Southeast Asian cities, so the role of religious affiliations in the social life of urban peoples therein has also not been explored in any systematic way. What evidence exists suggests that although traditional religious structures may have lost or be losing their importance for urban dwellers, new types of religious-based associations often gain in importance. In the study of slums in Bangkok mentioned earlier, it is reported that " slum dwellers, who often work seven days a week, do not have time or energy to take their children to the local *wat* [Buddhist temple monastery]; they may never go themselves."[212] In a study made in Chiang Mai, the second largest city in Thailand, it is reported that abbots were united in their complaint that the temple monastery had declined in importance as an institution around which the social life of the people of Chiang Mai was organized.[213] On the other hand, Chiang Mai also had one of the more active lay Buddhist Associations in the country, and meditation centers associated with modernist Buddhism have gained increasing numbers of adherents throughout Thailand in recent years. Similarly, in Saigon Buddhist associations, Hoa Hao associations and Catholic associations, which are all products of the late colonial period, continued to play important roles in the urban life of Vietnam at least until the end of the war in 1975.[214]

The new type of religious associations are representative of a type of social organization that has emerged in the city and is rarely found in the villages of mainland Southeast Asia—namely, the voluntary association. From what data is available, it would appear that recent migrants to the city rarely join voluntary associations. A study made in 1954 among migrants from northeastern Thailand who had become pedicab drivers in Bangkok reported that the migrants belonged to no formal groups although they did belong to such informal groups as " parking gangs."[215] Over half of a sample of recent migrants to Saigon interviewed in 1972 were unaware of such associations as those based on friendship, mutual welfare, funeral arrangements, and church affiliation that existed in their neighborhoods, and less than half of those who did know of such groups were members.[216]

Membership in a voluntary association appears to presuppose a commitment to the city as a place of permanent residence. Moreover, in all Southeast Asian cities voluntary associations are particularly evident among the middle and upper classes and among the long-resident ethnic minorities.

Regarding the latter, Willmott found a great variety of voluntary associations among the Chinese in Phnom Penh in the early 1960s: language group associations, locality associations, sports clubs (the most important Chinese association in Phnom Penh), a hospital committee, and a mutual aid association. He also lists the clan association as a type of voluntary association, thus revealing something of the change that Chinese kinship patterns had undergone in the overseas Chinese community in Cambodia.[217] Woodside has described a voluntary association, the " Society for Nourishing Children," which flourished in Saigon in the 1930s. Although this association was a phenomenon of the late colonial period, it is still typical of the type of association found among elites in Bangkok to the present day and in Saigon and Phnom Penh until the end of the war in Indochina. The Saigon Society for Nourishing Children was a women's association, the members being drawn from the Vietnamese and Sino-Vietnamese upper classes of the time. Through dues, through charitable donations, through moneylending, and through the sponsorship of such " society " events as women's fairs, the association attempted to raise money to aid the children of the poor.

Hanoi. A parade of youth in 1973. *(Robert C. Stever, photograph; with permission).*

> The main point about the Saigon " society for nourishing children," however, was that it was an urban adaptive institution of a culturally inverted type. That is, it was one designed not to help rural immigrants adjust to the towns so much as to help the urban upper class adjust to the customs and needs of the impoverished countryside, without having to acknowledge the necessity of changing the social structure. [218]

There are, or have been, associations that cater entirely to the interests of the elite. The Cercle Sportif in Saigon was filled with upper class Vietnamese and a few remaining Frenchmen, playing tennis, sipping Pernod, or lounging at the pool, right up to the last days before the fall of Saigon. But there are also urban voluntary associations with a membership drawn primarily from those of middle and upper class background who would like to effect radical changes in the social structure of their societies. The student movement in Saigon was a voluntary association; so too is the student movement in Rangoon; and the student movement in Bangkok, as in other Thai cities, has been, since it led the Revolution of October 1973 at the vanguard of groups within Thai society pushing for the implementation of radical reforms.

City, Village, and Society in Mainland Southeast Asia

Although Southeast Asian societies have experienced rapid urbanization since the 1940s and early 1950s when the colonial period came to an end, they still remain overwhelmingly rural. Even in Vietnam, the most urbanized country in mainland Southeast Asia, approximately 75 per cent of the people still live, or have returned to live, in rural communities. Although it is possible that marked increases in economic growth based on industrialization may lead to greatly intensified urbanization in one or another of the Southeast Asian countries, it is much more likely that these countries will remain predominantly rural for many years to come. On the other hand, despite the purported efforts of the Khmer Rouge to empty the cities of Cambodia and transform the country into a totally rural society, the city has become a permanent part of all societies in mainland Southeast Asia.

To dichotomize the populations of mainland Southeast Asia into " urban " and " rural " is, of course, to oversimplify the picture. The rural populations of mainland Southeast Asia, as we have seen from earlier chapters in this book, are divided between tribal peoples and lowland peasants and, in each of these categories, divided between different ethnic groups. There are also different types of urban centers. In addition to the great primate cities, and the network of roughly equivalent provincial and district centers linked in administrative hierarchies to the primate cities, there are some other cities that are distinctive because of a particular economic function (e.g., Moulmein, Danang, Haiphong, or Thai Nguyen) or a cultural role (Mandalay, Hué, or Chaing Mai, for example). Nonetheless, by viewing contemporary Southeast Asian societies with reference to the rural/urban contrast, certain processes of change are thrown into relief.

In premodern times, city and village existed as part of an organic society. The city defined the meaningful world for city dwellers and peasants alike, since it was the sacred center of the world. Forces unleashed in the colonial period shattered the organic unity of the traditional world and stimulated a process whereby the predomiant political, cultural, and economic roles of the city in mainland Southeast Asia were fragmented, being defined in part with reference to a European-dominated context, in part with reference to the interest situation of migrants from non-Southeast Asian countries, and only residually with regard to the social demand of the natives of the country. This fragmentation of roles played by the cities of mainland Southeast Asia—and most intensely by the great cities of the region—persisted into the postcolonial period.

The revolutions that have swept mainland Southeast Asia can be understood, in part, as efforts to effect a new integration of the roles of the city relative to the whole of the society, rural and urban included. The Southeast Asian city has been both the locus of revolutions and the object of revolution.

The intrusion of Western influence into mainland Southeast Asia brought the first major revolutionary change—the revolution of the market economy. Beginning first with the port cities, then spreading into the countryside nearest these ports, and then on to more distant rural areas, the people of mainland Southeast Asia were increasingly brought into an economy in which production was organized, at least in part, with reference to market demand. The revolution of the market economy has resulted in the freeing of land, labor, and capital from their embeddedness in kinship structures in all but the most remote villages of the region. The stagnation of the Burmese economy and the policy of economic self-sufficiency initiated by the new government of Cambodia not-withstanding, there will be no restoration of premodern economic systems in mainland Southeast Asia. The governments of mainland Southeast Asia, however much they differ regarding the ownership of the means of production, the mobilization of labor, the generation of and uses of capital, and the control of the market are all committed to increasing production for the market. Such commitments have not yet succeeded in effecting the completion of the revolution of the market economy. Economic dualism, that is, the coexistence of bazaar-based and firm-based economies, characterizes all of the economies of the region, including that of North Vietnam. Although the bazaar-based economy is more likely to be characteristic of rural villages, it is also found in the cities of the region as well. In turn, firm-based enterprises can sometimes be found in rural areas but more commonly in the cities.

The economic revolution that occurred in mainland Southeast Asia effected marked changes in the nature of social inequality in the societies of the region. Whereas traditional class differences in the region had been predicated upon a distinction between those few who held the power to rule and the vast majority who were the subjects the creation of a market economy stimulated the emergence of a new class whose membership was defined by occupation in trade. This new class was ethnically distinctive in all of the countries of the region. While the ethnic division of labor was most conspicuous in the cities, it was also manifest in the Chinese- or Indian-owned shops found in upcountry market centers.

In the postcolonial period, the stratification of mainland Southeast Asian societies have undergone yet further changes. Although foreign trading firms still operate in Thailand and while ethnic specialization in internal trade occupations still persists in all countries save in North Vietnam, trade has been " nationalized " to some extent in every country of the region. This nationalization has led to a weakening of the ethnic specialization in trade. In Burma, Indians involved in trade have been either forced to leave the country or, for those who remained, to accept a subordinate position within the Burman-dominated government trade corporations. In North Vietnam trade has also been taken over by the government and Chinese who, prior to 1954, were in trade and either have left the country or have taken new jobs within this socialist society. Even in Thailand where trade is still in private hands, those who occupy positions in trade have in the post World War II period begun to become more conscious of their class position than of their ethnic position within Thai society. There has also been a movement of ethnic Thai into many entrepreneurial roles in contemporary Thailand.

With industrialization, although carried out only to a limited degree, a new class has emerged in several of the countries of mainland Southeast Asia. The economic interest of workers in manufacturing, mining, and other such modern enterprises are not those of any in other classes, including those who are peasants or who are city dwellers engaged in bazaar-type enterprises. Although the distinctive place accorded workers in Vietnam is well-known, the role of workers in contemporary Thailand has also proved to be of particular importance. It was workers' resistance to initiatives to raise the price of rice (thus benefiting peasants) that led to the collapse of the government of Kukrit Pramoj in early 1976.

Although a number of new classes have been added to the social systems of Southeast Asian countries as a consequence of economic transformations of these societies, the vast majority of the populations of the societies of mainland Southeast Asia have continued to be peasants. There have, however, been radical changes in the class of people that possess the right to rule in these societies. In other words, societies in mainland Southeast Asia have been transformed by political as well as by economic revolutions.

Revolutions to establish new modes of political legitimacy have generated much of the conflict that has characterized recent Southeast Asian history. In Vietnam and in Burma, where colonial domination resulted in the irrevocable destruction of premodern forms of legitimacy, there were no necessarily obvious successors to the colonial rulers. Only after a prolonged civil war, complicated and magnified by American involvement, did the Lao Dong Party succeed in establishing itself as the new legitimate source of power in Vietnam. In Burma, a consensus that had been forged among the nationalist leaders during World War II has been shattered several times over. Although the Ne Win government enjoys a supremacy in arms, it has yet to surround itself with an aura of legitimacy (now based, in theory, on a constitution) that is recognized by a majority of the populace of the country. Similar situations also obtain in Laos and Cambodia where the respective Communist parties have yet to acquire the stature of their Vietnamese counterpart. In Thailand, where continuity with the past has been the greatest, there has still been conflict (most marked in 1932 and 1973) regarding the nature of a legitimacy expressed through the institution of the monarchy.

Even when the right to rule has not been in dispute in the centers of political authority, it has often not been recognized in peripheral areas where tribal and ethnic minorities have only a tenuous sense of belonging to a modern nation-state. As a consequence, the new rulers of mainland Southeast Asian states have been faced with the necessity of instituting ways that will succeed in integrating the diverse segments of the populations living within boundaries defined, rather arbitrarily, during the colonial period into unified polities.

Political revolutions that succeed in establishing new modes of legitimacy and in integrating all segments of a population into a single polity, and economic revolutions that succeed in orienting people toward production for the market, must necessarily involve radical cultural change. All governments of mainland Southeast Asia have created systems of education whose purposes include the inculcation of national identity and of knowledge and skills necessary to operate in the market economy. Although modern education has been made available in all urban centers in the region and has been extended to rural areas—more successfully in Thailand and Vietnam and least successfully in Laos—there remain major differences in educational opportunities for the populaces of all the societies of the region.

At the most fundamental level, cultural change necessitates a change in worldview and as worldviews in premodern Southeast Asia were grounded in the various religions of the region, cultural change has entailed a challenge to traditional religions. This challenge has sometimes been seen, simplistically, as a challenge posed by Western culture. However, the emergent cultures of Southeast Asia can no more be seen as transplanted Western traditions than past traditions in the region could be seen as transplanted Indian or Chinese traditions. In Thailand, in Burma, and perhaps also in Cambodia and Laos, the emergent traditions are ones that interweave Western thought with Buddhist thought. Vietnamese Communism has involved a similar interweaving, having meaning for the peasantry as well as for those few educated in the Western tradition because it has been couched in an idiom that has been drawn from the premodern Vietnamese tradition. The new traditions of modern mainland Southeast Asia are still best understood by the well-educated populace who are found mainly in the towns and cities. Since one may still find people mainly living in rural areas but also sometimes found in urban areas who seek meaning in the cultural traditions of the past, one might speak of mainland Southeast Asian societies as being characterized by both cultural and economic dualism.

The revolutions in both the conditions to which people in mainland Southeast Asia must adapt and in the cultures that make such adaptation meaningful, even if not fully concluded, have rendered it impossible for there to be a restoration of what Max Weber called the magical garden; that is, the context in which the world as experienced is also the world as it is culturally conceived. The world as it is now experienced is an ever-changing world. Yet, in this very experience not a few in mainland Southeast Asia have found meaning in the wellsprings of their own cultures.

> *Sabhe sankhārā aniccā, sabhe dhammā anattāti*
> All compounded things are impermanent;
> All phenomena are without permanent essence.

NOTES

Chapter 5

1. On Chansen, see Bennet Bronson and George F. Dales, " Excavations at Chansen, Thailand, 1968 and 1969: A Preliminary Report," *Asian Perspectives*, XV, 1 (1972), pp. 15–46. On Beikthano see U Aung Thaw, *Report on the Excavations at Beikthano* (Rangoon: Revolutionary Government of the Union of Burma, Ministry of Union Culture, 1969). Chansen did not become an urban center until about the seventh century, but it had been occupied since about 200 B.C. A comb found at Chansen, and dated from about the beginning of the Christian era, provides " the earliest solid date . . . for the presence of Indian influence in Southeast Asia . . . and . . . for the earliest appearance of Buddhism in Thailand "

(Bronson and Dales, *op. cit.*, p.30). Radiocarbon dates from several of the sites at Beikthano suggest strongly that Beikthano was an Indianized city during the first three centuries of the Christian era (U Aung Thaw, *op. cit.*, pp. 61–62).

2. For a typology of ancient cities in mainland Southeast Asia, see T. G. McGee, *The Southeast Asian City* (London: G. Bell and Sons, 1969), pp. 30–31. The fullest examination of the ancient Southeast Asian City is to be found in the work of Paul Wheatley. See Wheatley, *The Golden Khersonese* (Kuala Lumpur: University of Malaya Press, 1961); " ' What the Greatness of a City is Said to Be ': Reflections on Sjoberg's ' Preindustrial City '," *Pacific Viewpoint* 4.2:1633–89, 1963; and *The Pivot of the Four Corners* (Chicago: Aldine, 1971). Also see Paul Wheatley, " Satyānṛta in Suvarṇadvīpa: From Reciprocity to Redistribution in Ancient Southeast Asia," in *Ancient Civilization and Trade*, ed. by Jeremy A. Sabloff and C. C. Lamberg-Karlovsky (Albuquerque: University of New Mexico Press, 1975), pp. 227–83.

3. Wheatley, *The Pivot of the Four Corners, op. cit.*, pp. 248–57.

4. *Ibid.*, 436.

5. Wheatley, " ' What the Greatness of the City . . . ' ," p. 178; see also Wheatley, *Pivot of the Four Corners*, pp. 425–38.

6. Michael D. Coe, " Social Typology and Tropical Forest Civilizations," *Comp. Studies in Society and History*, IV, 1 (1961), pp. 65–85.

7. McGee, *The Southeast Asian City*, pp. 30–31.

8. The debate about the location of Takkola is summarized by Larry Sternstein in " ' Krung Kao ': The Old Capital of Ayutthaya," *Journal of the Siam Society*, LIII, 1 (1965), pp. 109–10.

9. McGee, *The Southeast Asian City*, p. 31.

10. G. Coedès, *The Making of South East Asia* (Berkeley and Los Angeles: University of California Press, 1966), p. 81.

11. *Ibid.*, p. 87.

12. Cf. E. Sarkisyanz, *Buddhist Backgrounds of the Burmese Revolution* (The Hague: Marinus Nijhoff, 1965), ch. XII.

13. Until recently, the most well known translation of the inscription of King Ram Khamhaeng was that done by George Coedès in *Receuil des Inscriptions du Siam, Première Partie: Inscriptions de Sukhodaya* (Bangkok, 1924), pp. 37–48. An English translations of Coedès' translation was made by Prince Wan Waithayakon and published as *Stone Inscriptions of Sukhothai* (Bangkok: The Siam Society, 1965). A new translation, which takes into account Coedès work as well as more recent archaeological and epigraphical research, has been published by A. B. Griswold and Prasert na Nagara in " Epigraphic and Historical Studies No. 9: The Inscription of Ramkamhaeng of Sukhothai (A.D. 1292), " *J. Siam Society*, LIX, 2 (1971), pp. 179–228. A discussion of the inscription appears in this last article as well as in *Towards a History of Sukhodaya Art* by A. B. Griswold (Bangkok: The Fine Arts Department, 1967).

14. Griswold and Prasert, *op. cit.*, p. 209.

15. *Ibid.*, p. 212.

16. Griswold, *Towards a History of Sukhodaya Art*, p. 3.

17. Griswold and Prasert, *op. cit.*, p. 211.

18. *Ibid.*, p. 213; Griswold, *op. cit.*, p. 9.

19. Griswold and Prasert, *op. cit.*, p. 214.

20. On shrine centers, see Charles F. Keyes, " Buddhist Pilgrimage Centers and the Twelve-Year Cycle: Northern Thai Moral Orders in Space and Time," *History of Religion*, 15.1:71–89, 1975 and James B. Pruess, *Veneration and Merit-Seeking at Sacred Places: Buddhist Pilgrimage in Contemporary Thailand* (Ph.D. Thesis, University of Washington, 1974).

21. Larry Sternstein, " ' Krung Kao ': The Old Capital of Ayutthaya," *J. Siam Society*, LII (1965), p. 108.

22. For the history of the changing positions of cities in traditional Southeast Asia, see Coedès, *op. cit.* and D. G. E. Hall, *A History of South-East Asia*, 3rd ed. (London: Macmillan, 1968).

23. The following discussion of cities in late traditional Burma is based on G. E. Harvey, *A History of Burma* (London: Frank Cass and Co., 1967; orig. 1925); V. C. Scott O'Connor, *Mandalay and other Cities of Burma* (London: Hutchinson and Co., 1907); E. C. Foucar, *Mandalay the Golden* (London: Dennis Dobson, 1963); and " Shway Yoe " (J. G. Scott, *The Burman* (New York: W. W. Norton, 1963; reprint of 3rd ed., 1909).

24. The date of February 1857 as the date for the beginning of construction of Mandalay is given in O'Connor, *op. cit.*, p. 6; the date of June 1857 for the occupation of Mandalay is from Foucar, *op. ciy.*, p. 26. Scott (Shway Yoe, *op. cit.*, p. 482) states: " Mandalay was commenced in 1858, and two years later the seat of government was transferred from Amarapura, some five or six miles down the river." 1857 is generally accepted by historians as the date when Mandalay was occupied.

25. " Shway Yoe", *op. cit.*, p, 197. Scott reports that the image was burnt after the British annexation, but it was rebuilt and still stands half-way up Mandalay Hill.

26. *Ibid.*, pp. 169–70.

27. E. Sarkisyanz, *Buddhist Backgrounds of the Burmese Revolution*, *op. cit.*, pp. 84–85. Cf. " Shway Yoe," *op. cit.*, pp. 477–79.

28. " Shway Yoe," *op. cit.*, pp. 481–82.

29. Whereas Scott and others have claimed that the practice was observed at Mandalay, O'Connor asserts that: " We have it upon the authority of the King, that this ancient custom was not followed at Mandalay. . . . The King would have no victims associated with the outset of his reign of peace." O'Connor, *op. cit.*, p. 6.

30. See E. Michael Mendelson, *Sangha and State in Burma* (Ithaca, N.Y.: Cornell University Press, 1975), pp. 111–12.

31. O'Connor, *op. cit.*, p. 48.

32. Scott ("Shway Yoe," *op. cit.*, p. 172) says that the Kutho-daw temple monastery was built by an uncle of King Thibaw. However this may be, the greatest merit involved was acquired by Mindon in his sponsoring of the Fifth Council, which made it possible for the scriptures to be so permanently recorded.

33. " Shway Yoe," *op. cit.*, p. 172.

34. Foucar, *op. cit.*, pp. 25–26.

35. See " Shway Yoe," *op. cit.*, pp. 540–41.

36. *Ibid.*, pp. 545–46.

37. *Ibid.*, p. 541.

38. *Ibid.*, p. 545.

39. *Ibid.*, p. 484.

40. Alexander B. Woodside, *Vietnam and the Chinese Model* (Cambridge: Harvard University Press, 1971), p. 151.

41. John Crawfurd, *Journal of an Embassy to the Courts of Siam and Cochin China* (Kuala Lumpur and London: Oxford University Press, 1967; orig. 1828), p. 510.

42. Coedès, *The Making of South East Asia*, p. 198.

43. Crawfurd, *op. cit.*, pp. 213–14.

44. *Ibid.*, p. 470. Crawfurd places the total number of Chinese in Vietnam in 1822 at not less than 40,000.

45. Woodside, *op. cit.*, pp. 131–32.

46. Crawfurd, *op. cit.*, p. 251.

47. Woodside, *op. cit.*, p. 128.

48. Crawfurd, *op. cit.*, pp. 252 and 461.

49. *Ibid.*, p. 470.

50. *Ibid.*, p. 461.

51. Woodside, *op. cit.*, p. 127.

52. McGee, *Southeast Asian City*, pp. 44–45. Malacca in Malaya was the foremost example of the " garrison fort settlement," whereas Manila in the Philippines and Batavia in Java were examples of " permanent stabilized centers of colonial power."

53. On the development of " primate cities " during the colonial period, see McGee, *The Southeast Asian City*, and Rhodes Murphy, " Traditionalism and Colonialism: Changing Roles in Asia," *J. Asian Studies*, XXIX, 1 (1969), pp. 67–84.

54. In Thailand, for example, at the end of the nineteenth century it took 15 days for a messenger to travel by fast boat and horse from Bangkok to Nongkhai located on the Mekong River across from Vientiane in Laos. It took ordinary travelers 40 days to go by boat from Bangkok to Chiang Mai located 545 miles to the north. See Tej Bunnag, " The Provincial Administration of Siam from 1892 to 1915 " (D. Phil. Thesis, Oxford, 1968), pp. 6–7.

55. J. Russell Andrus, *Burmese Economic Life* (Stanford: Stanford University Press, 1948), p. 237.

56. On the political centralization and concomitant bureaucratization of government in Burma, see F. S. V. Donnison, *Public Administration in Burma* (London: Royal Institute of International Affairs, 1953) and James F. Guyot, " Bureaucratic Transformation in Burma," in *Asian Bureaucratic Systems Emergent from the British Imperial Tradition* by Ralph Braibanti and Associates (Durham, N. C.: Duke University Press, 1966). For Thailand, see Tej Bunnag, *op. cit.;* Fred W. Riggs, *Thailand: The Modernization of a Bureaucratic Polity* (Honolulu:

East-West Center Press, 1966); and William J. Siffin, *The Thai Bureaucracy* (Honolulu: East-West Center Press, 1966). For Indochina, see Nghiem Dang, *Viet-Nam: Politics and Public Administration* (Honolulu: East-West Center Press, 1966) and Roger Pinto, *Aspects de l'évolution gouvernementale de l'Indochine française* (Paris: Librairie de Receuil Sirey, 1946).

57. See McGee, *The Southeast Asian City*, pp. 54–55.

58. The contrast between the "firm-centered economy" and "bazaar-centered economy" in Southeast Asian cities has been discussed by Clifford Geertz in *Peddlers and Princes* (Chicago: University of Chicago Press, 1963). Geertz' terms have been used by McGee in his discussion in *The Southeast Asian City* (*op. cit.*, p. 126f.).

59. Geertz, *op. cit.*, p. 28.

60. T. G. McGee, "Peasants in the Cities: A Paradox, A Paradox, a Most Ingenious Paradox," *Human Organization*, XXXII, 2 (1973), pp. 135–42; also see McGee, *The Urbanization Process in the Third World* (London: G. Bell and Sons, 1971).

61. In his formulation, McGee draws heavily on a paper by S. H. Franklin, "Systems of Production; Systems of Appropriation," *Pacific Viewpoint*, VI, 2 (1965), pp. 145–66.

62. The concept of economic "dualism" was first developed by the Dutch economist, J. H. Boeke in a thesis written in 1910 wherein he attempted to describe and explain the malintegration of the economy of the Dutch East Indies (what is today Indonesia). See J. H. Boeke, *Tropische-Koloniale Stadthuishoudkunde* (Dissertation, Amsterdam, 1910). Also see Clifford Geertz, *Agricultural Involution* (Berkeley and Los Angeles: University of California Press, 1966), p. 48. Boeke elaborated his ideas in subsequent studies, some of which have appeared in English: *The Evolution of the Netherlands Indies Economy* (Haarlem: H. D. Tjeenk Willink, 1947) and *Economics and Economic Policy of Dual Societies* (Haarlem: H. D. Tjeenk Willink, 1953). McGee (personal communication, February 25, 1976) has observed that there are some types of enterprises, such as are found in the construction industry, which are intermediate between firm-centered and bazaar-centered industries.

63. Andrus, *Burmese Ecomomic Life*, p. 142.

64. Great Britain. Admiralty, Naval Intelligence Division, *Indo-China* (London: H.M.S.O., 1943), p. 321f.

65. J. C. Ingram, *Economic Change in Thailand, 1830–1970* (Stanford: Stanford University Press, 1971), p. 144.

66. On handicraft production during the colonial period, see Andrus, *op. cit.*, ch. IX; Great Britain. Admiralty, Naval Intelligence Division, *op. cit.*, pp. 316–21; Ingram, *op. cit.*, pp. 112-23.

67. McGee, *The Southeast Asian City*, p. 58.

68. *Loc. cit.* McGee drew his data from Richard W. Redick, *A Demographic and Ecological Study of Rangoon Burma*, Ph.D. Thesis, University of Chicago, 1961.

69. McGee, *The Southeast Asian City*, p. 58.

70. *Ibid.*, pp. 67–68.

71. G. William Skinner, *Chinese Society in Thailand* (Ithaca, N. Y.: Cornell University Press, 1957), p. 81.

72. Data from Siam. Central Service of Statistics, *Statistical Year Book—Siam: No. 19, B.E. 2478 (1935–1936) and 2479 (1936–1937)* (Bangkok: Bangkok Times Press, 1939), pp. 7, 50. There is a considerable problem in using official statistics in estimating urban populations in Thailand prior to recent censuses, because data are differentiated by province rather than by type of settlement.

73. Crawfurd, *op. cit.*, pp. 213–14, 223–26.

74. Great Britain. Admiralty, Naval Intelligence Division, *op. cit.*, p. 248.

75. McGee, *The Southeast Asian City*, pp. 59–60; data from Redick, *op. cit.*

76. Great Britain. Admiralty, Naval Intelligence Division, *op. cit.*, pp. 248–55; Charles Robequain, *The Economic Development of French Indochina* (London: Oxford University Press, 1944), ch. I; William E. Willmott, *The Chinese in Cambodia* (Vancouver, B. C.: University of British Columbia Publications Centre, 1967), esp. ch. 2. Although the Vietnamese migrants in Phnom Penh were natives of Indochina, very few were native to Cambodia. They have long been considered " aliens " by the Khmer, even though the French did not consider them as such.

77. On the ethnic division of labor in Thailand with specific reference to the Chinese in Bangkok, see Skinner, *op. cit.*, esp. ch. 3.

78. Skinner, *op. cit.*, p. 91.

79. See J. S. Furnivall, *Netherlands India* (Cambridge University Press, 1939), esp. ch. XIII and Furnivall, *Colonial Policy and Practice* (New York: New York University Press, 1956; orig. 1948), esp. pp. 303–12. See also Furnivall, " Some Problems of Tropical Economy," in *Fabian Colonial Essays* ed. by R. Hinden (London: Allen and Unwin, 1945), pp. 167–71.

80. Furnivall, *Netherlands India*, p. 446.

81. Furnivall, *Colonial Policy and Practice*, pp. 308–309.

82. Furnivall, *Netherlands India*, p. 449.

83. *Loc. cit.*

84. *Ibid.*, p. 450.

85. Furnivall, *Colonial Policy and Practice*, p. 308.

86. *Ibid.*, p. 306.

87. In addition to Orwell's *Burmese Days* (first published in 1934), also see J. Hougron's *Reap the Whirlwind* (London: Hutchinson, 1958), which tells the story of a French community in a small colonial town in Laos. Although Somerset Maugham's stories rarely concern mainland Southeast Asia, those that do convey the flavor of what it was like to be a European living in Southeast Asia during the colonial period.

88. John Clement Koop, *The Eurasian Population in Burma* (New Haven: Yale University, Southeast Asia Studies, Cultural Report Series No. 6, 1960), pp. 1–2.

89. Koop, *op. cit.*, p. 22.

90. This type has been widely recognized and has been labeled variously as " pariah capitalist," " middleman minority," " Asian trading minority," etc. See Edna

Bonacich, " A Theory of Middleman Minorities," *Am. Sociological Review*, XXXVIII, 5 (1973), pp. 583–94 and Pierre L. van den Berghe, " Asian Africans Before and After Independence," unpublished paper, 1975.

91. For general overviews of overseas Chinese and overseas Indians in Southeast Asia, see Maurice Freedman, " The Chinese in Southeast Asia: A Longer View," *Occasional Papers of the China Society* (No. 14, London, 1964); reprinted in *Man, State, and Society in Contemporary Southeast Asia*, ed. by Robert O. Tilman (New York: Praeger, 1969), pp. 431–50; and R. Hatley, " The Overseas Indian in Southeast Asia: Burma, Malaysia, and Singapore," in Tilman, *op. cit.*, pp. 450–66.

92. Skinner, *op. cit.*, pp. 99–109.

93. Hatley, *op. cit.*, p. 452; Skinner, *op. cit.*, pp. 52–58. For details of the indenture system employed in recruiting Indians, see C. Kondapi, *Indians Overseas, 1838–1949* (Madras: Oxford University Press, 1951).

94. Skinner (*op. cit.*, pp. 91–99) drawns an excellent picture of the social basis for the values the Chinese migrants placed on industriousness and thrift. Also cf. Hatley, *op. cit.*, p. 453, for a similar argument about overseas Indians.

95. Hatley, *op. cit.*, p. 452.

96. Skinner, *op. cit.*, pp. 62–69; 172–80.

97. Cf. Freedman, in Tilman, *op. cit.*, p. 434; also see Furnivall, *Colonial Policy and Practice*, p. 307.

98. Skinner, *op. cit.*, p. 135.

99. G. W. Skinner, " Overseas Chinese Leadership: Paradigm for a Paradox," in *Leadership and Authority*, ed. by Gehan Wijeyewardene (Singapore: University of Malaya Press, 1968), pp. 191–207.

100. Freedman, *op. cit.*, p. 435, Cf. Hatley, *op. cit.*, p. 464. Furnivall (*Colonial Policy and Practice*, p. 307) also recognized that deracination was a concomitant of the plural society.

101. The term " double identity " is from the study of the Chinese in Thailand by Richard J. Coughlin: *Double Identity: The Chinese in Modern Thailand* (Hong Kong University Press, 1960). Also see Skinner, *op. cit.*, p. 315, for example.

102. The argument here is based in part on Furnivall's argument in *Colonial Policy and Practice*, pp. 306–307.

103. Regarding the Mons, see Brian Foster, *Ethnicity and Economy: The Case of the Mons in Thailand* (Ph.D. Thesis, University of Michigan, 1972); Foster, "Ethnic Identity of the Mons in Thailand," *J. Siam Society*, LXI, 1 (1973), pp. 203–226; Foster, " Ethnicity and Commerce," *American Ethnologist* I, 3 (1974), pp. 437–48.

104. The concept of the " cultural role " or "orthogenetic role " of cities is taken from Robert Redfield and Milton B. Singer, " The Culture Role of Cities," *Economic Development and Cultural Change III*, 1 (1954), pp. 53–73.

105. Alexander Woodside, " The Development of Social Organizations in Vietnamese Cities in the Late Colonial Period," *Pacific Affairs*, XLIV, 1 (1971), pp. 48–49.

106. Virginia Thompson, *Thailand: The New Siam*, 2nd ed. (New York; Paragon Book Reprint Corporation, 1967; orig., 1941), p. 645. On the nationalistic role played

by the YMBA and GCBA in Burma, see Donald E. Smith, *Religion and Politics in Burma* (Princeton, N.J.: Princeton University Press, 1965), esp. pp. 86–91.

107. Cf. McGee, *The Southeast Asian City*, pp. 100–101.

108. *Vietnamese Realities* (Saigon, 1969), pp. 147–50.

109. On traditional royal rituals practiced in Luang Prabang and Campasak, see Charles Archaimbault, " Religious Structures in Laos," *J. Siam Society*, LII, 1 (1964), pp. 57–74 and Archaimbault, *The New Year Ceremony at Basak* (*South Laos*) (Ithaca, N.Y.: Cornell University, Southeast Asia Program, Data Paper No. 78, 1971).

110. Donald E. Smith, *Religion and Politics in Burma*, p. 165. Also see E. Sarkisyanz, *Buddhist Backgrounds of the Burmese Revolution* (The Hague: Martinus Nijhoff, 1965), chs. XVIII–XXVIII and E. Michael Mendelson, *Sangha and State in Burma*, esp. chs. 4–6.

111. Mendelson, *op. cit.*, p. 273.

112. Roger Smith, " Prince Norodom Sihanouk of Cambodia," in *Man, State and Society in Contemporary Southeast Asia*, ed. by Robert O. Tilman (New York: Praeger, 1969), p. 398. Smith's article was originally published in *Asian Survey*, VII (1967), pp. 353-362.

113. On traditional royal ceremonies in Thailand, see H. G. Quaritch Wales, *Siamese State Ceremonies* (London: Bernard Quaritch, 1931).

114. Alexander Woodside, " Ideology and Integration in Post-Colonial Vietnamese Nationalism," *Pacific Affairs*, XLIV, 4 (1971–1972), p. 489.

115. See David K. Wyatt, *The Politics of Reform in Thailand* (New Haven: Yale University Press, 1969).

116. Skinner, *Chinese Society in Thailand*, pp. 228–30; Thompson, *Thailand: The New Siam*, pp. 775–76.

117. For a discussion of the role of compulsory education in the dissemination of national culture in a village in northeastern Thailand, see my " Peasant and Nation: A Thai-Lao Village in a Thai State " (Ph.D. Dissertation, Cornell University, 1967), pp. 161–84.

118. See Donald P. Whitaker, *et al.*, *Area Handbook for Laos* (Washington: U.S. Govt. Printing Office, DA Pam No. 550-58, 1967), pp. 108–16.

119. For some brief notices on education under the Pathet Lao, see Jacques Decornoy, " Life in the Pathet Lao Liberated Zone," in *Laos: War and Revolution*, ed. by Nina S. Adams and Alfred W. McCoy (N.Y.: Harper Colophon Books, 1970), pp. 411–23.

120. Frederick P. Munson, *et al.*, *Area Handbook for Cambodia* (Washington D.C.: U.S. Govt. Printing Office, DA Pam No. 550-50, 1968), pp. 110, 112.

121. American University, Foreign Area Studies, *Area Handbook for the Khmer Republic* (*Cambodia*) (Washington, D.C.: U.S. Govt. Printing Office, DA Pam 550-50, 1973), p. 114.

122. *Loc. cit.*

123. For a discussion of education in a rural area in 1959–1960, see Manning Nash, " Education in a New Nation: The Village School in Upper Burma," *International*

J. of Comparative Sociology, II (1961), pp. 135–43. Also see Manning Nash, *The Golden Road to Modernity: Village Life in Contemporary Burma* (New York: Wiley, 1965), pp. 94–97.

124. John W. Henderson, *et. al.*, *Area Handbook for Burma* (Washington: U.S. Govt Printing Office, DA Pam No. 550-61, 1968), p. 106.

125. *Ibid.*, pp. 109–10.

126. One of the most recent of such confrontations occurred in December 1974 on the occasion of funerary rites for U Thant, the late Secretary General of the United Nations. Ne Win had no great love for U Thant, and so he sought to have these funerary rites confined to the family alone. The students of Rangoon University, together with some supporters from the Sangha, saw the remains of U Thant as a symbol of their opposition to the Ne Win government. The students " stole " U Thant's body in order to give it a public funeral. In the ensuing struggle over the body, a number of students were killed or wounded and the University was temporarily closed. The students succeeded, however, given U Thant's international stature, in focusing attention from abroad on their protest. See Edwin Martin, "Socialist Republic of the Union of Burma," *Asian Survey*, XV, 2 (1975), pp. 130–131.

127. The following discussion of education in the two Vietnams is based on Alexander Woodside, " Ideology and Integration in Post-Colonial Vietnamese Nationalism," Harvey H. Smith, *et. al.*, *Area Handbook for South Vietnam* (Washington, D.C.: U.S. Govt. Printing Office, DA Pam No. 550-55, 1967; Harvey H. Smith, *et. al.*, *Area Handbook for North Vietnam* (Washington, D.C.: U.S. Govt. Printing Office, DA Pam No. 550-57, 1967). For a discussion of education in a South Vietnamese village in 1959, see Gerald C. Hickey, *Village in Vietnam* (New Haven: Yale University Press, 1964), pp. 51–52 and 205–209. The information on rural education in North Vietnam as observed by Gérard Chaliand in 1967 (*The Peasants of North Vietnam* [Harmondsworth, Middlesex, England: Penguin Books, 1969], esp. pp. 102–17) has been discussed in Chapter 5, pp. 243–44.

128. Woodside, " Ideology and Integration . . . ," p. 506.

129. *Ibid.*, p. 504.

130. See Ton That Thien, " Relations Between the Regional and the National Metropolitan University," in *Roles of Universities in Local and Regional Development in Southeast Asia*, ed. by Yip Yat Hoong (Singapore: Regional Institute of Higher Education and Development, 1973), 45–56.

131. Woodside, *op. cit.*, p. 498.

132. For an official interpretation of the anti-illiteracy program, especially as carried out during the period between 1945 and 1954, see *The Democratic Republic of Viet Nam* (Hanoi: Foreign Languages Publishing House, 1960), pp. 107–109; and *Lutte contre l'analphabétisme au Viet Nam* (Hanoi: Éditions en Langues Étrangères, 1959).

133. Woodside, " Ideology and Integration . . . ," p. 502.

134. *Ibid.*, p. 503.

135. *Ibid.*, pp. 503–504.

136. *Ibid.*, p. 504.

137. *Ibid.*, p. 499.

138. T. G. McGee, *The Southeast Asian City*, p. 175.

139. Figures from J. Russell Andrus, *Burmese Economic Life* (Stanford University Press, 1948), pp. 24–25; McGee, *The Southeast Asian City*, p. 54; Charles A. Fisher, *South-East Asia* (London: Methuen, 1964), p. 466; and D. W. Fryer, " The Primate Cities of Southeast Asia and Their Problems," in *Focus on Southeast Asia*, ed. by Alice Taylor (New York: Praeger, 1972), p. 32.

140. On the basis of 1955 data, Linsky (" Some Generalizations . . . ,"p. 293) ranked Bangkok second among the world's primate cities. On the basis of the same data, Mehta (" Some Demographic and Economic Correlates . . . ," p. 301) ranked it first. The fact that Bangkok has by 1970 increased its position vis-à-vis other cities in the country suggests that it probably still holds high ranking among the primate cities of the world.

141. " Urbanization and Economic Development: The Case of Thailand," by Sidney Goldstein, *LTC Newsletter*, No. 42 (1973), p. 2. Other statistics from McGee, *The Southeast Asian City*, pp. 79, 81.

142. Statistics on Laos are from Halpern, *Economy and Society of Laos*, Table 11, and from Laos, Royaume du Laos, Ministère du Plan et de la Cooperation, Service National de la Statistique, *Annuaire Statistique* (Vientiane 1970). The 1970 figures are estimates based on data for 1966–1968 given in the *Annuaire Statistique*. Fryer, in " The Primate Cities . . . ," also estimates Vientiane's population to have been about 200,000 in 1970.

143. Statistics for 1936 and 1960 from McGee, *The Southeast Asian City*, p. 81; that for 1970 from Fryer, *loc. cit.;* and that for 1975 from *Newsweek*, March 10, 1975, p. 25. In August 1975, a radio Phnom Penh broadcast reported that: " In Phnom Penh, textile mills, tyre factories, electric plants, water plants and food and dry-battery shops are now functioning and producing appreciable quality and quantity for local consumption." This report suggests that the city was beginning to be restored to its economic preeminence in the country. Moreover the same broadcast also said that the new government sought to promote industrialization in Cambodia. It would seem, thus, that the return to the land policy that was implemented after the takeover was only a temporary policy. The quotation and further information on this broadcast are from the *Asia 1976 Yearbook* (Hong Kong: Far Eastern Economic Review, 1976), p. 136.

144. Statistics from 1936 from Great Britain. Admiralty, Naval Intelligence Division, *op. cit.*, pp. 472, 474, 476. Statistics for 1960 and 1970 from *Between War and Peace: A Profile of Migrants to Saigon* by Allan E. Goodman and Lawrence M. Franks (New York: The Asia Society—SEADAG, SEADAG Papers on Problems of Development in Southeast Asia, 1974), Table 2, p. 29.

145. Statistics for South Vietnam from Goodman and Franks, *op. cit.*, Table 1, p. 26; those for Thailand from Goldstein, *loc. cit.* and from Fryer, *loc. cit.;* all others from Fryer, *loc. cit.*

146. A report prepared by the *Far Eastern Economic Review* states that: " Within four months [after the end of the war], more than 200,000 people from Saigon alone were reported to have gone back to the villages " (*Asia 1976 Yearbook*, p. 312).

147. Statistics for 1936 from Great Britain. Admiralty, Naval Intelligence Division, *op. cit.*, p. 473; those for 1962 from George L. Harris, *et. al.*, *U.S. Army Area Handbook for Vietnam* (Washington, D.C.: Headquarters, Department of Army,

DA Pam 550-40, 1962), pp. 51–52; those for 1970 from Fryer, *loc. cit.* and from T. G. McGee, "Hanoi," *Encylopaedia Britannica* (15th ed., Chicago: Encyclopaedia Britannica, 1974), p. 628. Nayan Chandra in an article entitled "Rebuilding Shattered Vietnam," *Far Eastern Economic Review* (February 13, 1975), p. 94, gives the population of Hanoi as being 736,211. The information on the expansion of the boundaries of Hanoi is from Harvey H. Smith, *et. al., Area Handbook for North Vietnam*, p. 27.

148. McGee, *The Southeast Asian City*, p. 82.

149. Skinner, *Chinese Society in Thailand*, p. 88.

150. W. E. Willmott, *The Chinese in Cambodia*, pp. 12, 14.

151. McGee, *The Southeast Asian City*, p. 68.

152. Joann L. Schrock, *et. al., Minority Groups in the Republic of Vietnam* (Washington, D.C.: Headquarters, Department of the Army, Department of the Army Pamphlet, No. 550-105, 1966), p. 934. See also Bernard Fall, "Vietnam's Chinese Problem," *Far Eastern Survey*, XXVII, 5 (1958), pp. 65–72.

153. Great Britain. Admiralty, Naval Intelligence Division, *Indo-China*, p. 254.

154. Joann L. Schrock, *et. al., Minority Groups in North Vietnam* (Washington: Headquarters, Department of the Army, DA Pam 550-110, 1972), pp. 558-59, 569.

155. Woodside, "Post-Colonial Vietnamese Nationalism . . . ," pp. 496–97.

156. Willmott, *The Chinese in Cambodia*, pp. 16–17.

157. *Ibid.*, pp. 80–83.

158. *Ibid.*, pp. 16–17.

159. Skinner, *Chinese Society in Thailand*, p. 174.

160. *Ibid.*, pp. 372–82; Skinner, "The Thailand Chinese: Assimilation in a Changing Society," *Asia* II (1964), pp. 80–92.

161. Skinner, *Chinese Society in Thailand*, p. 207.

162. Statistics from *Thailand Population Census*, 1960.

163. Boonsanong Punyodyana in *Chinese-Thai Differential Assimilation in Bangkok* (Ithaca, N.Y.: Cornell University, Southeast Asia Program, Data Paper No. 79, 1971) reports that assimilation of Chinese in Bangkok-Thonburi has been less rapid for those whose occupation is in trade and commerce than for those who attend Thai schools or become government civil servants. Although groups are not strictly comparable, the findings do suggest that the persistence of ethnic distinctiveness is a function of the ethnic division of labor rather than birth in a family whose parents both speak Chinese.

164. Information on the decline of the Indian population in Burma has been taken primarily from R. Hately, *op. cit.* See also, Usha Mahajani, *The Role of Indian Minorities in Burma and Malaya* (Bombay: Vora and Co. 1960). Hatley estimates (*op. cit.*, p. 458) that there were 450,000 Indians left in Burma in 1967. Kunstadter (*op. cit.*, p. 89) estimates that only 100,000 Indians remained in Burma in 1965. Another estimate is that 90 per cent of the Indian population of Burma left in the period between 1963 and 1965 (John W. Henderson, *et. al., Area Handbook for Burma.* Washington: U.S. Govt. Printing Office, DA Pam 550-61, 1968), pp. 44–45.

165. Goodman and Franks, *Between War and Peace . . .* , p. 14.

166. Lucien Pye, *Politics, Personality and Nation Building* (New Haven: Yale University Press, 1962), p. 93.

167. See Robert B. Textor, *From Peasant to Pedicab Driver* (New Haven: Yale University Southeast Asia Studies, Cultural Report Series, No. 9, 1961); Larry Sternstein, " A First Study of Migration in the Greater Bangkok Metropolitan Area," *Pacific Viewpoint*, XII, 4 (1971), pp. 41–67; E. C. Chapman and A. C. B. Allen, " Internal Migration in Thailand," (Paper delivered at the Hobart, Australia meeting of the Australian and New Zealand Association for the Advancement of Science, 1965, mimeo); Sidney Goldstein, " Urban Growth in Thailand, 1946–1967," *J. of the Social Sciences (Bangkok)*, VI, 3 (1969), pp. 100–18; Goldstein, *Urbanization in Thailand* (Bangkok: Chulalongkorn University, Population Research and Training Center, Research Report No. 2, 1970); Goldstein, " Urbanization and Economic Development . . . ," Susan Morell and David Morell, *Six Slums in Bangkok: Problems of Life and Options for Action* (2 vols., Bangkok: United Nations Children's Fund, 1972). Some summary data is also contained in J. C. Caldwell, " The Demographic Structure," in *Thailand: Social and Economic Studies in Development*, ed. by T. H. Silcock (Durham, N.C.: Duke University Press, 1967), pp. 27–64. Far more general discussion of urbanization in Southeast Asia with reference to migration, see McGee, *The Southeast Asian City*, McGee, *The Urbanization Process* . . . , esp. chs. 1–4. Some data on migration to Rangoon can be found in Richard W. Redick, *op. cit.;* on migration to Phnom Penh in R. Garry, " L'urbanization au Cambodge," *Civilisations*, XVII (1967), pp. 83–106; and on migration to Saigon-Cholon in Goodman and Franks, *Between War and Peace*. . . .

168. Sternstein, " A First Study of Migration . . . ," pp. 47–48.

169. Goldstein, " Urban Growth . . . ," p. 111.

170. Chapman and Allen, *op. cit.* p. 49.

171. Sternstein, "A First Study of Migration . . . ," p. 53.

172. Morell and Morell, *op. cit.,* Vol. II, Table II-10.

173. Goodman and Franks, *op. cit.,* p. 21.

174. Morell and Morell, *op. cit.,* Vol. II, Table II-15.

175. Goodman and Franks, *op. cit.,* p. 14.

176. McGee, *The Southeast Asian City*, p. 84.

177. *Ibid.*, pp. 90–96.

178. McGee makes considerable use of data on Rangoon in 1953 for his discussion of the postcolonial primate city—see *Ibid.*, pp. 88, 93–94, 98–99, for example.

179. See the article by Bob Tamarkin of the *Chicago Daily News*, which appeared in *The Seattle Times* under the title, " Beleaguered Cambodians find a scapegoat," March 2, 1975.

180. Quote from *Asia 1976 Yearbook*, p. 136.

181. Buu Hoan, " The South Vietnamese Economy in the Transition to Peace and After," *Asian Survey*, XI, 4 (1971), p. 314.

182. Goodman and Franks, *Between War and Peace* . . . , pp. 15, 33. Also see Frances Fitzgerald, *Fire in the Lake* (N.Y.: Vintage Books, 1973), pp. 569–71.

183. *Asia 1976 Yearbook*, p. 312.

184. Report cited in an article, " 2 Million to Work on Changing Saigon," *Seattle Times*, May 20, 1976.

185. Tran Nhu Trang, " The Transformation of the Peasantry in North Viet Nam " (Ph.D. Dissertation, University of Pittsburgh, 1972), pp. 389–94.

186. Woodside, " Ideology and Integration . . . ," p. 496. Also see McGee, " Hanoi."

187. Prachoom Chomchai, " Thailand's Industrial Development: Rationale, Strategy and Prospects," in *Studies of Contemporary Thailand*, ed. by Robert Ho and E. C. Chapman (Canberra: Australian National University, Research School of Pacific Studies, Department of Human Geography, Publication HG/8, 1973), p. 68. See also N. K. Sarkar, *Industrial Structure of Greater Bangkok* (Bangkok: United Nationals Asian Institute for Economic Development and Planning, 1974).

188. Sarkar, *op. cit.*, pp. 23–27.

189. *Ibid.*, pp. 5–6.

190. These facts are based on my own, unsystematic, observations.

191. Cf. in this regard the similar observations made by Evers with regard to Malaysia and Singapore in Hans-Dieter Evers, " Urbanization and Urban Conflict in Southeast Asia," *Asian Survey*, XV, 9 (1975), pp. 775–85; see esp., pp. 781–83. Also see, with regard to Bangkok, Boonsanong, *Chinese-Thai Differential Assimilation. . . .*

192. Statistics calculated from data given in Sarkar, *op. cit.*, p. 50. " Foreign firms " are here defined, following Sarkar, as those firms in which 26 per cent or more of the shares are foreign owned or which are subsidiaries of foreign companies. The most important foreign firms are Japanese, followed by American, British, and other European firms.

193. Statistics calculated from data in *ibid.*, p. 29.

194. See, in this connection, Hans-Dieter Evers, " The Formation of a Social Class Structure. Urbanization, Bureaucratization and Social Mobility in Thailand," *J. Southeast Asian History*, VII, 2 (1966), pp. 100–15.

195. See Bert F. Hoselitz, " Generative and Parasitic Cities," in Hoselitz, Sociological Aspects of Economic Growth (Glencoe, Ill.; Free Press, 1960) pp. 185–215. The debate about whether postcolonial Third World cities, including Southeast Asian cities, are or are not primate cities in the colonial mold and whether, if so, they are functioning as parasites or as catalysts for ecomonic development has generated a very large literature. See McGee, *The Southeast Asian City;* McGee, *The Urbanization Process in the Third World* (London: G. Bell and Sons, 1971), esp. chs. 3 and 4; McGee, " Catalysts or Cancers? The Role of Cities in Asian Socieities," in *Urbanization and National Development*, ed. by Leo Jakobson and Ved Prakash (Beverly Hills, Calif.: Sage Publications, South and Southeast Asia Urban Affairs Annuals, I, 1970); Arnold S. Linsky, " Some Generalizations Concerning Primate Cities," in *The City in Newly Developing Countries*, ed. by Gerald Breese (Englewood Cliffs, N. J.: Prentice-Hall, 1969); Surinder K. Mehta, " Some Demographic and Economic Correlates of Primate Cities," in *The City in Newly Developing Countries*; Carol Owen and Ronald A. Witton, " National

Division and Mobilization: A Reinterpretation of Primacy," *Economic Development and Cultural Change*, XXI (1973), pp. 325–37. For discussions focused specifically on capital cities in Southeast Asia, see D. J. Dwyer, ed., *The City as the Centre of Change in Asia* (Hong Kong: Hong Kong University Press, 1971); D. W. Fryer, " The ' Million City ' in Southeast Asia," *Geography Review*, XLIII (1953), pp. 474–94; reprinted in *Man, State and Society in Contemporary Southeast Asia*, ed. by Robert O. Tilman, pp. 72–87; Fryer, *Emerging Southeast Asia: A Study of Growth and Stagnation* (New York: McGraw-Hill, 1970), ch. 3; Fryer, " The Primate Cities of Southeast Asia and Their Problems"; Norton Ginsburg. " The Great City in Southeast Asia," *Am. J. of Sociology*, LX (1955), pp. 455–62; Ginsburg, " Planning the Future of the Southeast Asian City," in *Focus on Southeast Asia*, ed. by Alice Taylor, *op. cit.*, pp. 43–56; Rhoads Murphy, " New Capitals of Asia," *Economic Development and Cultural Change*, V, 3 (1957), pp. 216–43; and Murphy, "Traditionalism and Colonialism: Changing Roles in Asia."

196. Larry Sternstein, " The Image of Bangkok," *Pacific Viewpoint*, XII, 1 (1971), p. 68. Sternstein's inquiry was stimulated by the work of K. Lynch, *The Image of the City* (Cambridge, Mass.: M.I.T. Press, 1964).

197. Sternstein, " The Iamage of Bangkok," p. 74.

198. See Roger Teulieres and Nguyen Huy, " Une Agglomération de sampans habités à Saigon," *Cahiers d'Outre Mer* (Avril-Juin 1962), pp. 166–79.

199. McGee, *The Southeast Asian City*, p. 156.

200. Morell and Morell, *op. cit.*, I, p. 3.

201. Goodman and Franks, *Between War and Peace . . .*, p. 19.

202. Morell and Morell, *op. cit.*, I, p. 27.

203. Woodside, " Ideology and Integration . . . ," p. 496.

204. Goodman and Franks, *Between War and Peace . . .*, pp. 12, 19.

205. Morell and Morell, *op. cit.*, I, p. 31.

206. *Ibid.*, p. 32.

207. *Ibid.*, p. 34.

208. *Ibid.*, p. 35.

209. Skinner, *Chinese Society in Thailand*, pp. 256–57.

210. W. E. Willmott, *The Political Structure of the Chinese Comminity in Cambodia* (London: Athlone Press, London School of Economics, Monographs on Social Anthropology, No. 42, 1970), p. 50.

211. *Loc. cit.*

212. Morell and Morell, *op. cit.*, I, p. 34.

213. Charles F. Keyes, " Buddhism in a Secular City: A View from Chiang Mai," *Visakha Puja B.E. 2518* (Bangkok: The Buddhist Association of Thailand, 1975), pp. 62–72.

214. Woodside, " The Development of Social Organizations in Vietnamese Cities in the Late Colonial Period," pp. 48–49; Woodside, " Ideology and Integration . . . ," pp. 500–502.

215. Textor, *From Peasant to Pedicab Driver*, pp. 22–27.

216. Goodman and Franks, *op. cit.*, p. 20.

217. Willmott, *The Chinese in Cambodia*, pp. 88–90.

218. Woodside, " The Development of Social Organizations . . . ," p. 53.

APPENDIX A
LANGUAGE GROUPINGS IN
MAINLAND SOUTH-EAST ASIA

The following groupings of languages in mainland Southeast Asia differ somewhat from those that appear elsewhere in the literature partially because the languages of recent migrants to the region, which others have ignored, have been taken into account, and partially because those groupings whose ultimate affiliation is unclear have not been forced into one larger grouping or another. For other, and more detailed classifications, see Frank M. LeBar, Gerald C. Hickey, John K. Musgrave, and others, *Ethnic Groups of Mainland Southeast Asia* (New Haven: Human Relations Area Files Press, 1964) and Peter Kunstadter, ed. *Southeast Asian Tribes, Minorities and Nations* (Princeton: Princeton University Press, 1967), pp. 78–91. For recent surveys of the results of linguistic research on Southeast Asia, see H. L. Shorto, ed., *Linguistic Comparison in Southeast Asia and the Pacific* (London: School of Oriental and African Studies, University of London, 1963) and Thomas A. Sebeok, ed., *Current Trends in Linguistics,–II: Linguistics in East Asia and South East Asia* (The Hague: Mouton, 1967).

AUSTROASIATIC

Peoples speaking Austroasiatic languages are to be found throughout mainland Southeast Asia, from the Assamese hills and Nicobar islands in the west to the highlands of the Annamite Cordillera in the eastern part of the region. Major language groupings within the Austroasiatic language family include Khmer or Cambodian, and Mon.

AUSTRONESIAN

The languages of the Austronesian (or Malayo-Polynesian) family are to be found over an immense area stretching from Madagascar to Hawaii. In Southeast Asia, almost all the languages spoken in Indonesia, Malaysia and the

Philippines belong to this family. A relatively small number of Austronesian-language speakers are also to be found in Mainland Southeast Asia: they include some of the montagnard peoples of southern Vietnam (e.g., the Rhadé and Jarai) as well as the Chams, small numbers of whom still live in Cambodia and Vietnam.

SINO-TIBETAN

Linguists distinguish between two main subgroupings of the enormous Sino-Tibetan family: that is, Sinitic and Tibeto-Burman. Speakers of Tibeto-Burman languages in mainland Southeast Asia include not only the Burmese but also a number of tribal peoples such as the Chin and Kachin, who live in upland areas in the northern part of the region. Sinitic languages are not indigenous to the region, but overseas Chinese migrants have introduced a variety of Chinese languages into the region. Meo-Yao languages, spoken by some upland peoples found mainly in southern China but existing also in small numbers in northern mainland Southeast Asia, are assumed by most linguists to be part of the Sino-Tibetan language family. However, the connections linking them to this family have not yet been clearly demonstrated.

TAI (DAIC)

Tai languages are found from the Chinese provinces of Kweichow and Szechwan in the north to the middle of Malaya in the south and from Assam in the west to Hainan island in the east. The best known members of this language family include Siamese, Lao, and Shan. Two different theories have attempted to place Tai languages either within the greater Sino-Tibetan or alternatively within the Austronesian language family. Neither theory has yet been generally accepted, however, and the ultimate kinship of the Tai languages thus remains uncertain for the time being.

VIET-MUONG

The relationship of the Viet-Muong languages, of which Vietnamese is the best known representative, to one of the larger language groupings of mainland Southeast Asia is still a subject of debate. As yet no conclusive agreement has been reached among linguists as to whether or not these languages should be subsumed under the wider Sino-Tibetan, Austroasiatic, or Tai language families.

KAREN

Karen languages are spoken by people most of whom live in eastern Burma and across the frontier into western Thailand. Although there has been a marked tendency among linguists to place Karen languages within the Sino-Tibetan family, the accuracy of such an affiliation has yet to be substantiated. An alternative hypothesis, that Karen languages are ultimately related to Tai, also remains unsubstantiated as yet.

DRAVIDIAN

The homeland of Dravidian languages is South India and Ceylon, and Dravidian speakers in mainland Southeast Asia are limited to migrants from these areas of South Asia.

INDO-EUROPEAN

The fact that Indo-European languages, primarily English and French, still serve as the second language for a sizable proportion of the educated population of mainland Southeast Asia and in some cases as a first language, as for example in certain Eurasian communities, or among the French-trained elite in the area formerly comprised under Indochina, bears witness to the linguistic legacy of European colonialism to the region. Indo-European languages of South Asian origin are also spoken by a number of Indian and Pakistani migrants to mainland Southeast Asia.

APPENDIX B
SIZE, DENSITY, URBAN, COMPOSITION, AND ETHNIC COMPOSITION OF POPULATIONS IN THE COUNTRIES OF MAINLAND SOUTHEAST ASIA

Burma

Area	678,033 sq. km.
Total population	
1960	22.3 million
1970	27.6 million
Population density (1970)	41 persons per sq. km.
Areas of greatest density of population	Irrawaddy Delta, Sittang Delta, Central Dry Zone, Northern Tennasserim Coast
Urban population (per cent of total population)	
1960	9.6* or 5.3† per cent
1970	15.8‡ per cent
Ethnic minorities (per cent of total population)	
Tribal	15–17 per cent
(Karen 11 per cent)	
(Chin 2½ per cent)	
Indians	7–8 per cent in 1960; reduced to perhaps 2–3 per cent by 1970
Chinese	1–2 per cent
Others (Shans, Mons, Eurasians)	8½–9½ per cent

*Keith Buchanan, *The Southeast Asian World* (New York: Doubleday Anchor Books, 1968), p. 170.
† Donald W. Fryer, *Emerging Southeast Asia* (New York: McGraw-Hill, 1970), p. 83; Fryer's figure is based on the population of cities exceeding 100,000.
‡ Donald W. Fryer, " The Primate Cities of Southeast Asia and Their Problems," in *Focus on Southeast Asia*, ed. by Alice Taylor New York: Praeger, 1972), p. 32.

Cambodia

Area	172,511 sq. km.
Total population	
1960	5.6 million
1970	7.0 million
Population density (1970)	40½ persons per sq. km.
Areas of greatest density of population	Tonlé Sap Basin, the Flood Plains of the Mekong, Tonlé Sap, and Bassac Rivers, and the Coastal Lowlands along the Gulf of Siam
Urban population (per cent of total population)	
1960	13.0 per cent* or 8.7† per cent
1970	12.8‡ per cent
Ethnic minorities (per cent of total population)	
Tribal	1 per cent
Chinese	7½ per cent
Vietnamese	5–7 per cent (before anti-Vietnamese riots of 1970)
Chams (Muslims)	2 per cent
Others (mainland Thai and Lao)	1 per cent

* Buchanan, *op. cit,.* p. 170.
† Fryer, *op. cit.*, p. 83; Fryer's figure is based on the population of cities exceeding 100,000.
‡ Fryer in Taylor, *op. cit.*, p. 32.

Laos

Area	236,800 sq. km.
Total population	
1960	1.8 million
1970	3.0 million
Population density (1970)	13 persons per sq. km.
Areas of greatest density of population	The Flood Plain along the Mekong River
Urban population (per cent of total population)	
1960	3* per cent or 6.3† per cent
1970	13.4‡ per cent
Ethnic minorities (per cent of total population)	
Tribal	30 per cent +
(Tai 8–9 per cent)	
(Mon-Khmer 13 per cent)	
(Miao-Yao 9 per cent)	
Chinese	2 per cent
Vietnamese	1 per cent

* Buchanan, *op. cit.*, p. 172.
† Fryer, *op. cit.*, p. 83; Fryer's figure is based on the population of cities exceeding 100,000.
‡ Fryer in Taylor, *op. cit.*, p. 32. This figure impresses me as being too high, although from rural areas had begun to swell Vientiane by 1970.

Thailand

Area	514,000 sq. km.
Total population	
1960	26.4 million
1970	36.2 million
Population density (1970)	70 persons per sq. km.
Areas of greatest density of population	Lower Cao Phraya River Basin, Basins of Chi and Mun Rivers (northeastern Thailand), Basin of Ping River (northern Thailand), Coastal lowlands on eastern peninsula in southernmost Thailand
Urban population (per cent of total population)	
1960	9.1* per cent or 9.9† per cent
1970	13.0‡ per cent
Ethnic minorities (per cent of total population)	
Tribal	1–1½ per cent
Chinese	8–9 per cent
Malays	4 per cent

* Buchanan, *op. cit.*, p. 172.
† Fryer, *op. cit.*, p. 83; Fryer's figure is based on the population of cities exceeding 100,000.
‡ Fryer in Taylor, *op. cit.*, p. 32.

North Vietnam

Area	159,000 sq. km.
Total population	
1960	16.4 million
1970	21.2 million
Population density (1970)	132 persons per sq. km.
Areas of greatest density of population	Red River (Tonkin) Delta
Urban population (per cent of total population)	
1960	3.1* per cent or 7.1† per cent
1970	23.9‡ per cent
Ethnic minorities (per cent of total population)	
Tribal	14–14½ per cent
(Tai 7½–8 per cent)	
(Meo-Yao 2½ per cent)	
(Mu'ong 3 per cent)	
Chinese	1 per cent

* Buchanan, *op. cit.* p. 172.
† Fryer, *op. cit.*, p. 83; Fryer's figure is based on the population of cities exceeding 100,000.
‡ Fryer in Taylor, *op. cit.*, p. 32.

South Vietnam

Area	170,806 sq. km.
Total population	
1960	14.1 million
1970	18.3 million
Population density (1970)	107 persons per sq. km.
Areas of greatest density of population	Mekong Delta
Urban population (per cent of total population)	
1960	10.8* per cent
1970	27.1† per cent
Ethnic minorities (per cent of total population)	
Tribal	8–9 per cent
Chinese	5–6 per cent
Khmer	2–3 per cent

* Both Buchanan (*op. cit.*, p. 172) and Fryer (*op. cit.*, p. 83) give the same figure and both base their figure on the population of cities exceeding 100,000.
† Fryer in Taylor, *op. cit.*, p. 32; Fryer says that this figure may be too low.

APPENDIX B: SOURCES

BUCHANAN, KEITH. *The Southeast Asian World.* New York: Doubleday Anchor, 1968.

FISHER, CHARLES A. *South-East Asia: A Social Economic and Political Geography.* London: Methuen, 1964.

FRYER, DONALD W. *Emerging Southeast Asia: A Study in Growth and Stagnation.* New York: McGraw-Hill, 1970.

KUNSTADTER, PETER, ed. *Southeast Asian Tribes, Minorities and Nations.* Princeton: Princeton University Press, 1967.

LAOS, ROYAUME DE LAOS, Ministère du Plan et de la Cooperation, Service National de la Statistique. *Annuaire Statistique.* Vientiane, 1970.

TAYLOR, ALICE, ed. *Focus on Southeast Asia.* (New York: Praeger in Cooperation with the American Geographical Society, 1972).

UNITED NATIONS, Economic Commission for Asia and the Far East. *Statistical Yearbook for Asia and the Pacific.* Bangkok, 1973.

WILLIAMS, LEA E. *The Future of Overseas Chinese in Southeast Asia.* New York: McGraw-Hill, 1966.

WILLMOTT, WILLIAM E. *The Chinese in Cambodia.* Vancouver, B. C.: University of British Columbia Publications Centre, 1967.

AUTHOR INDEX

SUBJECT INDEX

Culture (*cont.*)
    bodia, 105; in Laos, 105; in Thailand, 105; in Theravada Buddhist societies, 100, 102, 105; in Vietnam, 214
    cultural forms, 9; in Theravada Buddhist societies, 100
    culture and adaptation, 8
    culture and meaning, 9, 12
    culture and personality, 7–8
    definition of culture, 9
    "two cultures," 101
    national culture, 291
    also see: Knowledge; Meaning; Symbol
Currency, in Theravada Buddhist societies, 144
Cybernetic relationship between culture and adaptation, 42

Dagon, former name of Rangoon, 264
Delat, town in the highlands of south Vietnam, 274
Damrong Rajanubhab, Thai Prince (1862–1948), 103
Dāna, Pali Buddhist term; meritorious or charitable offering, 118, 123
    also see: Merit
Danang (Tourane), city in Vietnam, 202, 208, 231, 269, 300, 320
Dance dramatization of myth among Shans, 122
Death customs and beliefs, among Chin, 47; among Semang, 37; among Theravada Buddhists, 119; among Vietnamese, 196
Defoliation by United States military in Vietnam, 229
Deities and divinities, belief in by Theravada Buddhists, 87
    also see: Deva; Gods; *Thewada*
Demerit, Buddhist concept, 89, 117, 118, 119, 125
    also see: Karma; *pappa*
    compare: Merit
Democratic Republic of Vietnam, 226
    founding of, 204, 226, 276
    influence in Cambodia and Laos, 106
Demography. *see* Birth control; Fertility; Migration; Mortality; Population
Depression, the great, impact on central Thailand, 144; impact on lower Burma, 143–144
Descent, system of, 5–6
    matrilineal descent in Theravada Buddhist societies, 131–132, 133, 174–175
    patrilineal descent in Theravada Buddhist societies, 131, 133–134, 153; in Vietnam, 186–188
    also see: Kinship; Patrilineage
Deva, Sanskrit term; god, 125, 155
    also see: God; *Thewada*
Devarāja, Sanskrit term; god king or divine king, 69, 77, 81, 262
Dharma, Buddhist concept; the teachings of the Buddha; the "Way" taught by the Buddha, 84, 89, 118
Dharma Society, association in Thailand during the colonial period, 284
Dien Bien Phu, site of battle in northern Vietnam, 23, 96, 205, 225
Diet, in Theravada Buddhist villages, 126–128, 129
    also see: Coffee; Drinks; Fish; Food; Fruits; Meat; Nutrition; Rice; Sweets; Tea; Vegetables
Diffusion, cultural, 3–4
Dinh, Vietnamese term; shrine dedicated to the cult of the village guardian spirit, 190, 191, 192, 199

Divorce, in Theravada Buddhist societies, 136
Dong-Son, prehistoric site in northern Vietnam, 16, 182
"Double identity," held by people of Chinese descent in Thailand, 280, 329
    also see: Assimilation
Drama, folk, in the Democratic Republic of Vietnam, 243, 257; in Theravada Buddhist villages, 122
Doumer, Paul, Governor-General of Indochina (1897–1902), 204
Dravidian language family, 341
Drinks, in diet of Theravada Buddhist villagers, 127–128
Dualism, economic, coexistence of "bazaar-centered" and "firm-centered" economies, 275, 321, 322
    also see: "Bazaar-centered" economy; "Firm-centered" economy
Dukkha, Pali Buddhist term; suffering, sorrow, 84, 109
    also see: Suffering
Dvaravati, ancient Mon-Buddhist kingdom located in central Thailand, 260

Earth Goddess, in Theravada Buddhist societies, 119, 120, 132
Ecology
    cultural ecology, 5
    ecological adaptation in central Thailand, 136; in Theravada Buddhist societies, 136–141; of Chins, 42–43; of tribal people, 5
Economic development
    and Buddhism in Theravada Buddhist societies, 149–151
    in Burma under colonialism, 98–99, 111; after independence, 306–307
    in Cambodia under colonialism, 99; after independence, 307–308
    under colonialism, 272
    in the Democratic Republic of Vietnam, 240, 310–311; during war in Indochina, 237–238, 310
    in Indochina under colonialism, 111–112
    in Laos under colonialism, 99–100; after independence, 308
    in the Republic of Vietnam, 309–310; during war in Indochina, 309
    in Thailand during the colonial period, 98–99, 111; since World War II, 311–313
    in Theravada Buddhist societies during the colonial period, 97–98
    in Vietnam under colonialism, 207–214
    under colonialism, 272
    also see: Industry
Education
    American influence on education in the Republic of Vietnam, 296
    among tribal peoples, 21
    in Cambodia under the National United Front of Cambodia, 294
    during colonial period, 100–101, 282; in Burma, 101; in Cambodia, 101, 293–294; in Laos, 101, 293; in Vietnam, 205, 215, 252, 296
    during the War in Indochina in Cambodia, 293–294
    educational policies towards minorities, in Burma, 295; in the Democratic Republic of Vietnam, 297
    educational reform in Thailand, 101, 112, 291
    extension education in Theravada Buddhist societies, 124

MACMILLAN PUBLISHING CO., INC.
866 Third Avenue, New York, N.Y. 10022

ISBN 0-02-364430-3